WOMEN IN TURBULENT TIMES

The last two decades have been marked by economic and social turmoil – from the global financial crash and the austerity turn to the Covid-19 pandemic, followed by cost-of-living crises, geopolitical conflicts and heightened political divisions. This succession of crises has destabilised economic and political systems and risks undermining the hard-won, albeit slow, progress towards gender equality in contemporary societies. At the same time, the way we live and work is being challenged by rapidly developing AI and digital technologies, the imperative to accelerate the transition to net zero emissions and unresolved pressures to transform care systems to support women's sustained participation in waged work. Against this backdrop, this volume offers a long-term perspective on turbulence, grounded on comparative and country evidence from Europe, the USA, Australia and the Global South. The chapters trace how acute shocks, chronic crises and systemic transformations reverberate through labour markets, households and state policies, reshaping gender inequalities and vulnerabilities and their intersections. The concluding discussion argues that turmoil is evolving into a polycrisis – an entanglement of economic, social and ecological disruptions – while exposing a critical but neglected dimension of turbulence: the crisis of social reproduction and women's pivotal role in managing the tensions between production and the social reproduction spheres. By introducing a gender perspective into the polycrisis debate, this volume speaks to scholars in socioeconomics and gender studies; policy experts and advisors on gender equality; and activists, educators and the general public seeking to understand and address the challenges to gender equality in turbulent times.

Jill Rubery is professor of comparative employment systems and Executive Director of the Work and Equalities Institute at Alliance Manchester Business School, University of Manchester, Manchester, UK. She is an international expert on gender and employment and has worked extensively as a consultant for the ILO and the EU. Her research focuses on wages, working time, precarious work and the gendered impact of crises and she has edited books on Women and Recession and Women and Austerity (published by Routledge). She is a Fellow of the British Academy.

Núria Sánchez-Mira is professor of sociology at the University of Neuchâtel, Neuchâtel, Switzerland. Her research focuses on gender inequalities at the work–family interface and across the life course, using quantitative, qualitative and mixed-methods approaches. She has worked on the gendered impacts of crises on labour markets and household divisions of labour, precarious work in female-dominated sectors, and the digital transformation of work. She currently serves as Co-Editor-in-Chief of the *Swiss Journal of Sociology*.

Valeria Insarauto is lecturer in work and employment, Centre for Decent Work, Sheffield University Management School, Sheffield, UK, and affiliated researcher, Institute of Labour Economics and Industrial Sociology (LEST), Aix-Marseille University, Aix-en-Provence, France. Her research focuses on gender inequalities in the labour market from an international comparative and quantitative perspective, particularly around socio-economic vulnerability among marginal workers, discrimination and sexual harassment, and the work–family interface. She serves on the editorial boards of *Work, Employment and Society* and of *Papers. Revista de Sociologia*.

Routledge IAFFE Advances in Feminist Economics

IAFFE aims to increase the visibility and range of economic research on gender; facilitate communication among scholars, policymakers, and activists concerned with women's wellbeing and empowerment; promote discussions among policy makers about interventions which serve women's needs; educate economists, policymakers, and the general public about feminist perspectives on economic issues; foster feminist evaluations of economics as a discipline; expose the gender blindness characteristic of much social science and the ways in which this impoverishes all research - even research that does not explicitly concern women's issues; help expand opportunities for women, especially women from underrepresented groups, within economics; and, encourage the inclusion of feminist perspectives in the teaching of economics. The IAFFE book series pursues the aims of the organization by providing a forum in which scholars have space to develop their ideas at length and in detail. The series exemplifies the value of feminist research and the high standard of IAFFE sponsored scholarship.

19 Informal Women Workers in the Global South
Policies and Practices for the Formalisation of Women's Employment in Developing Economies
Edited by Jayati Ghosh

20 The Political Economy of Same-Sex Marriage
A Feminist Critique
Bronwyn Winter

21 Women's Economic Thought in the Romantic Age
Towards a Transdisciplinary Herstory of Economic Thought
Joanna Rostek

22 First-Wave Feminism and Women's Civil and Political Rights in South America
Carmen Diana Deere

23 Women in Turbulent Times
Crises, Transitions and Challenges for Gender Equality
Edited by Jill Rubery, Núria Sánchez-Mira and Valeria Insarauto

For more information about this series, please visit www.routledge.com/Routledge-IAFFE-Advances-in-Feminist-Economics/book-series/IAFFE

WOMEN IN TURBULENT TIMES

Crises, Transitions and Challenges for Gender Equality

Edited by
Jill Rubery, Núria Sánchez-Mira and Valeria Insarauto

Routledge
Taylor & Francis Group
LONDON AND NEW YORK

Designed cover image: Getty Images / stellalevi

First published 2026
by Routledge
4 Park Square, Milton Park, Abingdon, Oxon OX14 4RN

and by Routledge
605 Third Avenue, New York, NY 10158

Routledge is an imprint of the Taylor & Francis Group, an informa business

British Library Cataloguing-in-Publication Data
A catalogue record for this book is available from the British Library

ISBN: 978-1-032-86585-0 (hbk)
ISBN: 978-1-032-86583-6 (pbk)
ISBN: 978-1-003-52821-0 (ebk)

DOI: 10.4324/9781003528210

Typeset in Times New Roman
by Deanta Global Publishing Services, Chennai, India

Access the Support Material: www.routledge.com/9781032865836

CONTENTS

FIGURES

TABLES

CONTRIBUTORS

Janeen Baxter is the Director of the Australian Research Council (ARC) Centre of Excellence for Children and Families over the Life Course (Life Course Centre) at University of Queensland, Brisbane, Australia, and an ARC Kathleen Fitzpatrick Laureate Fellow. She is a sociologist with research interests in social disadvantage, gender, family dynamics, life course and longitudinal studies.

Sonja Bekker is professor of European social policy at the Law School of Utrecht University, Utrecht, the Netherlands. She is the coordinator of the interdisciplinary Sector Plan on Welfare, Participation and Citizenship in a Digital World. Bekker publishes on temporary and part-time work, youth, women and European Union socioeconomic governance.

Marija Bashevska is a postdoctoral research fellow at the University of Turin, Turin, Italy. Her research focuses on gender and socio-economic inequalities in the labour market, unpaid work and work–family dynamics. She explores how social contexts and crises shape these inequalities from a comparative and life course perspective.

Ioulia Bessa is associate professor at the University of Leeds in the Centre for Employment Relations Innovation and Change (CERIC), Leeds, UK. Her research looks at non-standard forms of employment and working conditions linked to precarity, underemployment/unemployment in insecure environments, such as during Covid-19, in platforms and when considering specific socio-economic groups.

Fei Bian is a postdoctoral researcher at the Institute of Sociology, University of Neuchâtel, Neuchâtel, Switzerland. She holds a PhD in social sciences from the University of Lausanne, Lausanne, Switzerland. Her research focuses on family behaviour and social inequalities, using longitudinal data and quantitative analyses.

Alice Campbell is a lecturer in social research at the University of Tasmania, Hobart, Australia. Alice's research expertise includes the sociology of gender and sexuality, family dynamics, social inequalities and longitudinal and life-course studies. Her current research is focused on gender-based violence, care work and post-separation families.

Jack Daly is a postdoctoral research fellow in the Centre for Employment Relations, Innovation and Change (CERIC) at the University of Leeds, Leeds, UK. His research focuses on equality, diversity and inclusion in male-dominated occupations and industries, exploring the role of men in facilitating and/or resisting the implementation of equality work.

Giulia Dotti Sani is associate professor of sociology at the University of Milan, Milan, Italy. Her research focuses on gender, family and work–life balance, with expertise in quantitative methods. She currently leads the MatGuilt project, investigating maternal and paternal guilt and its impact on employment and fertility decisions in Italy.

Hugo Figueiredo is an economist with a PhD from the Manchester Business School. He is a lecturer at Department of Economics, Management, Industrial Engineering and Tourism, University of Aveiro, Aveiro, Portugal and a researcher at the Centre for Research in Higher Education Policies (CIPES). His research interests are in the areas of labour, (higher) education economics and inequality.

Nora Gobel is a junior research officer at the Research Department of the International Labour Organization (ILO), Geneva, Switzerland. She holds a master's degree in Economic Policy in Global Markets from Central European University, Vienna, Austria.

Mattia Guarnerio is a doctoral student at the University of Lausanne, Lausanne, Switzerland. His research analyses how the intersectional gender-migration composition of occupations shapes wage penalties over time and across countries. He applies advanced quantitative methods to document cumulative inequalities and inform policies promoting labour market equality and inclusion.

Savannah Hunter is a senior researcher at the University of California, Berkeley Labor Center, Berkeley, USA. A sociologist, Dr. Hunter leads research and technical assistance projects on job quality, working conditions and labour policy, particularly focused on low-wage industries and jobs.

Valeria Insarauto is a lecturer in work and employment, Centre for Decent Work, Sheffield University Management School, Sheffield, UK, and an affiliated researcher, Institute of Labour Economics and Industrial Sociology (LEST), Aix-Marseille University, Aix-en-Provence, France. Her research focuses on gender inequalities in the labour market from an international comparative and quantitative perspective, particularly around socio-economic vulnerability among marginal workers, discrimination and sexual harassment, and the work–family interface. She serves on the editorial boards of *Work, Employment and Society* and of *Papers. Revista de Sociologia*.

Maria Karamessini is professor of labour economics and economics of social policy at the Panteion University of Social and Political Sciences, Athens, Greece, as well as the Director of the Centre for Gender Studies and the President of the Gender Equality and Anti-Discrimination Committee of the same university.

Trine P. Larsen is professor in employment relations at Institute for Employment Research, Warwick University, Coventry, UK. She specialises in comparative employment and industrial relations, family policies, non-standard work and digitalisation. Her research has been published in various outlets, most recently in *Socio-Economic Review* and the *European Journal of Industrial Relations*.

Rennie Lee is a senior research fellow in the Life Course Centre at the University of Queensland, Brisbane, Australia. She is a sociologist with interests in immigrant integration, the children of immigrants and migration policy. She is currently working on a comparative project of the children of immigrants in the United Kingdom, Australia, Canada and the United States.

Janine Leschke is professor in political economy of labour markets at the Department of Management, Society and Communication in Copenhagen Business School, Copenhagen, Denmark. She is a board member of European Social Policy Analysis Network (ESPAnet) and co-chair of Nordic ESPAnet. She has published widely on employment, welfare and migration, and co-edited several volumes.

Madison Lloyd is a doctoral student in the Life Course Centre at the University of Queensland, Brisbane, Australia. She has research interests in gender inequality, family dynamics and domestic and family violence.

Martí López-Andreu is a senior lecturer in human resource management and employment relations at Newcastle University, Newcastle upon Tyne, UK. His research focuses on precarity, changing employment regulation and collective action in fragmented European labour markets. His work has been published in leading journals including *Work, Employment and Society* and the *British Journal of Industrial Relations*.

Enrique Lopezlira is the Director of the Low-Wage Work Program at the University of California, Berkeley Labor Center, Berkeley, USA. A labour economist, Dr. Lopezlira conducts research on how policies affect labour market outcomes for low-income workers, with a particular focus on how these policies impact economic inequality.

Luana Marx is a postdoctoral researcher at the University of Neuchâtel, Neuchâtel,Switzerland. She holds a PhD in sociology from the University of Oxford, and a master's in Social Policy from the London School of Economics and Political Science (LSE). She has expertise in social policy analysis and quantitative methods.

Agnieszka Piasna is a senior researcher at the European Trade Union Institute (ETUI) in Brussels, Belgium, and is associated with the Centre for Sociological Research at Katholieke Universiteit Leuven (KU Leuven), Leuven, Belgium. Her research interests include job quality, labour market policies and regulation, digitalisation and gender equality. She has a PhD in sociology from the University of Cambridge, Cambridge, UK.

Ania Plomien, associate professor at the London School of Economics Department of Gender Studies, London, UK, is a feminist political economist focusing on social reproduction, the nexus of paid and unpaid work, employment, care and labour migration and the role of policy in shaping these processes in the EU, the UK, Poland and Ukraine.

Uma Rani is senior economist at the Research Department of the International Labour Office, Geneva, Switzerland. Since 2016, she has been working on digital transformations in the world of work, wherein she tries to explore how labour and social institutions could be strengthened to address economic and social inequality.

Jill Rubery is professor of comparative employment systems and Executive Director of the Work and Equalities Institute at Alliance Manchester Business School, University of Manchester, Manchester, UK. She is an international expert on gender and employment and has worked extensively as a consultant for the ILO and the EU. Her research focuses on wages, working time, precarious work and the gendered impact of crises, and she has edited books on *Women and Recession* and *Women and Austerity* (published by Routledge). She is a Fellow of the British Academy.

Núria Sánchez-Mira is professor of sociology at the University of Neuchâtel, Neuchâtel, Switzerland. Her research focuses on gender inequalities at the work–family interface and across the life course, using quantitative, qualitative and mixed-methods approaches. She has worked on the gendered impacts of crises on labour markets and household divisions of labour, precarious work in female-dominated sectors and the digital transformation of work. She currently serves as Co-Editor-in-Chief of the *Swiss Journal of Sociology*.

Gregory Schwartz, senior lecturer at the University of Bristol Business School, Bristol, UK, is a labour sociologist focusing on the effects of transformations of global political economy on the social organisation of labour, workers' subjectivities, class, gender and migration, and social reproduction in the process of Europeanisation of Eastern Europe.

Stephanie Steinmetz is associate professor of sociology at the University of Lausanne, Lausanne, Switzerland, and University of Amsterdam, Amsterdam, the Netherlands. Her research examines educational and labour market vulnerabilities from cross-national and intersectional perspectives, focusing on female migrants' integration and discrimination. Her work has been published in leading journals, including the *European Sociological Review* and *Social Forces*.

Jennifer Tomlinson is professor of gender and employment relations at the University of Leeds, Leeds, UK. She has researched and published on topics including gender inequalities and part-time work; flexible working time arrangements and flexible careers; women returners and occupational gender segregation; gender and ethnicity in the legal profession.

Vera Trappmann is professor at the University of Leeds, Leeds, UK, and leads a Just Transition Competence Centre funded by the Hans-Böckler Foundation. Her research focuses on how macroeconomic labour market changes affect workers' lives regarding the climate crisis, precarious employment and platform work, examining both professional and personal impacts on individuals.

Luis Torres is associate professor at the Nottingham University Business School, Nottingham, the UK, and at Universidad del Desarrollo, Santiago, Chile. His expertise lies in the governance and management of sustainable organisations. Key themes in his work are corporate social responsibility/ESG, labour inequalities and compliance management.

Sueda Uludag is consulting associate at Charles River Associates. Prior to her current role, she was an intern at the Research Department of the International Labour Organisation, Geneva,Switzerland, and served as a research assistant at the AXA Research Lab on Gender Equality at Bocconi University, Milan, Italy.

Tracey Warren is professor in the Nottingham University Business School, Nottingham, UK. Her research focuses on inequalities of work–time, work–life balance, job quality and financial security. Tracey is a Fellow of the UK's Academy of Social Sciences and an Academic Fellow of the Chartered Institute of Personnel and Development.

ACKNOWLEDGEMENTS

This book is the outcome of a journey spanning over three years, during which time we convened a series of academic events to discuss and refine its themes: a panel of experts in November 2022 at the University of Lausanne; two special sessions at the ILO's *Regulating for Decent Work* Conferences 2023 and 2025 in Geneva; and an international workshop with the book's contributors at the University of Neuchâtel in June 2024.

We are very grateful to all colleagues who, along with the authors of this volume, contributed to these discussions as speakers, chairs or discussants: Stephanie Barrientos, Janine Berg, Nicky Le Feuvre, Jane Gray, Ania Plomien and Stephanie Steinmetz. Their insights greatly enriched the debates that shaped this volume. Our appreciation also goes to the institutions that supported these events: the Faculty of Social and Political Sciences of the University of Lausanne, the Faculty of Arts and Humanities of the University of Neuchâtel, the Swiss National Science Foundation (Scientific Exchanges Programme) and the Professorial Grant Monique de Meuron (Sandoz Foundation).

The open-access publication of this volume was made possible through the co-funding of the University of Neuchâtel and the Professorial Grant Monique de Meuron.

Finally, we owe special thanks to Felipe Corredor, whose careful coordination and attention to detail were invaluable in the final preparation of the manuscript.

Introduction

1

GENDER EQUALITY IN TURBULENT TIMES

From the financial crash to polycrisis

Jill Rubery, Valeria Insarauto and Núria Sánchez-Mira

This book addresses the impact of turbulence in the economic, social and environmental context on gender equality in the labour market and the social and family system in the Global North. Our starting plan for the book was to explore and take stock of how successive crises experienced from the late 2000s onwards have affected the realisation of and prospects for gender equality by applying and developing concepts drawn from earlier contributions on gender equality under crises (Bettio et al., 2013; Karamessini & Rubery, 2014a; Rubery, 1988). Specifically, this involved reviewing the effects of the financial crisis, through the austerity turn to the Covid-19 pandemic and recovery in stalling, accelerating or even reversing trends in women's economic and social position. These crises are all overt economic crises and have been labelled and recognised as such even where their origins diverged.

The book focuses on both women's contribution to and their treatment within the production and the social reproduction spheres. By making the interactions between production and social reproduction visible, the aim is to provide a feminist-informed perspective on economic crises that can be distinguished from a mainstream or neoliberal economic approach to crises where often only the production sphere is analysed (see concluding chapter Sánchez-Mira et al., 2026, this volume, for further explanation). We characterise this period of successive crises as turbulent times due to both the frequency and the variety of recent challenges to economic and social stability. In the space of only 15 years we have moved from a global financial crisis caused in large part by an out-of-control financial system to an austerity crisis where political preferences for shrinking the state may have exaggerated the need for fiscal restraints, to a major health crisis, originating in the transfer of disease from the animal kingdom to humans but exacerbated by a

DOI: 10.4324/9781003528210-2

lack of readiness, in operational and political terms, to manage such a pandemic, even in the richest countries. Furthermore, the period of recovery from the pandemic, far from offering a respite from turbulence, was becoming quickly dominated by a cost-of-living crisis associated with the Russo-Ukrainian war.

At an early stage in the development of the book, it became clear that a wider consideration of turbulence was needed to capture a range of challenges to the ways in which we live and work. These challenges are much discussed and anticipated but not yet fully realised and include, first, the potential impact from digitalisation and AI on the volume and nature of jobs, particularly as the Covid-19 pandemic had itself induced significant changes in ways of working, at least in white-collar jobs. Platform work was expanding into female-dominated areas such as care work, and an acceleration in the application of AI appeared to be just around the corner. These developments had already induced considerable debate on their gender equality impact, particularly as on the surface they appear in some respects to facilitate combining work and family. Consequently, some scrutiny of the evidence in relation to actual gender equality impacts was called for. The second long-term challenge, that is how to control and even reverse climate change, also has major significance for how we work and live and thus for the system of gender relations. Yet, in practice, the plans for implementing national and international commitments to net zero have hardly discussed changes to our ways of living and instead focus on a straightforward transfer of mainly male workers in high-polluting sectors into newly created green jobs. Not only might this approach reproduce current gender inequalities, but also this technology-driven solution might prove unattainable or insufficient. Hence, again there was a need to bring women's interests into consideration in how this transformation was to be designed and managed.

The third challenge is the by now longstanding need to change ways of working and living to fit changes in women's working patterns. This challenge may be considered a crisis in care provision but a crisis that often remains invisible, particularly at times of difficulty or crisis in the production sphere. The implicit assumption is that women will find some way to manage their responsibilities for both wage work and social reproduction (Elson, 2012) and that addressing the care crisis can therefore wait until times of economic prosperity. However, care crises keep emerging, whether in the form of stress on the health system or harm to children's education and development, not to mention stress on households and women. From these concerns we decided to include chapters on each of these challenges to the current order.

Our focus in the book is on experiences in the Global North. This reflects editorial and thematic choices that inevitably delimit the scope of the volume, leaving perspectives from and on the Global South less visible. Indeed, we recognise that even what is labelled a global crisis is often determined by a Global North perspective, while crises in the Global South may remain largely invisible.

Women in the South struggled at an earlier stage with structural adjustment policies (Elson, 2014) but this received relatively little recognition until women in the Global North faced similar problems under the austerity policies imposed after the financial crash. Some chapters do consider aspects of the multiple sources of interactions between changing dynamics in the North, related to crises and to technological, ecological and social changes, and the Global South. One chapter (Rani et al., 2026, this volume) focuses in detail on the role of digital platforms in opening up access for those located in the Global South to work that is paid for and organised in the Global North.

Importantly, the development of a distinctive feminist lens on the impact of crises also requires recognition of differences in experiences of crises within genders. This applies to spatial difference, not only between the Global North and Global South, as discussed, but also between developed economies where national or local specific institutional arrangements shape the environment in which women are located and their experience of crises (Karamessini & Rubery, 2014a; Rubery, 1988) so that no universal gender effect can be expected. Moreover, despite some commonalities by gender, there are also very different experiences by, for example, social class, ethnicity, race and migration status, age and generation among other factors, and indeed circumstances where the advance of some women's interests comes at the expense of other women. Contributors were encouraged to trace empirical impacts across social as well as spatial divides, to consider who within each gender benefits or loses under turbulence, and along which lines of stratification (class, migration, racialisation, etc.). Hence, while intersectionality was not adopted as a central conceptual framework in the book, and the available data did not always allow for a fully developed intersectional analysis, the overall aim was to be intersectionally sensitive (McBride et al., 2015) wherever possible.

The following sections of this chapter flesh out this introduction to the book project. In the next section, we outline our conceptual approach to gender relations and our understandings of the complex ways in which crises may influence trends in gender equality. This is followed by a brief historical review, starting from the 1970s to the present, of how these interactions between gender relations and crises have changed over time. These changes are linked to the nature of the crises, to the evolving political, social and economic context that is shaping women's position both in the wage economy and the domestic economy and finally, but by no means least important, to the changing aspirations, expectations and behaviours of women (and indeed men) over this time period. This review identifies how the core questions for gender equality have changed along with the changing world order and the more permanent integration of women into wage labour markets. This section is followed by a parallel review of developments over recent decades and into the present day in the three key challenges to how we live and work, namely from digitalisation and AI, from climate change and from failures to address support for care and social reproduction. This review immediately draws us into the intensifying sense of turbulence since the end of the

Covid-19 crisis. The most recent period has been characterised by numerous and dangerous conflicts, from the Russia–Ukraine war to the Israel–Palestine conflict and other flashpoints that may be further destabilised by the ongoing remaking of the world economic and political order. Moreover, the long-term challenges that we identified are themselves part of the observed and experienced turbulence, as they involve the complex problems of how to regulate the new technologies to protect human interests and decent work, how to transition to net zero and how to address the chronic care deficits. While these are longstanding and unresolved policy objectives, the new era has seen threats to the rights of nation states to regulate technologies, the tearing up of international agreements on implementing net zero and the emergence of a significant backlash against gender equality that calls into question even the need to make institutional changes to support developments in gender relations and instead favours a reversal of gender equality policies. In the conclusions of the volume, we take up the implications of what is widely considered to be a polycrisis of unresolved and interrelated crises, yet a polycrisis without a developed gender analysis. This introductory chapter ends by outlining the structure of this volume and explains how the analysis and synthesis of the contributions is provided in the final concluding chapter.

A conceptual lens for analysing the gendered impacts of crises

Before the impact of turbulence on paths to gender equality can be investigated, it is important to locate the analysis in the now rather vast literature on how, why and with what effects gender relations have been changing over recent decades. A key issue is the concept of gender relations which we regard as a social construct (Rubery, 2014) and therefore not related to any essentialist notions of gender differences. This social construct can and does vary over time, place and within genders so there can be no expectation of a uniform response to changes in economic conditions. For example, a rise or a fall in demand for labour does not indicate a uniform response resulting in either higher participation (an added worker effect) or withdrawal of labour (a reserve army effect). Uniform responses can only be expected under essentialist notions of gender, for example with women always being carers first, workers second or always being contingent rather than permanent members of the labour force (see Bruegel, 1979; Humphries, 1983; Rubery, 2011).

These essentialist approaches stand in opposition to the contrary belief, implicit in the influential World Economic Forum reports (see for example World Economic Forum, 2023), that most of the hard battles to achieve gender equality have effectively been won, with only the somewhat myopic views of established elites in business and politics standing in the way of full realisation of the benefits of gender equality for both capitalism and society. From this perspective, progress towards gender equality is a win-win for all, by adding to the available talent, with only outdated social norms the barrier to progress. This optimistic approach also sits in stark contrast to views that the forces of patriarchy are such that any indications of apparent progress towards gender equality are at best a mirage unless it stems from changes in male norms and values. That said, it is important in these turbulent times to be concerned with the potential for backlash against gender equality (Edström et al., 2024). This may be particularly likely where gender hierarchies are put at risk because patriarchy "is also not only about gender but about the maintenance and management of a multidimensional hierarchical status quo" (Edström et al., 2024, p. 281). Moreover, backlash may not always be reactive to new rights but can also be preemptive and with the objective of establishing a more misogynistic society than previously prevailed, as can be identified in developments in the United States from the formation of the Tea Party to the concerted attacks on gender equality policies and practices unleashed in the second Trump term of office. In analysing the notion of backlash, it is important to recognise that divergent positions on gender equality have always been present including hard-wired misogyny; turbulence may lead to changes in overt or even dominant positions and ideologies (Crouch & Keune, 2005).

Despite the risk of reversals, we take the view that positive change is also possible, supported by beliefs that substantive differences in the form of gender relations can be found across space and time. By regarding gender relations as a social construct, we take the view that gender relations are shaped by different and even divergent national models that follow path-specific patterns of development, reflecting interactions between institutional, social and political as well as economic factors. Research on path-specific developments in gender relations has both challenged and enriched understandings of differences between national models. For example, the varieties of capitalism literature has been critiqued for not accounting for diversity in approaches to social reproduction and the public sector (Mandel & Shalev, 2009), which are critical factors in understanding recent patterns of growth and development and in women's integration into employment. Likewise, feminist scholars at an early stage in the varieties of welfare state literature identified the need to view these systems not only from an apparently gender-neutral perspective of the decommodification of labour, but to include the issues of whether or not female labour had been commodified in the first place and whether systems of social support were based on strong or weak male breadwinner models (Lewis, 1992; Orloff, 1993; Sainsbury, 1996). Analysis of welfare systems is now more firmly grounded in its effects on women in both paid and unpaid work roles (Saraceno & Keck, 2011). Furthermore, changes in labour markets towards new forms of segmentation or dualisation reflect the divergent processes of women's integration into wage employment, linked to varieties of production, social reproduction and cultural systems (Pfau-Effinger, 1998; Rubery et al., 1999).

In taking a view that positive change is possible, it is also important to recognise that not all women benefit from apparent changes towards gender equality and that the experiences of change for women are strongly differentiated by race, ethnicity, migration status, age and social class (Warren, 2015) and other factors within the same employment systems. What constitutes progress for some women may be less advantageous for others (Gheaus, 2020) and could even be reliant on the exploitation of those supporting increased care demands, often female migrant labour (Bettio et al., 2006; Rodríguez-Modroño et al., 2022). This intersectional perspective needs to be kept in mind in all comparative analyses of, for example, gender relations within and between countries and according to the nature of the crisis or transition. Moreover, this standpoint also makes clear that if gender equality is to benefit most women, it is important to pursue overall equality in the labour market, both to protect vulnerable groups of women from absolute low employment standards and because to pursue gender equality in an unequal labour market is harder as it involves "swimming against the tide" (Blau & Kahn, 1992; Rubery & Koukiadaki, 2016).

In adopting an institutionalist approach to understanding variations in gender equality, we may be considered to be neglecting arguments that the influence of national institutions and models has been significantly weakened due to, for example, globalisation, the financialisation of neoliberal capitalism or the dominance of tech giants, all of which challenge the persistence of distinct varieties of capitalism. However, despite evidence of significant change within national models, the processes of reshaping have also demonstrated the resilience of national models even in the face of globalisation and their continued capacity to shape experiences of work, employment and social relations (Bosch et al., 2009), including gender relations. Furthermore, the current political turbulence is strongly related to the rejection of notions of globalisation and a resurgence of neonationalism.

These debates on the nature and form of change are in themselves linked to issues of how economies and societies respond to crises and turbulence and how the challenges to current ways of living and working stemming from technological, ecological and social changes are being addressed. It is to this topic that we now turn. Crises may play a role in the reshaping of gender relations over the long term but there can be no expectation of deterministic effects. For example, in the case of a political crisis such as war, one can identify how in the case of Portugal the mobilisation of women to fill the labour gaps caused by men fighting overseas led to women undertaking wage work on a full-time basis. This in part explains the exceptionalism of Portugal among the southern European countries in its record of high full-time work, although this characteristic was reinforced by the associated growth of the Portuguese textile, apparel and footwear industries, where women have provided an important source of labour (Tavora & Rubery, 2013). Yet the mobilisation of women for the Second World War effort across the UK and the United States, for example, had limited long-term impact on women's employment as most left their jobs after the war.

Change in gender relations may emerge from the labour market impacts of crises or may be shaped by policies enacted by the state in response to crises.

For example, in Spain, Insarauto (2021) argues that the development of part-time work in response to the financial crisis reinforced women's position as vulnerable economic dependants within the household. The role of the state can be expected to vary according to context; in the financial crisis, most European countries prioritised the implementation of neoliberal policies of flexibility, privatisation and fiscal constraint. Instead, during the Covid-19 pandemic there was widespread recognition of the importance of maintaining macroeconomic stability by supporting a wider range of social groups, including women who were excluded from work (Rubery & Tavora, 2021) to maintain consumption levels both for the well-being of citizens and to maintain demand for businesses. Indeed, the overwhelming need for the state to act during the Covid-19 pandemic perhaps called into question, at least temporarily, the neoliberal preference for market dominance and a small state.

The household is another site of potential change in gender relations for long-term trends towards more equal participation in wage work by couples (despite limited change in unpaid work) may be further strengthened by the experience of crises. This is particularly the case where unemployment risks are high for men (Sánchez-Mira & O'Reilly, 2019; Vitali & Arpino, 2016), putting sole male breadwinner households at high risk of severe income loss. Induced changes in family income generation in response to crises may serve to normalise a wider variety of household breadwinning arrangements but may also be regarded as unwanted and temporary (Sánchez-Mira, 2024).

There is now a wide literature on how economic crises may have gender impacts in both the short and the longer term. In reviewing this body of knowledge, it is clear that each crisis, depending on its nature, has given rise to different problems and challenges for gender equality. The impact is also dependent, on the one hand, on structural and political changes in the organisation of labour markets and, on the other hand, on changes in the strategies and behaviours of women and men. A gap may also exist between these behaviours and the social and institutional context in which people are living. Institutional arrangements may remain stuck in the shadow of the sole male breadwinner model of family organisation long after this has become largely an irrelevance for how people live and work. The following section thus traces the evolution of the context in which crises have occurred as well as changes in the nature of crises and their consequences starting from the 1970s up until the present day.

A brief history of crises and gender equality

Crises in the 1970s and 80s: women's labour as a flexible reserve?

Studies exploring the gender impact of crises in the 1970s and 1980s in the Global North were mainly concerned with the short-term labour market effects, to explore and, if appropriate, refute the notion of women mainly acting as a flexible reserve that could be turned off and on according to the needs of capitalism (Bruegel, 1979; Humphries, 1983; Rubery, 1988). At this point in the post-war development of women's integration into the wage labour market, the notion that their increased participation might only be a temporary response to high labour demand was still prevalent, at least for those working in low value-added jobs in manufacturing or services. In practice research found that some women did appear to provide a buffer but mainly in some parts of manufacturing and not across the occupational structure. Indeed, Milkman (1976) had argued that gender segregation, particularly into administrative and clerical work, provided protection, for at that time these employees were regarded as fixed overheads in many organisations. In addition, women were also entering expanding female-dominated professional work in public services such as nursing or primary teaching.

A process of desegregation of male-dominated jobs was also taking place, particularly in the United States (Reskin & Roos, 1990) but also in professional-type jobs in the UK (Crompton & Sanderson, 1990) as women were increasingly using investments in education to enter a wider range of occupations. A key question in relation to crises in this period was thus whether substitution effects, that is the process of desegregation and possible subsequent feminisation, were more likely in times of labour shortage. Alternatively, substitution effects might be stronger in the aftermath of recession as employers sought to reduce labour costs through employing cheaper labour or deskilling of work. In both cases women could provide a source of potential lower wage cost labour and a means of resegregation through the creation of more deskilled or routinised work, as found by Reskin and Roos (1990) in the United States.

These early analyses thus effectively focused on the processes by which women have integrated into wage employment, whether through "buffer-type" jobs, due to their apparent characteristics as contingent labour market participants; through expanding feminised professions and occupations; or through processes of desegregation and substitution that might involve internal restructuring of the occupation and some devaluation of those parts of the jobs that were becoming feminised.

With respect to women's position in the household, there was limited attention to impacts on unpaid work in these earlier stages of integration, perhaps reflecting low expectations of changes in entrenched social norms. Change was nevertheless taking place in household provisioning, with an increased reliance on wage goods as direct substitutes for domestic labour (for example through ready-made food) and as support for domestic labour (through household appliances). This change in consumption meant that there could be no easy reversal of women's participation simply because of a downturn in demand (Humphries & Rubery, 1984), a resistance that was reinforced by the evolving aspirations of women for education and wage work for their own personal development.

From Beijing to the financial crisis: the normalisation of women's employment integration?

In the two decades between the publication of the book on women and recession (Rubery, 1988) by one of this volume's editors and the onset of the financial crash in 2008, there was limited attention paid to the implications of crisis for gender equality in the Global North. This period was regarded as one of relative stability for the Organisation for Economic Co-operation and Development economies, characterised by a general sustained rise in female employment rates (OECD, 2018), reflecting women's greater investment in education and their changing aspirations towards careers. There was also more development of policies to promote gender equality; the high point of optimism was the aftermath of the UN's 1995 Beijing World Conference on Women where an agreement on commitments to gender mainstreaming of all policy was reached and endorsed by the EU, as reflected in the adoption of an equal opportunities pillar in the EU's employment strategy in 1998 (Rubery, 2015). While these developments suggested that policymakers did see merit in promoting gender equality simply for the benefit of women, there was always an economic rationale for this support, particularly that of addressing the problems of sustaining an ageing population. This economic justification for supporting women's employment came to dominate EU policymaking in the 2000s. Moreover, supposed benefits for equal opportunities and work–life balance were used to justify further development of neoliberal flexible labour market policies (Stratigaki, 2004). Nevertheless, the identification of economic benefits led to a widespread assumption that women's participation would continue to increase (in line with the EU's Lisbon target for higher women's employment by 2010) and, importantly, would be permanent.

However, the characterisation of this period as one of stability and progress does not hold up once a more intersectionally-sensitive lens is adopted, for this was also a period of deregulation and movement towards more flexible labour markets. The associated growth of precarious work had negative consequences for women, particularly in lower-skilled work. Changes were also evident in what types of jobs could be considered protected: the increased digitalisation of administrative and clerical work had undermined the protection that Milkman (1976) had argued was attached to these kinds of jobs in the 1970s. Instead, they were transformed into outsourced and offshored call centres or tasks were devolved to all who worked with a computer on a daily basis. Social class divisions were also widening at the household level, as middle-class women, often married to middle-class men, invested more in education and pursued professional careers. Moroever the disintegration of state-socialism from 1989 onwards in Europe caused major turbulence as these countries made the transition to capitalism. When eight of the post-socialist countries joined the EU in 2004, the conditions were set for a major expansion of EU migration flows due to severe problems encountered in adopting Western economic and social models (see Plomien & Schwartz, 2026, this volume). Migration offered perceived opportunities to improve household income because of the wide wage gaps (though offset by price gaps) within the EU. Moreover, through processes of both EU and non-EU migration by women, a temporary and partial resolution of the care crisis in advanced countries was provided by inflows of exploitable female migrant labour (Bettio et al., 2006).

However, perhaps the most serious way in which this characterisation of stability fails is in its neglect of instability in the Global South. This became more evident as the 2008 financial crisis started and parallels then began to be made, for example to the financial crisis in Asia in 1997. Crucially for the analysis of the subsequent austerity crisis in the Global North, the focus turned to the important critiques of structural adjustment policies implemented in the Global South by the World Bank and the IMF which had negative impacts on women (Elson, 2014). Moreover, women's further integration into wage employment was closely entwined with the further implementation of neoliberal approaches to economic management and financial market deregulation which may be considered to have set the conditions for the financial crash. For example, the consumption and housing booms that predated it were only sustained through the growth of household debt (Roberts, 2016), which in turn reinforced women's increasingly important role in supporting households' wage income and debt financing.

The financial and sovereign debt crises

By the time of the financial crash, earlier concerns over whether women's integration into wage work was temporary or permanent appeared less salient, though the growth of new forms of precarious work meant that many permanent members of the labour force, both male and female, might have little choice but to take jobs on contingent contracts. In the initial phase of the financial crisis, men's jobs were more affected than women's, even though research has found that in the badly affected male-dominated sectors of manufacturing and construction, women still lost more jobs than would be predicted if job loss was strictly proportional to gender shares of employment (Razzu & Singleton, 2018). Nevertheless, research suggested that the main sources of flexible labour supply or buffers in the financial crash proved to be young people and migrant workers (Bettio et al., 2013).

The research focus on gender equality issues turned more to household strategies to address the large loss of male jobs and incomes, particularly in badly hit countries. Women's income became more relevant for the economies of many families. Across Europe, there was an observed increase in the share of households where the woman was the main or sole breadwinner, which was particularly strong in the countries most affected by the crisis, such as Southern Europe, and among working-class couples (Dotti Sani, 2017; Sánchez-Mira & O'Reilly, 2019). Moreover, qualitative research found that household resilience strategies against the generalised reduction in household expenditures over the recessionary period were highly gendered, relying on an increase in (female) unpaid labour and with women more likely to deprive themselves of their own needs to safeguard their children and other family members (Castrillo et al., 2020). Even within the growing female breadwinner households during the financial crisis, shifts in the division of housework and care tasks were limited as female breadwinning was mostly perceived as an undesired and temporary situation, as research on the Spanish context has shown (Sánchez-Mira, 2024). Research showing the association of female breadwinning with economic hardship and decreased well-being may explain why this arrangement was considered undesirable by women as well as men (Kowalewska & Vitali, 2020; Kowalewska & Vitali, 2024). Nevertheless, women's persistent and increased labour market involvement over the crisis is likely to have reinforced the extension of the dual-earner model over the long run as a key way for couple households to gain protection from labour market risks (Marx et al., 2026, this volume).

The intensity of the crisis made it inevitable that it would spread to more gender-mixed private services from 2010 onwards, but it was the political response that particularly contributed to strengthening the impact of the crisis on women's employment (Bettio et al., 2013; Karamessini & Rubery, 2014b). The austerity policy response that followed can be seen as an effort to reinforce neoliberal policies through stronger fiscal rules and an effort to explain the neoliberal failures behind the crash as due to too high public spending and insufficient reform of labour markets towards the ideal flexible model. This movement was accompanied by a general downscaling of gender equality policies in the EU, endorsing the idea that equality should be perceived as a "luxury for good times", (Kantola & Lombardo, 2017; Karamessini & Rubery, 2014b) and gender mainstreaming was virtually absent from the political response to the crisis (Bettio et al., 2013). The implementation of austerity was facilitated by the state bailout policies that converted private debt into sovereign debt and enabled the EU, in conjunction with the European Central Bank and the IMF, to impose neoliberal reforms of industrial relations and cuts to public expenditure as conditions for financial support. These strategies were copied in some cases, such as the UK, even when not imposed by international organisations. However, other countries followed different strategies; for example, Obama in the United States applied a more expansive fiscal policy (Karamessini & Rubery, 2014b).

The euphemistically-named austerity policies directed attention to new issues and problems for gender equality, including the cuts to public services from 2010 onwards, that implicitly expected women to add unpaid labour to pick up the slack (Karamessini & Rubery, 2014b). This reduced public support for social care and childcare heightened pre-existing pressures on dual-earning and single-parent families. Furthermore, the long-term public sector employment and wage freezes directed attention to the important role played by the public sector in women's integration into employment and into professional jobs for those with higher education. Public sector cuts also resulted in a degradation of employment conditions in a female-dominated sector (Rubery, 2013) and favoured a refamiliarisation of care in countries where the long-term care system was still under development (Cunningham, 2015; Díaz Gorfinkiel & Elizalde San Miguel, 2015; Karamessini, 2026, this volume).

Overall in this period, any perceived reduction in gender inequalities, for example in gender gaps in employment, unemployment, activity or job quality, especially for the lower skilled, was the result of a downward levelling of men's position in the labour market, particularly for the lower skilled (Rubery, 2015; Visser, 2019). In addition, it was during this crisis period that a trend towards the reversal of gender-progressive ideologies emerged, fuelled by the rise of far-right parties and movements in the aftermath of the crisis across Europe and the United States. Most paradigmatic examples are the major backlash against women's social, sexual and reproductive rights, along with those of the LGBTQI community, in East-Central European post-socialist countries such as Poland or Hungary (Grabowska, 2015; Kováts, 2020). This trend against the perceived threat of "gender ideology" has now become stronger throughout Europe, with conservative and fundamentalist movements on the rise in countries as diverse as Austria, Croatia, France, Germany, Hungary, Poland, Spain, Slovenia and Slovakia and the United States (Köttig et al., 2017; Kováts, 2018; Stein, 2023).

From austerity to Covid-19

In the exit from the intense austerity period, many different political responses to the period of crises emerged so that overall policy directions have varied between and within continents, in part shaped by who was in power when the crisis hit as a change of government seems to be common during or just after crises (Bartels, 2012). Variation in political priorities can also be found within international institutions that in part govern the world economy; thus international organisations such as the IMF encouraged the EU to pursue strong austerity policies in response to the financial crisis but in the subsequent recovery period and into the Covid-19 pandemic, there was some stepping back from a full embrace of neoliberalism and financial orthodoxy. In the EU's case, this has been labelled the EU's social turn (Piasna & Theodoropoulou, 2024) that started with the development of the European Pillar of Social Rights in 2017 onwards. It is also found, for example, in the OECD's conversion to the idea that collective bargaining and social dialogue could provide a positive contribution to the reshaping of labour markets in a period of turbulence (OECD, 2019).

It is beyond the scope of this volume to track, let alone analyse, all these twists and turns in the recovery period; where these feature strongly in particular contributions to this volume, they are highlighted in the conclusions (see, for example, Figueiredo & López-Andreu, 2026, this volume; Karamessini, 2026, this volume). However, these variations in themselves are cause for scepticism (Bosch et al., 2009) with respect to any simplistic model of global convergence towards a neoliberal state.

The Covid-19 pandemic

An important factor likely to shape impacts by gender is the specific nature of the crisis; this effect was particularly evident in the Covid-19 pandemic, when a health crisis became almost immediately also an economic and social crisis due to social distancing measures. Three main new challenges for gender equality could be identified. First, the rapid rollout and effective success of remote working became an important potential long-term legacy, raising issues of how we would work in the future and whether that would be different for women and men. Second, household arrangements were destabilised because of the rise in telework that ensued from the lockdowns, and which placed men as well as women in the space where the increased domestic and care work was taking place. Third, the pandemic led to the possibility of reevaluating how work was organised and rewarded as public recognition of the role played by care workers in keeping people safe raised awareness of the poor conditions of work in essential sectors.

In practice, the overall job loss during the Covid-19 pandemic proved to be relatively gender neutral, at least at an aggregate level, largely because women were more likely than men to work in teleworkable sectors and in sectors that were deemed essential (Eurofound, 2022a). However, remote working widened divisions among women as this option was mainly available to those in white-collar occupations (Eurofound, 2022b) and it was working-class women, particularly those with children, who were more exposed to job loss (Eurofound, 2022b; Rubery & Tavora, 2021). Indeed, well-paid jobs even expanded, reflecting broader pre-existing trends towards occupational upgrading (Eurofound and European Commission Joint Research Centre, 2021), and indicating how gender inequalities interact with class dynamics. Moreover, compared to the financial crisis, a much higher share of women was covered by short-term income support policies (Rubery & Tavora, 2021), though some groups of women still remained outside these protective supports. The legacy of remote working, however, is unlikely to be fully positive even for women who can take advantage of the option. Research is indicating that remote working along with other forms of flexible working may even add to women's working days as women feel under pressure to prove their continued value to the company under increasing competitive conditions to overcome the risk that remote workers may be more invisible (Chung, 2022).

The compulsory lockdowns combined with the closure of childcare facilities resulted in enforced re-familiarisation with care and domestic tasks, triggering consequences such as poor work–life balance and time poverty for parents, especially women. Several European and national-level studies found that more women than men reduced their working hours or left the labour market altogether due to increased unpaid work demands (Eurofound, 2022a; Collins et al., 2021).

Moreover, even though men also often worked at home, evidence suggests that women undertook a disproportionate amount of housework and childcare even when both parents were working remotely and schools were closed. Only when the father worked from home but the mother did not (Eurofound, 2022a) did fathers' childcare share increase.

Care work was at the centre of this pandemic, whether paid or unpaid. For paid care workers, there was increased public recognition of the social importance of this work and the prevailing poor working conditions. However, efforts in practice to improve rewards for care staff often amounted to only very short-term financial bonuses (Eurofound, 2022a). Nonetheless, these considerations may have influenced the EU's later adoption of new measures to raise minimum wages, of particular importance to care staff.

From the pandemic to new sources of turbulence

The expectation during the Covid-19 pandemic was that the experience of lockdown might encourage people – both men and women – to reconsider how they worked and lived. However, while discussions continued, for example on opportunities to change the spatio-temporal organisation of work and the benefits and risks of blurring boundaries between work and home, such reflections were soon eclipsed by new concerns over the outbreak of war in Ukraine and the rapidly accelerating cost of living. Women were particularly vulnerable to rises in the cost of living, described by some as the "shock absorbers" of poverty (Topping, 2022). The cost rises particularly affected essential goods like housing, food and energy (International Labour Office [ILO], 2022) and these increases in essential goods had a particularly negative impact on single parent households, a majority of which are headed by women (Sologon et al., 2024). Women often have more responsibility for managing budgets (Women's Budget Group [WBG], 2024) as well as for energy-intensive household tasks such as cooking. Across many countries in Europe, substantial minimum wage increases were introduced to support low-wage workers in the face of high inflation although in almost half of all those countries with a statutory minimum wage the nominal increases were insufficient to preserve purchasing power during the cost-of-living crisis (Müller, 2023). Nevertheless, this can be seen to have heralded a new era of higher minimum wages, of definite benefit to women who almost always gain most from increases in wage floors. The 2022 adoption of the European Minimum Wage Directive (European Parliament and Council of the European Union, 2022), with its dual objective of ensuring adequate minimum wages and strengthening collective bargaining, should consolidate this trend towards a higher wage floor in Europe, though further improvements in women's pay are highly dependent on whether the aim of extending collective bargaining coverage is actively pursued.

Since the cost-of-living crisis that followed the Covid-19 pandemic, the world has become even more turbulent, notably due to the Israel–Palestine war to add to the ongoing war in Ukraine, to the related energy crisis and refugee crises, and to the multi-faceted and unpredictable changes to United States policy in Trump's second term. Contributing to the perception of persistent turbulence are the ongoing long-term crises related to the impact of new technologies, the increasingly evident process of climate change and environmental degradation and continuing gaps in the provision of care. The political turbulence that has accelerated in the three years since we started planning this book in 2022 has added to the uncertainty, putting in question the capacity of policymakers at national and international levels to address these challenges in a systematic way, let alone address their undoubted gender equality implications.

To take first the impact of digital and AI technologies, research over the last 15 years or so has revealed increasing cause for concern over the consequences of these developments for employment and associated risks for gender equality. These concerns include the inequalities and insecurities associated with the platform economy, especially the threat to the survival of the standard employment relationship, which is not only the main institution for providing some economic security and supporting social reproduction but also an essential vehicle for equal opportunities policy such as maternity leave and equal pay. Likewise, extended use of AI may be embedding gender bias as well as increasing risks of job displacement, applying now as much in knowledge workdue due to generative AI as routine work (Fernandez Macias et al., 2025; ILO, 2025). The impact of these developments by gender is not yet fully known and while digitally-enabled remote and flexible work for women may be providing some new opportunities, there are also some new risks. Indeed, far from solving problems of combining work and family care, the traditional gender division of labour may be being reinforced and working days more extended. Yet, despite both wide agreement that new regulatory frameworks are urgently needed to protect humanity against the potential negative impacts of these developments and also some progress being made in developing new regulations (for example the EU directive and the proposed ILO new standard on platform work), US threats to impose high tariffs on sovereign states attempting to regulate the US-owned tech giants may significantly destabilise regulatory efforts. Moreover, these problems may soon be eclipsed by the intensified competition between China and the United States for technological, economic and political dominance. In this context, gender equality concerns may well be overlooked.

There is just as much turbulence over the planned move to net zero. After the Paris Accords to move the world economy to net zero, there was optimism that the conflict between climate sceptics and climate scientists could be brought to an end, and the hard job of the transition could start. Trump's withdrawal from the Paris Accords in his first term was a warning of what might yet come, and at the moment of writing this introduction, a serious backlash is growing against net zero by all far-right and even some supposedly mainstream conservative parties.

Yet without a concerted move to implement planned changes both to the technologies in use and our ways of living and consuming, catastrophic changes to our way of life can be anticipated. The implications for gender equality of either a planned transition to net zero or an unplanned change in environmental conditions are unclear, not only because these outcomes are in essence still unknowable but also because there has been little consideration of the environmental crisis from a gender perspective. This applies to changes in the wage labour market but perhaps even more importantly to changes in how we consume and their implications for unpaid work in the home. Gender equality so far has hardly featured in net zero discussions (see Daly et al., 2026, this volume) but the likelihood of initiating such a discussion may be diminishing as we face the task of rediscussing what were thought to be settled debates, for example, that the world needs to use less, not more, fossil fuels.

Finally, if we consider the social reproduction and care challenge, political and economic turbulence is also creating contradictory pressures. Women's integration into wage work on similar terms to men is proving unsustainable in the longer term without a new social contract based on both more social support for care from the state (Pearson, 2014) and changes to men's involvement in unpaid work, in turn facilitated by changes in workplace norms. However, a stable political system may be a necessary condition for progress to be made in bringing about the essential changes in welfare systems and in working practices to improve the institutional match with changing gender regimes. The positive shift towards a more active social policy in the EU from 2017 (Piasna & Theodoropoulou, 2024) importantly included a new EU care strategy, but the realisation of that strategy may be put in question by recent fiscal restraints and by the priority accorded to investment in defence over investment in care. Even more challenging is the backlash in the United States and other far-right dominated countries against the whole implicit commitment to support care rather than expect women to undertake double shifts. In some countries, the preferred option might be to reverse women's involvement in the wage economy or at least rescind the implicit social contract to provide more support for their unpaid work.

Thus the mounting evidence of political, social, technological and ecological sources of both disruption and resistance has highlighted the risks of taking for granted both a political commitment, even if weak, towards gender equality and also the continued existence of institutions in the labour market, welfare and public services systems through which progress to gender equality can be both promoted and monitored. At the same time, current turbulence may also be calling into question the globalisation of the world economy and dominance of neoliberalism. Women's employment may have expanded on the back of neoliberalism, but this economic ideology also prevented the development of a more rounded gender equality programme. Furthermore, these fast-paced changes gave weight to the notion of polycrisis (Lawrence et al., 2024; Parnell et al., 2024) or permacrisis

(Brown et al., 2023) which have begun to be widely mooted in political and academic circles as appropriate descriptions of the current and likely future state of the world. These concerns have amplified as the book project progressed and in writing our conclusions presented in Chapter 15 (Sánchez-Mira et al., 2026), we have sought to not only consider the lessons of the recent past, as outlined in this introductory chapter and as explored and elaborated in the chapters to this volume, but also to consider the prospects of further turbulence and how gender issues interact with both the sources of turbulence and the outcomes stemming from multi-dimensional and contradictory pressures for change.

The plan of the book

This volume is topped and tailed by two substantive chapters by the editors; this introductory chapter provides information on how we think about conceptualising gender relations and gender equality and offers a brief overview of how the nature and the impact of crises on gender equality have changed over time. These changes are reflective of long-term changes in women's roles in both wage work and the household economy.

These themes in the introduction are then picked up in the commissioned contributions to the volume. The first set of chapters under the title "Labour markets in crises and intersecting inequalities" includes three contributions primarily focused on employment change and one focused on trends in the gender pay gap. Two provide a pan-European perspective (Steinmetz & Guarnerio, 2026; Bashevska & Dotti Sani, 2026) while two offer country case studies, one on the UK (Torres & Warren, 2026) and the other on two southern European countries, Spain and Portugal (Figueiredo & López-Andreu, 2026). This section reveals a range of intersectional impacts, whether by gender and migrant status (Steinmetz & Guarnerio, 2026) or by gender and social class (Torres & Warren, 2026; Figueiredo & López-Andreu, 2026).

The second set of chapters – the largest grouping in the volume – focuses on issues of social reproduction under the title "The crisis of social reproduction: households and the state". The first two look at different sides of women's position in the household; the first takes a pan-European look at changes in breadwinning strategies as affected by crisis (Marx et al., 2026); the second takes a longitudinal approach to studying change in domestic and care labour in Australia (Baxter et al., 2026). A third chapter (Plomien & Schwartz, 2026) addresses the fallout from the rupture in the economic and social system in post-socialist countries, with Poland and Ukraine the examples where the market transition undermined the social reproduction system. The chapter explores the gendered responses by citizens to this chronic crisis. This example of how the market transition failed to provide for sustainable social reproduction is mirrored in the example of social care arrangements in California discussed in the fourth chapter by Lopezlira and Hunter. The United States is probably the most market-driven economy in the world, but this system has been unable to develop a workable care system for an ageing population, leading in California to innovative solutions based around both paying for unwaged work and developing new systems of collective bargaining. The final two chapters in this set take up the issues of transforming the care systems (Karamessini, 2026) and the welfare systems (Larsen et al., 2026) to match the changing behaviour of women as they move away from being primarily carers to long-term participants in wage work. Here the EU has been important in finally pushing for further change in care systems across Europe (Karamessini, 2026), but Larsen et al. find that at the nation-state level the legacy of the male breadwinner household model can still be found in welfare arrangements across a wide variety of countries, including even in the Nordic countries, prized for their gender equality records.

The final set of three chapters under the title "Gendering the digital and net zero transitions" explores the gender equality impacts of both the AI and digital challenges and the movement to net zero. The first chapter (Piasna, 2026) shows how two forms of remote working – telework and platform work – are not solving but often reinforcing gender inequality, while the chapter by Rani et al. (2026) further strengthens these conclusions in relation to all forms of gig work, especially in the Global South, where opportunities to work for clients in the Global North are further exploiting and underutilising women's capacities. The section concludes with a review (Daly et al., 2026) of the lack of a gender perspective on debates on the transition to net zero and the potential consequence of this absence for gender equality.

The final concluding chapter (Sánchez-Mira et al., 2026) not only reviews the implications of these contributions in relation to previous work on gender equality and crises but also describes how this gender lens needs to be extended in the current developing debates on polycrisis, which has remained so far largely gender-blind. This is found to have the effect of maintaining the invisibility of the crisis in social reproduction. The introduction of a gender lens on polycrises extends attention beyond the production system by focusing on women's role in both production and social production spheres and their interconnections. Against this background, the chapter discusses the prospects for gender equality in turbulent times.

References

Bartels, L. (2012, May 16). Elections in hard times. *Progressive Review, 137*. https://www.ippr.org/articles/elections-in-hard-times

Bashevska, M., & Dotti Sani, G. (2026). The gendered impact of the Covid-19 pandemic on labor market outcomes: A comparative European perspective. In J. Rubery, N. Sánchez-Mira, & V. Insarauto (Eds.), *Women in turbulent times. Crises, transitions, and challenges for gender equality* (pp. 52–72). Routledge.

Baxter, J., Campbell, A., Lee, R., & Lloyd, M. (2026). Covid-19 and gender gaps in paid and unpaid work. In J. Rubery, N. Sánchez-Mira, & V. Insarauto (Eds.), *Women in turbulent times. Crises, transitions, and challenges for gender equality* (pp.141–161). Routledge.

Bettio, F., Corsi, M., D'Ippoliti, C., Lyberaki, A., Samek Lodovici, M., & Verashchagina, A. (2013). *The impact of the economic crisis on the situation of women and men and on gender equality policies: Synthesis report*. Publications Office of the European Union.

Bettio, F., Simonazzi, A., & Villa, P. (2006). Change in care regimes and female migration: The "care drain" in the Mediterranean. *Journal of European Social Policy*, *16*(3), 271–285. https://doi.org/10.1177/0958928706065598

Blau, F. D., & Kahn, L. M. (1992). The gender earnings gap: Learning from international comparisons. *American Economic Review*, *82*(2), 533–538. https://doi.org/10.3386/w4224

Bosch, G., Lehndorff, S., & Rubery, J. (2009). European employment models in flux: Pressures for change and prospects for survival and revitalization. In G. Bosch, S. Lehndorff, & J. Rubery (Eds.), *European employment models in flux* (pp. 1–56). Palgrave Macmillan. https://doi.org/10.1057/9780230237001_1

Brown, G., El-Erian, M., & Spence, M. (2023). *Permacrisis: A plan to fix a fractured world*. Simon and Shuster.

Bruegel, I. (1979). Women as a reserve army of labour: A note on recent British experience. *Feminist Review*, *3*(1), 12–23. https://doi.org/10.1057/fr.1979.18

Castrillo, C., Martín, M. P., Arnal, M., & Serrano, A. (2020). Gender regimes in vulnerable households during the recession-what has changed and what not. In M. Boost, J. Dagg, J. Gray, & M. Promberger (Eds.), *Poverty, crisis and resilience* (pp. 143–160). Elgar. https://doi.org/10.4337/9781788973205.00019

Chung, H. (2022). *The flexibility paradox: Why flexible working leads to (self-) exploitation*. Policy Press. https://doi.org/10.1332/policypress/9781447354772.001.0001

Collins, C., Landivar, L. C., Ruppanner, L., & Scarborough, W. J. (2021). COVID-19 and the gender gap in work hours. *Gender, Work & Organization*, *28*(S1), 549–560. https://doi.org/10.1111/gwao.12506

Crompton, R., & Sanderson, K. (1990). *Gendered jobs and social change*. Routledge.

Crouch, C., & Keune, M. (2005). Changing dominant practice: Making use of institutional diversity in Hungary and the UK. In W. Streeck & K. Thelen (Eds.), *Beyond continuity: Institutional change in advanced political economies* (pp. 83–102). Oxford University Press. https://doi.org/10.1093/oso/9780199280452.003.0003

Cunningham, I. (2015). Austerity, personalization and the degradation of voluntary sector employment conditions. *Competition & Change*, *19*(3), 228–245. https://doi.org/10.1177/1024529415580261

Daly, J., Trappmann, V., Bessa, I., & Tomlinson, J. (2026). Unpacking the green economy: Worker justice without gender justice? In J. Rubery, N. Sánchez-Mira, & V. Insarauto (Eds.), *Women in turbulent times. Crises, transitions, and challenges for gender equality* (pp.297–315). Routledge.

Díaz Gorfinkiel, M., & Elizalde San Miguel, B. (2015). Desprofesionalizando el servicio público de asistencia a domicilio en los cuidados de larga duración: Análisis de la reconfiguración del sector en la región de Madrid. *Zerbitzuan: Gizarte zerbitzuetarako aldizkaria= Revista de servicios sociales*, *60*, 131–141. https://doi.org/10.5569/1134-7147.60.09

Dotti Sani, G. M. (2017). The economic crisis and changes in work–family arrangements in six European countries. *Journal of European Social Policy*, *28*(2), 177–193. https://doi.org/10.1177/0958928717700566

Edström, J., Greig, A., & Skinner, C. (2024). Patriarchal (dis)orders: Backlash as crisis management. *Signs: Journal of Women in Culture and Society*, *49*(2), 277–309. https://doi.org/10.1086/726744

Elson, D. (2012). Social reproduction in the global crisis: Rapid recovery or long-lasting depletion? In P. Utting, S. Razavi, & R. V. Buchholz (Eds.), *The global crisis and transformative social change* (pp. 63–80). Palgrave Macmillan. https://doi.org/10.1057/9781137002501_4

Elson, D. (2014). Economic crises from the 1980s to the 2010s. In S. Rai & G. Waylen (Eds.), *New frontiers in feminist political economy* (pp. 189–212). Routledge.

Eurofound, & European Commission Joint Research Centre. (2021). *European jobs monitor 2021: Gender gaps and the employment structure*. Publications Office of the European Union.

Eurofound. (2022a). *COVID-19 pandemic and the gender divide at work and home*. Publications Office of the European Union.

Eurofound. (2022b). *Recovery from COVID-19: The changing structure of employment in the EU*. Publications Office of the European Union.

European Parliament, & Council of the European Union. (2022). *Directive (EU) 2022/2041 of the European Parliament and of the Council of 19 October 2022 on adequate minimum wages in the European Union* (L 275, 33–47). Official Journal of the European Union. https://eur-lex.europa.eu/eli/dir/2022/2041/oj

Fernandez Macias, E., Gonzalez Vazquez, I., Torrejon Perez, S., & Nurski, L. (2025). *Work in the digital era: How technology is transforming work and occupations*. Publications Office of the European Union. https://data.europa.eu/doi/10.2760/0956105

Figueiredo, H., & López-Andreu, M. (2026). Gender pay inequality and wage setting institutions through crises and recoveries: A Southern European success story? In J. Rubery, N. Sánchez-Mira, & V. Insarauto (Eds.), *Women in turbulent times. Crises, transitions, and challenges for gender equality* (pp. 94–116). Routledge.

Gheaus, A. (2020, February 10). Feminism for working-class women is the best feminism [blog post]. *Northern Notes*. https://northernnotes.leeds.ac.uk/feminism-for-working-class-women-is-the-best-feminism/

Grabowska, M. (2015). Cultural war or "business as usual"? Recent instances, and the historical origins of a "backlash" against women's and sexual rights in Poland. In Heinrich Böll Foundation (Eds.), *Anti-gender movements on the rise? Strategising for gender equality in Central and Eastern Europe* (pp. 54–64). Heinrich-Böll-Stiftung.

Humphries, J. (1983). The "emancipation" of women in the 1970s and 1980s: From the latent to the floating. *Capital and Class*, *7*(2), 6–28. https://doi.org/10.1177/030981688302000101

Humphries, J., & Rubery, J. (1984). The reconstitution of the supply side of the labour market: The relative autonomy of social reproduction. *Cambridge Journal of Economics*, *8*(4), 331–346. https://doi.org/10.1093/oxfordjournals.cje.a035554

Insarauto, V. (2021). Women's vulnerability to the economic crisis through the lens of part-time work in Spain. *Work, Employment and Society*, *35*(4), 621–639. https://doi.org/10.1177/09500170211001271

International Labour Office. (2022). *Global wage report 2022–23: The impact of inflation and COVID-19 on wages and purchasing power*.

International Labour Office. (2025). *Generative AI and jobs: A refined global index of occupational exposure* (Working Paper No. 140). https://www.ilo.org/sites/default/files/2025-05/WP140_web.pdf

Kantola, J., & Lombardo, E. (Eds.). (2017). *Gender and the economic crisis in Europe: Politics, institutions and intersectionality*. Springer. https://doi.org/10.1007/978-3-319-50778-1

Karamessini, M. (2026). The "care transition" in turbulent times. In J. Rubery, N. Sánchez-Mira, & V. Insarauto (Eds.), *Women in turbulent times. Crises, transitions, and challenges for gender equality* (pp. 207–228). Routledge.

Karamessini, M., & Rubery, J. (Eds.). (2014a). *Women and austerity: The economic crisis and the future for gender equality.* Routledge. https://doi.org/10.4324/9780203066294

Karamessini, M., & Rubery, J. (2014b). Economic crisis and austerity: Challenges to gender equality. In M. Karamessini & J. Rubery (Eds.), *Women and austerity: The economic crisis and the future for gender equality* (pp. 314–351). Routledge. https://doi.org/10.4324/9780203066294

Köttig, M., Bitzan, R., & Pető, A. (Eds.). (2017). *Gender and far right politics in Europe.* Palgrave Macmillan. https://doi.org/10.1007/978-3-319-43533-6

Kováts, E. (2018). Questioning consensuses: Right-wing populism, anti-populism, and the threat of "gender ideology". *Sociological Research Online*, *23*(2), 528–538. https://doi.org/10.1177/1360780418764735

Kováts, E. (2020). Post-socialist conditions and the Orbán government's gender politics between 2010 and 2019 in Hungary. In G. Dietze & J. Roth (Eds.), *Right-wing populism and gender: European perspectives and beyond* (pp. 75–100). Transcript Verlag. https://doi.org/10.1515/9783839449806-005

Kowalewska, H., & Vitali, A. (2020). Breadwinning or on the breadline? Female breadwinners' economic characteristics across 20 welfare states. *Journal of European Social Policy*, *31*(2), 125–142. https://doi.org/10.1177/0958928720971094

Kowalewska, H., & Vitali, A. (2024). The female-breadwinner well-being "penalty": Differences by men's (un)employment and country. *European Sociological Review*, *40*(2), 293–308. https://doi.org/10.1093/esr/jcad034

Larsen, T. P., Leschke, J., & Bekker, S. (2026). Unemployment and care risks in times of crisis: Gender (in)equalities at the intersection of unemployment benefits, childcare and leave policies. In J. Rubery, N. Sánchez-Mira, & V. Insarauto (Eds.), *Women in turbulent times. Crises, transitions, and challenges for gender equality* (pp. 229–254). Routledge.

Lawrence, M., Homer-Dixon, T., Janzwood, S., Rockström, J., Renn, O., & Donges, J. F. (2024). Global polycrisis: The causal mechanisms of crisis entanglement. *Global Sustainability*, *7*, Article e6. https://doi.org/10.1017/sus.2024.1

Lewis, J. (1992). Gender and the development of welfare regimes. *Journal of European Social Policy*, *2*(3), 159–173. https://doi.org/10.1177/095892879200200301

Lopezlira, E., & Hunter, S. (2026). Enhancing dignity and equity: Homecare workforce challenges amidst the cost of living crisis, with a focus on California. In J. Rubery, N. Sánchez-Mira, & V. Insarauto (Eds.), *Women in turbulent times. Crises, transitions, and challenges for gender equality* (pp.184–206). Routledge.

Mandel, H., & Shalev, M. (2009). Gender, class, and varieties of capitalism. *Social Politics: International Studies in Gender, State & Society*, *16*(2), 161–181. https://doi.org/10.1093/sp/jxp006

Marx, L., Bian, F., & Sánchez-Mira, N. (2026). Crises as drivers of change in couples' paid work arrangements in Europe. In J. Rubery, N. Sánchez-Mira, & V. Insarauto (Eds.), *Women in turbulent times. Crises, transitions, and challenges for gender equality* (pp. 119–140). Routledge.

McBride, A., Hebson, G., & Holgate, J. (2015). Intersectionality: Are we taking enough notice in the field of work and employment relations? *Work, Employment and Society*, *29*(2), 331–341. https://doi.org/10.1177/0950017014538337

Milkman, R. (1976). Women's work and economic crisis: Some lessons of the great depression. *Review of Radical Political Economics*, *8*(1), 73–97. https://doi.org/10.1177/048661347600800107

Müller, T. (2023). *Minimum wage developments in 2022 - fighting the cost-of-living crisis* (Report). ETUI. https://www.etui.org/sites/default/files/2023-03/Minimum%20wage%20developments%20in%202022-fighting%20the%20cost-of-living%20crisis_2023.pdf

Organisation for Economic Co-operation and Development. (2018). *Is the last mile the longest? Economic gains from gender equality in nordic countries* (Report). https://doi.org/10.1787/9789264300040-en

Organisation for Economic Co-operation and Development. (2019). *Negotiating our way up: Collective bargaining in a changing world of work.*

Orloff, A. S. (1993). Gender and the social rights of citizenship: The comparative analysis of gender relations and welfare states. *American Sociological Review*, *58*(3), 303–328. https://doi.org/10.2307/2095903

Parnell, T., Van Hout, T., & Del Fante, D. (2024). Critical discursive responses to polycrisis. In T. Parnell, T. Van Hout, & D. Del Fante (Eds.), *Critical approaches to polycrisis* (pp. 1–14). Palgrave Macmillan. https://doi.org/10.1007/978-3-031-76966-5_1

Pearson, R. (2014). Gender, globalisation and the reproduction of labour: Bringing the state back in. In S. Rai & G. Waylen (Eds.), *New frontiers in feminist political economy* (pp. 19–43). Routledge.

Pfau-Effinger, B. (1998). Culture or structure as explanations for differences in part-time work in Germany, Finland and the Netherlands? In C. Fagan & J. O'Reilly (Eds.), *Part-time prospects* (pp. 177–198). Routledge.

Piasna, A. (2026). Digitalisation and remote work: Gendered outcomes in job quality and the role of persistent gender inequalities in paid and unpaid work. In J. Rubery, N. Sánchez-Mira, & V. Insarauto (Eds.), *Women in turbulent times. Crises, transitions, and challenges for gender equality* (pp. 257–274). Routledge.

Piasna, A., & Theodoropoulou, S. (2024). *Benchmarking working Europe 2024: The ongoing quest for Social Europe*. ETUI.

Plomien, A., & Schwartz, G. (2026). The crisis of social reproduction provisioning: Gender, class and migration in Poland and Ukraine. In J. Rubery, N. Sánchez-Mira, & V. Insarauto (Eds.), *Women in turbulent times. Crises, transitions, and challenges for gender equality* (pp. 162–183). Routledge.

Rani, U., Gobel, N., & Uludag, S. (2026). Unmasking gender disparities in the digital economy: Beyond access and numbers. In J. Rubery, N. Sánchez-Mira, & V. Insarauto (Eds.), *Women in turbulent times. Crises, transitions, and challenges for gender equality* (pp. 275–296). Routledge.

Razzu, G., & Singleton, C. (2018). Segregation and gender gaps in the United Kingdom's great recession and recovery. *Feminist Economics*, *24*(4), 31–55. https://doi.org/10.1080/13545701.2018.1451907

Reskin, B., & Roos, P. (Eds.). (1990). *Job queues, gender queues.* Temple University Press.

Roberts, A. (2016). Household debt and the financialization of social reproduction: Theorizing the UK housing and hunger crises. In S. Soederberg (Ed.), *Risking capitalism Research in Political Economy* 31: 35-164.https://doi.org/10.1108/S0161-7230201631

Rodríguez-Modroño, P., Agenjo-Calderón, A., & López-Igual, P. (2022). Platform work in the domestic and home care sector: New mechanisms of invisibility and exploitation

of women migrant workers. *Gender & Development*, *30*(3), 619–635. https://doi.org/10.1080/13552074.2022.2121060
Rubery, J. (Ed.). (1988). *Women and recession*. Routledge.
Rubery, J. (2011). Towards a gendering of the labour market regulation debate. *Cambridge Journal of Economics*, *35*(6), 1103–1126. https://doi.org/10.1093/cje/ber001
Rubery, J. (2013). Public sector adjustment and the threat to gender equality. In D. Vaughan-Whitehead (Ed.), *Public sector shock: The impact of policy retrenchment in Europe* (pp. 43–83). Edward Elgar Publishing. https://doi.org/10.4337/9781781955352.00007
Rubery, J. (2014). From "women and recession" to "women and austerity": A framework for analysis. In M. Karamessini & J. Rubery (Eds.), *Women and austerity: The economic crisis and the future for gender equality* (pp. 17–36). Routledge.
Rubery, J. (2015). Austerity and the future for gender equality in Europe. *ILR Review*, *68*(4), 715–741. https://doi.org/10.1177/0019793915588892
Rubery, J., & Koukiadaki, A. (2016). *Closing the gender pay gap: A review of the issues, policy mechanism and international evidence*. International Labour Office (ILO).
Rubery, J., Smith, M., & Fagan, C. (1999). *Women's employment in Europe. Trends and prospects*. Routledge.
Rubery, J., & Tavora, I. (2021). The Covid-19 crisis and gender equality: Risks and opportunities. In B. Vanhercke, S. Spasova, & B. Fronteddu (Eds.), *Social policy in the European Union: State of play 2020* (pp. 71–96). European Trade Union Institute (ETUI) and European Social Observatory (OSE). https://www.etui.org/sites/default/files/2020-12/Social%20policy%20in%20the%20European%20Union%20state%20of%20play%202020-web.pdf
Sainsbury, D. (1996). *Gender, equality and welfare states*. Cambridge University Press. https://doi.org/10.1017/CBO9780511520921
Sánchez-Mira, N. (2024). (Un)doing gender in female breadwinner households: Gender relations and structural change. *Gender, Work & Organization*, *31*(4), 1196–1213. https://doi.org/10.1111/gwao.12775
Sánchez-Mira, N., & O'Reilly, J. (2019). Household employment and the crisis in Europe. *Work, Employment and Society*, *33*(3), 422–443. https://doi.org/10.1177/0950017018809324
Sánchez-Mira, N., Rubery, J., & Insarauto, V. (2026). The future of gender equality in turbulent times: Why we need a gender lens on polycrisis. In J. Rubery, N. Sánchez-Mira, & V. Insarauto (Eds.), *Women in turbulent times. Crises, transitions, and challenges for gender equality* (pp. 319–347). Routledge.
Saraceno, C., & Keck, W. (2011). Towards an integrated approach for the analysis of gender equity in policies supporting paid work and care responsibilities. *Demographic Research*, *25*(11), 371–406. https://doi.org/10.4054/DemRes.2011.25.11
Sologon, D. M., Doorley, K., O'Donoghue, C., & Peluso, E. (2024). *The gendered nature of the cost-of-living crisis in Europe* (IZA Discussion Paper No. 16820). IZA Institute of Labor Economics. https://doi.org/10.2139/ssrn.4737330
Stein, A. (2023). Gender, authoritarian populisms, and the attack on democracy. *Sociological Forum*, *38*(4), 1340–1348. https://doi.org/10.1111/socf.12947
Steinmetz, S., & Guarnerio, M. (2026). Intersecting inequalities. The role of gender and migration background in women's labour market vulnerability during crises. In J. Rubery, N. Sánchez-Mira, & V. Insarauto (Eds.), *Women in turbulent times. Crises, transitions, and challenges for gender equality* (pp. 29–51). Routledge.

Stratigaki, M. (2004). The co-optation of gender concepts in EU policies: The case of "reconciliation of work and family". *Social Politics*, *11*(1), 30–56. https://doi.org/10.1093/sp/jxh025

Tavora, I., & Rubery, J. (2013). Female employment, labour market institutions and gender culture in Portugal. *European Journal of Industrial Relations*, *19*(3), 221–237.

Topping, A. (2022, April 17). "Shock absorbers of poverty": Women's lives cut short by their unequal position in society. *The Guardian*. https://www.theguardian.com/inequality/2022/apr/17/shock-absorbers-of-poverty-womens-lives-cut-short-by-their-unequal-position-in-society

Torres, L., & Warren, T. (2026). Working lives and livelihoods in turbulent times: Intersecting inequalities of gender and class in the UK. In J. Rubery, N. Sánchez-Mira, & V. Insarauto (Eds.), *Women in turbulent times. Crises, transitions, and challenges for gender equality* (pp. 73–93). Routledge.

Visser, M. A. (2019). Restructuring opportunity: Employment change and job quality in the United States during the great recession. *Socio-Economic Review*, *17*(3), 545–572. https://doi.org/10.1093/ser/mwy002

Vitali, A., & Arpino, B. (2016). Who brings home the bacon? The influence of context on partners' contributions to the household income. *Demographic Research*, *35*, 1213–1244. https://doi.org/10.4054/DemRes.2016.35.41

Warren, T. (2015). Work-life balance/imbalance: The dominance of the middle class and the neglect of the working class. *British Journal of Sociology*, *66*(4), 691–717. https://doi.org/10.1111/1468-4446.12160

Women's Budget Group. (2024). *The cost of living and gender* (Briefing paper). https://www.wbg.org.uk/publication/the-cost-of-living-and-gender-briefing-for-a-new-government/

World Economic Forum (WEF). (2023). *Global gender gap report 2023*. https://www.weforum.org/publications/global-gender-gap-report-2023/digest/

PART 1

Labour markets in crises and intersecting inequalities

2

INTERSECTING INEQUALITIES

The role of gender and migration background in women's labour market vulnerability during crises

Stephanie Steinmetz and Mattia Guarnerio

Introduction

The unequal impact of crises, such as the Great Recession or the Covid-19 pandemic, on gender inequalities in work and other life domains is well documented. Crises destabilise economies, instigate political instability and pose immediate and long-term threats to employment, social protection and personal well-being (Bernal-Verdugo et al., 2013; Blanton et al., 2015; Choudhry et al., 2012; Mohindra et al., 2011; Serieux et al., 2012). However, these effects are not experienced uniformly. While research has examined how, for instance, the Great Recession and the subsequent austerity policies, as well as the Covid-19 pandemic, affected women and men differently over time and across countries (Alon et al., 2020; Kantola & Lombardo, 2017; Karamessini & Rubery, 2014), most studies continue to treat women as a homogeneous group. This overlooks notable changes in the ethnic composition of the female workforce in European labour markets. Moreover, such an approach risks obscuring the ways that gendered inequalities intersect with other social hierarchies – especially migration background – to shape labour market vulnerability in times of crisis. Migrant women have become an increasingly important part of European labour markets, especially in sectors such as healthcare, hospitality and domestic work, highlighting their crucial role in filling labour shortages, particularly in low-skilled and care-related jobs with more precarious working conditions. Yet, their specific experiences during crises remain underexplored.

This chapter adopts an *intersectional lens* (Crenshaw, 1989) to address the gap in contemporary analyses of crises consequences, by examining how gender and migration background jointly shape exposure to labour market disadvantages during and after periods of crisis. Focusing on two severe shocks, the Great

DOI: 10.4324/9781003528210-4

Recession (2007–2012) and the Covid-19 pandemic (2019–2022), the chapter critically examines their short- and long-term impacts on key labour market indicators, such as employment status, working hours, temporality and segregation patterns, tracing how dynamics in European countries have evolved and changed over the period 2007–2022. Drawing on feminist crisis literature and classic crisis impact hypotheses – buffer, substitution and segmentation – this chapter argues that these frameworks need to be re-evaluated through an intersectional lens. In doing so, it also builds on the concept of "double disadvantage" (Boyd, 1984; Evans, 1984) to describe how migrant women, particularly those from non-EU countries, encounter layered forms of labour market exclusion during times of crisis. Integrating this perspective contributes to the volume's broader aim of assessing how crises reshape gender inequalities in employment, and how multiple structural axes of inequality mediate these processes.

Theoretical considerations and empirical evidence

The gendered labour market consequences of economic crises have been widely analysed. During the Great Recession, initial job losses were concentrated in male-dominated sectors such as construction and manufacturing. In contrast, the impact on women's employment became more pronounced in later stages of the downturn, when the financial crisis evolved into a sovereign debt crisis, prompting austerity measures and widespread cuts to public services – sectors where women are overrepresented (Eydoux, 2014; Karamessini & Koutentakis, 2014; Karamessini & Rubery, 2014). These dynamics undermined women's labour market position, contributing to rising employment insecurity, including increases in part-time work (Insarauto, 2021), temporary contracts (Bettio & Verashchagina, 2014) and persistent wage stagnation (Antonopoulos, 2014). However, the magnitude and nature of these effects varied significantly across countries, underscoring the mediating role of national welfare regimes and gender equality policies in shaping crisis outcomes (Périvier, 2018; Sánchez-Mira & O'Reilly, 2019). The Covid-19 pandemic followed a distinct pattern. Women's overrepresentation in essential occupations, particularly in healthcare, hospitality, caregiving and retail, exposed them to higher risks of infection, stress and burnout (Goldin, 2022), while also increasing their vulnerability to job losses and income reductions (Alon et al., 2020; Dang & Nguyen, 2021). Limited access to remote work in many female-dominated occupations and increased caregiving responsibilities further deepened these disparities (Adams-Prassl et al., 2020; Kim et al., 2022; Petts et al., 2021; Reichelt et al., 2021). Consequently, many women reduced their working hours or exited the labour force altogether, prolonging their re-entry into employment (Collins et al., 2021; Gezici & Ozay, 2020).

Both crises exposed the enduring structural vulnerabilities embedded in gendered employment patterns, which feminist scholars have long sought to explain through well-established theoretical frameworks. Notably, three main hypotheses have been proposed to account for the gendered impact of crises. First, the *buffer hypothesis* suggests that women, who are often overrepresented in labour-intensive and precarious jobs, function as a flexible labour reserve (i.e., as a buffer). Following this argument, women are more likely to enter the workforce during economic upturns and are frequently dismissed in periods of downturn (Galli & Kucera, 2008), which would typically result in declining female employment and unemployment and rising inactivity rates throughout recessions. Second, the *substitution hypothesis* posits that during economic downturns, employers may replace "expensive" male workers with "cheaper" female workers. While this can exacerbate occupational segregation and widen gender wage disparities, it may also lead to increased female labour force participation and moderate female unemployment in the aftermath of recessions (Bettio et al., 2013). Finally, the *segmentation hypothesis* suggests that women's employment patterns during recessions are largely dependent on the exposure of gender-segregated sectors and occupations to economic shocks and fluctuations (Smith & Villa, 2014). If women are concentrated in more crisis-resilient sectors, their employment may be less affected or more stable than that of men, while the opposite should hold for more crisis-sensitive sectors. Importantly, these explanations are not mutually exclusive, and their relevance may vary depending on the nature of the crisis and the broader institutional contexts.

However, these hypotheses tend to overlook how intersecting social positions shape individuals' exposure to crisis-related labour market dynamics. In that regard, migration background alongside gender constitutes a critical axis of inequality that significantly influences labour market experiences, especially during periods of economic disruption. Evidence shows that migrant workers faced disproportionate disadvantages throughout both the Great Recession and the Covid-19 pandemic, including greater job losses, higher unemployment risks and more frequent occupational downgrading and skill underutilisation compared to native workers (Fromentin, 2016; Koser, 2016; Panichella, 2018). During the Covid-19 crisis, migrants were notably overrepresented in essential sectors, often in roles that were low-paid, temporary and less adaptable to remote work. Non-EU migrants, in particular, experienced significantly higher levels of economic vulnerability, losing their jobs at twice the rate of native-born workers. EU migrants were also disproportionately affected, being 1.6 times more likely to be displaced (Bossavie et al., 2022). These patterns reflect a process of labour market shielding, where migrant workers disproportionately absorb employment risks, allowing native workers to transition into safer, more teleworkable occupations.

Within this broader context, migrant women face a *double disadvantage* rooted in the intersecting dimensions of gender and migration (King, 1988). Their over-representation in highly segregated, low-status and precarious forms of employment – such as domestic work, personal care and hospitality – renders them particularly susceptible to job loss, exploitation and economic insecurity during times of crisis (Kofman et al., 2009; Rubin et al., 2008; Palencia-Esteban, 2022).

This vulnerability is not incidental but is reinforced by a range of structural barriers: restrictive immigration policies, weak or poorly enforced labour protections, lack of recognition of foreign qualifications, racialised gender norms and limited access to public services (Adib & Guerrier, 2003; England et al., 2004; Palencia-Esteban & Del Río, 2020). Consequently, there is a need to critically re-evaluate the classical crisis hypotheses – buffer, substitution and segmentation – via an intersectional lens. Without accounting for the compounded effects of gender and migration background, existing frameworks risk obscuring the mechanisms through which crisis-related inequalities are produced and sustained. For example, migrant women may indeed function as a buffer group, entering or exiting the labour force in response to shifting economic demands, but often under conditions of far greater precarity than their native counterparts. Similarly, the substitution hypothesis may unfold differently for migrant women. Whereas employers might replace higher-paid native men with native women as a cost-cutting strategy, migrant women may be perceived as less viable substitutes due to language barriers, non-recognition of educational or professional qualifications, precarious legal status or discriminatory hiring practices. Finally, the segmentation hypothesis may apply more severely to migrant women, who are disproportionately concentrated in highly vulnerable and poorly protected sectors and occupations, such as domestic work, caregiving and hospitality. These sectors are marked by informal employment, low wages and limited social protections. Against this backdrop, the double disadvantage faced by migrant women, particularly those from non-EU countries, can be understood as a result of these overlapping mechanisms. Such patterns also underscore the need to re-conceptualise the labour market consequences of economic crises as shaped by compounded and intersecting gender-migration inequalities.

Data and analysis

The following exploratory analyses employ data from the European Union Statistics on Income and Living Conditions survey (EU-SILC, Eurostat, 2024) which provides comparable micro-data on income, poverty, social exclusion and living conditions across Europe. Pooled cross-sectional waves from 2007–2012 (Great Recession), 2015, 2018 (between-crisis years) and 2019–2022[1] (Covid-19 pandemic) are used to ensure adequate migrant sample sizes and to capture key crisis and non-crisis periods. The study covers 20 European countries: Austria, Belgium, Cyprus, the Czech Republic, Denmark, Estonia, Finland, France, Greece, Hungary, Ireland, Lithuania, Luxembourg, Latvia, the Netherlands, Poland, Portugal, Spain, Slovakia and Sweden. It utilises two analytical samples of individuals aged 16–64, excluding self-employed, retirees, students and military personnel, respectively comprising all the labour force and only employed people.

Furthermore, labour market vulnerabilities are assessed through an intersectional lens following McCall's *inter-categorical approach* (McCall, 2005) which focuses on analysing and confronting systematic relationships of power and inequality among clearly defined social categories. It often involves cross-group comparisons to highlight how systems of oppression operate differently across intersecting identities such as gender and migration background. In the framework of this chapter, six gender-migration groups – native women, native men, EU migrant women, EU migrant men, non-EU migrant women and non-EU migrant men – are compared to reveal how these intersecting identities collectively shape labour market vulnerabilities, offering a more comprehensive understanding of structural inequalities. While gender[2] is operationalised based on the dichotomous measure of biological sex, migrant categories are defined using a combination of country of birth and citizenship, which allows for the inclusion of more diverse migrant profiles. More specifically, migrants are defined either as individuals who do not hold the citizenship of their country of residence, or as citizens whose country of birth lies outside their country of residence. Further distinctions are made based on region of origin, categorising migrants as either EU or non-EU origin. However, due to data limitations and sample size constraints, more granular operationalisations (e.g., by legal status or duration of stay) were not possible, preventing the utilisation of more detailed cross-classifications of migration and gender.

As indicated, trends and changes in key labour market outcomes – identified in the literature as potentially crisis-sensitive – are examined to assess how gender and migration background jointly shape labour market vulnerability across crisis and non-crisis periods. *Employment status* distinguishes between employment, unemployment and inactivity rates. *Employment quality* is captured by average weekly working hours and contract type (permanent vs. temporary). Given the importance of occupational segregation in shaping the gendered and migratory effects of crises, the evolution of multi-group occupational segregation patterns is examined using the *Mutual Information Index* (M), based on the 2-digit ISCO (International Standard Classification of Occupations, ILO) codes (Alonso-Villar & Del Río, 2010). M measures occupational segregation by assessing how unevenly groups, such as men and women or those with and without a migration background, are distributed across occupations. It captures how much knowing a person's group reduces uncertainty about their job (Guinea-Martin et al., 2015). A value of zero indicates perfect integration, while higher values reflect greater segregation. M is especially useful as it summarises overall segregation in a single measure, allows the inclusion of multiple dimensions (e.g., sex and migration background) and can be decomposed to show each group's contribution to overall segregation. In addition, changes in *occupational concentration of gender-migrant groups* (defined as the extent to which employment of these groups is distributed or clustered within specific occupations) are traced, using the 1-digit ISCO code to provide a deeper insight into which occupational groups experienced significant shifts. With a particular focus on the Covid-19 pandemic, the share of individuals employed in *essential or non-essential occupations*[3] is also assessed. All figures and tables are weighted with cross-sectional personal weights to ensure representativeness of the survey estimates. The code used to produce analytical samples, figures and tables, along with a reproducible technical report, is available in a dedicated open-access repository (see Guarnerio, 2026).

Intersecting inequalities in labour market vulnerability during times of crisis

Changes and trends in employment status

Starting with an examination of changes and trends in employment, unemployment and inactivity rates between 2007 and 2022, this subsection assesses how the Great Recession and the Covid-19 pandemic affected labour market participation. The patterns of workforce entry and exit across gender-migration groups may provide valuable insight into whether these groups served as a flexible labour reserve (buffer), faced job displacement (substitution) or were protected by sectoral clustering (segmentation). Figures 2.1 A–C (Tables A2-1 and A2-2, online appendix) illustrate how these dynamics evolve over time, allowing crisis-specific effects to be distinguished from long-term structural trends.

Among natives, both women and men saw rising employment rates, with 2022 levels surpassing those of 2007. Native women, in particular, showed steady gains from 2015 onward. The impact of the Great Recession was moderate. Employment rates fell by 5.8% for men and 1.5% for women (2007–2012), but a recovery started from 2015. The Covid-19 pandemic caused a brief setback, followed by a rebound in 2021, reaching a new high. In contrast, non-natives, especially non-EU migrants, faced greater volatility. Non-EU migrant men (−18.3%) and women (−11.0%) experienced sharp employment declines during the Great Recession, with women reaching the lowest levels across all groups by 2012 and 2015. After a partial recovery (2015–2019), Covid-19 disrupted employment again. However, by 2022, non-EU migrant men (+8.1%) and women (+12.1%) recorded the strongest employment gains, likely driven by labour shortages in key sectors like hospitality, healthcare, manufacturing and transportation. EU migrants followed similar employment patterns, though with less pronounced shifts. While changes in employment rates reflect the immediate effects of crises, it is also important to examine whether job losses led to rising unemployment or inactivity, which may indicate that certain groups function as flexible labour reserves during economic downturns. Throughout the Great Recession and the subsequent austerity period (2007–2012), unemployment rose across all groups, but migrants, especially non-EU migrants, were hit hardest: rates increased by 16.0% for men and 10.6% for women. From 2012, unemployment declined steadily, reflecting labour market recovery, until

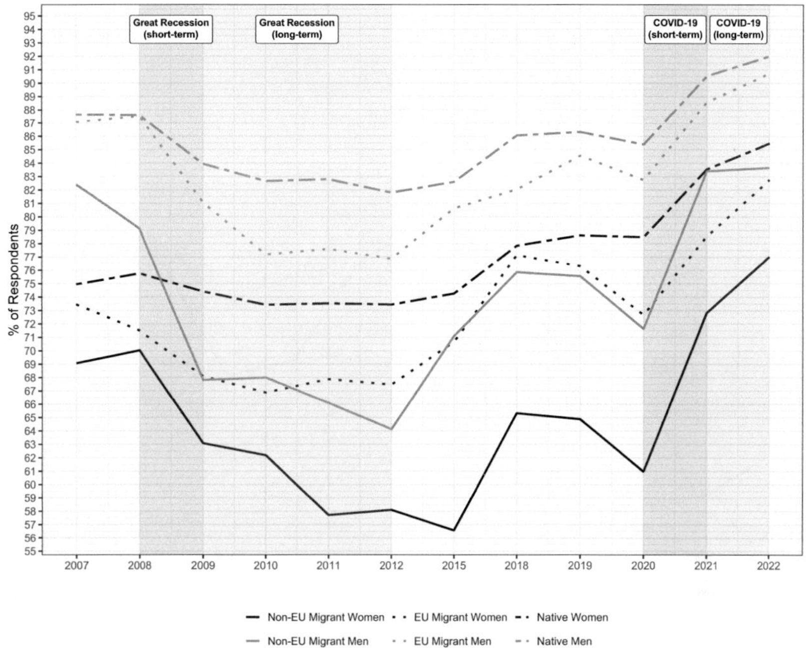

FIGURE 2.1A Yearly Trends in Rates of Employment by Sex and Migration Background.

Source: Own elaboration based on data from EU-SILC 2007–2022 (N = 1.838.684); weighted sample (Eurostat, 2024).

briefly spiking again across all groups during the Covid-19 pandemic. Once more, non-EU migrant men (+2.8%) and women (+5.5%) were most affected. These effects proved temporary, with unemployment falling across all groups in the post-pandemic period. Inactivity rates, often seen as the clearest indicator of the buffer hypothesis, declined across all groups between 2007 and 2022, especially among women. Male inactivity remained low and stable across both crises. Native women saw a steady downward trend in inactivity, staying below migrant women throughout most of the period, though this decline did not boost employment during the Great Recession. In contrast, migrant women's inactivity rates showed more crisis-specific fluctuations. Non-EU migrant women saw a sharp rise from 2007 to 2015, suggesting a buffer function, before gradually declining, while EU migrant women's inactivity dropped at the onset of the Great Recession, followed by a rise until 2010, and a steady decrease similar to native women until 2018. The Covid-19 pandemic reversed earlier trends, with sharp inactivity declines for all female groups – most notably non-EU migrant women (−8.8%) – while male inactivity slightly increased, highlighting persistent gendered labour market patterns.

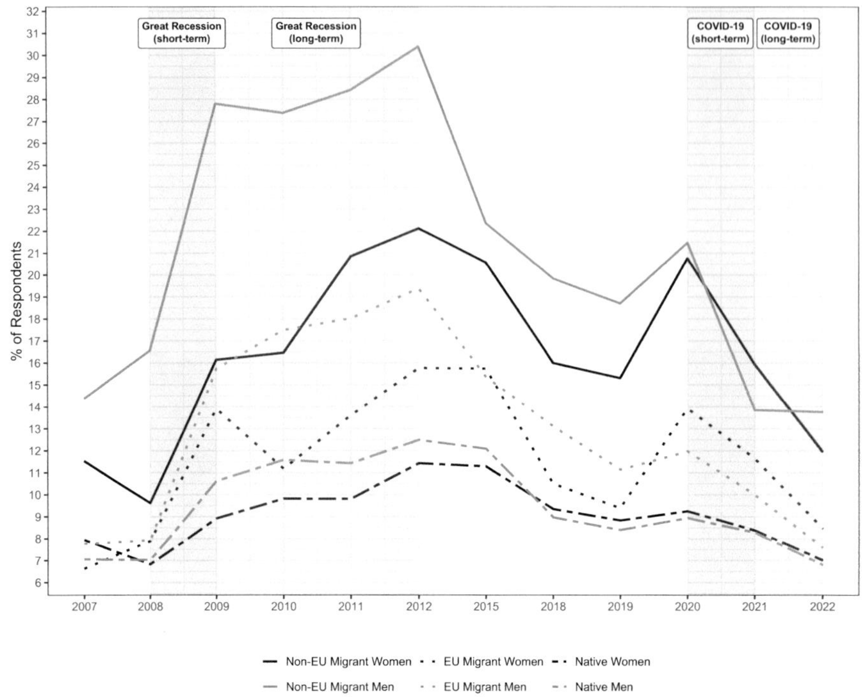

FIGURE 2.1B Yearly Trends in Rates of Unemployment by Sex and Migration Background.

Source: Own elaboration based on data from EU-SILC 2007–2022 (N = 1.838.684); weighted sample (Eurostat, 2024).

Overall, the analysis reveals distinct patterns of resilience and vulnerability across intersecting gender-migration groups. Native men and women, along with EU migrants, showed relatively stable employment trends, reflecting structural protection likely linked to their concentration in more secure occupational and sectoral segments of the labour market. In contrast, non-EU migrants, especially women, faced greater volatility, with sharp rises in unemployment and inactivity, consistent with the buffer hypothesis, suggesting that they acted as a flexible labour reserve. Non-EU migrant women emerged as the most vulnerable group, frequently shifting between workforce participation and inactivity in times of crisis. Their heightened exposure suggests a double disadvantage, shaped by precarious employment and exclusion from protected segments of the labour market, supporting the segmentation hypothesis. The substitution hypothesis finds limited support, as there is little evidence that migrant women gained from the displacement of other groups. From an intersectional perspective, the results indicate that migration background consistently had a stronger impact than gender on labour force participation during both crises. However, the gendered effects observed within migrant groups suggest differentiated roles that warrant deeper exploration.

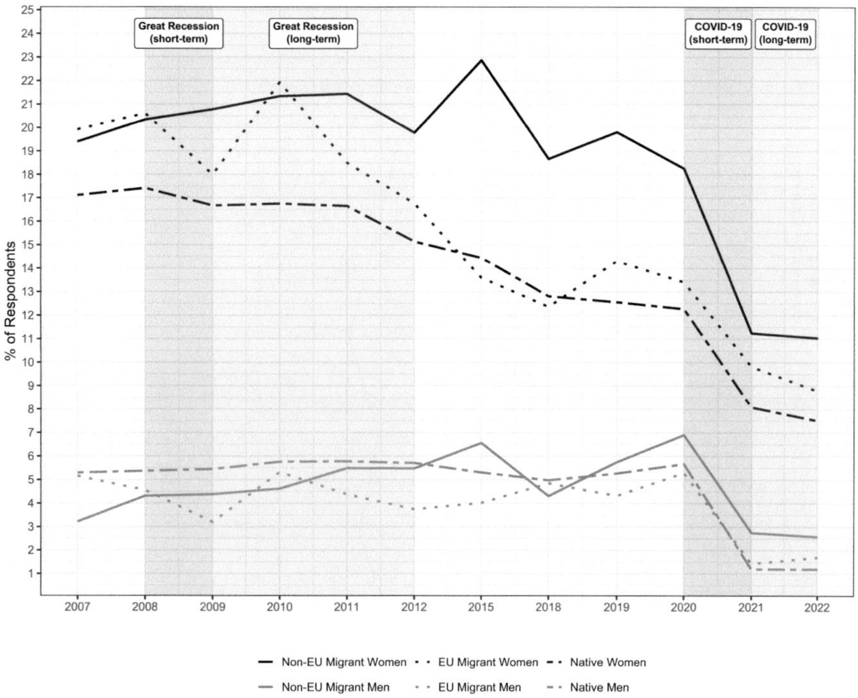

FIGURE 2.1C Yearly Trends in Rates of Inactivity by Sex and Migration Background.

Source: Own elaboration based on data from EU-SILC 2007–2022 (N = 1.838.684); weighted sample (Eurostat, 2024).

Changes and trends in job quality

In times of economic upheaval, changes in job quality indicators reflect shifts in occupational stability, income security and access to social protection. Therefore, drawing on the buffer and segmentation hypotheses, this subsection examines whether certain gender-migration groups, but particularly migrant women, absorbed crisis-provoked shocks by moving into more precarious forms of employment, such as part-time or temporary work (Bettio et al., 2013; Galli & Kucera, 2008). Although distinguishing between voluntary and involuntary changes is not possible, tracking variations in these two key indicators across the two crises may uncover critical patterns shaped by the intersection of gender and migration background.

Figure 2.2 (Tables A2-3 and A2-4, online appendix) presents changes and trends in average weekly working hours for women and men from 2007 to 2022. While gender gaps in working time persisted – albeit narrowing over time – migration background had a stronger influence on crisis-specific outcomes. Native women saw a slight but steady increase in working hours, largely unaffected by either the

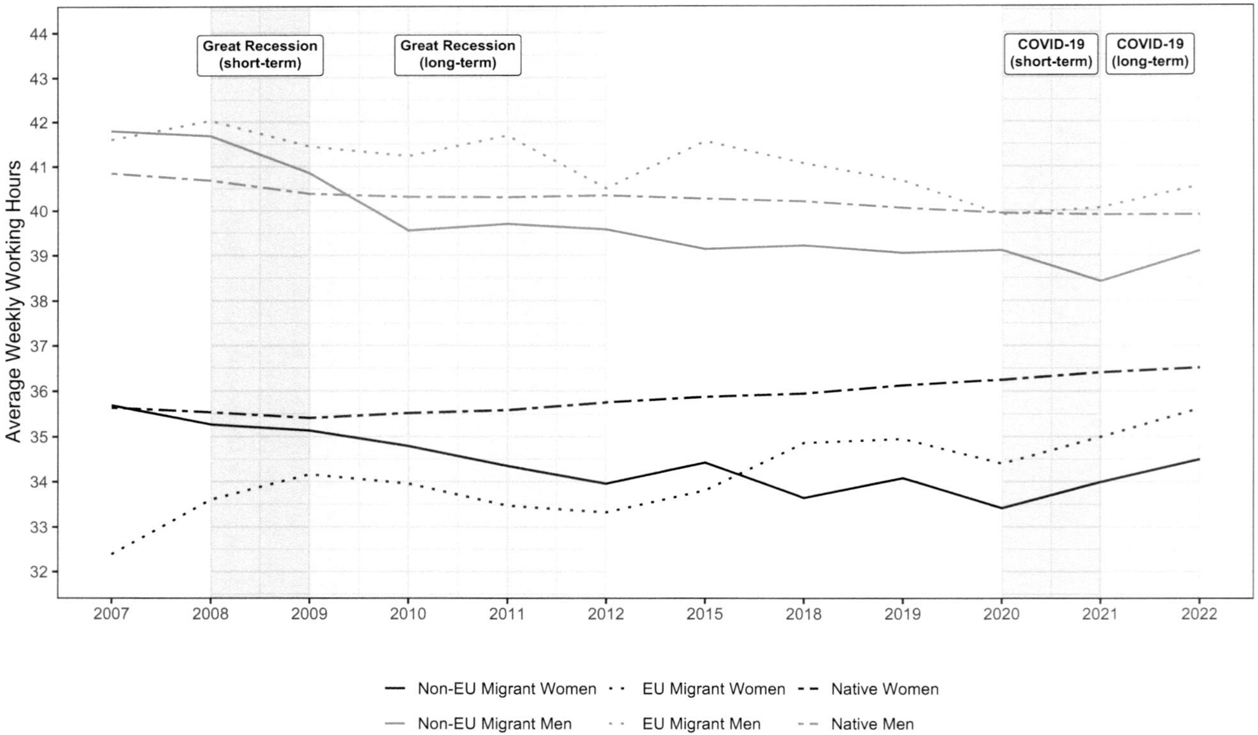

FIGURE 2.2 Yearly Trends in Average Weekly Working Hours by Sex and Migration Background.

Source: Own elaboration based on data from EU-SILC 2007–2022 (N = 1.296.594); weighted sample (Eurostat, 2024).

Note: Only employed respondents.

Great Recession or the Covid-19 pandemic. In contrast, migrant women's working hours were more volatile. Non-EU migrant women, who began at similar levels to natives in 2007, experienced a sustained decline following austerity-driven contractions in the service sector (post-2009) and again during the peak of the Covid-19 crisis. However, their working hours rebounded post-pandemic, returning to 2015 levels, suggesting a rapid recovery. EU migrant women started with the lowest working hours in 2007 but showed a consistent rise until 2022, surpassing their non-EU counterparts. Notably, during the Great Recession, their working time increased by 1.8 hours, possibly reflecting increased labour market participation to compensate for household income loss. Although briefly disrupted during the Covid-19 peak, this trend quickly resumed by 2021. The overall rise in working hours among non-native women during the pandemic likely reflects their concentration in essential sectors, where labour demand remained high despite wider economic disruptions.

Among men, changes in average weekly working hours between 2007 and 2022 reveal a pattern of relative stability for natives. As shown in Figure 2.2 (Tables A2-3 and A2-4, online appendix), native men started with lower working hours than migrant men in 2007, followed by a steady but moderate decline, largely unaffected by either the Great Recession or the Covid-19 pandemic. EU migrant men displayed a similar, though slightly less consistent, downward trend over the same period. In contrast, non-EU migrant men, who initially had the highest working hours, faced the most pronounced crisis-related changes. During the Great Recession, their working time dropped by 2.2 hours per week, falling below those of native men, likely due to their concentration in sectors hit hardest by the downturn. A further decline occurred during the Covid-19 outbreak, though this too was temporary, with working hours rebounding to pre-pandemic levels by 2022.

Looking at changes and trends in temporary employment, Figure 2.3 (Tables A2-3 and A2-5, online appendix) shows a continuous decline in non-permanent contracts among native women and men between 2007 and 2022. Already at low levels in 2007, their share in non-permanent contracts remained largely unaffected by the Great Recession and the Covid-19 pandemic. In contrast, non-EU migrants, especially women, started with the highest shares and experienced the most pronounced changes. Temporary employment among this group dropped sharply during the Great Recession (2008–2009) and again after the peak of the Covid-19 pandemic, particularly for women. By 2022, non-EU migrants reached their lowest levels of temporary employment since 2007. While this trend may appear positive, the earlier drop during the Great Recession likely reflects employment destruction rather than a shift to stable employment. However, the rise in permanent contracts for non-EU migrant men and women during the Covid-19 pandemic may suggest a more favourable shift, potentially driven by increased demand in essential sectors where these groups were overrepresented.

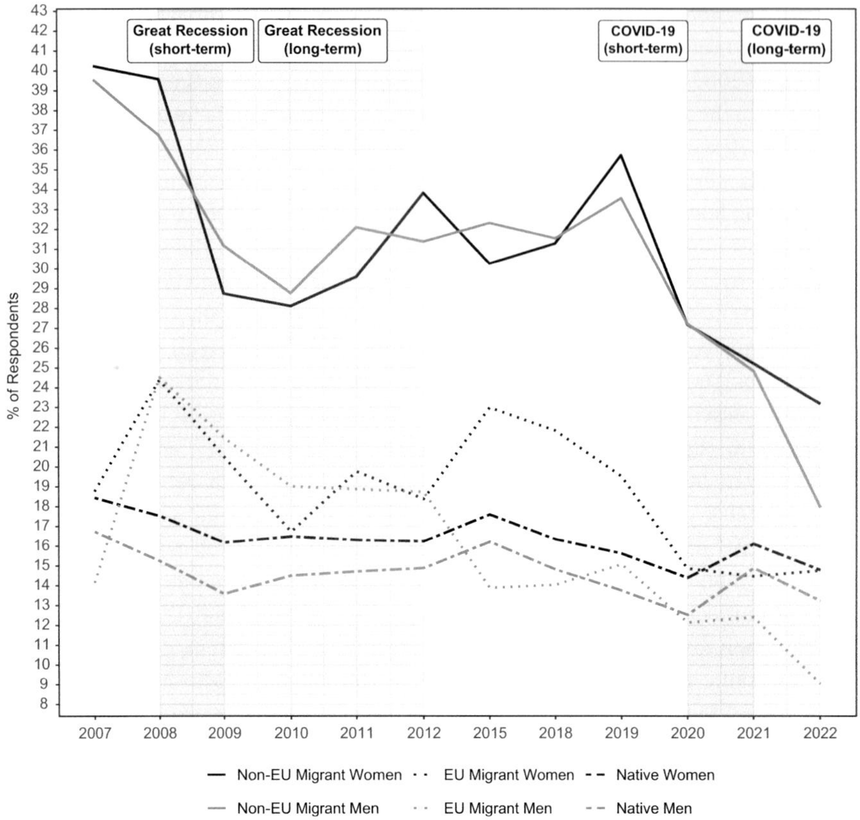

FIGURE 2.3 Yearly Trends in Temporary Employment Rates by Sex and Migration Background.

Source: Own elaboration based on data from EU-SILC 2007–2022 (N = 1.296.594); weighted sample (Eurostat, 2024).

Note: Only employed respondents.

In sum, the findings demonstrate that, while gender remains a key dimension of labour market vulnerability, migration background, particularly non-EU origin, emerges as a more salient axis of crisis-related disadvantage. Furthermore, the intersection of gender and migration shaped distinct patterns of exposure, with non-EU migrant women facing a clear double disadvantage: greater volatility in working hours and higher reliance on temporary contracts. Conversely, native workers were largely shielded from crisis-specific repercussions on job quality, with changes reflecting broader structural trends rather than the immediate effects of the two crises. These patterns lend support to the segmentation hypothesis, highlighting persistent structural inequalities that confine non-EU migrant women to the most crisis-sensitive sectors. Evidence of a buffer effect is scant, but appears strongest during the Great Recession and is not exclusive to women. Improvements in job quality for migrant women often coincided with broader employment losses, weakening the case for the substitution hypothesis. Nevertheless, the post-Covid rise in employment among non-EU migrants may signal a shift, potentially driven by increased demand in essential sectors that native workers are less willing to enter under deteriorating working conditions.

Changes and trends in occupational segregation and concentration

Sectoral and occupational segregation and concentration significantly influence vulnerability to labour market shocks, as certain gender-migration groups may be systematically confined to more crisis-sensitive sectors and occupations. This subsection, therefore, examines how overall segregation patterns evolved between 2007 and 2022, shaping gender- and migration-specific labour market conditions during times of crisis. Additionally, analysing the unequal distribution of gender-migration groups across essential occupations during the Covid-19 pandemic might provide valuable insights into how crisis-induced economic shocks reinforced or altered pre-existing inequality patterns.

Analysis of overall segregation patterns using the M Index (Table A2-6, online appendix) indicates that joint occupational segregation by gender and migration background remained relatively stable between 2007 and 2022. While a modest decline is observable over time, it does not appear to be closely associated with either the Great Recession or the Covid-19 pandemic.[4] To unpack these aggregate trends, Tables 2.1 and 2.2 examine short- and long-term changes in occupational concentration across nine major occupational groups[5] (1-digit ISCO) for the different gender-migrant groups. The supplementary Tables A2.7a and A2.7b (online appendix) explore whether these changes reflect not only crisis-related but also deeper structural transformations in labour markets between 2007 and 2022.

Starting with the results for women (Tables 2.1 and 2.2, A2-7a., online appendix), the strong concentration of non-EU migrant women in low-status occupations is confirmed. In 2007, approximately 75.3% were employed in just two occupational groups: elementary occupations (48.3%) and service jobs (27.0%). While the share in elementary occupations steadily declined between 2007 and 2022, modest gains were made in professional and technical occupations over the same period. These changes primarily reflect gradual, long-term structural trends, which appear to have been amplified by the onset of the Covid-19 pandemic. In contrast, service and clerical occupations proved to be more crisis-sensitive. Notable fluctuations in the concentration of non-EU migrant women in these occupations were observed during the Great Recession, with a sharp concentration decline in service occupations, and during the Covid-19 pandemic, with an increase in clerical occupations. By comparison, EU migrant women were more evenly distributed across four, generally higher-status occupational groups: service, clerical,

TABLE 2.1 Changes in Occupational Concentration (1-digit ISCO) during the Great Recession, by Sex and Migration Background

Occupation (1-digit ISCO)	*Non-EU Migrant Women (%)*	*EU Migrant Women (%)*	*Native Women (%)*	*Non-EU Migrant Men (%)*	*EU Migrant Men (%)*	*Native Men (%)*
Great Recession (2007–2009, short-term)						
Managers	+0.77	+0.35	+0.33	+0.05	−1.50	+0.48
Professionals	−0.27	−3.82	+0.96	+1.46	−3.50	+0.41
Technicians	+2.60	−1.14	+0.98	+1.85	−0.52	+0.76
Clerical workers	+0.88	−3.19	−0.97	+0.22	+1.31	−0.07
Service workers	−3.69	+3.67	−0.04	+2.16	−0.51	−0.11
Skilled workers	−0.23	−0.05	+0.02	−1.35	+0.21	−0.07
Craft and related trade workers	−0.48	+1.72	−1.04	−3.05	+0.59	−0.66
Operators	+0.93	+1.36	+0.29	+1.58	−0.08	−0.20
Elementary workers	−0.50	+1.10	−0.52	−2.91	+4.20	−0.55
Great Recession (2007–2012, long-term)						
Managers	+0.20	+0.02	+0.51	−0.85	−0.07	+0.32
Professionals	+3.56	−0.66	+4.55	+2.01	−1.52	+1.76
Technicians	+2.69	−1.90	−1.13	+2.34	−1.19	+1.11
Clerical workers	−1.06	−4.47	−2.90	+1.77	−1.19	−0.42
Service workers	+2.31	+4.11	+1.52	+6.35	+3.54	+2.32
Skilled workers	+0.86	+1.27	+0.11	+0.14	+1.01	−0.24
Craft and related trade workers	−0.03	+0.73	−1.16	−2.75	−4.29	−2.71
Operators	−1.51	+1.10	−0.22	−1.92	−1.49	−1.48
Elementary workers	−7.02	−0.23	−1.28	−7.08	+5.21	−0.65

Source: Own elaboration based on data from EU-SILC 2007–2022 (N = 1.838.684); weighted sample (Eurostat, 2024).

Note: Occupations are classified using 1-digit ISCO-88 (2007–2010) or ISCO-08 (2011–2022).

professional and elementary occupations. Changes observed between 2007 and 2022 reflect a combination of long-term structural developments and short-term, crisis-specific responses. For instance, the sharp decline in their concentration in elementary occupations between 2019 and 2022 appears to be linked to the Covid-19 pandemic. Meanwhile, the pronounced increase in their concentration

TABLE 2.2 Changes in Occupational Concentration (1-digit ISCO) during the Covid-19 Pandemic, by Sex and Migration Background

Occupation (1-digit ISCO)	*Non-EU Migrant Women (%)*	*EU Migrant Women (%)*	*Native Women (%)*	*Non-EU Migrant Men (%)*	*EU Migrant Men (%)*	*Native Men (%)*
		Covid-19 (2019–2020, short-term)				
Managers	−0.42	−0.38	−0.34	−0.07	−0.31	−0.71
Professionals	+0.58	+1.84	+1.69	+2.08	−0.85	+2.10
Technicians	+0.45	−0.32	+0.06	+0.24	+1.98	−0.41
Clerical workers	+0.24	+0.22	+0.22	+0.12	−0.81	+0.21
Service workers	−0.07	+0.90	−1.06	−0.98	+0.00	−0.08
Skilled workers	+0.14	+0.60	+0.01	−1.03	+1.16	−0.29
Craft and related trade workers	−0.34	+0.39	−0.07	−0.54	−0.08	−0.38
Operators	−0.67	−3.25	−0.25	−0.26	+0.75	−0.53
Elementary workers	+0.09	+0.01	−0.28	+0.44	−1.83	+0.08
		Covid-19 (2019–2022, long-term)				
Managers	+1.06	−0.49	+0.76	+1.58	−0.38	+0.62
Professionals	+5.34	+7.12	+3.96	+6.94	+1.70	+3.80
Technicians	+1.87	+1.86	+1.41	+2.94	+0.08	−0.16
Clerical workers	+1.93	+4.21	+0.77	+3.02	+1.08	+0.75
Service workers	−2.37	−1.16	−3.43	+0.21	−1.94	−0.94
Skilled workers	−0.64	+0.74	+0.07	−1.56	−0.19	−0.46
Craft and related trade workers	−1.07	+0.03	−0.31	−3.88	+1.67	−1.36
Operators	−0.53	−3.13	−0.54	+0.30	+1.78	−1.46
Elementary workers	−5.58	−9.17	−2.69	−9.54	−3.80	−0.78

Source: Own elaboration based on data from EU-SILC 2007–2022 (N = 1.838.684); weighted sample (Eurostat, 2024).

Note: Occupations are classified using 1-digit ISCO-88 (2007–2010) or ISCO-08 (2011–2022).

in professional occupations – while amplified by the pandemic – also reflects a broader, long-term structural upward trend. A similar development was observed among native women. However, their occupational concentration remained relatively stable over time, with most changes reflecting gradual structural transformations in the labour market rather than direct responses to the crises.

Examining male workers (Tables 2.1 and 2.2, A2-7b, online appendix) reveals a similar pattern to that seen among women. In 2007, non-EU migrant men were predominantly concentrated in three low-status occupational groups: crafts and trade-related occupations (36.1%), elementary occupations (29.7%) and machine operators (12.0%). Most changes in the concentration over time reflect long-term structural labour market shifts rather than direct crisis effects. However, as with women, the Covid-19 pandemic appears to have intensified existing trends in both lowest-status – particularly elementary occupations – and higher-status occupations, such as professional and clerical occupations. In contrast, by 2007, EU migrant and native men had a more dispersed occupational distribution. While craft and trade-related occupations remained prominent for both groups, higher shares were also observed for machine operators, technical and professional occupations. Crisis-related changes in occupational concentration between 2007 and 2022 were limited, particularly among native men. Their greater occupational stability suggests that they were more likely to hold secure and insulated positions in the labour market.

Additionally, the Covid-19 pandemic highlighted the central role of "essential occupations" in sustaining societal functioning, while exposing persistent gender- and migration-related inequalities. Essential jobs in sectors like healthcare, transport and retail were low-paid and lacked protections, leaving many, especially women, overworked, stressed and burdened with extra caregiving at home. The overrepresentation of migrant women, and in particular of non-EU migrants, in essential jobs is confirmed by Figure 2.4 (Tables A2-8 and A2-9, online appendix). Although the share of non-EU migrant women decreased slightly by 1.8% between 2019 and 2022, it remained relatively high at 51.4%. EU migrant women followed a similar but more pronounced downward trend, with a 3.2% drop between 2019 and 2022. In contrast, native women and men had consistently lower shares in these occupations (~39%), with no clear indication that the Covid-19 pandemic had any repercussions. Notably, EU migrant men saw a 5.7% decline in essential employment between 2019 and 2022, while non-EU migrant men experienced a 4.5% increase during the peak of the outbreak (2019–2020), underscoring the unequal distribution of labour market risks also among men.

In sum, changes and trends in occupational segregation and concentration point to deeply entrenched structural inequalities shaped by the intersection of gender and migration background across both crises. Non-EU migrant women remained heavily concentrated in low-status occupations throughout the observed period, with only modest changes over time. During the Covid-19 pandemic, they were disproportionately represented in essential yet undervalued jobs. In contrast, EU migrant and native women were more evenly distributed across higher-status occupations, and changes between 2007 and 2022 reflect both long-term structural shifts and short-term crisis impacts. Among men, non-EU migrants were also concentrated in low-status occupations, such as craft and elementary jobs, although some upward occupational mobility was evident before the Covid-19 outbreak. The pandemic appeared to reinforce existing inequalities, with non-EU

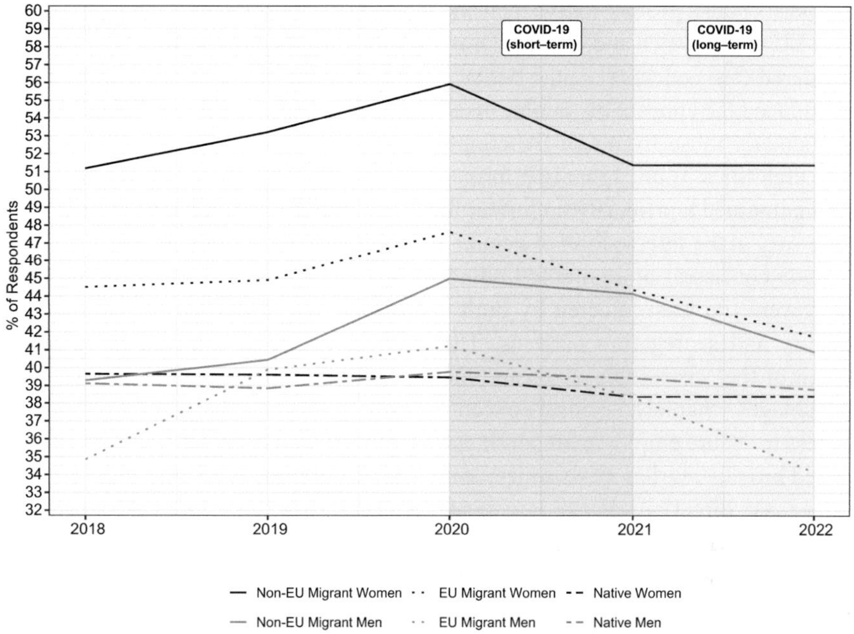

FIGURE 2.4 Yearly Trends in Employment in Essential Occupations by Sex and Migration Background.

Source: Own elaboration based on data from EU-SILC 2007–2022 (N = 1.296.594); weighted sample (Eurostat, 2024).

Note: Only employed respondents.

migrants disproportionately absorbing labour market risks through their concentration in essential occupations. A more diverse occupational distribution was observed among EU migrant and native men, with native men experiencing the least crisis-related disruption. Overall, while both the Great Recession and Covid-19 pandemic reinforced certain trends – especially for non-EU migrants – most occupational changes reflect long-standing structural dynamics rather than short-term, crisis-specific shocks. This lends stronger support to the segmentation hypothesis over the substitution or buffer hypotheses, as patterns of occupational disadvantage remained relatively stable and stratified. The findings underscore again the need to interpret crisis effects through the lens of compounded structural positioning, rather than viewing them as solely driven by crisis-related volatility.

Discussion and conclusion

This chapter has explored how two major crises, the Great Recession (2007–2012) and the Covid-19 pandemic (2019–2022), have shaped key labour market outcomes across six social groups: native men and women; EU migrant men and women; and non-EU migrant men and women. Drawing on established frameworks that explain gendered crisis effects (i.e., the buffer, substitution and segregation hypotheses), it introduced the concept of "double disadvantage" to examine how migrant women, particularly those from non-EU countries, may face compounded labour market vulnerabilities. While broadly informed by an intersectional perspective, the chapter maintained a primarily empirical focus, examining how patterns of disadvantage vary at the intersection of gender and migration background.

One consistent and notable finding of this chapter is that native women and men were the least affected by both crises in terms of employment status, job quality and segregation patterns. This relative resilience appears to be less a result of the crises themselves and more a reflection of long-standing structural advantages – namely, sectoral concentration in more stable industries and greater access to secure employment contracts. Moreover, native women and men experienced broadly similar crisis trajectories, with differences emerging more in scale rather than direction, shaped largely by their pre-crisis labour market positioning. Importantly, results confirm that native women are no longer acting as a "buffer" during economic downturns, a role they have historically played. Instead, the evidence highlights a marked shift in the distribution of labour market risks towards non-EU migrants, among whom both women and men consistently faced the most severe labour market impacts during the crises. For women in particular, this often resulted in a "double disadvantage", as the intersection of gender and migration background amplified their exposure to precarious employment conditions. This heightened vulnerability of non-EU migrants reflects a structural positioning that aligns with the buffer hypothesis, wherein migrants function as a flexible labour reserve. However, this buffering function was not exclusive to women: non-EU migrant men also experienced shifts in employment, supporting existing evidence (Bettio & Verashchagina, 2014) and reinforcing the argument that structural labour market segmentation, more than gender alone, shapes vulnerability in times of crisis.

Building on this, the analysis reveals that the nature and extent of disadvantage experienced by non-EU migrants – particularly women – evolved differently across crises. While their persistent concentration in low-status, precarious and crisis-sensitive sectors and occupations consistently led to sharp employment losses and rising unemployment during both the Great Recession and the Covid-19 pandemic, the indicators of job quality diverged. Throughout the Great Recession, declines in temporary employment among this group most likely reflected job destruction. In contrast, the post-pandemic decline in temporary contracts may signal modest gains in job quality and bargaining power. These improvements appear to be associated with labour shortages in essential sectors, where employers have encountered difficulties in attracting native workers, as well as occupational restructuring, driven by the increasing demand for high-skilled labour in expanding industries such as IT and logistics. This shift underscores that structural disadvantage is not fixed but is shaped by the dynamic interplay between sectoral developments, policy responses and broader labour market transformations. In relation to EU migrants, the impact of the crises was found to be comparable for both women and men, albeit generally less pronounced when compared with non-EU migrants. As with non-EU migrants, their vulnerability during both the Great Recession and the Covid-19 pandemic was closely linked to their concentration in certain sectors and occupations. However, a notable trend emerged during the pandemic: EU migrants' employment patterns began to more closely resemble those of native workers, particularly regarding job stability and quality. This shift may signal a gradual integration into more resilient labour market segments, potentially reflecting differences in legal status, mobility rights or employment trajectories over time. It also underscores the heterogeneity of migrant experiences and reinforces the need for disaggregating migrant groups when assessing exposure to crisis-related shocks and structural disadvantage.

The findings highlight the importance and complexity of applying an intersectional lens to understand how crises affect the labour market. While the analysis primarily relied on disaggregated group comparisons, it reveals how the intersection of gender and migration background shapes distinct patterns of vulnerability and resilience. These positions are not fixed but evolve over time, meaning that past vulnerabilities may not predict future outcomes. For example, the buffering role once played by native women has diminished, while non-EU migrant women have become increasingly exposed – though the nature and extent of their disadvantage differ across crises and sectors. This underscores the need to understand intersectional disadvantage as shaped by broader structural transformations, policy changes, and evolving gender regimes. Rather than yielding static or universally applicable conclusions, the results emphasise the evolving labour market configurations and the diverse trajectories of social groups within them, reinforcing the need to approach the contours of "double disadvantage" as historically and contextually dynamic.

Finally, as an explorative contribution, this chapter serves as a starting point for more in-depth research. Future studies should further exploit existing cross-national comparative data to examine how variations in national labour markets, welfare systems and cultural climates influence the impact of crises on different social groups. Such analyses could provide valuable insights into how institutional settings shape trajectories of labour market vulnerability in times of crisis. Moreover, given the often long-lasting effects of crises, it is essential to evaluate how these shocks interact with broader transformations in employment and welfare systems. Even relatively short-term occupational changes can have profound and enduring consequences for individuals and economies. Attention should also be directed towards the social groups under study. As previously mentioned, the categorisation of migrant groups within this chapter was constrained by the limitations of the available data. Future research would benefit from more refined classifications that consider additional factors, such as generational status, ethnicity or migration motive, to better capture the complexities of intersectional disadvantage. Despite these challenges, the chapter makes a meaningful contribution to the book's overarching aim: to unpack the uneven social consequences of crises and to deepen the understanding of how structural inequalities are reinforced – or reshaped – at the intersection of gender and migration background in times of economic upheaval.

Notes

1 The Covid-19 crisis significantly affected the fieldwork of EU-SILC 2020. Measures taken during the pandemic, such as switching from face-to-face to telephone interviews and potential sample biases due to household availability, impacted data collection. As a result, comparisons with EU-SILC 2019 and 2021 are limited. It is also important to note that, due to widespread temporary unemployment during the Covid-19 pandemic, the EU-SILC 2021 "unemployed" category includes both long-term unemployed individuals and those temporarily unemployed for over six months – many of whom were in less precarious situations.
2 In referring to women and men, the authors understand gender as a socially assigned position, which may or may not align with individuals' self-identified gender. Genders beyond these binary categories are not included, as the data sources employed classify individuals exclusively within these two categories.
3 The classification of essential and non-essential sectors during Covid-19 was typically based on national lockdown measures, which varied by country. As a result, cross-country comparisons have been difficult due to differing laws and classifications (Barbieri et al., 2022; Fana et al., 2020). To improve comparability, Flisi and Santangelo (2022) rely on the European Commission's 2020 guidelines on "critical occupations" to define key workers as those likely permitted to work during strict lockdowns (Fasani & Mazza, 2023; 2024).
4 The only notable increase occurred between 2010 and 2011, likely reflecting a methodological artefact resulting from the transition from ISCO-88 to ISCO-08 in the EU-SILC.
5 These occupational groups can be broadly ranked from highest status (e.g., managers) to lowest status positions (e.g., elementary occupations).

References

Adams-Prassl, A., Boneva, T., Golin, M., & Rauh, C. (2020). Inequality in the impact of the coronavirus shock: Evidence from real time surveys. *Journal of Public Economics*, *189*, 104245. https://doi.org/10.1016/j.jpubeco.2020.104245

Adib, A., & Guerrier, Y. (2003). The interlocking of gender with nationality, race, ethnicity and class: The narratives of women in hotel work. *Gender, Work & Organization*, *10*(4), 413–432. https://doi.org/10.1111/1468-0432.00204

Alon, T., Doepke, M., Olmstead-Rumsey, J., & Tertilt, M. (2020). *The impact of COVID-19 on gender equality* (No. w26947). National Bureau of Economic Research. https://doi.org/10.3386/w26947

Alonso-Villar, O., & Del Río, C. (2010). Local versus overall segregation measures. *Mathematical Social Sciences*, *60*(1), 30–38. https://doi.org/10.1016/j.mathsocsci.2010.03.002

Antonopoulos, R. (Ed.). (2014). *Gender perspectives and gender impacts of the global economic crisis*. Routledge. https://doi.org/10.4324/9780203436288

Barbieri, T., Basso, G., & Scicchitano, S. (2022). Italian workers at risk during the COVID-19 epidemic. *Italian Economic Journal*, *8*(1), 175–195. https://doi.org/10.1007/s40797-021-00164-1

Bernal-Verdugo, L. E., Furceri, D., & Guillaume, D. (2013). Banking crises, labor reforms, and unemployment. *Journal of Comparative Economics, 41*(4), 1202–1219. https://doi.org/10.1016/j.jce.2013.03.001

Bettio, F., Corsi, M., D'Ippoliti, C., Lyberaki, A., Lodovici, M. S., & Verashchagina, A. (2013). *The impact of the economic crisis on the situation of women and men and on gender equality policies: Synthesis report*. Publications Office of the European Union. https://data.europa.eu/doi/10.2838/53123

Bettio, F., & Verashchagina, A. (2014). Women and men in the "Great European Recession". In M. Karamessini & J. Rubery (Eds.), *Women and austerity: The economic crisis and the future for gender equality* (pp. 57–81). Routledge. https://doi.org/10.4324/9780203066294

Blanton, R. G., Blanton, S. L., & Peksen, D. (2015). Financial crises and labor: Does tight money loosen labor rights? *World Development*, *76*, 1–12. https://doi.org/10.1016/j.worlddev.2015.06.005

Bossavie, L., Garrote-Sanchez, D., Makovec, M., & Özden, Ç. (2022). Do immigrants shield the locals? Exposure to COVID-related risks in the European Union. *Review of International Economics*, *30*(5), 1478–1514. https://doi.org/10.1111/roie.12609

Boyd, M. (1984). At a disadvantage: The occupational attainments of foreign born women in Canada. *International Migration Review*, *18*(4), 1091–1119. https://doi.org/10.2307/2546074

Choudhry, M. T., Marelli, E., & Signorelli, M. (2012). Youth unemployment rate and impact of financial crises. *International Journal of Manpower*, *33*(1), 76–95. https://doi.org/10.1108/01437721211212538

Collins, C., Landivar, L. C., Ruppanner, L., & Scarborough, W. J. (2021). COVID-19 and the gender gap in work hours. *Gender, Work & Organization*, *28*(S1), 101–112. https://doi.org/10.1111/gwao.12506

Crenshaw, K. (1989). Demarginalizing the intersection of race and sex: A Black feminist critique of antidiscrimination doctrine, feminist theory and antiracist politics. *University of Chicago Legal Forum*, *1989*(1), 139–167. http://chicagounbound.uchicago.edu/uclf/vol1989/iss1/8

Dang, H.-A. H., & Nguyen, C. (2021). Gender inequality during the COVID-19 pandemic: Income, expenditure, savings, and job loss. *World Development*, *140*, 105296. https://doi.org/10.1016/j.worlddev.2020.105296

England, P., Garcia-Beaulieu, C., & Ross, M. (2004). Women's employment among Blacks, Whites, and three groups of Latinas: Do more privileged women have higher employment? *Gender & Society*, *18*(4), 494–509. https://doi.org/10.1177/0891243204265632

Eurostat. (2024). *EU statistics on income and living conditions (EU-SILC)* [Data set]. https://ec.europa.eu/eurostat/web/microdata/european-union-statistics-on-income-and-living-conditions. https://doi.org/10.2907/EUSILC2004-2023

Evans, M. D. R. (1984). Immigrant women in Australia: Resources, family, and work. *International Migration Review*, *18*(4), 1063–1090. https://doi.org/10.1177/019791838401800409

Eydoux, A. (2014). Women during recessions in France and Germany: The gender biases of public policies. *Revue de l'OFCE*, *133*(2), 153–188. https://doi.org/10.3917/reof.133.0153

Fana, M., Tolan, S., Torrejón, S., Urzi Brancati, C., & Fernández-Macías, E. (2020). *The COVID confinement measures and EU labour markets*. Publications Office of the European Union. https://data.europa.eu/doi/10.2760/079230

Fasani, F., & Mazza, J. (2023). Being on the frontline? Immigrant workers in Europe and the COVID-19 pandemic. *ILR Review*, *76*(5), 890–918. https://doi.org/10.1177/00197939231173676

Fasani, F., & Mazza, J. (2024). Immigrant key workers: *Their contribution to Europe's COVID-19 response* (IZA Discussion Papers No. 16884). Institute of Labor Economics (IZA). https://hdl.handle.net/10419/295907

Flisi, S., & Santangelo, G. (2022). Occupations in the European labour market during the COVID-19 pandemic. *Intereconomics*, *57*(2), 120–126. https://doi.org/10.1007/s10272-022-1040-y

Fromentin, V. (2016). The global economic crisis and migrant workers: The case of the construction sector in Europe. *International Economic Journal*, *30*(1), 147–163. https://doi.org/10.1080/10168737.2014.894550

Galli, R., & Kucera, D. (2008). *Gender, informality and employment adjustment in Latin America* (Policy Integration and Statistics Department Working Paper No. 85). International Labour Organization.

Gezici, A., & Ozay, O. (2020). An intersectional analysis of COVID-19 unemployment. *Journal of Economics, Race, and Policy*, *3*(4), 270–281. https://doi.org/10.1007/s41996-020-00075-w

Goldin, C. (2022). Understanding the economic impact of COVID-19 on women. *Brookings Papers on Economic Activity*, *2022*(1), 65–139. https://doi.org/10.1353/eca.2022.0019

Guarnerio, M. (2026). *Intersecting inequalities – Supplementary Materials* [Source code]. GitHub. https://github.com/MattiaGuarnerio/Intersecting-Inequalities

Guinea-Martin, D., Mora, R., & Ruiz-Castillo, J. (2015). The joint effect of ethnicity and gender on occupational segregation: An approach based on the Mutual Information Index. *Social Science Research*, *49*, 167–178. https://doi.org/10.1016/j.ssresearch.2014.08.007

Insarauto, V. (2021). Women's vulnerability to the economic crisis through the lens of part-time work in Spain. *Work, Employment and Society*, *35*(4), 621–639. https://doi.org/10.1177/09500170211001271

Kantola, J., & Lombardo, E. (2017). Gender and the politics of the economic crisis in Europe. In J. Kantola & E. Lombardo (Eds.), *Gender and the economic crisis in Europe* (pp. 1–25). Springer International Publishing. https://doi.org/10.1007/978-3-319-50778-1_1

Karamessini, M., & Koutentakis, F. (2014). Labour market flows and unemployment dynamics by sex in Greece during the crisis. *Revue de l'OFCE*, *133*(2), 215–239. https://doi.org/10.3917/reof.133.0215

Karamessini, M., & Rubery, J. (2014). The challenge of austerity for equality: A consideration of eight European countries in the crisis. *Revue de l'OFCE*, *133*(2), 15–39. https://doi.org/10.3917/reof.133.0015

Kim, A. T., Erickson, M., Zhang, Y., & Kim, C. (2022). Who is the "she" in the pandemic "she-cession"? Variation in COVID-19 labor market outcomes by gender and family status. *Population Research and Policy Review*, *41*(3), 1325–1358. https://doi.org/10.1007/s11113-021-09693-0

King, D. K. (1988). Multiple jeopardy, multiple consciousness: The context of a Black feminist ideology. *Signs: Journal of Women in Culture and Society, 14*(1), 42–72. https://doi.org/10.1086/494491

Kofman, E., Roosblaad, J., & Keuzenkamp, S. (2009). Migrant and minority women, inequalities and discrimination in the labour market. In J. Roosblaad, K. Kraal, & J. Wrench (Eds.), *Equal opportunities and ethnic inequality in European labour markets: Discrimination, gender and policies of diversity* (1st ed., pp. 47–68). Amsterdam University Press. https://doi.org/10.2307/j.ctt46n0zz.6

Koser, K. (2016). The impacts of the global economic and financial crisis. In G. Lazaridis (Ed.), *Security, insecurity and migration in Europe* (pp. 67–80). Routledge.

McCall, L. (2005). The complexity of intersectionality. *Signs: Journal of Women in Culture and Society, 30*(3), 1771–1800. https://doi.org/10.1086/426800

Mohindra, K. S., Labonté, R., & Spitzer, D. (2011). The global financial crisis: Whither women's health? *Critical Public Health, 21*(3), 273–287. https://doi.org/10.1080/09581596.2010.539593

Palencia-Esteban, A. (2022). Occupational segregation of female and male immigrants in Europe: Accounting for cross-country differences. *International Labour Review, 161*(3), 341–373. https://doi.org/10.1111/ilr.12207

Palencia-Esteban, A., & Del Río, C. (2020). *The earnings effects of occupational segregation in Europe: The role of gender and migration status* (ECINEQ Working Paper Series No. 2020-533). Society for the Study of Economic Inequality. http://www.ecineq.org/milano/WP/ECINEQ2020-533.pdf

Panichella, N. (2018). Economic crisis and occupational integration of recent immigrants in Western Europe. *International Sociology, 33*(1), 64–85. https://doi.org/10.1177/0268580917742002

Périvier, H. (2018). Recession, austerity and gender: A comparison of eight European labour markets. *International Labour Review, 157*(1), 1–37. https://doi.org/10.1111/ilr.12032

Petts, R. J., Carlson, D. L., & Pepin, J. R. (2021). A gendered pandemic: Childcare, homeschooling, and parents' employment during COVID-19. *Gender, Work & Organization, 28*(S2), 515–534. https://doi.org/10.1111/gwao.12614

Reichelt, M., Makovi, K., & Sargsyan, A. (2021). The impact of COVID-19 on gender inequality in the labour market and gender-role attitudes. *European Societies, 23*(supl), S228–S245. https://doi.org/10.1080/14616696.2020.1823010

Rubin, J., Rendall, M., Rabonovitch, L., Tsang, F., Oranje-Nassau, C., & Janta, B. (2008). *Migrant women in the European labour force*. RAND Europe.

Sánchez-Mira, N., & O'Reilly, J. (2019). Household employment and the crisis in Europe. *Work, Employment and Society, 33*(3), 422–443. https://doi.org/10.1177/0950017018809324

Serieux, J. E., Munthali, S., Sepehri, A., & White, R. (2012). The impact of the global economic crisis on HIV and AIDS programs in a high prevalence country: The case of Malawi. *World Development, 40*(3), 501–515. https://doi.org/10.1016/j.worlddev.2011.07.006

Smith, M., & Villa, P. (2014). The long tail of the Great Recession: Foregone employment and foregone policies. *Revue de l'OFCE, 133*(2), 85–119. https://doi.org/10.3917/reof.133.0085

3

THE GENDERED IMPACT OF THE COVID-19 PANDEMIC ON LABOUR MARKET OUTCOMES

A comparative European perspective

Marija Bashevska and Giulia Dotti Sani

Introduction

The Covid-19 pandemic triggered a series of global crises, affecting health, economies and societies. Unlike the 2008–2009 global economic crisis, where men initially faced a sharper decline in employment (Bettio & Verashchagina, 2014), the pandemic hit sectors with a higher concentration of female workers, although the impact on gendered labour market outcomes varied across countries (Alon et al., 2021; Hupkau & Petrongolo, 2020).

This shift has led to two contrasting hypotheses in the literature on gender equality. The pessimistic view suggests a potential "re-traditionalisation" with women facing greater setbacks in both employment and unpaid household labour. This could lead to increased gender inequality in the labour market, greater economic vulnerability for women and possibly undo decades of progress (Alon et al., 2021; Carlson et al., 2021). In contrast, the optimistic view highlights potential gains for gender equality. Changes driven by the pandemic, such as flexible work arrangements, remote or hybrid work and the recognition of critical and essential occupations, could improve women's employment outcomes and enhance work–family balance in the post-pandemic era (Del Boca et al., 2020; Carlson et al., 2021; Chung et al., 2021; Hupkau & Petrongolo 2020).

Recent studies have found mixed evidence supporting both pessimistic and optimistic outlooks regarding the impact of the pandemic. However, these findings vary significantly based on: a) the country context, b) the phase of the pandemic and c) the socio-economic characteristics of the individuals studied. For instance, early research from the United States (US) indicates a widening gender gap in wages (Alon et al., 2021), unemployment and labour force participation (Albanesi & Kim, 2021) during and following the pandemic recession. In

DOI: 10.4324/9781003528210-5

contrast, later US studies and research from other countries suggest that the negative effects on women's labour market participation were transitory (Bluedorn et al., 2023; Brini et al., 2021), and that women actually faced smaller reductions in work hours and earnings overall (Hupkau & Petrongolo, 2020). Ultimately, these findings indicate that outcomes varied significantly not only by country and stage of the pandemic but also according to individual characteristics, such as level of education, parental status and the ability to telework (Dias et al., 2020; Collins et al., 2021; Mesiäislehto et al., 2022).

These variations underscore the importance of adopting an intersectional gender lens that considers how gender interacts with class, education and caregiving responsibilities. Crucially, they highlight the extent to which significant differences in study designs, measured outcomes and the timing of data collection across different phases of the pandemic make it impossible to conclusively confirm or reject either of the two competing hypotheses. This lack of clarity is critical, as it leaves unresolved whether the notion of a generalized "she-cession" – representing the pandemic's disproportionate negative impact on women – accurately reflects the experience of women overall, and if not, whether it applies differently to women across diverse socio-economic backgrounds and contexts.

This issue is especially important in the European context, as women may have fared better in some countries than in others, underscoring the need to address these disparities to fully grasp the pandemic's broader implications for gender inequality in Europe, also considering that many European countries as well as the European Union as a whole have included gender equality among their targets on several occasions in recent decades. Critically, the well-documented disparities across European countries regarding welfare support, gender equality and female labour force participation (Esping-Andersen, 2009; Eurostat, 2023; European Institute for Gender Equality [EIGE], 2023), combined with the varying responses to the pandemic, particularly the length and strictness of restrictive measures, may have led to a more severe economic impact on women than on men in certain countries compared to others, thereby widening between-gender inequalities. Furthermore, it is plausible that the pandemic also widened within-gender gaps, as certain groups of citizens, particularly the low skilled, are more vulnerable to economic shocks, further exacerbating existing social inequalities.

This study leverages data from Round 10 of the European Social Survey (ESS, 2023) to explore these issues. Specifically, we examine gender differences in negative employment outcomes during the pandemic (including redundancy or job loss, reduced income or working hours, being forced to take unpaid leave or holiday) by analysing the role of individual characteristics, such as education, employment sector, contract type and presence of children. We also assess cross-national differences across Europe, with a particular focus on variations linked to work–family arrangements and degree of familialism of welfare state policies.

On this basis, and building on previous analyses of gendered labour outcomes during crises, this chapter offers a comparative and intersectional perspective on the labour market impacts of the Covid-19 crisis in Europe, assessing whether and how women were affected. In doing so, it contributes to the volume by examining how crises – specifically a global health shock – interact with pre-existing gendered labour market structures and welfare systems to either reinforce or reshape inequalities.

Pre-pandemic gender differences in employment: labour market outcomes during the Great Recession

Before looking at the pandemic's effects in detail, in this section we review research on the gendered consequences of the Great Recession across Europe. This literature provides key insights into the complex factors shaping gendered labour market vulnerabilities during crises, providing a reference for approaching and understanding the impacts of the Covid-19 crisis, particularly in terms of potentially recurring or emerging patterns of disadvantage across gender groups.

The literature on the gendered impact of the 2008 crisis highlights a reversal in the rising trends of women's employment, alongside increased unemployment for both genders across Europe. However, the extent of the impact and recovery varied, depending on country contexts, gender relations and women's position within labour markets. Initially, male-dominated sectors, like manufacturing and construction, were most affected, reducing gender gaps in the labour market, a phenomenon largely attributed to sectoral and occupational segregation (Bettio & Verashchagina, 2014). As subsequent austerity measures were implemented, the impact shifted towards female-dominated public sector and services, increasing job insecurity and economic vulnerability for women (Karamessini & Rubery, 2014).

Comparative analyses on work–family arrangements across Europe also revealed divergent impacts (Sánchez-Mira & O'Reilly, 2019; Dotti Sani, 2018). In Southern Europe, particularly Greece and Spain, where the crisis hit hardest, dual-earner households declined while no-earner households increased, indicating widespread job losses across genders and social groups (Dotti Sani, 2018). Sánchez-Mira and O'Reilly (2019) identified similar patterns, emphasising the role of labour market structures and employment opportunities in conjunction with policy and gender cultures. In these countries, the increase in "male-breadwinner-female-unemployed" households affected women across all educational backgrounds, highlighting the rise in women's unemployment due to austerity policies. Central European countries exhibited similar shifts but experienced a quicker recovery by 2012, particularly in full-time dual-earner households (Sánchez-Mira & O'Reilly, 2019). Here, the increase in male-breadwinner households was more pronounced among lower-educated households, indicating greater job vulnerability for less-educated women.

Beyond household arrangements, other factors like employment sector, contract type and parenthood status further shaped women's labour market vulnerability (Karamessini & Rubery, 2014). While gender segregation initially sheltered women in the public sector from immediate job losses, the austerity phase disproportionately impacted them by shrinking public services, deteriorating working conditions and undermining salary levels and job security, particularly for women with caregiving responsibilities. Additionally, women's overrepresentation in part-time, self-employed and temporary positions added to their vulnerability due to limited job protections (Insarauto, 2021; Karamessini & Rubery, 2014).

Gendered employment outcomes during the Covid-19 pandemic

In contrast to the Great Recession, the Covid-19 pandemic immediately raised serious concerns about its disproportionate effects on women, both in paid work and unpaid domestic responsibilities. Lockdowns and sector-specific closures, including those in hospitality, leisure, entertainment and residential care, alongside school and childcare facility shutdowns, heightened fears of a "she-cession". Women, overrepresented in the hardest-hit sectors, also faced increased demands for unpaid housework and childcare. This double burden jeopardised their employment prospects and labour supply, leading many to reduce working hours or exit the labour market altogether (Alon et al., 2021; Eurofound, 2022). Indeed, early estimates showed a global decline in women's employment by 4.2% between 2019 and 2020, compared to just 0.3% for men (International Labour Organization [ILO], 2021).

Closer examination of national contexts reveals that women generally experienced greater employment losses than men during the pandemic. Comparative studies from the United Kingdom (UK), US, and Germany indicate that the pandemic exacerbated pre-existing inequalities in employment and earnings, with women and less-educated workers being the most affected (Adams-Prassl et al., 2020). In the US, the initial impact was particularly harsh on mothers, who were more likely than fathers to exit the labour market, lose their jobs or face reductions in working hours (Dias et al., 2020). In Italy and Spain, women also experienced greater job losses than men during the initial lockdown (Bettin et al., 2024; Blázquez et al., 2023). In Finland, women's part-time employment was disproportionately affected in the pandemic's early stages (Mesiäislehto et al., 2022). Studies in the US, UK, and the Netherlands also confirm that during the first phases of the pandemic, gender gaps were largely pronounced among workers unable to work from home, with mothers being particularly affected (Alon et al., 2021).

These findings underscore the critical need for more systematic, cross-national comparative research into the gendered labour market impacts of the pandemic, particularly in light of pre-existing gender norms and national work–family arrangements. Further investigation into the factors that influenced varying employment outcomes across European countries is essential not only to grasp the consequences of this specific global crisis, but also to build resilience against future disruptions. Drawing on this background, in the next section we present a set of hypotheses on how the pandemic may have affected the employment outcomes for women and men at two distinct levels of analysis: the individual and the contextual. These hypotheses guide the empirical analysis that follows.

Gendered employment outcomes at the individual level

We initially anticipate observing gender disparities in employment outcomes during the pandemic in Europe, with women being more likely to experience negative employment outcomes compared to men (H1). This expectation is based on women's overrepresentation in sectors most affected by early lockdowns (e.g., hospitality, care and retail) (Eurofound, 2022). Moreover, given that the lockdown measures implied the closure of schools and childcare facilities and led to an increase in unpaid work (Kulic et al., 2021), which is typically shouldered by women, a more severe effect of the pandemic on women's labour market outcomes appears inevitable.

Drawing on previous findings on the role of education during economic crises (Karamessini & Rubery, 2014), we also expect higher education to serve as a protective factor. Specifically, we hypothesise that both women and men with tertiary education are less likely to face negative employment outcomes than those with lower levels of education (primary and secondary) (H2).

Given the disproportionate increase in unpaid childcare and domestic work during lockdowns due to school and childcare facility closures, along with the primary caregiver role still predominantly assumed by women before and during crises (Sánchez-Mira & O'Reilly, 2019), we anticipate that women with children in the household (0–4 years old and 5–15 years old) are more likely to face negative employment outcomes compared to women without children (H3a). We do not expect a similar pattern for men (H3b).

Based on evidence that workers in the public sector are generally more protected from job loss than workers in the private sector of the economy, we expect that both women and men working in the public sector (i.e., central and local government, including healthcare and education) are less likely to face negative employment outcomes compared to those in private firms, businesses or self-employed individuals (H4).

Moreover, we expect that both women and men employed with unlimited job contracts are less likely to face negative employment outcomes compared to those with limited or no contracts (H5a). However, considering women's disproportionate concentration in temporary and atypical jobs, as well as findings from the Great Recession indicating greater vulnerability among women in these roles (Insarauto, 2021; Karamessini & Rubery, 2014), we hypothesize that the protective effect of an open-ended contract may be greater for women than for men (H5b).

Gendered employment outcomes at the contextual level

To examine employment outcomes at the contextual level and explore cross-country differences, we rely on typologies. Comparative studies on gender relations and employment have highlighted the heuristic value of typologies in identifying and understanding cross-national variations in the structural and policy factors shaping gender inequalities in the labour market, including variations in and the influence of responses to systemic shocks like the 2008 crisis and the Covid-19 pandemic (Sánchez-Mira & O'Reilly, 2019; Dotti Sani et al., 2025). Typologies enable a more nuanced understanding of the systemic barriers women face in the labour market, including the compounded effects of unpaid care responsibilities. They also highlight the importance of conceiving policies that acknowledge and address both labour market inequalities and the unequal distribution of unpaid work. Studies in this domain have often relied on two dimensions to classify national models across Europe: differences in work–family arrangements (namely breadwinning models, as seen in Lewis, 1992) and degree of familialism in public policies (as seen in Esping-Andersen, 1999; Leitner, 2003; Saraceno, 2016). Although countries often exhibit characteristics from multiple clusters with respect to these two dimensions, cross-national typologies usually identify five main groups: Nordic, Liberal, Continental, Southern, and Eastern countries.

Nordic countries, such as Sweden and Norway, are characterised by a strong de-familialisation approach, underpinned by a robust public sector that fosters gender equality (Hook, 2015; Korpi et al., 2013; Saraceno, 2016) and a prevalent dual earner model. Liberal countries, like the UK and Ireland, follow market-oriented family policies, coupled with a lack of state support for caring responsibilities, which limits assistance for women's employment, particularly for less educated and socially disadvantaged women, who often turn to part-time jobs to juggle care and paid work (Korpi et al., 2013; Saraceno, 2016). In Continental countries such as Germany, familialist public policies continue to prevail despite some attempts at renovation (Hook, 2015; Kowalewska, 2023; Saraceno, 2016), resulting in comparatively lower women's labour market participation, even among the highly educated. Southern countries, such as Italy and Spain, exhibit a clear familialist approach, with insufficient public care services, strong gendered caregiving norms and limited availability of part-time work (Dotti Sani, 2018; Saraceno, 2016). Cross-national studies reveal that in these countries households tend to polarise between the dual full-time earner model and the male-breadwinner model, often mirroring class divides as indicated by women's education levels (Hook, 2015). Finally, Eastern countries form a diverse and less-studied cluster comprising post-Soviet and post-Yugoslav countries, featuring regional sub-groups with hybrid welfare and work–family characteristics. Within this group, the Visegrad countries (Czech Republic, Hungary, Poland and

Slovakia) are more familialist compared to the Baltic and post-Yugoslav states, with higher gender employment gaps (Kowalewska, 2023). Nonetheless, studies indicate that the dual-earner-full-time model remained dominant across Eastern countries before and after the Great Recession (Sánchez-Mira & O'Reilly, 2019).

Drawing on these typologies – and building on cross-national studies on work–family arrangements and the gendered impact of the 2008 crisis across different country clusters in Europe (Sánchez-Mira & O'Reilly, 2019; Dotti Sani, 2018) – we expect to find differences between countries in terms of the negative employment outcomes triggered by the Covid-19 pandemic. In particular, we expect negative employment outcomes to be the least common in Nordic and Continental countries and more prevalent in Liberal, Eastern and Southern countries (H6), for both men and women. This expectation is based on the differences in welfare state provisions between these regions. Nordic and Continental countries are characterised by comprehensive and well-developed welfare systems designed to mitigate negative employment outcomes. In contrast, Liberal, Eastern and Southern countries tend to have less developed welfare states, with more limited social support and protections, leading to higher risks of adverse employment consequences especially in times like those of the Covid-19 pandemic. However, we expect women in the Southern countries to be the most affected (H7), considering that these countries are characterised by higher degrees of familialism, less supportive environments for working women, comparatively higher gender gaps in employment prior to the pandemic and prolonged lockdown closures in the early phase of the pandemic.

Data and methods

Data

For this research, we rely on data from the European Social Survey (Round 10 – 2020, edition 3.2) (ESS ERIC, 2023). Round 10 includes a rotating module on the impact of the Covid-19 pandemic enabling insights into the negative employment outcomes individuals faced during the pandemic. The module was optional, with 29 out of 31 countries participating, while France and Montenegro opted out and are therefore excluded from the analysis. Additionally, since our focus is on European countries, Israel was also removed from the final sample. The Covid-19 pandemic impacted the timing and implementation of fieldwork for ESS Round 10, resulting in a longer completion period compared to previous rounds (ESS, 2023). The fieldwork took place from September 2020 to August 2022, with different fieldwork start and completion timelines across countries within this time frame (ESS, 2023). This variation is not expected to significantly impact our results as the majority of the countries considered completed fieldwork at a time when vaccines had already been rolled out and the pandemic was well under control. In other words, by the time the interviews were carried out, the harshest pandemic phase had passed in all countries and we are able to capture a broad range of employment impacts across all contexts.

Dependent variable

To assess the impact of the Covid-19 pandemic on employment outcomes, the dependent variable is constructed as an individual-level measure indicating self-reported negative employment outcomes since the beginning of the pandemic. This measure is operationalised using a survey question about work-related events occurring due to the pandemic, with multiple-choice options including: made redundant/lost job, income from job reduced, working hours reduced, furloughed, forced to take unpaid leave/holiday, none of these and not in work since the start of the pandemic.

Due to low statistical power for each specific outcome – each category representing less than 10 per cent of responses – exploring the impact of the pandemic on these negative employment outcomes separately was not feasible. Therefore, the negative employment categories were pooled into a binary variable: category 0 – no change in employment status or conditions; and category 1 – occurrence of any of the listed negative outcomes.

Independent variables and controls

The following predictors are used to test the individual level hypotheses. Level of education is operationalised through a question regarding the highest education level attained by respondents, classified according to the International Standard Classification of Education (ISCED) (ESS ERIC, 2022). The variable contrasts those with less than tertiary education (primary and secondary levels) against those with tertiary education or higher.

Employment sector is constructed based on respondents' last employment type. We distinguish between more protected sectors (i.e., public sector, education and health and state-owned enterprises) and other sectors (e.g., private firms, self-employment and other types), which serve as the reference category. The predictor for the type of employment contract is operationalised with the question on the duration of the work contract, with the following categories: unlimited contract, as the reference category; limited contract; and no contract.

Finally, two parenthood status variables are constructed using the household grid question from the ESS: the first one accounts for the presence of pre-school children aged 0–4 years in the household, while the second one accounts for the presence of children aged 5–15 years.

To test the hypothesis on differences in employment outcomes during the pandemic across various country clusters, we construct a variable with five categories, guided by the cross-national typologies in work–family arrangements and degrees of familialism in European countries discussed in the previous section.

The Continental cluster includes Austria, Belgium, Switzerland, Germany and the Netherlands; the Nordic cluster comprises Finland, Iceland, Norway and Sweden; the Liberal cluster consists of the United Kingdom and Ireland; the Eastern cluster encompasses Bulgaria, Czechia, Estonia, Croatia, Hungary, Lithuania, Latvia, North Macedonia, Poland, Serbia, Slovenia and Slovakia; and the Southern cluster includes Cyprus, Spain, Greece, Italy and Portugal.

Individual-level control variables include migrant status and age categories. Migrant status is a binary categorical variable with non-migrant vs migrant. An individual's status as a non-migrant is defined by holding citizenship and being born in the country, whereas migrant status is identified by the absence of citizenship and birth outside of the country. The second control variable is age, recoded as a categorical variable with the following categories: 20–35 years old (reference category), 36–50 years old, and 51–65 years old.

Analytical strategy and sample

This research applies descriptive statistics and binomial logistic regression models to estimate the probability of experiencing negative employment outcomes during the Covid-19 pandemic for women and men in Europe. To investigate gender differences in negative employment outcomes, we first employ a binomial logistic regression model using pooled samples of women and men from various countries, adjusted for individual-level predictors, including education, sector of employment, type of employment contract and parenthood status. Then, a second set of binomial logistic regression models is applied separately for women and men to explore the effects of these individual-level characteristics on employment outcomes during the pandemic. Finally, a third set of models introduces a contextual-level predictor for country clusters, aiming to identify differences in employment outcomes for women and men across various country contexts, which we also present in terms of predicted probabilities. These models enable us to test the proposed hypotheses and assess how the pandemic shock has affected employment outcomes for women and men in Europe at both individual and contextual levels. For the analysis, the sample is restricted to individuals aged 20 to 65 years, resulting in a final analytical sample of 29,832 individuals: 13,796 men and 16,036 women (see Table A3-2 in the appendix for descriptive statistics).

Results

The role of individual characteristics in shaping gendered employment patterns

The descriptive findings reveal significant variation in the incidence of negative employment outcomes experienced by women and men across European countries since the onset of the Covid-19 pandemic. As illustrated in Figure 3.1,

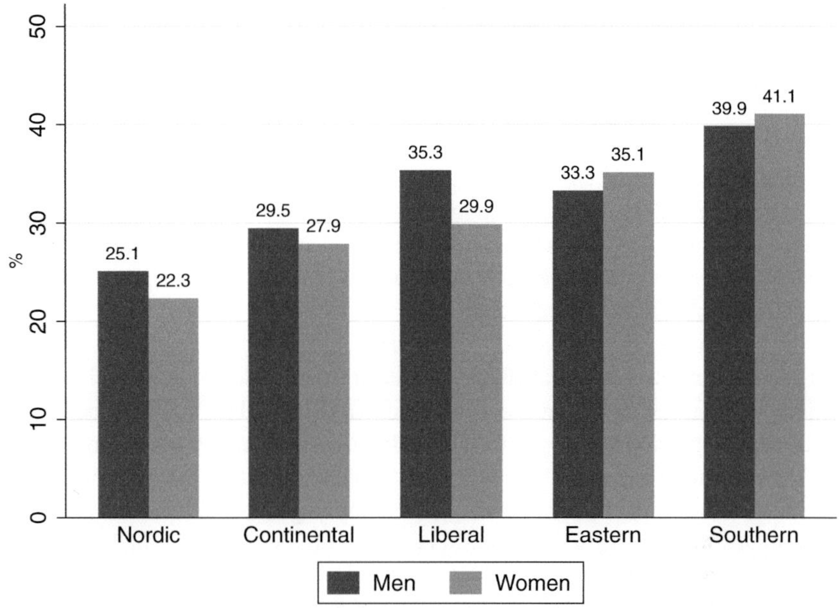

FIGURE 3.1 Percentage of Women and Men Experiencing a Negative Employment Outcome, by Country Cluster.

Source: Authors' calculations based on data from the European Social Survey (Round 10 – 2020, edition 3.2) (ESS ERIC, 2023).

a considerable proportion of women and men faced negative employment outcomes in Southern and Eastern European countries. In contrast, Continental and Nordic countries report the lowest percentages of both women and men experiencing negative employment outcomes during the pandemic. Overall, while gender gaps favouring men are evident in Southern and Eastern European countries, these gaps are relatively small in magnitude, suggesting that the pandemic had widespread effects across genders. Conversely, the findings suggest that in Continental, Northern and Liberal European countries, the impact of the pandemic was less severe overall, yet men experienced somewhat more significant negative employment outcomes compared to women. These findings provide preliminary indication that welfare regime characteristics shape the extent of employment disruptions, though the expected female disadvantage is not uniformly strong.

Beyond gender differences in aggregate outcomes, we also expected within-gender differences, with negative employment outcomes being more prevalent among individuals with lower levels of education, those working in sectors with limited job security (private sector or self-employed) and those under precarious job contracts (limited or no contract).

Table 3.1 presents the results from the three sets of binomial logistic regression models. The results for the first pooled model indicate that, overall, women were more likely to experience negative employment outcomes compared to men (coefficient for gender $\beta = 0.100$, $p < 0.001$). However, the magnitude of this effect is rather small, as the probability of experiencing a negative employment outcome is 0.33 among women versus 0.31 among men. This result aligns with the descriptive findings presented above, which showed that while gender gaps exist, their magnitude varies across contexts and is relatively modest overall – suggesting that the pandemic negatively affected both men and women, though in slightly different ways depending on the national context.

The results for the second set of models, estimated separately for women and men, examine the relationship between individual-level characteristics and employment outcomes during the pandemic (Model 2, Table 3.1). The coefficients for tertiary education are negative and statistically significant for both women ($\beta = -0.374$, $p < 0.001$) and men ($\beta = -0.357$, $p < 0.001$), indicating that higher levels of education reduced the likelihood of experiencing negative employment outcomes. This suggests that tertiary education served as a protective factor during the pandemic across genders.

The results further confirm the anticipated relationship between job precariousness (measured through employment sector and contract type) and negative employment outcomes during the pandemic. Women employed in the less protected private sector were more likely to experience negative employment outcomes compared to those in the public sector ($\beta = 0.764$, $p < 0.001$). The same pattern is observed for men, with a similar magnitude ($\beta = 0.752$, $p < 0.001$), suggesting minimal gender differences in this respect. Furthermore, women with limited contracts ($\beta = 0.470$, $p < 0.001$) and no contracts ($\beta = 0.458$, $p < 0.001$) faced higher risks of negative outcomes than those with unlimited contracts. Men exhibited a similar pattern, but in this case, the effect was stronger for women, confirming the anticipated gender difference. These findings are consistent with prior research documenting the increased job vulnerability of individuals involved in precarious employment forms, particularly women, and especially during economic crises (Karamessini & Rubery, 2014).

Finally, our findings reveal that both women and men with school-age children (5–15 years) were less likely to experience negative employment outcomes during the pandemic ($\beta = -0.102$, $p < 0.05$ for women; $\beta = -0.134$, $p < 0.01$ for men). However, no significant association was found between the presence of children under four years old and the likelihood of negative employment outcomes ($\beta = 0.032$, $p > 0.05$ for women; $\beta = 0.005$, $p > 0.05$ for men). These results contradict our expectations, which anticipated a more negative impact of childcare responsibilities – particularly for women. While the effects are statistically significant for school-age children, their magnitude is relatively modest (approximately two percentage points for both women and men).

TABLE 3.1 Logistic Regression Models

	Model 1	*Model 2*		*Model 3*	
	Pooled Women and Men	*Women*	*Men*	*Women*	*Men*
Constant	−1.280***	−1.174***	−1.281***	−1.338***	−1.349***
	(0.0423)	(0.0529)	(0.0602)	(0.0599)	(0.0678)
Individual level					
Gender [ref. Men]					
Women	0.100***				
	(0.0257)				
Education [ref. Primary and Secondary]					
Tertiary	−0.366***	−0.374***	−0.357***	−0.355***	−0.341***
	(0.0269)	(0.0368)	(0.0395)	(0.0372)	(0.0402)
Employment sector [ref. More protected]					
Less protected	0.761***	0.764***	0.752***	0.729***	0.742***
	(0.0298)	(0.0386)	(0.0472)	(0.0390)	(0.0474)
Employment contract type [ref. Unlimited]					
Limited	0.432***	0.470***	0.377***	0.427***	0.348***
	(0.0352)	(0.0461)	(0.0544)	(0.0466)	(0.0547)
No contract	0.445***	0.458***	0.431***	0.380***	0.352***
	(0.0576)	(0.0791)	(0.0841)	(0.0808)	(0.0849)
Children in household (0–4 years old) [ref. No children]					
Yes	0.0224	0.0319	0.00506	0.0432	0.00758
	(0.0464)	(0.0632)	(0.0686)	(0.0636)	(0.0688)
Children in household (5–15 years old) [ref. No children]					
Yes	−0.114***	−0.102*	−0.134**	−0.0918*	−0.113*
	(0.0344)	(0.0463)	(0.0517)	(0.0465)	(0.0519)
Migrant [ref. No]					
Yes	0.152*	0.0878	0.217*	0.168	0.202*

(Continued)

TABLE 3.1 *(Continued)*

	Model 1	*Model 2*		*Model 3*	
	Pooled Women and Men	*Women*	*Men*	*Women*	*Men*
	(0.0609)	(0.0863)	(0.0861)	(0.0877)	(0.0874)
Age category [ref. 20–35]					
36–50	0.0469	0.0315	0.0658	−0.0100	0.0271
	(0.0343)	(0.0468)	(0.0505)	(0.0471)	(0.0509)
51–65	0.0211	−0.00131	0.0452	−0.0193	0.0253
	(0.0334)	(0.0466)	(0.0482)	(0.0469)	(0.0484)
Country clusters [ref. Continental]					
Nordic				−0.129	−0.200**
				(0.0664)	(0.0667)
Liberal				0.0839	0.216*
				(0.0839)	(0.0893)
Eastern				0.336***	0.116*
				(0.0442)	(0.0472)
Southern				0.457***	0.370***
				(0.0538)	(0.0563)
Log-likelihood	−18099.47	−9677.12	−8420.27	−9610.62	−8382.42
Pseudo R2	0.0360	0.0414	0.0301	0.0479	0.0344
N	29832	16036	13796	16036	13796

Source: Authors' calculations based on data from the European Social Survey (Round 10 – 2020, edition 3.2) (ESS ERIC, 2023).

Note: *p < 0.05, **p < 0.01, ***p < 0.001. Logistic regression model (pooled women and men) (M1), logistic regression models for women and men with individual-level predictors (Model 2) and macro-level country cluster predictor (Model 3). B coefficients with standard errors in parentheses.

Especially surprising is the lack of a negative impact on employment among women with young children (0–4 years), a group often cited in the literature as especially vulnerable to work–family conflict. To further explore this finding, we included an interaction between country cluster and presence of children aged 0–4 in the models. The results indicate some relevant nuances. Indeed, the presence of young children in the household entails a slightly higher (albeit not statistically significant) probability of experiencing a negative employment outcome among women in Nordic (0.31 vs. 0.25), Liberal (0.33 vs. 0.29) and especially Southern European countries (0.43 vs. 0.37) compared to not having children in the household. No such difference emerges among women in Continental and Eastern countries, nor among men (see full results in Figure A3-1 in the online appendix). Thus, the result indicates that the presence of young children may have had some negative effect on mothers' employment outcomes, but not on fathers', partially aligning with existing literature on gendered caregiving responsibilities. However, further research is needed to better assess this outcome. Indeed, it should be kept in mind that the relatively small number of respondents with young children in the household might affect the overall reliability of the estimate.

Gendered employment impacts across European country clusters

Beyond individual-level determinants, the comparison across European country clusters reveals significant differences in employment outcomes during the pandemic. As shown in the top panel of Figure 3.2, the probability of experiencing negative employment outcomes is lower in Nordic and Continental countries compared to Liberal, Eastern and Southern European countries. This pattern generally holds when results are disaggregated by gender, as shown in the bottom panel. Women in Nordic and Continental countries show the lowest probability of experiencing a negative employment outcome – 0.26 and 0.28 respectively. By contrast, women in Southern countries were the most likely to face negative employment outcomes (0.38), followed by those from Eastern European countries (0.35). Women in Liberal countries fall in between, with a predicted probability of experiencing a negative employment outcome close to 0.30. The findings for men reveal a similar pattern, with men in Southern countries having the highest probability of negative employment outcomes (0.38), while men in Continental (0.30) and Nordic (0.26) countries had the lowest. Interestingly, in contrast to the pattern observed among women, men in the Liberal cluster had a higher probability of negative employment outcomes (0.35) than those in Eastern European countries (0.33). These results are in line with our general expectation that negative employment outcomes would be most common in Southern European countries, partly due to prolonged lockdown closures during the initial phase of the pandemic. However, our results do not indicate significantly worse outcomes for women as compared to men. Indeed, the probability of experiencing a negative employment outcome among women and men in the Southern group of countries is quite

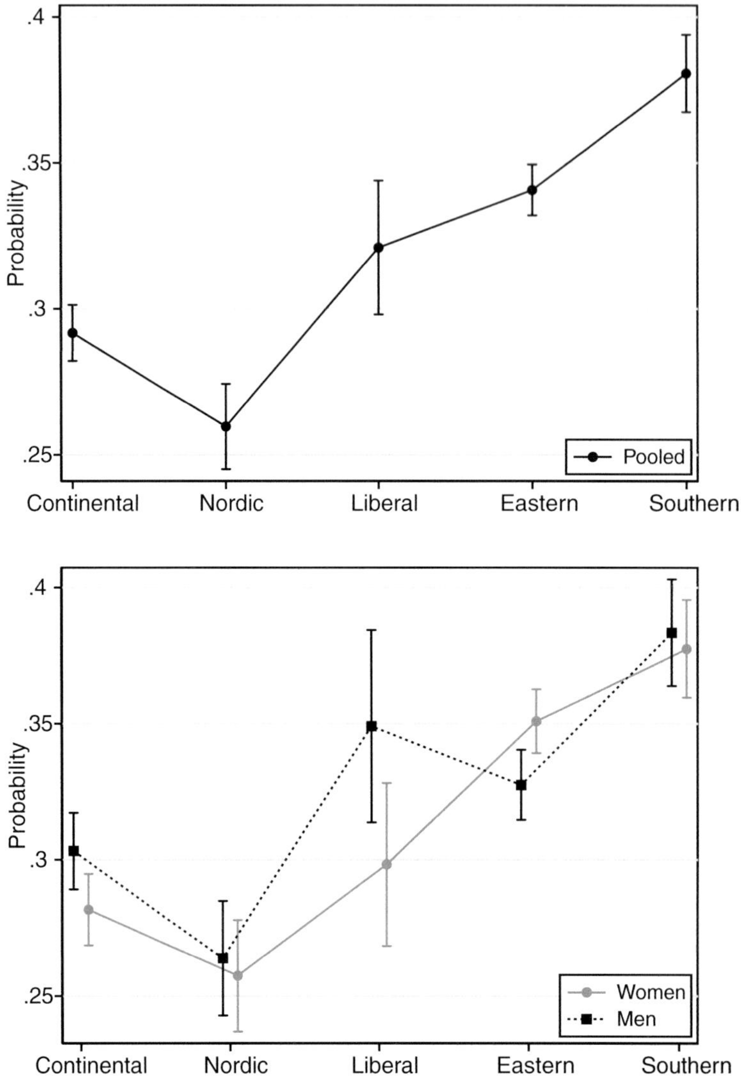

FIGURE 3.2 Predicted Probabilities of Experiencing a Negative Employment Outcome by Country Clusters in the Overall Sample (Top Panel) and by Gender (Bottom Panel).

Source: European Social Survey (2023), Round 10. Women N = 16,036, Men N = 13,796.

Note: 95% confidence intervals.

similar and the difference is not statistically significant[1] at the 5% level. Thus, it appears that women in this cluster were not disproportionately penalised in terms of labour market outcomes. Interestingly, we also find evidence of a small, though non-statistically significant, gender gap favouring women in the Liberal group.

This unexpected pattern requires further investigation, particularly in relation to sectoral composition and policy responses in these countries.

In summary, the results highlight both individual- and contextual-level factors shaping gendered employment outcomes during the Covid-19 pandemic in Europe. They underscore the complexity of gendered labour market vulnerability and set the stage for a more in-depth interpretation in the following discussion.

Discussion

How do these results map onto our hypotheses? First, and contrary to our expectation of observing substantial gender disparities in employment outcomes during the pandemic in Europe (H1), our results show that women were only slightly more likely than men to suffer from negative labour market outcomes – and this pattern was not consistent across all country contexts. Instead, our findings highlight the role of structural employment characteristics in shaping vulnerability to negative labour market outcomes, beyond gender alone. In line with hypotheses H2, H4 and H5, higher education, public sector employment and holding an unlimited job contract all acted as protective factors against negative employment outcomes for both women and men. These findings align with prior research on the buffering role of education and employment sector during exogenous shocks (Karamessini & Rubery, 2014; Alon et al., 2021; Qian et al., 2023) and suggest that, beyond a modest baseline gender gap, these individual and employment factors offered consistent protection across gender groups. However, our expectation that holding an unlimited contract would offer additional protection to women (H5b) was not confirmed.

This finding invites further reflection on the structural barriers that limit women's access to secure employment in the first place, rather than on differential returns to stability once achieved. While women are more likely to be concentrated in precarious forms of employment, the benefits of job stability – once attained – are not necessarily greater for them than for men.

Similarly, findings related to parental status only partially met our expectations: while having a school-aged child (5–15 years) entailed a lower risk of experiencing a negative employment outcome for both women and men, the presence of younger children (aged 0–4) showed a modest and context-dependent effect. Specifically, a slightly higher risk was observed among mothers in certain countries (e.g., Southern and Liberal clusters), but not for fathers, and not consistently across all clusters. Hence, Hypotheses H3a and H3b receive only partial support. This result raises questions about how care infrastructures, gender norms and lockdown policy stringency intersected to shape mothers' labour market vulnerability in different national contexts.

Considering differences across European country clusters, our expectations that employment outcomes would be more negative in Southern, Eastern and Liberal countries – compared to Nordic and Continental ones – was largely confirmed for both women and men, in line with Hypothesis H6. Southern countries, in particular, faced the most severe employment impacts. However, contrary to Hypothesis H7, we did not find evidence of a more pronounced gender gap in this cluster: in other words, women and men in Southern countries were similarly affected by negative employment outcomes. In contrast, Eastern countries exhibited a more marked gender gap, with women experiencing worse employment outcomes than men. This divergence suggests that the gendered impact of the pandemic was not uniformly structured by welfare regimes or familialism models, and that other factors – such as labour market segmentation or country-specific policy responses – may have played a critical role in shaping gendered outcomes within these clusters.

Overall, while we did not find clear evidence of a generalised "she-cession" (Alon et al., 2021; Carlson et al., 2021), our findings reveal that the negative employment effects of the Covid-19 pandemic were unevenly distributed, both within and between European countries. At the individual level, our results align with previous research, showing that individuals with stronger labour market positions – such as higher education and secure job contracts – were less likely to face adverse employment outcomes across all the country clusters we analysed. At the contextual level, by adopting a comparative approach, our study highlights the pandemic's unequal impact across different welfare regimes. Specifically, the impacts were less severe in Continental and Nordic European countries, where robust welfare support systems and – especially in the latter case – strong commitments to gender equality, appear to have buffered against widespread negative employment outcomes. It is plausible that a combination of factors – such as work protection schemes implemented during the initial lockdowns, robust public sector employment, strong labour market protections, supportive gender equality policies, the prevalence of good quality part-time jobs among women (notably in Germany and the Netherlands) and high pre-pandemic female employment rates (especially in Nordic countries) – contributed to mitigating the negative impacts of the pandemic on labour market outcomes in these contexts.

Conclusion

The Covid-19 pandemic triggered global crises that disrupted health systems and economies, disproportionately affecting industries with high concentrations of female workers, unlike the 2008–2009 economic crisis, which initially impacted male employment more severely (Alon et al., 2021; Bettio & Verashchagina, 2014; Hupkau & Petrongolo, 2020). This shift has led to contrasting views on gender equality: a pessimistic perspective warns of "re-traditionalisation," with setbacks in women's employment and unpaid labour potentially worsening economic vulnerability and reversing progress (Alon et al., 2021; Carlson et al., 2021). Conversely, an optimistic view highlights opportunities arising from flexible work arrangements, hybrid models and greater recognition of essential roles, which could enhance women's labour market outcomes and work–family balance (Hupkau & Petrongolo, 2020; Del Boca et al., 2020). This chapter draws on recent European Social Survey data (2023, ESS10) to search for evidence in support of either side of the debate.

Our results suggest that the risk of a generalised "she-cession" has been avoided. However, we do not find support for the optimistic view that the pandemic functioned as a catalyst for greater gender equality in employment. Rather, we observe a more nuanced picture where vulnerabilities were shaped not only by gender but also by the intersection of individual characteristics – particularly education, contract type and employment sector – with country-level institutions and welfare models. On this basis, we conclude that, in the immediate aftermath of the Covid-19 pandemic, progress towards gender equality in employment outcomes was stalled.

These findings hold significant relevance for the academic community, policymakers and the broader public. As one of the few large-scale comparative studies to date, this research underscores the critical interplay between individual characteristics and the broader socio-economic context in which individuals operate. While individual characteristics and personal labour market positions play a crucial role in shaping employment outcomes, the degree of protection offered during crises also depends on welfare and gender equality frameworks, particularly during crises like the Covid-19 pandemic. The study demonstrates that countries with robust welfare support systems and strong commitments to gender equality – which in this study are represented by the Nordic and Continental clusters – provide a more protective and supportive environment for both women and men against adverse employment impacts. However, our study also suggests important gender nuances: in some contexts, especially in Eastern Europe, women experienced greater vulnerability than men, while in others, gender differences were minimal.

These patterns reinforce the need to understand gender as one upon many of the key dimensions of inequality and to study it in interaction with socio-economic position, family roles and national policy structures. This insight is vital for policymakers as it emphasises the need to invest in comprehensive welfare programmes and gender equality initiatives that can buffer against future crises and avoid exacerbating gender inequalities during systemic shocks. Lessons from countries that fared better during the pandemic should inform the development of policies to better protect workers from exogenous shocks, promote more equitable labour market participation and strengthen gender equality within households. For instance, enhancing the quality and accessibility of part-time jobs and promoting more equitable divisions of care within households are policy areas with the potential to reduce gendered labour market disadvantage.

This study has some limitations that should be acknowledged. First, due to sample size constraints, we could not disaggregate types of negative employment outcomes or examine interactions between multiple individual-level variables (e.g., differences across generations as well as smaller geographical areas). Future research with ad hoc samples on the working population could fruitfully address which adverse employment outcomes were more likely among different groups of respondents. Second, since the ESS data on the effects of the Covid-19 pandemic were collected in a single round of data collection, our analyses inevitably reflect short-term changes only. Future research should address whether the gendered impact of the pandemic on labour market outcomes persisted, deepened or shifted over time and, if so, for which groups of respondents. A longitudinal within-individual approach would allow for more accurately disentangling the long-term effects of the pandemic on employment outcomes in a comparative European context.

In summary, this chapter emphasises that understanding employment outcomes in times of crisis requires attention to both individual vulnerabilities and the socio-institutional conditions they are embedded in. It calls for a comprehensive and inclusive policy-making approach that considers gender as a transversal axis of inequality at the intersection of both individual and structural factors. Such an approach is essential not only to promote equality in future crises, but also to build resilient, equitable labour markets in the long run.

To conclude, the study of crises and unexpected shocks on individuals' employment remains a critical area of research. In an interconnected world characterised by global markets, increased mobility and the rapid exchange of goods, the spread of pathogens is accelerated, heightening the likelihood of future pandemics for which welfare states should and must be prepared. Furthermore, future disruptions may produce similarly destabilising effects: for example, climate change may necessitate lockdown-like measures, as extreme weather events – such as heatwaves and floods – could result in localised mobility restrictions, school closures and disruptions to daily life. As countries prepare for such challenges, understanding how various policy frameworks influence gendered labour market impacts is crucial for developing policies that minimise gender inequality and mitigate longer-term disadvantages at both individual and societal levels.

Note

1 An additional model was run to test the interaction between gender and cluster of countries and is reported in Table A3-1 in the online appendix.

References

Adams-Prassl, A., Boneva, T., Golin, M., & Rauh, C. (2020). Inequality in the impact of the coronavirus shock: Evidence from real-time surveys. *Journal of Public Economics*, *189*, 104245. https://doi.org/10.1016/j.jpubeco.2020.104245

Albanesi, S., & Kim, J. (2021). Effects of the COVID-19 recession on the US labor market: Occupation, family, and gender. *Journal of Economic Perspectives*, *35*(3), 3–24. https://doi.org/10.1257/jep.35.3.3

Alon, T., Doepke, M., Olmstead-Rumsey, J., & Tertilt, M. (2021). From mancession to shecession: Women's employment in regular and pandemic recessions. *NBER Macroeconomics Annual*, *36*, 83–151. https://doi.org/10.1086/718660

Bettin, G., Giorgetti, I., & Staffolani, S. (2024). The impact of Covid-19 lockdown on the gender gap in the Italian labour market. *Review of Economics of the Household*, *22*, 1–33. https://doi.org/10.1007/s11150-023-09659-5

Bettio, F., & Verashchagina, A. (2014). Women and men in the Great European Recession. In Karamessini, M., & Rubery, J. (Eds.), *Women and austerity: The economic crisis and the future for gender equality* (pp. 17–36). Routledge.

Blázquez, M., Herrarte, A., & Moro-Egido, A. I. (2023). Gender differences in the effect of teleworking on job loss during the COVID-19 pandemic in Spain. *Economics and Human Biology*, *51*, 101299. https://doi.org/10.1016/j.ehb.2023.101299

Bluedorn, J., Caselli, F., Hansen, N.-J. H., Shibata, I., & Tavares, M. M. (2023). Gender and employment in the COVID-19 recession: Cross-country evidence on "she-cessions". *Labour Economics*, *81*, 102308. https://doi.org/10.1016/j.labeco.2022.102308

Brini, E., Lenko, M., Scherer, S., & Vitali, A. (2021). Retraditionalisation? Work patterns of families with children during the pandemic in Italy. *Demographic Research*, *45*, 957–972. https://doi.org/10.4054/DemRes.2021.45.31

Carlson, D. L., Petts, R., & Pepin, J. R. (2021). Changes in US parents' domestic labor during the early days of the COVID-19 pandemic. *Sociological Inquiry*, *92*(3), 1217–1244. https://doi.org/10.1111/soin.12459

Chung, H., Birkett, H., Forbes, S., & Seo, H. (2021). COVID-19, flexible working, and implications for gender equality in the United Kingdom. *Gender & Society*, *35*(2), 218–232. https://doi.org/10.1177/08912432211001304

Collins, C., Landivar, L. C., Ruppanner, L., & Scarborough, W. J. (2021). The gendered consequences of a weak infrastructure of care: School reopening plans and parents' employment during the COVID-19 pandemic. *Gender & Society*, *35*(2), 180–193. https://doi.org/10.1177/08912432211001300

Del Boca, D., Oggero, N., Profeta, P., & Rossi, M. (2020). Women's and men's work, housework and childcare, before and during COVID-19. *Review of Economics of the Household*, *18*, 1001–1017. https://doi.org/10.1007/s11150-020-09502-1

Dias, F. A., Chance, J., & Buchanan, A. (2020). The motherhood penalty and the fatherhood premium in employment during covid-19: Evidence from the United States. *Research in Social Stratification and Mobility*, *69*, 100542. https://doi.org/10.1016/j.rssm.2020.100542

Dotti Sani, G. M. (2018). The economic crisis and changes in work–family arrangements in six European countries. *Journal of European Social Policy*, *28*(2), 177–193. https://doi.org/10.1177/0958928717700566

Dotti Sani, G. M., Bertogg, A., Besamusca, J., Yerkes, M. A., & Zamberlan, A. (2025). To the fifties and back again? A comparative analysis of changes in breadwinning arrangements during the first year of the COVID-19 pandemic in four European countries. *Work, Employment and Society*, *39*(4), 972–996.. https://doi.org/10.1177/09500170251322684

Esping-Andersen, G. (1999). *Social foundations of postindustrial economies*. Oxford University Press.

Esping-Andersen, G. (2009). *The incomplete revolution: Adapting to women's new roles*. Polity Press.

Eurofound. (2022). *COVID-19 pandemic and the gender divide at work and home*. Publications Office of the European Union. https://www.eurofound.europa.eu/en/publications/2022/covid-19-pandemic-and-gender-divide-work-and-home

European Institute for Gender Equality (EIGE). (2023). *Gender equality index 2023 – Towards a green transition in transport and energy*. Publications Office of the European Union. https://eige.europa.eu/sites/default/files/documents/Gender%20Equality%20Index%202023.pdf?utm_source=chatgpt.com

European Social Survey European Research Infrastructure (ESS ERIC). (2023). *ESS10 integrated file, edition 3.2* [Data set]. Sikt – Norwegian Agency for Shared Services in Education and Research. https://doi.org/10.21338/ess10e03_2

Eurostat. (2023). *Employment rate by sex (20–64 years), EU Labour Force Survey*. https://ec.europa.eu/eurostat/databrowser/view/lfsi_emp_a/default/table?lang=en

Hook, J. L. (2015). Incorporating "class" into work–family arrangements: Insights from and for three worlds. *Journal of European Social Policy*, *25*(1), 14–31. https://doi.org/10.1177/0958928714556968

Hupkau, C., & Petrongolo, B. (2020). Work, care and gender during the COVID-19 crisis. *Fiscal Studies*, *41*(3), 623–651. https://doi.org/10.1111/1475-5890.12245

International Labour Organization. (2021). *Building forward fairer: Women's rights to work and at work at the core of the COVID-19 recovery*. https://www.ilo.org/publications/building-forward-fairer-women's-rights-work-and-work-core-covid-19-recovery

Insarauto, V. (2021). Women's vulnerability to the economic crisis through the lens of part-time work in Spain. *Work, Employment and Society*, *35*(4), 621–639. https://doi.org/10.1177/09500170211001271

Karamessini, M., & Rubery, J. (Eds.). (2014). *Women and austerity: The economic crisis and the future for gender equality*. Routledge.

Korpi, W., Ferrarini, T., & Englund, S. (2013). Women's opportunities under different family policy constellations: Gender, class and inequality tradeoffs in Western countries re-examined. *Social Politics: International Studies in Gender, State & Society*, *20*(1), 1–40. https://doi.org/10.1093/sp/jxs028

Kowalewska, H. (2023). Gendered employment patterns: Women's labour market outcomes across 24 countries. *Journal of European Social Policy*, *33*(2), 151–168. https://doi.org/10.1177/09589287221148336

Kulic, N., Dotti Sani, G. M., & Scherer, S. (2021). Economic disturbances in the COVID-19 crisis and their gendered impact on unpaid activities in Germany and Italy. *European Societies*, *23*(supl), S400–S416. https://doi.org/10.1080/14616696.2020.1828974

Leitner, S. (2003). Varieties of familialism: The caring function of the family in comparative perspective. *European Societies*, *5*(4), 353–375. https://doi.org/10.1080/1461669032000127642

Lewis, J. (1992). Gender and the development of welfare regimes. *Journal of European Social Policy*, *2*(3), 159–173. https://doi.org/10.1177/095892879200200301

Mesiäislehto, M., Saari, J., & Vänskä, J. (2022). *The gendered impacts of the Covid-19 crisis in Finland and the effectiveness of the policy responses* (Discussion Paper 2/2022). Finnish Institute for Health and Welfare (THL). https://urn.fi/URN:ISBN:978-952-343-800-2

Qian, Y., Shen, J., & Wang, H. (2023). COVID-19 job loss and re-employment among partnered parents: Gender and educational variations. *Journal of Marriage and Family*, *85*(2), 438–458. https://doi.org/10.1111/jomf.12927

Sánchez-Mira, N., & O'Reilly, J. (2019). Household employment and the crisis in Europe. *Work, Employment and Society*, *33*(3), 422–443. https://doi.org/10.1177/0950017018809324

Saraceno, C. (2016). Varieties of familialism: Comparing four southern European and East Asian welfare regimes. *Journal of European Social Policy*, *26*(4), 314–326. https://doi.org/10.1177/0958928716657275

4

WORKING LIVES AND LIVELIHOODS IN TURBULENT TIMES

Intersecting inequalities of gender and class in the UK

Luis Torres and Tracey Warren

Introduction

The chapter examines gender and class equality in working lives and livelihoods in the UK over two decades of turbulence. We focus on the period of financial crisis and austerity, the Covid-19 pandemic and the cost-of-living crisis. Each period of turmoil led to serious academic, policy and public interest in identifying those who were most affected by, and those most protected from, its negative ramifications. Turbulent times provide unique insights into the structure and experience of work and employment, including the extent and nature of inequalities. They raise fundamental questions about the potential deepening of gendered inequalities in work, stalling or undoing progress for women (Elson, 2013) and, for this chapter too, the classed ramifications for women's and men's working lives and livelihoods.

The impact of economic turbulence is frequently measured by tracking levels of unemployment. During the 2008–2009 recessionary turbulence, for example, this approach led to the problematic widespread use of the "man-cession" and "he-cession" labels because men were falsely predicted to lose their jobs in greater numbers than women (Rubery & Rafferty, 2013; Zhang et al., 2015). In the UK, far more women than men leave the labour force on job loss due to their greater responsibilities for essential unpaid domestic work and caring, and in a welfare system with a strong male-breadwinner legacy (Chanfreau, 2023; Lewis, 2001), and so a pure focus on unemployment levels disguises the full impact of turmoil on work and workers. This can include threats to worktime and/or wages, and rising precarious work arrangements, all potentially impacting women and men differently (Rubery & Távora, 2021), which is our threefold focus in this chapter.

DOI: 10.4324/9781003528210-6

It is also important to note that the gendered impact of recession varies according to socio-economic context. There have been valuable studies focused on variation across national socio-economic contexts and the sectors most affected by specific crises (Rubery, 1988; Rubery & Rafferty, 2013). This chapter takes up an under-researched issue: the differential impact of relentless turbulence on female and male workers from diverse social classes. Class has critical implications in the contemporary workplace: it strongly shapes workers' achievements and opportunities in the short and longer terms (Kish-Gephart et al., 2023). Despite the significance of class, Milkman et al. (2021) argue that studies using the gender-class nexus remain too rare in research into working lives. This nexus shows that the experience of paid work is distinctly gendered: women and men work in highly segregated occupations, for example, tending to concentrate in different types of jobs and with men dominating higher levels within organisations (Andrew et al., 2024; Francis-Devine, 2024; Razzu & Singleton, 2018). However, adding in class enriches our understanding of work and inequalities. It reveals, for example, that working-class women, at the intersection of both gender and class disadvantage (McBride et al., 2015), are far more narrowly clustered than other workers. They are frequently found doing essential but undervalued and underpaid work (Farris & Bergfeld, 2022; International Labour Organization [ILO], 2023).

In the UK, in addition to the above, working-class women are heavily over-concentrated in part-time employment, especially when they have dependent children. Compared with the middle classes, working-class parents are less likely to use full-time childcare, shaped by prohibitive costs of private provision (Organisation for Economic Co-operation and Development [OECD], 2022). Accordingly, as main carers, working-class mothers tend instead to reduce their hours to be able to patch together doing childcare themselves alongside shift parenting if they have a partner, informal childcare from relatives and friends, and part-time state-funded formal care. These complex patchworks shape the women's paid working lives when their children are young, but they have lengthier ramifications too because the women can become trapped in part-time jobs even when they want to increase their hours (Wood & Bennett, 2022; Warren & Lyonette, 2018). Such worktime underemployment impairs workplace progression and brings short- and longer-term financial risks (Kamerāde & Richardson, 2018; Warren, 2015).

This chapter examines gender and class inequalities in paid work during continuing turbulence in the UK. It shows that inequalities in some aspects of working lives remained relatively stable, but others widened. Most notably, working-class women, at the intersections of gender and class inequalities, saw the deepest disadvantages across the decades, working the fewest hours, earning the least and at rising risks of precarious employment. We conclude that it remains essential to move beyond solely gendered analyses to reveal how class also shapes workers' achievements and opportunities in both the short and longer terms, and to expose unequal working lives amid turmoil.

Gender, class and paid work in the UK in turbulent times

This section reviews the three periods of turmoil, identifying their potential ramifications for gender and class inequalities in paid working lives.

Financial crisis and austerity

Before the turbulence of the 2008–2009 recession, the UK was characterised by clear gendered inequalities in working lives and livelihoods. There were deep gender gaps in paid worktime and wages, to women's disadvantage, and a real risk was that the financial crisis would widen these gaps, stalling progress towards gender equality or undoing hard-won gains. With earnings, for example, the Equal Pay Act in 1970 and the 1975 Sex Discrimination Act (amalgamated in the 2010 Equality Act) had been passed to tackle discrimination and, by law, women and men doing equal work (like work, equivalent work or work of equal value) should receive equal pay. Amid the recession, however, women faced new threats to their wages and job security. While women workers in some sectors (e.g., public administration, education, health and social care) were better protected than men in many male-dominated sectors, as Rubery and Rafferty (2013) show, women employed elsewhere saw heightened insecurity, sometimes even more so than their male peers working in the same sector (e.g., wholesale, retail and restaurants, financial and insurance activities). Women workers were further disproportionately impacted in the sustained years of austerity that followed the recessionary period. Deep cuts in public expenditure and state-funded services that led to job loss and a freezing of pay hit women's work harder because of their heavy concentration in employment in these sectors (Durbin et al., 2017; Rake, 2009; Rubery, 2015; Rubery & Rafferty, 2013).

Class inequalities were also substantial in the UK before the recession hit, with wide class gaps in workers' earnings and living standards (Brewer et al., 2009). It was notable that the financial crisis was predicted to bring the first recession in which middle-class workers would be most affected. In reality, the recession impacted those employed in lower-level occupations to a larger extent, producing substantial increases in their economic insecurity (Warren, 2015). The post-recessionary period widened societal class gaps further (Dorling, 2015), with questions about disparities amplified in the years leading up to and in the aftermath of the 2016 Brexit referendum. Employment grew more precarious, and a rising number of working-class workers were stuck in "low-pay, no-pay" cycles, facing in-work poverty (Garthwaite, 2016; Hall, 2019; Shildrick et al., 2012). The final years of the post-recessionary decade saw a sharp rise in inflation and the freezing of and then deep cuts to welfare support, impacting lower earners disproportionately (Okeke et al., 2021). More positively, levels of unemployment remained low and so fewer people were without any earnings at all (Bourquin et al., 2024) while pay for the lowest earners including working-class women (e.g., in social care) was supported by the national minimum wage (NMW) (introduced in 1999). Since 2016, those aged 21 years and over are covered by a higher National Living Wage (Richardson & Witteveen, 2024).

Covid-19

Even when compared with the decade of deep financial turbulence preceding it, the Covid-19 pandemic brought extraordinary challenges for workers (Beck et al., 2020), with severely unequal effects by gender, class and other intersecting social inequalities (Rubery, Távora et al., 2024). Three pandemic developments had clear gender and class ramifications for working lives.

The gender impact of the first development, furloughing or the "Coronavirus Job Retention Scheme", changed over the course of the early pandemic months. This scheme enabled employers to put workers on a temporary full or partial leave, paid at 80% of their wages (capped at £2,500 a month, unless otherwise agreed [HM Revenue & Customs, 2020]). While initially more men than women were furloughed as work in, for example, building and construction and manufacturing was halted, this phase lasted for a short time while lengthier restrictions on face-to-face work in non-essential travel and services saw women also stopping or reducing work and for longer periods (Wielgoszewska, 2024). The next development was the extraordinary rise in working from home due to pandemic restrictions. More men than women had worked from home before 2020, but women overtook men (albeit only slightly) during the pandemic months (Chung et al., 2021). The third development, the new categorisation of workers as critical, key or essential, also had a gendered impact, here very strongly affecting more women than men. In designating who was still allowed to go out to work during lockdowns, positively, the classification recognised the necessity of the roles that many women do, such as in health and care (ILO, 2023; Kim et al., 2024), and women were better protected against redundancies or even saw an increase in employment. Yet being essential also meant that many had to leave their homes for work, heightening their exposure to the virus (Connor et al., 2020).

These pandemic-induced changes to paid work were also firmly classed. Furlough, for example, was taken up largely by employers of working-class workers, and, while it gave those on furlough some job protection (Witteveen, 2020), the lower paid (many of whom were women) were less likely to have their pay topped up than were higher earners (Adams-Prassl et al., 2020; Brewer & Patrick, 2021). Places of work were also classed during Covid, with distinct inequalities in where work was carried out amid pandemic restrictions. Pre-pandemic, the jobs held by many working-class workers were less open to being carried out in their own home and the workers had limited access to other quality flexible working arrangements (Chung et al., 2021; Felstead, 2022). This classed patterning persisted into the pandemic even during strict lockdowns, with working-class workers more likely to still be going out to work than managerial and professional staff, and with far fewer opportunities to flex their work in other ways (Warren et al., 2021). The third pandemic development, key working, saw the roles of more people in working- than middle-class jobs deemed essential (e.g., in social care, transport, the production/distribution of essential goods) and, additionally, among the key workers, the working class were disproportionately found in frontline roles which required face-to-face interaction and brought health risks (ILO, 2023).

Cost-of-living crisis

The pandemic was followed rapidly by the cost-of-living crisis. For Dorling (2023), while some countries in Europe were in a much better position to weather the cost-of-living storm, more people in the UK (alongside Hungary and Poland) reported finding it harder to "get by" as the crisis deepened. The UK crisis was characterised by substantial drops in disposable incomes as the prices of necessities spiralled, leading to the biggest decline in living standards since official records began in 1956 (Brown et al., 2023; Florisson, 2024; Hick & Collins, 2024).

The fallout from economic insecurity was heavily gendered. Women workers faced higher risks of in-work poverty than men due to their lower pay rates, intensified for part-timers and, within the home, women more often acted as the household "shock absorbers" in careful budgeting, going without themselves and feeding families within their more restricted means (Pinto, & Reis, 2024). These pressures were clearly classed as well. UK living standards were collectively affected, but the crisis hit heaviest those on lower incomes because they spend a larger proportion of their incomes on necessities like food (Edmiston, 2025). The Insecure Work Index 2024 showed people in insecure work experiencing huge financial pressure to make ends meet (Florisson, 2024) and a cost-of-living tracker found that the poorest were seeking to take on more work (and turning to high-cost credit) to get by day to day (Joseph Rowntree Foundation [JRF], 2024). Pressures were not eased by the Conservative government's decision to end the £20 a week uplift to basic benefits for those unemployed or with insufficient wage income that had been introduced at the start of the pandemic due to the very low levels of these benefits in the UK (Edmiston, 2025). Amid labour shortages across such key sectors as health and social care (where working-class women often work), and rising economic inactivity linked to widening ill-health (Brown et al., 2023), the government also prioritised a "Back to Work" agenda that included increasing levels of welfare conditionality and harsh sanctions for those failing to find employment (Wright, 2023). Alongside these "sticks" to get more people into paid work, there was a promised "carrot" of a new Employment Bill. This could have increased access to guaranteed minimum hours (helping young people and working-class women in particular), but it was repeatedly delayed and then abandoned by Prime Minister Rishi Sunak when he called an early general election (July 2024). More positively, in October 2024, the new Labour government introduced an Employment Rights Bill, aiming to help people stay in paid work, support productivity and improve living standards (Department for Business and Trade et al., 2025).

Summary

The above three periods of turmoil are alleged to have created a permacrisis across decades of unrest, with highly unequal ramifications (Edmiston et al., 2025; Hoff & Happer, 2025). This chapter next questions the extent of gender and class inequalities in work amid perma-turmoil. We focus on risks of insecurity in three aspects of working lives: worktime, wages and employment contracts.

Data and methods

The chapter draws on analysis of data gathered in the UK Labour Force Survey (LFS) (Office for National Statistics, 2024) on workers' (main) jobs. Respondents are interviewed for five successive waves at three-month intervals. Four releases are supported in a typical year and enable overall population trends from 2006 to 2022 to be tracked (i.e., from pre-recession to mid cost-of-living crisis). Our analyses consider employees aged between 18 to 64 years old who provide valid responses to the survey questions that we focus on. We exclude the self-employed because their worktime, systems of remuneration and levels of autonomy vary substantially from those of employees.

Operationalisation of social class and sample description

We use occupational class to explore inequalities among female and male employees, drawing on Crompton's (2010) influential argument that, for most people, class outcomes are strongly related to the kinds of occupations available to them. We used the Office for National Statistics' National Statistics Socio-economic Classification (NS-SEC) to operationalise occupational class. NS-SEC aims to differentiate workers by labour market situation (source of income, economic security and prospects of economic advancement) and work situation (location in systems of authority and control at work, Office of National Statistics [ONS], 2022a).

To facilitate the analysis, we distinguish between occupations that can be regarded as working class in this schema, namely "semi-routine" (e.g., care workers, retail assistants) and "routine" workers (e.g., cleaners, waiting staff, bar staff) and treat all other occupations as non-working-class. As the sample characteristics show (Table 4.1), as a share of all employees, the working-class category declined among men over time, and fell slightly more among the women, but in our final year of analysis, still over a fifth of the UK workforce was working class (21.5% women, 23.6% men).

Among the non-working class categories, over this period, the already substantial managerial/professional category expanded further, particularly for women.

TABLE 4.1 Sample Characteristics for Selected Years of the LFS

Gender	*Occupational Category*	*2006*	*2010*	*2014*	*2018*	*2022*
Men	Management/professional	48.1%	49.3%	48.6%	50.9%	56.1%
	Intermediate	7.6%	7.7%	9.3%	9.7%	10.3%
	Lower supervisory/technical	17.0%	15.5%	13.7%	13.1%	10.0%
	Routine/semi-routine	27.3%	27.4%	28.4%	26.3%	23.6%
	Total	12,107,123	11,952,038	12,447,293	13,059,321	13,340,736
Women	Management/professional	43.8%	45.2%	44.8%	47.7%	54.1%
	Intermediate	20.8%	19.3%	23.4%	22.3%	20.8%
	Lower supervisory/technical	7.0%	6.5%	4.7%	4.6%	3.0%
	Routine/semi-routine	28.4%	29.0%	27.0%	24.4%	21.5%
	Total	11,432,907	11,497,420	12,028,514	12,675,280	12,876,721

Source: Own elaboration based on UK Labour Force Survey data.

Notes: Percentages and totals are calculated considering the last quarter each year (Oct–Dec). Population estimates (weighted data).

By 2022, over half of women and men employees (54.1% and 56.1% respectively) were in this highest occupational grouping, though women were still concentrated within its lower levels. Around a fifth of women and up to 10% of men were employed in intermediate jobs (e.g., clerical, sales and service roles with no authority) with even lower and falling percentages of men, and very small percentages of women, in lower supervisory/technical jobs (e.g., as "foremen" or supervisors or in technical jobs with some work autonomy).

Data analysis

R software (version 4.4.2) was used to analyse the data to track the overarching patterns in employment conditions across the turbulent years, differentiated by gender and class. We produced descriptive statistics on worktime, earnings and job precariousness, focusing on average hours worked per week in the main job; levels of part-time employment (and reasons for working part-time); average hourly pay; and levels of involuntary temporary jobs and zero-hours contracts.

Findings

Worktime in turbulent times

Our analyses show clearly how women employees in the UK spend fewer hours in paid work than men, on average (Figure 4.1(a)). They show too how, amid turmoil, median usual weekly hours remained steady (at 30.5 hours for women and 38.3 hours for men). Working-class women consistently worked shorter weeks than all the other groups. In 2022 (Oct–Dec), for example, they averaged 26.5 hours, fully 10 hours fewer per week than their male working-class counterparts. The gender hours gap among the non-working class occupational group was much narrower at approximately five hours (33.7 hours median for women versus 38.8 for men). These figures reflect that while most women employees have full-time jobs in the UK (and so work over 30 hours a week), women full-timers average a shorter week than their male peers and substantially more women than men work part-time, especially working-class women (Warren & Lyonette, 2018). As Figure 4.1(b) shows too, (self-reported) part-time employment continued to be more of a feature of working-class women's work.

Employees' typical worktime remained relatively stable over the crisis periods. However, our analysis of median hours will necessarily under-report any developments in very short or long hours employment, and our focus on the main job does not include hours spent in additional jobs. Other studies report workers facing unwelcome changes to their hours over the years of turbulence, with concerns raised over potential increases in worktime underemployment (Bell & Blanchflower, 2013) and workers trying to take on more work to get by, particularly the lowest waged (JRF, 2024). Because most of the worktime underemployed in the UK work part-time hours but would prefer full-time (ONS, 2022b), we explore involuntary part-time employment next.

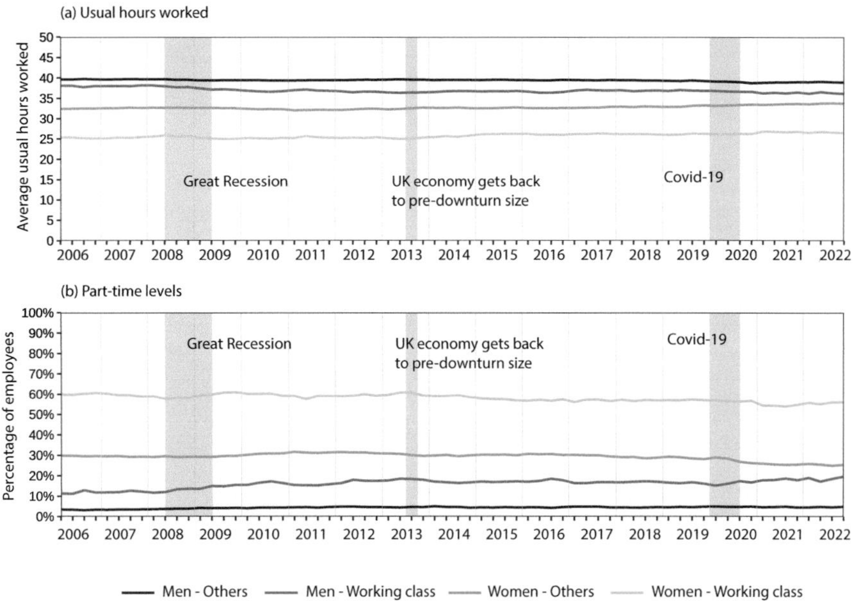

FIGURE 4.1 Average Usual Hours Worked (a) and Levels of Part-Time Employment (b) among Employees by Gender and Class (2006–2022).

Source: Own elaboration based on UK Labour Force Survey data.

Figure 4.2 shows that involuntary part-time working remained a strongly gendered and classed phenomenon over the crisis decades. Levels of involuntary part-time working rose after the recession (up to 2013), and again during the pandemic, yet stable amid these changes was that, while most female part-timers did not want full-time hours, a larger percentage of male part-timers did desire full-time work but could not find it. A key factor contributing to this tenacious disparity is that women more often work part-time to fit around other roles in their lives, including caring for children and others, that constrain their options (Rubery, Bi-Swinglehurst et al., 2024; Rubery & Rafferty, 2013; Warren and Lyonette, 2018). This form of worktime underemployment is also markedly and steadfastly classed, for women and men, with the result that, in each year studied, working-class men stood out from the other part-timers in how many were doing so involuntarily.

Earnings in turbulent times

Women workers as a group earn less than men, per hour, week and over their lifetimes (Andrew et al., 2024), but women in working-class occupations face a combination of even lower hourly wages, shorter paid working weeks and more interrupted labour force participation. We examine whether gender- and

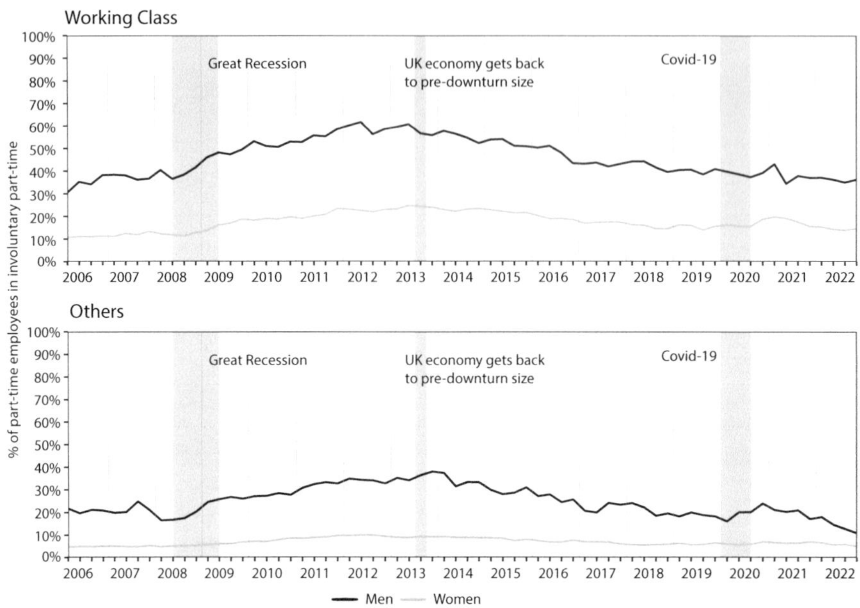

FIGURE 4.2 Trends in Involuntary Part-Time Working among Part-Time Employees, by Gender and Class (2006–2022).

Source: Own elaboration based on UK Labour Force Survey data.

class-based earnings disparities persisted amid turbulence when employers cut bonuses, enacted wage freezes and negotiated wage reductions (Fabiani et al., 2015). We calculate the pound difference from the overall median gross hourly pay: scores below zero indicate which workers were earning below median hourly earnings each year (and how far below average), scores above show who was paid above the average.

Figure 4.3 shows that overall gender wage gaps within social classes were relatively stable over the three periods of turbulence. Male employees in higher occupational classes continued to earn far more per hour than the median, with middle-class women (at some distance) behind (Figure 4.3 bottom panel). In marked contrast, working-class employees, women and men both, earned far below the median hourly pay, each year, and their relative earnings declined progressively over time, despite women's pay being much lower to start with. Moreover, for both sexes, the pandemic and cost-of-living crisis exacerbated this downward trend for working-class workers. Bringing together gender and class also shows clearly just how poorly working-class women were faring. They had by far the lowest hourly earnings of all workers each year, and, like working-class men, their relative positions weakened over time and particularly in the aftermath of the pandemic.

Hourly wage gaps persisted amid turbulence and even widened into 2022 when lower-paid workers were facing the steepest cost-of-living pressures. A

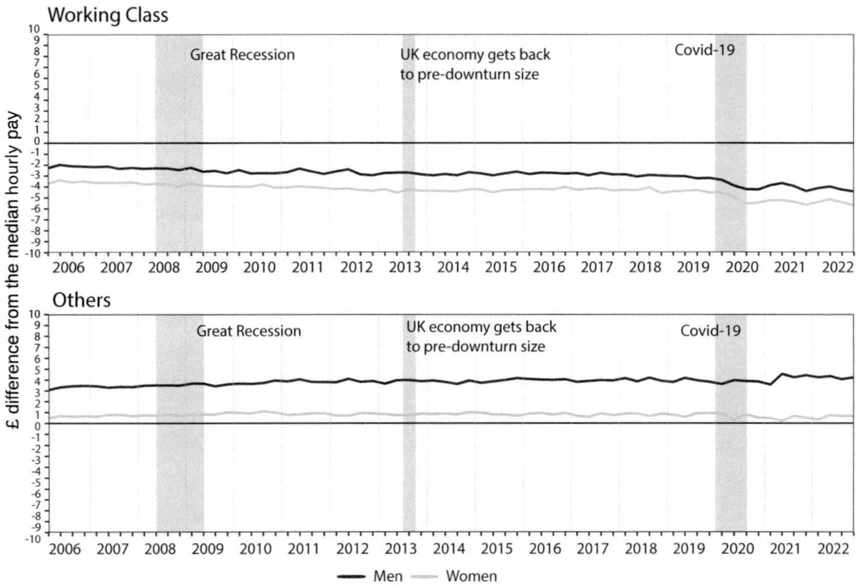

FIGURE 4.3 Differences from the Overall Median Hourly Pay Each Quarter (£), by Gender and Class (2006–2022).

Source: Own elaboration based on UK Labour Force Survey data.

progressive deterioration in the relative wages of working-class employees, given the floor established by the NMW, points to wage increases among the middle classes widening the wage gap and leaving working-class employees even further behind, despite the positive outcomes of the NMW (Living Wage Foundation, 2024). Furthermore, while a minimum hourly wage is an invaluable support for the lowest-paid employees, workers also need to work enough hours to bring home an adequate weekly wage. ONS data show that average weekly earnings in the UK also fell over the post-recessionary period (after adjusting for inflation [House of Commons, 2024]). The Trades Union Congress (Chung et al., 2024) argues that the mantra that having a job is the best route out of poverty has grown increasingly untrue in the UK. Gendered and classed inequalities in hourly wages and worktime result in day-to-day hardship plus an inability to save and plan securely for the future.

Job precariousness in turbulent times

In this final section, we examine the chances of being employed in the most precarious forms of work across the decades of perma-turmoil. Precarious work can grow more prevalent during turbulent times, bringing unequal risks of deeper social and/or economic vulnerability (Rubery et al., 2018; Wilson & Ebert, 2013).

We explore two types of work arrangements: involuntary temporary jobs and zero-hours contracts. Both increase the risks of precariousness and neither arrangement allows workers to plan in the long-term (Florisson, 2024). A temporary contract is one that has a specific end date, where the worker is only employed for a certain period of time, for example, fixed-term contracts, agency work and casual and seasonal work. We identify which of these temporary workers said that they could not find a permanent job. Zero-hours contracts are the most casual of contracts, highly contentious because a worker has no guarantee of any work at all: they are only paid for the number of hours that they work. Zero-hours contracts have been increasing in prevalence in the UK, especially in non-unionised work in, for example, care, hospitality and warehouses. Employers use these contracts to gain organisational flexibility and often report that their workers also value them for flexible reasons, but there has been much criticism of their widespread use and the insecurity they create (Chartered Institute of Personnel and Development, 2023; Martin et al., 2024; Slaughter, 2024).

Figure 4.4A shows levels of involuntary temporary employment over time, comparing women with men within both the working-class and the non-working-class

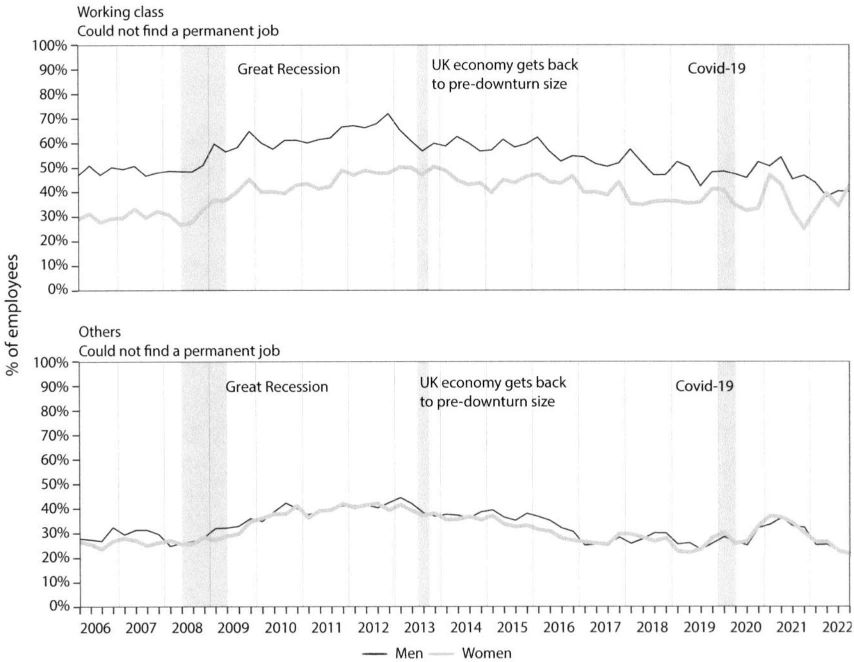

FIGURE 4.4A Trends in Involuntary Temporary Jobs among Employees, by Gender and Class (2006–2022).

Source: Own elaboration based on UK Labour Force Survey data.

employed groups. This illustrates how involuntary temporary work increased after the recession for all groups but more so for working-class women and men, then began to fall from 2013 as the economy started to recover. This downward trend was disrupted by Covid-19, and involuntary temporary work again rose in 2020 and into 2021, for both women and men. Working-class men stood out as the most likely to be involuntary temporary employees, followed closely by working-class women. Over the 2021–2022 period, levels began to diverge for women and men in this occupational group, with involuntary temporary work decreasing for men, but working-class women seeing subsequent jumps. This increase was driven by greater numbers of working-class women on fixed-term contracts and in casual work, reflecting the residual unequal effect of the pandemic on a challenging and uncertain economic landscape, fuelled by the cost-of-living crisis, with employers pursuing a flexible workforce and the most disadvantaged of workers having to accept the most insecure jobs to make ends meet (Florisson, 2024).

Figure 4.4B then shows just how dramatically zero-hours contracts escalated in the post-recessionary UK. While part of this increase is due to pre-pandemic

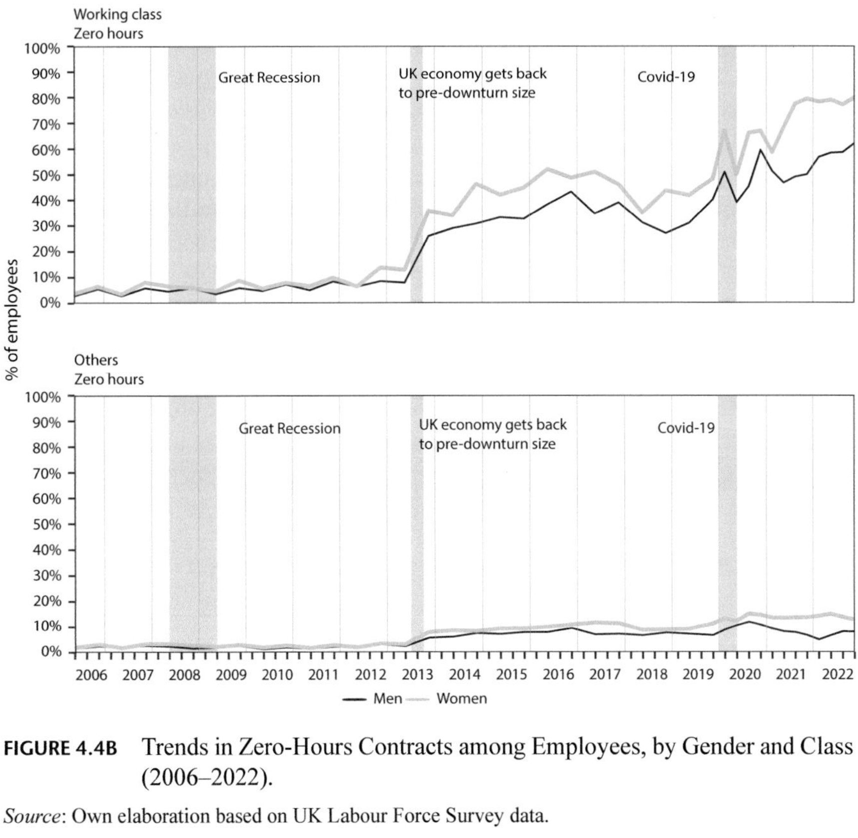

FIGURE 4.4B Trends in Zero-Hours Contracts among Employees, by Gender and Class (2006–2022).

Source: Own elaboration based on UK Labour Force Survey data.

changes in the way that zero hours were measured in the LFS, our findings still illustrate that the percentage of employees with zero-hours contracts increased after the pandemic hit and the cost-of-living crisis began, leading to greater numbers facing limited hours and risks of low pay and uncertainty. Zero-hours contracts are a strongly classed phenomenon, as they virtually only affect working-class groups. Yet, not only did the classed gap widen as zero-hours contracts multiplied, so too did the gender gap, with working-class female employees most affected (our analysis of the LFS showed that approximately 216,400 working-class women were on zero-hours contracts at the close of 2022 compared with 195,700 of their male peers).

Conclusions

Turbulent times provide unique insights into the structure and experience of work and employment, including the extent and nature of inequalities. They raise fundamental questions that we address in this chapter about the potential deepening of gendered inequalities in working lives and livelihoods amid turbulence, and classed ramifications. We focus on turmoil resulting from the financial crisis and austerity, the Covid-19 pandemic and the cost-of-living crisis.

The first period of turmoil was initially heralded as a larger threat to male than female workers, to the middle-class more than the working-class. Yet, despite early predictions of a man- or he-cession, and of the first middle-class recession to hit the UK, the financial crisis was in reality not kind to women workers, and with working-class women the least protected from its damaging effects (Bradley, 2020). Unequal gendered and classed outcomes resulted from the pandemic and cost-of-living crises too, and so, while working lives and livelihoods weakened for many across the full crisis period, workers who were already faring poorly retained their disadvantage or saw it intensify and then recovered more slowly when crises eased. In each crisis, studies show working-class women workers shouldering a very heavy burden of turmoil, experiencing double disadvantage as both gender and class inequalities deepened in work. In every instance, women were disproportionately impacted by growing job insecurity while having to manage homes on tighter incomes and amid heightened pressures as state-funded services were cut (Durbin et al., 2017; Rake, 2009; Rubery, 2015). Moreover, recurring crises have served to wear away the scant resources of the most precarious in society, intensifying the risks to their livelihoods (Edmiston et al., 2025). Turbulence has not been kind to women workers in many ways, as this edited collection demonstrates, but the intersectional gender and class approach adopted in our chapter shows who had the unkindest experiences.

We examined working hours, earnings and precarious employment. During each period of turmoil, workers faced potentially unwelcome changes to the number of hours that they worked: hours might have been cut for some leading to increased worktime underemployment while other workers may have experienced worktime extensification, working extra hours to earn more in hard times and in more pressurised organisational contexts (Beck et al., 2024; Gregg & Wadsworth 2010; Rubery & Távora, 2021; Warren, 2015). Each period of turmoil also raised concerns about possibly deepening inequalities in earnings as labour markets grew tighter, wages were frozen or reduced and bonuses and overtime cut back; although the NMW may have counterbalanced some of these negative effects. Finally, the risk of precarious work can grow across turbulent years. When employers and employees find themselves operating in a more uncertain context, new hiring can take place on the basis of atypical work that offers weak conditions, bringing short- and longer-term instability, insecurity and social and/or economic vulnerability (Rubery et al., 2018; Wilson & Ebert, 2013).

Our analysis of gender, class and working hours, earnings and precarious employment, using data from the UK's LFS, shows that working-class women remained the group of workers with the shortest working weeks across all the turbulent years, their already very low hourly wages deteriorated further (relative to other workers), and the women faced intensifying risks of precarious work. During "normal" times, working a short week in a low-waged and precarious job brings the risk of financial hardship and, if this work pattern is sustained, serious lasting consequences. Turmoil cemented these pre-existing inequalities, but its negative effects also impacted highly unevenly on daily working lives and brought unequal threats to workers' current and future livelihoods, with heightening risks for working-class women.

The chapter makes the case that purely gendered analyses of paid work are inadequate because they disregard the key role that class plays, including amid hard times. Class continues to strongly shape workers' achievements and opportunities in normal times, but its importance grows more critical during turbulence as workplaces and livelihoods are under greater and unequal pressures. Solely gendered analyses, in conflating their experiences with those of class-privileged women, overlook the deeper challenges that working-class women face in terms of their lowering relative earnings and rising job precariousness amid persistent shorter hours. Similarly, comparing women only with men also obscures how middle-class women's paid work patterns, with more full-time employment over their careers than working-class women, are contingent upon the jobs undertaken disproportionately by working-class women who provide, for example, caring and cleaning for middle-class families. Crucially too, adding in class also reveals disparities in various aspects of men's paid work. Working-class men experienced weaker and weakening earnings and job security than middle-class men. Often the principal breadwinner in their homes, working-class men can carry a heavy burden of provisioning, amplified in times of hardship and resulting in elevated worktime underemployment, as we show, that is known to negatively impact the well-being of male workers and their families (Kamerāde & Richardson, 2018).

These findings are based on analysis of employees working within the UK, but with ramifications beyond. We show how, within a society characterised by overarching gender norms around working and caring, and with very unequal experiences for women and men, there are nevertheless distinct variations by class, raising questions about working lives and gender, class and their intersections in other societal contexts. Recognising class alongside gender inequalities also raises questions around the most effective ways to advance women's work, including whether gender-targeted or generalist measures produce the best outcomes for (all groups of) women. There is certainly support for a generalist strategy that focuses on improving labour standards and regulation, such as the establishment of a NMW, to help narrow wage differentials by providing uplifts to the typically lower earnings of women workers, particularly those in working-class jobs, while also benefitting low-waged working-class men (Rubery, 1992). Minimum wage rates must be set carefully and updated regularly, and work in tandem with sufficient or "living" hours (Living Wage Foundation, 2024), else hourly and weekly earnings disparities can widen further, especially amid turbulence, and gender and class inequalities in livelihoods deepen.

Our analysis of paid work, gender and class across years of turmoil opens many possibilities for further research within and beyond the UK. In our attention to paid workers, we did not explore those who lost jobs or were looking for employment amid intense economic pressures. Nor have we had space to examine other critical differences among workers, including resulting from their specific occupational locations or due to such intersecting social divisions as ethnic group, race, migrant status, age, disability and more (see Steinmetz & Guarnerio, 2026, this volume, for intersections between gender and migration).

Times of turbulence can lead us to reflect whether we can or even should return to "business as usual". What lessons can be learned, and might those lessons help to create an economy in which all can flourish? We can see that economic recovery does not mean that the quality of work also improves. It is in the interests of society that we strengthen our economic, labour market and welfare systems to enable a sharing of risks and benefits among all people.

References

Adams-Prassl, A., Boneva, T., Golin, M., & Rauh, C. (2020). Inequality in the impact of the coronavirus shock. *Journal of Public Economics*, *189*, 1–33. https://doi.org/10.1016/j.jpubeco.2020.104245

Andrew, A., Bandiera, O., Costa Dias, M., & Landais, C. (2024). Women and men at work. *Oxford Open Economics*, *3*(1), i294–i322. https://doi.org/10.1093/ooec/odad034

Beck, V., Fuertes, V., Kamerāde, D., Lyonette, C., & Warren, T. (2020). Work and life after Covid. In M. Parker (Ed.), *Life after Covid: Essays towards a better future* (pp. 53–62). Bristol University Press.

Beck, V., Warren, T., & Lyonette, C. (2024). Is any job better than no job? Utilising Jahoda's latent deprivation theory to reconceptualise underemployment. *Work, Employment and Society, 39*(2), 404–425. https://doi.org/10.1177/09500170241254794

Bell, D., & Blanchflower, D. (2013). Underemployment in the UK revisited. *National Institute Economic Review, 224*(1), F8–F22. https://doi.org/10.1177/002795011322400110

Bourquin, P., Brewer, M., & Wernham, T. (2024). Trends in income and wealth inequalities. *Oxford Open Economics, 3*(1), i103–i146. https://doi.org/10.1093/ooec/odad100

Bradley, H. (2020). Crisis at work: Gender, class, and the dehumanization of jobs. *Historical Studies in Industrial Relations, 41*(1), 109–135. https://doi.org/10.3828/hsir.2020.41.5

Brewer, M., Muriel, A., Phillips, D., & Sibieta, L. (2009). *Poverty and inequality in the UK: 2009*. Institute for Fiscal Studies. https://ifs.org.uk/sites/default/files/output_url_files/c109.pdf

Brewer, M., & Patrick, R. (2021). *Pandemic pressures: Why families on a low income are spending more during Covid-19*. Resolution Foundation. https://www.resolutionfoundation.org/app/uploads/2021/01/Pandemic-pressures.pdf

Brown, R., Wilson, C., & Begum, Y. (2023). *The social impact of the cost-of-living crisis*. NatCen. https://natcen.ac.uk/sites/default/files/2023-07/Society%20Watch%202023_The%20Price%20We%20Pay_the%20social%20impact%20of%20the%20cost%20of%20living%20crisis.pdf

Chanfreau, J. (2023). The persistence in gendering: Work-family policy in Britain since Beveridge. *Journal of Social Policy, 52*(4), 981–998. https://doi.org/10.1017/S0047279422000125

Chartered Institute of Personnel and Development. (2023). *Zero hours contracts.* . https://www.cipd.org/uk/knowledge/factsheets/zero-hours-reality-report/

Chung, H., Birkett, H., Forbes, S., & Seo, H. (2021). Covid-19, flexible working, and implications for gender equality in the United Kingdom. *Gender & Society, 35*(2), 218–232. https://doi.org/10.1177/08912432211001304

Chung, H., Yuan, S., & Arkwright, A. (2024). *Making hybrid work inclusive*. Trades Union Congress. https://www.tuc.org.uk/sites/default/files/2024-02/inclusivehybridworking.pdf

Connor, J., Madhavan, S., Mokashi, M., Amanuel, H., Johnson, N. R., Pace, L. E., & Bartz, D. (2020). Health risks and outcomes that disproportionately affect women during the Covid-19 pandemic: A review. *Social Science & Medicine, 266*, 113364. https://doi.org/10.1016/j.socscimed.2020.113364

Crompton, R. (2010). Class and employment. *Work, Employment and Society, 4*(1), 9–26. https://doi.org/10.1177/0950017009353667

Department for Business and Trade, The Rt Hon Jonathan Reynolds MP & The Rt Hon Angela Rayner MP. (2025, March 4). *Employment Rights Bill to boost productivity for British workers and grow the economy*. Gov UK. https://www.gov.uk/government/news/employment-rights-bill-to-boost-productivity-for-british-workers-and-grow-the-economy

Dorling, D. (2015). *Injustice. Why social inequality still persists*. Policy Press.

Dorling, D. (2023). From the pandemic to the cost-of-living crisis. In K. Arabadjieva, N. Countouris, B. L. Fabris, & W. Zwysen (Eds.), *Transformative ideas: Ensuring a just share of progress for all* (pp. 21–37). ETUI. https://www.etui.org/sites/default/files/2023

-05/Transformative%20ideas-ensuring%20a%20just%20share%20of%20progress%20for%20all_2023.pdf

Durbin, S., Page, M., & Walby, S. (2017). Gender equality and "austerity": Vulnerabilities, resistance and change. *Gender, Work & Organization*, *24*(1), 1–6. https://doi.org/10.1111/gwao.12173

Edmiston, D. (2025). Indentured: Benefit deductions, debt recovery and welfare disciplining. *Social Policy & Administration*, *59*(2), 360–375. https://doi.org/10.1111/spol.13021

Edmiston, D., Hyde, E., & Adnan-Smith, T. (2025). Submerged: Surfacing deep poverty during permacrisis. *Sociology*, *59*(4), 782–800. https://doi.org/10.1177/00380385251320564

Elson, D. (2013). Economic crises from the 1980s to the 2010s: A gender analysis. In S. Rai & G. Waylen (Eds.), *New frontiers in feminist political economy* (pp. 189–212). Routledge. https://doi.org/10.4324/9781315884745

Fabiani, S., Lamo, A., Messina, J., & Rõõm, T. (2015). European firm adjustment during times of economic crisis. *IZA Journal of Labor Policy*, *4*, 24. https://doi.org/10.1186/s40173-015-0048-3

Farris, S. R., & Bergfeld, M. (2022). Low-skill no more! Essential workers, social reproduction and the legitimacy-crisis of the division of labour. *Distinktion: Journal of Social Theory*, *23*(2–3), 342–358. https://doi.org/10.1080/1600910X.2022.2077400

Felstead, A. (2022). *Remote working*. Routledge. https://doi.org/10.4324/9781003247050

Florisson, R. (2024). *The UK insecure work index 2024*. The Work Foundation. https://www.lancaster.ac.uk/work-foundation/publications/the-uk-insecure-work-index-2024

Francis-Devine, B. (2024). *The gender pay gap. House of Commons Library*. https://researchbriefings.files.parliament.uk/documents/SN07068/SN07068.pdf

Garthwaite, K. (2016). *Hunger pains: Life inside foodbank Britain*. Policy Press.

Gregg, P., & Wadsworth, J. (2010). Employment in the 2008–2009 recession. *Economic and Labour Market Review*, *4*(8), 37–43. https://doi.org/10.1057/elmr.2010.111

Hall, S. M. (2019). A very personal crisis: Family fragilities and everyday conjunctures within lived experiences of austerity. *Transactions of the Institute of British Geographers*, *44*, 479–492. https://doi.org/10.1111/tran.12300

Hick, R., & Collins, M. L. (2024). The cost-of-living crisis in the UK and Ireland. *Social Policy and Society*, *23*(1), 189–203. https://doi.org/10.1017/S1474746423000453

HM Revenue & Customs. (2020, April 20). *Claim for wages through the Coronavirus Job Retention Scheme*. GOV.UK. https://www.gov.uk/guidance/claim-for-wages-through-the-coronavirus-job-retention-scheme

Hoff, I., & Happer, C. (2025). Mediating the cost-of-living crisis. *Critical Sociology*. Advance online publication. https://doi.org/10.1177/08969205241311560

House of Commons Library. (2024). *Average earnings by age and region*. https://commonslibrary.parliament.uk/research-briefings/cbp-8456/

International Labour Organization. (2023). *The value of essential work*. Author. https://www.ilo.org/sites/default/files/wcmsp5/groups/public/@dgreports/@dcomm/@publ/documents/publication/wcms_871017.pdf

Joseph Rowntree Foundation. (2024). *The JRF's pre-election cost of living tracker*. JRF. https://www.jrf.org.uk/cost-of-living/jrfs-pre-election-cost-of-living-tracker

Kamerāde, D., & Richardson, H. (2018). Gender segregation, underemployment and subjective well-being in the UK labour market. *Human Relations*, *71*(2), 285–309. https://doi.org/10.1177/0018726717713829

Kim, J. H., Kuk, J., & Kweon, Y. (2024). Did low-income essential workers during COVID-19 increase public support for redistribution? *Policy & Politics*, *52*(3), 430–452. https://doi.org/10.1332/03055736Y2023D000000008

Kish-Gephart, J. J., Moergen, K. J. N., Tilton, J. D., & Gray, B. (2023). Social class and work. *Journal of Management*, *49*(1), 509–565. https://doi.org/10.1177/01492063221076822

Lewis, J. (2001). The decline of the male breadwinner model. *Social Politics*, *8*(2), 152–170. https://doi.org/10.1093/sp/8.2.152

Living Wage Foundation. (2024). *What is the real living wage?* https://www.livingwage.org.uk/what-real-living-wage

Martin, A., Williams, G. D., Atay, A., & Florisson, R. (2024). *Zero choices: Swapping zero-hour contracts for secure, flexible working.* The Work Foundation. https://www.lancaster.ac.uk/media/lancaster-university/content-assets/documents/lums/work-foundation/reports/ZeroChoices.pdf

McBride, A., Hebson, G., & Holgate, J. (2015). Intersectionality: Are we taking enough notice in the field of work and employment relations? *Work, Employment & Society*, *29*(2), 331–341. https://doi.org/10.1177/0950017014538337

Milkman, R., Elliott-Negri, L., Griesbach, K., & Reich, A. (2021). Gender, class, and the gig economy. *Critical Sociology*, *47*(3), 357–372. https://doi.org/10.1177/0896920520949631

Office for National Statistics. (2022a). *SOC2010 volume 3: The National Statistics Socio-economic Classification (NS-SEC rebased on SOC2010).* Author. https://www.ons.gov.uk/methodology/classificationsandstandards/otherclassifications/thenationalstatisticssocioeconomicclassificationnssecrebasedonsoc2010

Office for National Statistics. (2022b). *Alternative measures of underutilisation in the UK labour market.* Author https://www.ons.gov.uk/employmentandlabourmarket/peoplenotinwork/unemployment/articles/alternativemeasuresofunderutilisationintheuklabourmarket/2022-09-05

Office for National Statistics. (2024). Labour Force Survey. [data series]. 11th Release. UK Data Service. SN: 200002. https://doi.org/10.5255/UKDA-Series-2000026

Okeke, A., Alexiou, C., & Nellis, J. (2021). Austerity effects on national output and income inequality. *Review of Economics*, *72*(2), 97–148. https://doi.org/10.1515/roe-2021-0012

Organisation for Economic Co-operation and Development. (2022). *Net childcare costs.* https://www.oecd.org/en/data/indicators/net-childcare-costs.html

Pinto, I. & Reis, S. (2024). *An intersectional analysis of women's living standards since 2010.* Women's Budget Group. https://www.wbg.org.uk/publication/where-do-we-go-from-here-an-intersectional-analysis-of-womens-living-standards-since-2010/

Rake, K. (2009). *Are women bearing the burden of the recession?* Fawcett Society.

Razzu, G., & Singleton, C. (2018). Segregation and gender gaps in the United Kingdom's great recession and recovery. *Feminist Economics, 24*(4), 31–55. https://doi.org/10.1080/13545701.2018.1451907

Richardson, J., & Witteveen, A. (2024). *Employee jobs paid below the living wage 2023.* Living Wage Foundation. https://www.livingwage.org.uk/sites/default/files/2025-02/Employee%20Jobs%20Paid%20Below%20the%20Real%20Living%20Wage%202024%20-%20Living%20Wage%20Foundation%20Research%202025.pdf

Rubery, J. (1988). Women and recession: A comparative perspective. In J. Rubery (Ed.), *Women and recession* (pp. 253–286). Routledge and Kegan Paul.

Rubery, J. (1992). Pay, gender and the social dimension to Europe. *British Journal of Industrial Relations*, *30*, 605–621. https://doi.org/10.1111/j.1467-8543.1992.tb00794.x

Rubery, J. (2015). Austerity and the future for gender equality in Europe. *ILR Review, 68*(4), 715–741. https://doi.org/10.1177/0019793915588892

Rubery, J., Bi-Swinglehurst, I., & Rafferty, A. (2024). *Part-time work and productivity.* The Productivity Institute. https://www.productivity.ac.uk/research/part-time-work-and-productivity/

Rubery, J., Grimshaw, D., Keizer, A., & Johnson, M. (2018). Challenges and contradictions in the "normalising" of precarious work. *Work, Employment and Society, 32*(3), 509–527. https://doi.org/10.1177/0950017017751790

Rubery, J., & Rafferty, A. (2013). Women and recession revisited. *Work, Employment & Society, 27*(3), 414–432. https://doi.org/10.1177/0950017012460314

Rubery, J., & Távora, I. (2021). The Covid-19 crisis and gender equality: Risks and opportunities. In B. Vanhercke, S. Spasova, & B. Fronteddu (Eds.), *Social policy in the European Union* (pp. 71–96). ETUI. https://www.etui.org/sites/default/files/2021-01/06-Chapter4-The%20Covid%E2%80%9119%20crisis%20and%20gender%20equality.pdf

Rubery, J., Távora, I., Herman, E., Winton, A., & Castillo Larrain, A. (2024). Women workers on the frontline and the coronavirus pandemic. In M. Rönnmar & S. Hayter (Eds.), *Making and breaking gender inequalities in work* (pp. 54–74). Edward Elgar and ILO.

Shildrick, T., MacDonald, R., Webster, C., & Garthwaite, K. (2012). *Poverty and insecurity: Life in low-pay, no-pay Britain.* Policy Press.

Slaughter, H. (2024). *Firm foundations: Understanding why employers use flexible contracts.* Resolution Foundation. https://www.resolutionfoundation.org/app/uploads/2024/04/Firm-foundations.pdf

Steinmetz, S., & Guarnerio, M. (2026). Intersecting inequalities. The role of gender and migration background in women's labour market vulnerability during crises. In J. Rubery, N. Sánchez-Mira, & V. Insarauto (Eds.), *Women in turbulent times. Crises, transitions, and challenges for gender equality* (pp. 29–51). Routledge.

Warren, T. (2015). Work-time underemployment and financial hardship: Class inequalities and recession in the UK. *Work, Employment and Society, 29*(2), 191–212. https://doi.org/10.1177/0950017014559264

Warren, T., & Lyonette, C. (2018). Good, bad and very bad part-time jobs for women? Re-examining the importance of occupational class for job quality since the 'great recession' in Britain. *Work, Employment and Society, 32*(4), 747–767. https://doi.org/10.1177/0950017018762289

Warren, T., Lyonette, C., & The UK Women's Budget Group. (2021). *Carrying the work burden of the Covid-19 pandemic: Working class women in the UK.* Nottingham University Business School. https://www.nottingham.ac.uk/business/documents/research/carrying-the-work-burden-of-covid-19/final-report-working-class-women-and-covid.pdf

Wielgoszewska, B. (2024). *The gender furlough gap.* LSE. https://blog.ukdataservice.ac.uk/the-gender-furlough-gap/

Wilson, S., & Ebert, N. (2013). Precarious work: Economic, sociological and political perspectives. *The Economic and Labour Relations Review, 24*(3), 263–278. https://doi.org/10.1177/1035304613500434

Witteveen, D. (2020). Sociodemographic inequality in exposure to COVID-19-induced economic hardship in the United Kingdom. *Research in Social Stratification and Mobility, 69*, 100551. https://doi.org/10.1016/j.rssm.2020.100551

Wood, M., & Bennett, F. (2022). Parenting in the pandemic: Exploring the experiences of families with children on Universal Credit. *Families, Relationships and Societies*, *12*(2), 163–179. https://doi.org/10.1332/204674321X16528527479429

Wright, S. (2023). *Women and welfare conditionality*. Policy Press.

Zhang, M. M., Peppas, S., Peppas, S., & Tyler, T. Y. (2015). The great recession: A statistical analysis of its effects on unemployment. *International Journal of Business and Economics Perspectives*, *10*(1), 44–55. https://link.gale.com/apps/doc/A430547672/AONE?u=anon~259a6f50&sid=googleScholar&xid=1bbde689

5

GENDER PAY INEQUALITY AND WAGE SETTING INSTITUTIONS THROUGH CRISES AND RECOVERIES

A Southern European success story?

Hugo Figueiredo and Martí López-Andreu

Introduction

Gender Pay Gaps (GPGs) have significantly decreased in Portugal and Spain throughout the last two cycles of crisis and recovery, that is from the financial crisis and the ensuing austerity years through the following recovery period and its interruption by the Covid-19 pandemic. This chapter questions this apparent success story. It does so by documenting how changes in full-time equivalent real earnings for men and women across the job spectrum since 2010 have interacted with two fundamental drivers of earnings, namely first the wider structural transformations in the composition of both jobs and the labour supply including the increased educational attainment of workers and the fast tertiarisation of economic activity. These long-term trends are analysed alongside the direct effects of the crises in reinforcing or delaying the trends, paying attention to differences both between and within genders, particularly by educational level. Second, we consider how wage setting institutions evolved over this period, focusing first on the period of 2010–2014 when austerity conditions shaped both changes to collective bargaining and to wage setting for the public sector. We then explore the subsequent reactions to this period, particularly after the rise to power of left-of-centre governments in both countries that led to political decisions to increase real minimum wages and to restore social dialogue, albeit in Spain under the continuing influence of pressures towards wage moderation. The focus here is both on the similarities and differences across the two countries and on the gender-specific effects of these changes. In doing so, the chapter sheds light on how crisis-driven transformations in labour market structures and wage setting institutions may intersect with evolving gender dynamics, offering insight into the national pathways through which structural inequalities are reproduced or recalibrated.

DOI: 10.4324/9781003528210-7

The chapter is organised as follows. The next section provides a brief overview of the employment and earnings data used as well as the general methodological approach to the calculation of gender pay gaps and associated earnings trends. We then present the significant reduction between 2010 and 2022 in average gender pay gaps, followed by analyses that indicate the apparent success story may have been driven by the restructuring of both the job landscape and the structure of the labour supply. In the subsequent section, we describe how real earnings levels developed across sectors and occupations through these two cycles of crisis and recovery. The next section considers how these patterns have also been, in part, shaped by the transformation of wage setting institutions during the austerity years and the subsequent recovery and pandemic periods. We focus on three dimensions: the loss of bargaining power among men; the role of minimum wages in contributing to greater pay equality and its further reach in Portugal; and the resilience and recovery of public-sector employment and pay post-austerity. The final section summarises our main arguments, showing how this chapter contributes to the book's broader aim of understanding the ways in which crises reshape gendered inequalities, not only through changes in employment and pay structures, but also through the institutional reconfiguration of wage setting and labour market governance in Southern Europe.

Data and methods

This chapter uses two main sources of employment and earnings data. For Spain, we use Structure of Earnings Survey data (Encuesta Cuatrienal de Estructura Salarial – ECES [Instituto Nacional de Estadística, n.d.]). This survey is conducted every four years (with 2022 being the latest data available). It collects information on gross monthly and annual earnings provided by establishments through questionnaires and covers both private and public-sector employees whose pay conditions fall under the General Social Security Regime. For Portugal, we use mostly administrative gross monthly earnings logs (Quadros de Pessoal – QP [Gabinete de Estratégia e Planeamento, n.d.]) compiled by the Ministry of Labour and Social Security, which covers practically the universe of private-sector firms and third sector organisations with wage-earning employees, which are required by law to provide such information. Crucially, QP data excludes the Public Administration workers that are not covered by the standard labour code. The dataset includes, however, public-sector employees (at the country, regional or local levels) if their work contracts fall under such standard. The coverage of health, education and other state-run activities is, however, incomplete due to significant numbers of workers in such sectors being under the specific labour code for public servants. The two datasets are, therefore, not strictly comparable. Spanish data, while covering the whole job structure, is based on a sample survey, which can reduce precision – particularly for smaller groups – and introduce a degree of random variability across waves. The exclusion of a significant share of public administration workers in the Portuguese data limits our ability to capture the full gender impact of the crises, particularly since many relatively qualified women are concentrated in the public sector. However, we draw information on broader public sector pay trends from published reports based on administrative data from all public sector entities in Portugal.

Gender Pay Gaps are calculated as the difference between male and female earnings as a percentage of male earnings. All earnings data used here refer to full-time equivalent (FTE) monthly real earnings.[1] These are calculated by considering all gross nominal wage components (regular and irregular) reported in both surveys, deflated using Harmonised Consumer Price Index data from Eurostat (n.d.) with 2021 as the reference year and adjusted to account for differences in weekly working hours relative to the standard of 40 weekly hours.[2] Monthly wages of workers working below (above) such hours are adjusted upwards (downwards). This is an important issue to bear in mind since working time is not evenly distributed by gender as most workers with shorter weekly hours are women. Unadjusted monthly earnings pay gaps can, therefore, be larger than those reported here, as they also consider such differences in working time.[3] Our estimates reflect, in that sense, mostly real hourly pay gaps.

A success story?

Declining gender pay gaps

Figures 5.1 and 5.2 present the evolution of full-time equivalent (FTE) real monthly earnings and the corresponding gender pay gaps (GPG) since 2010 for both Portugal and Spain. Both countries saw significant decreases in average gender pay gaps since the financial crisis, albeit at different speeds. The financial crisis is known to have had a strong direct impact on employment, leading to increases in redundancies and growing unemployment, particularly as austerity policies took effect. Whereas during the first phase of the crisis, male-dominated sectors were strongly hit (mainly construction and manufacturing); in contrast, austerity policies initiated in 2010 directly impacted women-dominated sectors in the public sector and public sector dependent activities (Karamessini & Rubery, 2014). This further coincides with a period of deterioration in gender pay equality due to a decrease in female monthly wages relative to male earnings. As the data show, in Portugal, the austerity years failed to promote improvements in women's pay relative to men. In 2014, women's monthly earnings were still over 22% lower than men's, showing a slight deterioration since 2010. In Spain, FTE equivalent gender pay gaps declined as a result of faster decreases in real earnings for men.

However, significant improvements occurred in gender pay gaps in both countries in the post-intervention years. In Portugal, the reduction was close to five percentage points, with women's earnings reaching 83% of men's by 2022, while in Spain the gap closed by more than six percentage points and reached 92% of men's

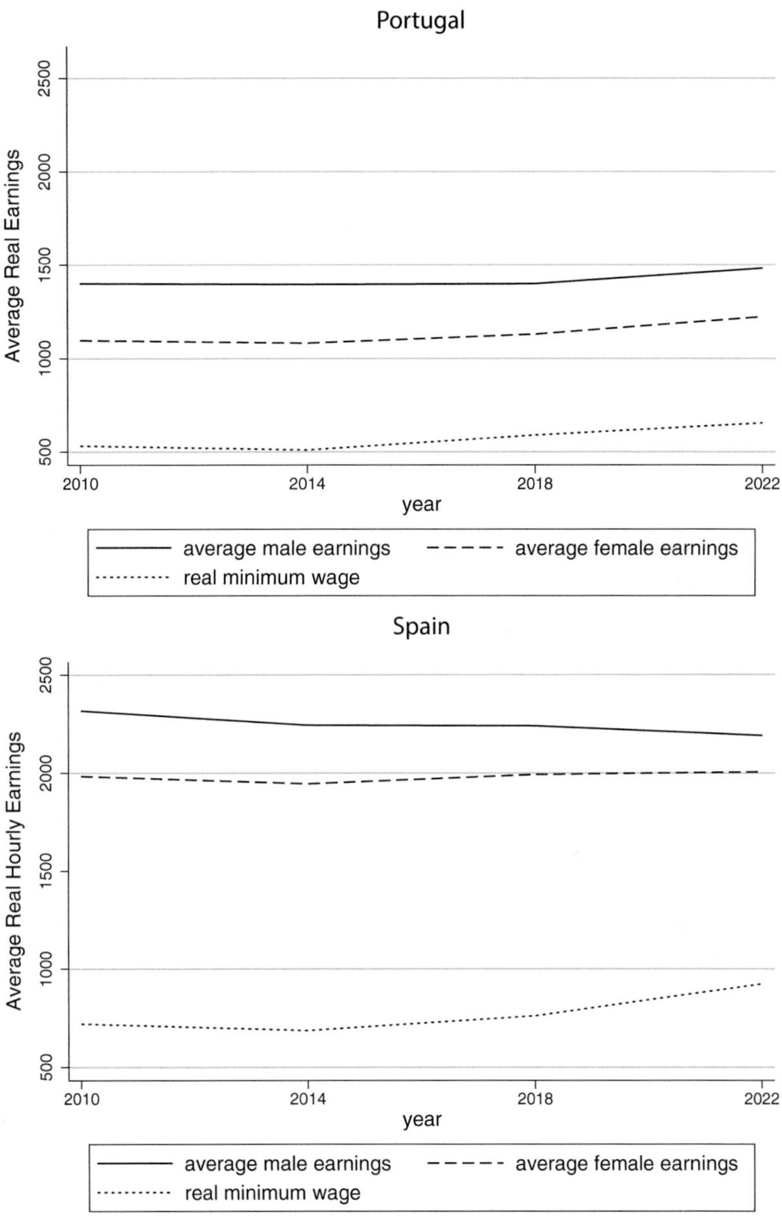

FIGURE 5.1 Real Average Gross Monthly Earnings and the Minimum Wage, 2010–2022.

Source: Own elaboration based on data from Gabinete de Estratégia e Planeamento (n.d.) and Instituto Nacional de Estadística (n.d.).

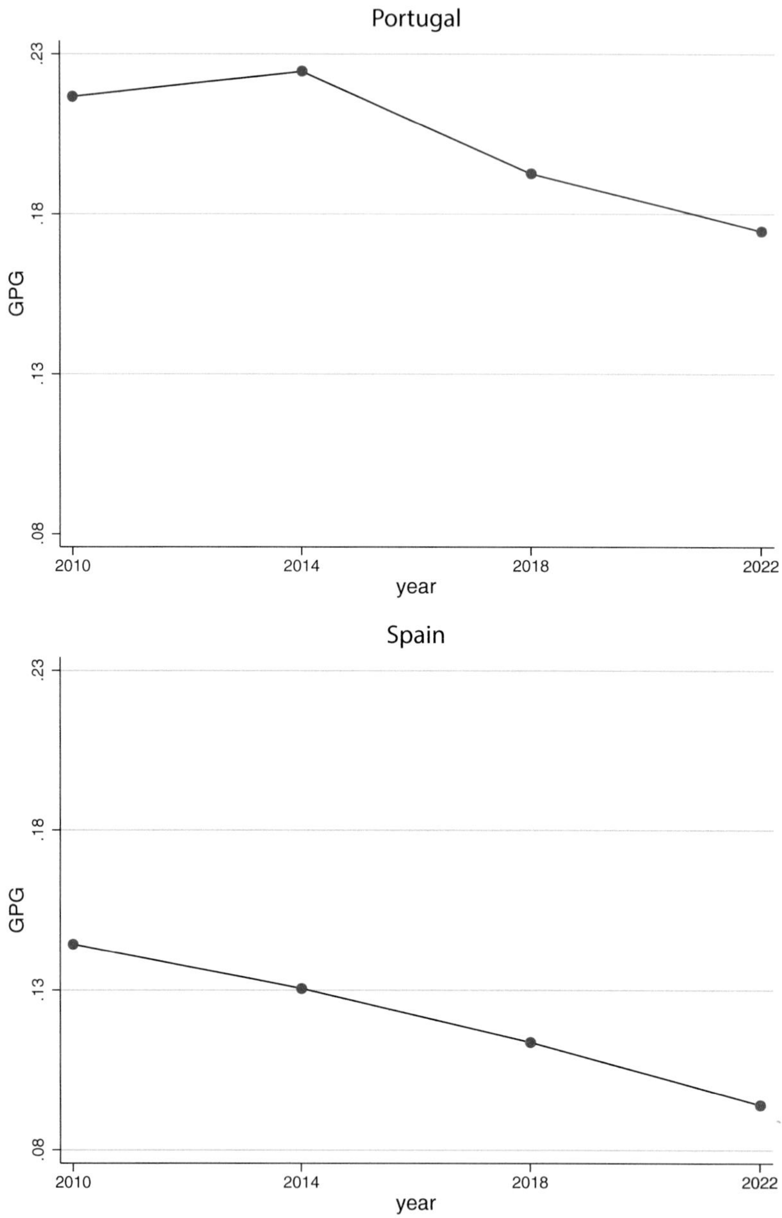

FIGURE 5.2 Gender Pay Gaps (FTE Average Monthly Gross Earnings), 2010–2022.

Source: Own elaboration based on data from Gabinete de Estratégia e Planeamento (n.d.) and Instituto Nacional de Estadística (n.d.).

earnings by 2022. However, while in Portugal both men's and women's earnings improved in real terms, in Spain, the narrowing of the gender pay gap is mostly the product of increases in real average earnings for women since 2014 alongside decreasing average monthly real earnings for men in FTE throughout the period. The acceleration of the convergence of average wages for men and women also coincided with faster increases in real minimum wages since 2019.

A counterfactual story

A significant part of the decrease in the GPG in both countries stems, however, from the significant recomposition of employment along three fundamental and interrelated dimensions: the job mix and the age and educational attainment of the labour force. To demonstrate these recomposition effects, we start by comparing actual GPGs with two counterfactual measures that, first, hold the sector and occupation composition of employment (job mix) constant over time and, second, also the age and education mix (Figure 5.3). We do so by calculating the employment shares of specific occupation*sector*education*age cells[4] and holding such shares of employment constant from 2010. The difference between these two measures highlights the relative importance of changes in the education and age mix of the workforce compared to changes in the job mix of the economy since that base period.

In both countries, the job mix adjustment considerably reduces the decline in the gender pay gap over this period but still shows a narrowing of around 2 pp in Portugal (remaining at around 20% in 2022) and 3 pp in Spain (remaining at just over 10%). However, in Spain, the overall downward trend disappears completely once both age and education and job mix composition effects are considered, with education and age effects assuming a more crucial role and resulting in GPGs close to 16% when adjusted for such composition effects. In Portugal, the decrease of the GPG that remains is just above one third of the overall trend, with a significant part associated with the interaction between the transformation of the job structure and shifts in the educational structure of the workforce. Furthermore, gender pay gaps increased significantly in both countries during the austerity years once such composition effects are considered, confirming growing gender inequality within jobs.

Changes in the composition of employment

Women are leading the qualifications race

Table 5.1 provides a description of changes in the age and the education mix of these two labour markets since 2010. Not only has education expansion happened much faster among women, but also this trend is associated with faster increases in the average worker's age among women. These tendencies are intertwined with the decision to stay longer in education and with changes in the skill composition

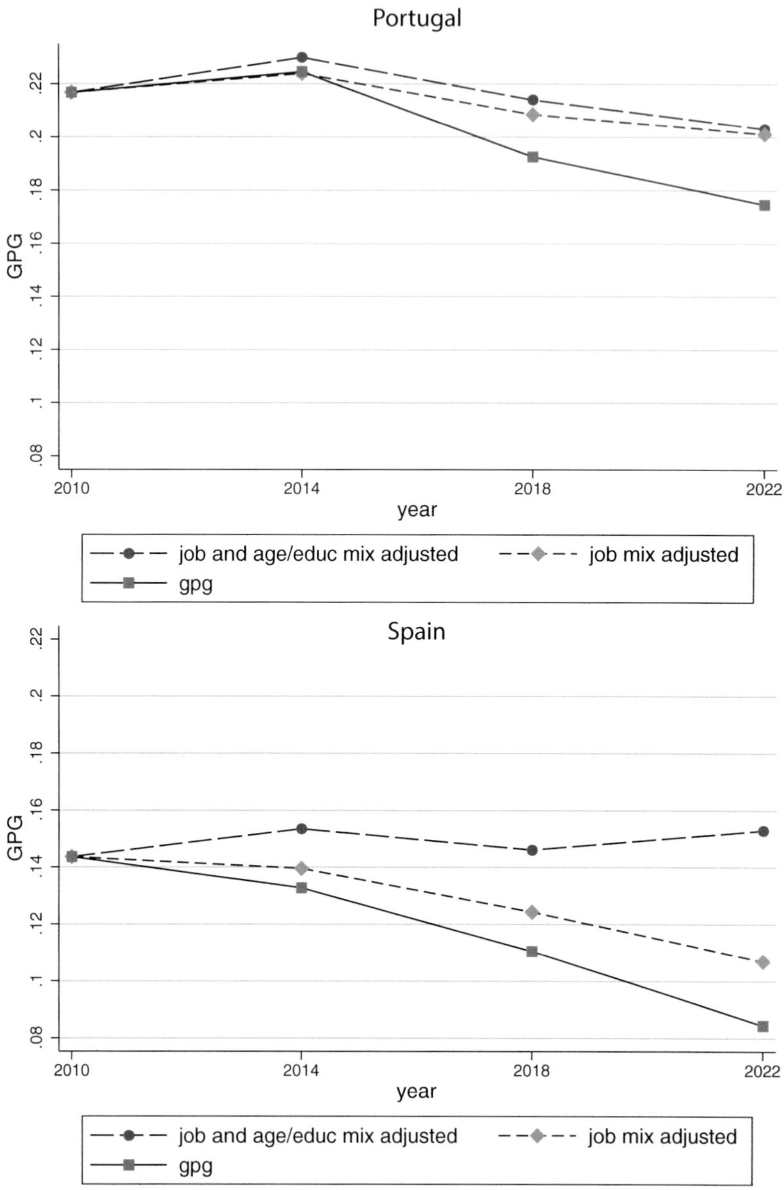

FIGURE 5.3 Composition Adjusted Gender Pay Gaps, 2010–2022.

Source: Own elaboration based on data from Gabinete de Estratégia e Planeamento (n.d.) and Instituto Nacional de Estadística (n.d.).

TABLE 5.1 Changes in the Age and Education Mix of Employment, 2010–2022

		Portugal				*Spain*			
		2010	*2014*	*2018*	*2022*	*2010*	*2014*	*2018*	*2022*
Share of university graduates in employment (%)	Women	15.9	19.5	22.2	25.5	21.7	32.4	32.6	35.5
	Men	10.7	13.4	14.8	17.0	16.4	22.8	22.2	24.3
Intergenerational change in share of uni graduates (20–39/50+)	Women	4.9	4.6	4.1	3.2	1.5	1.6	1.4	1.2
	Men	2.1	2.3	2.4	2.1	1.4	1.2	1.2	1.1
Share of workers in employment aged 30 or under	Women	27.4	22.1	22.7	22.6	18.7	12.7	11.8	11.5
	Men	25.5	21.7	23.2	23.6	16.1	11.4	11.8	12.3
Share of workers in employment aged 50 or over	Women	17.3	20.8	23.8	26.9	19.8	24.0	30.1	35.6
	Men	20.4	22.8	25.4	27.2	22.9	26.7	31.5	35.2

Source: Own elaboration based on data from Gabinete de Estratégia e Planeamento (n.d.) and Instituto Nacional de Estadística (n.d.).

of employment. The crises, particularly the financial crisis and the austerity years in Spain, were associated with significant upticks in workers' qualifications, particularly among women. Between 2010 and 2014, the share of female workers with a tertiary degree rose from around one fifth to close to one third. Because educational expansion had started much earlier in Spain, by 2022, older and younger generations already shared broadly similar educational levels. Portugal, however, was still characterised by massive intergenerational differences in the educational attainment of its workforce, particularly among women.

Two labour markets in flux

Such changes reflect not only structural trends in educational attainment but also decisions to stay in education or work. These flows into and out of employment are shaped directly by the crises and depend on the patterns of job creation and destruction. In this respect, the Portuguese and Spanish labour markets were considerably shaken first by the financial and second by the pandemic crises. Such processes of recomposition were gender- and skill-biased.

Tables 5.2 and 5.3 present data on which jobs, using a detailed classification, experienced the most significant swings in their share of total employment. A few common threads are immediately apparent in both countries. The first is the crisis in the construction sector during the austerity years and the massive job losses in the sector. Second, there were signs of deindustrialisation throughout the whole period, including through the pandemic and affecting, mostly, less technology-intensive manufacturing. Third, the technological and knowledge intensity of work grew in both countries during both crises, for example in information and communication and scientific and technical knowledge services. Fourth, there was a recovery and expansion of low-skill employment in the growth period between the two crises, particularly in hospitality. Finally, welfare-related professional jobs (education, health and social services) accounted for a growing share of employment throughout the whole period.

Such changes in the job mix had the effect of decreasing gender segregation in the two labour markets as women made inroads into higher paid jobs. The overall trends were remarkably similar in both countries. The driving force towards lower gender segregation in the labour market after the financial crisis was the fall in the share of men employed in industry and construction. This impacted mostly qualified blue collar occupations and male workers saw their concentration levels in such occupations decreasing considerably. Feminisation levels, in turn, decreased significantly in personal and low-skill service jobs (above all in retail and hospitality in Portugal) as well as to a lesser extent in feminised manufacturing jobs. Among the highly skilled, knowledge services have shown opposing entrenchment trends with increasing feminisation in sectors such as Consulting, Finance and Insurance and increasing clustering of men in ICT-related professional jobs.

TABLE 5.2 Most Representative Jobs in the Recomposition of Employment in Portugal, 2010–2022

	2010–2014	*(pp)*	*2014–2018*	*(pp)*	*2018–2022*	*(pp)*
↑	Service Clerks in Health and Social Services	+0.56	Service Clerks in Hospitality	+0.76	Professionals in Information and Communication	+0.74
↑	Professionals in Health and Social Services	+0.48	Elementary Jobs in Admin Services	+0.46	Qualified Blue Collar in Construction	+0.45
↑	Elementary Jobs in Industry	+0.39	Elementary Jobs in Hospitality	+0.46	Professionals in Scientific and Technical Consultancy	+0.40
↓	Qualified Blue Collar in Construction	−1.88	Qualified Blue Collar Workers in Industry	−0.97	Qualified Blue Collar in Industry	−1.23
↓	Elementary Jobs in Construction	−0.49	Service Clerks in Retail	−0.38	Elementary Jobs in Admin Services	−0.38
↓	Technicians in Construction	−0.31	Administrative Staff in Finance and Insurance	−0.34	Qualified Blue Collar in High Tech Industry	−0.21

Source: Own elaboration based on data from Gabinete de Estratégia e Planeamento (n.d.).

Changes in real earnings across the job structure

How did such changes in labour supply and demand influence real earnings within jobs and across the earnings distribution? Figure 5.4 first looks at the evolution of average monthly FTE real earnings for men and women across job earnings deciles. Detailed jobs (a job being defined as an occupation within a sector) are first ranked into deciles according to their average earnings levels (including male and female earnings) in the initial year (2010). The graph then shows the average earnings separately for men and women in 2010 and 2022 at each decile, keeping detailed jobs constant within deciles.

There is a significant contrast between the trends for Portugal and Spain, even if both are consistent with decreasing gender pay gaps. Thus, while real FTE monthly earnings appear to have risen considerably throughout the earnings structure in Portugal (except for jobs in the top two deciles of the earnings distribution), they have mostly decreased in Spain, again particularly so as we move to the top of the earnings distribution and mainly for men. The pattern of wage

TABLE 5.3 Most Representative Jobs in the Recomposition of Employment in Spain, 2010–2022

	2010–2014	*(pp)*	*2014–2018*	*(pp)*	*2018–2022*	*(pp)*
↑	Professionals in Education	+0.61	Elementary Jobs in Hospitality	+0.64	Professionals in Education	+0.56
↑	Professionals in Health and Social Services	+0.45	Elementary Jobs in High Tech Industry	+0.61	Technicians in Information and Communication	+0.32
↑	Professionals in Retail	+0.37	Professionals in Education	+0.60	Professionals in Information and Communication	+0.29
↓	Qualified Blue Collar in Construction	−1.76	Blue Collar in Retail	−0.52	Service Clerks in Retail	−0.75
↓	Elementary in Construction	−0.51	Technicians in Public Administration	−0.44	Qualified Blue Collar in High Tech Industry	−0.42
↓	Technicians in Construction	−0.38	Technicians in Industry	−0.44	Technicians in Retail	−0.32

Source: Own elaboration based on data from Instituto Nacional de Estadística (n.d.).

progression is considerably tilted towards higher earnings increases in lower paid jobs in Portugal, affecting both men and women but with women experiencing higher relative increases. These trends are compatible with a reduction of bargaining power particularly among men, throughout the distribution in Spain and at the top of the earnings distribution in Portugal. The hollowing-out of male employment has compounded this trend, namely in lower pay deciles. They're equally compatible with rising wage floors among the low-paid, particularly in Portugal, that conceivably benefited mostly women.

Changes in wage setting institutions

A full story of the reduction of GPGs in Portugal and Spain needs to consider the interactions between structural trends in the supply and demand of labour and changes in wage setting mechanisms, and how these have been shaped by the crises and responses to the crises. These institutional shifts are not gender-neutral: they are both shaped by and contribute to reshaping gender relations in the labour market, particularly through their effects on wage hierarchies, sectoral employment and bargaining power. We first consider what the impact of the financial crisis and subsequent austerity period was on wage setting. First, we consider the effects on collective bargaining and social dialogue, followed by consideration of changes in minimum wage setting and pay for public sector workers. Second, we

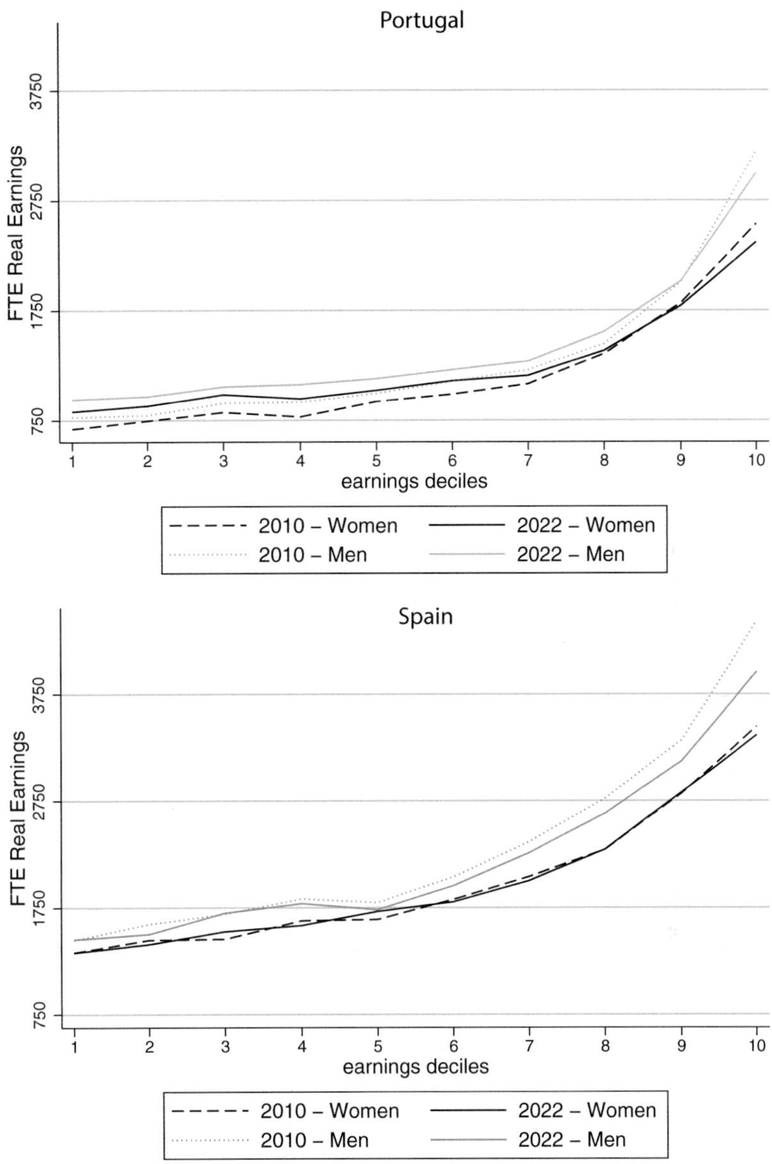

FIGURE 5.4 Change in Real FTE Earnings by Gender and Earnings Deciles, 2010–2022.

Source: Own elaboration based on data from Gabinete de Estratégia e Planeamento (n.d.) and Instituto Nacional de Estadística (n.d.).

consider the response to austerity regarding wage setting institutions, focusing particularly on the impact of the change to more left of centre governments that came earlier in Portugal than Spain (2016 versus 2019) and the influence of the Covid-19 pandemic years. In both time periods, we consider the impacts by gender and by job type.

The impact of austerity: increased pay gaps and reduced men's bargaining power

Southern European labour markets provided the centrepiece of the austerity narrative that became dominant after the 2008 financial crisis (Fernandez-Rodriguez & Martinez Lucio, 2023; López-Andreu, 2023). As a trade-off for the external support of their financial system, Portugal and Spain both had to commit to significant structural reforms and implemented austerity policies on a similar timescale, even if with different external support configurations, as only Portugal entered an official and more encompassing bail-out programme (López-Andreu, 2019a; Távora, 2019). This "austerity turn" led to several reforms in employment-related institutions that can be expected to have influenced gender pay equality along at least three dimensions: through public spending cuts which resulted in job and pay cuts in the public sector; through greater decentralisation and wage moderation in collective bargaining and its influence on men and women's bargaining power; and through reinforcing the trend towards greater labour market flexibility and its interaction with shifts in the composition of employment.

First, due to the concentration of relatively "good jobs" for women in the public sector, employment cuts in the public sector and nominal pay freezes eroded pay equality dynamics in Portugal and Spain. Welfare-related sectors experienced very significant drops in real earnings across the earnings distribution from 2010 to 2014 in both countries. However, at the top of the earnings distribution, both countries saw steep drops in average real earnings levels among male managers and professionals in welfare-related sectors, which were steeper relative to women in similar positions. Although women are overrepresented in the public sector relative to men, they are also less likely to be in the highest paid jobs so the austerity measures had mixed effects. Thus, pay cuts in the public sector in Portugal applied to higher salaries (above €1,500 in 2011) with a progressive incidence of cuts up to a maximum of 10%. In Spain, public sector wages were cut on average by 5% already in 2010 but high-ranked officials experienced much sharper cuts (between 8 and 15%) (Malo, 2015). As a result, there was a stronger contraction of real earnings among men, who were disproportionately concentrated in high paid positions.

Pay cuts and minimum wage freezes also disproportionately affected low-educated women due to stronger female concentration in such jobs (Távora & Rodríguez-Modroño, 2018). In Spain decreases in real earnings for female low-paid blue collar workers were even steeper than those experienced by male blue collar workers.

Second, the austerity years reduced the reach of collective bargaining and accelerated a trend towards its decentralisation. This potentially increases pay inequality as sector-level agreements have traditionally led towards greater pay equality, whereas organisational level negotiation has tended to increase pay inequality due to higher managerial discretion (Sánchez-Mira et al., 2020). From 2010 to 2012, Spain introduced reforms to give priority to company-level agreements over multi-employer agreements in setting working conditions (López-Andreu, 2019b). In Portugal such arrangements have existed since 2003, but progressive legislative changes, after 2009, introduced the possibility of non-union representative structures to conclude agreements at the company level and eased the requirements for non-union bodies to be granted bargaining powers (Távora & González, 2016). Companies also gained more powers to unilaterally opt out of agreements, and further reforms allowed for such agreements to expire. These reforms were accelerated when, under the Troika (the European Commission, the European Central Bank and the International Monetary Fund), Portugal was affected by drastic legislative regulation between 2011 and 2014 (Távora & González, 2016). "Opt-out" options, in particular, have been found to have led to nominal as well as real pay decreases (López-Andreu, 2019b). Legislative changes also limited automatic extensions such that, in Portugal, extensions required employers' associations to be employing at least 50% of the workers potentially covered by the agreement (Campos Lima, 2019). This change greatly reduced the reach of collective bargaining to the private sector and to more dispersed sectors (with greater presence of small and medium enterprises). Also, new limits on the impact of expired collective agreements were introduced (in Portugal, in 2009, for no more than five years and in Spain, in 2014, for up to 13 months). This gave greater bargaining power to employers and reinforced the trend towards decentralised bargaining.

The effects of such losses in the workers' bargaining power on pay equality need to be understood in tandem with the wider trends in job destruction and the recomposition of employment explored above. In this context, the bargaining power of men was further reduced by the collapse of employment in male-dominated sectors (manufacturing and construction, in particular) during this period. In this context, there were stronger pressures for prioritising job security over pay with disproportionate effects in male-dominated and relatively unionised sectors (see Las Heras et al., 2025).

Third, the reduction of bargaining power and the trend towards bargaining decentralisation were compounded by reform measures that further increased employer-driven flexibility to set working conditions in both countries. Among other aspects, such changes facilitated temporary employment and reduced the costs (severance payments) and requirements for dismissals, namely for "economic" or "objective" reasons. The reforms also led to a decrease in overtime payments, particularly in Portugal, through the creation of working time banks to accommodate working time flexibility and directly reducing overtime payments, especially affecting men. Regular working hours in the public sector were also extended from 35 to 40 hours, mainly affecting women. Such effects are only partially captured in our GPG estimates for Portugal, considering the low incidence of public administration workers, constituting one further factor decreasing real earnings. These trends therefore generalised lower bargaining power across the occupational structure, creating further pressures for reductions in FTE real earnings. Such generalised loss of bargaining power conceivably created further pressures towards the reduction of male pay in private service sectors. The already low pay of women in female-dominated sectors may have indirectly contributed to greater earnings stability among women due to a greater concentration of women in lower-paid jobs.

After austerity: the impact of political and economic change

The post-austerity years, coinciding with a slow but progressive economic recovery, witnessed the emergence of left-of-centre government coalitions in both Portugal (in 2015) and, later (2019), in Spain. This led to a progressive reversal of some of the austerity reforms and significant changes in policy regarding wage setting mechanisms. However, this did not mean an immediate and full reversal of the previous trend towards flexibility and wage moderation.

In Spain, for example, no major legislative changes took place, although several agreements establishing maximum pay increases were agreed in 2012, 2015 and 2018 by the main unions and the employers' organisations (setting the negotiations at sector and company level) linked to issues such as productivity. These resulted in modest nominal pay increases. The period is best described, therefore, as a continuation of the pattern of concession bargaining through which unions, despite intense mobilisation (including several strikes) during the austerity years, focused their resources and developed practices to maintain the space for social dialogue, especially with the employers (Rigby & García Calavia, 2017), thereby accommodating wage moderation and employers' flexibility in wage setting as central themes.

Despite the reforms, collective bargaining coverage remained relatively stable, particularly in Spain (Visser, 2016). Portugal appears to have experienced a much stronger decline in bargaining coverage, but the continued application, even after the formal expiration of agreements (Addison et al., 2017; Organisation for Economic Co-operation and Development [OECD], 2017), puts the extent of that decline in question. Moreover, after 2014, coverage in Portugal recovered considerably (International Labour Organization [ILO], 2018), albeit not to pre-crisis levels and with a weakened role for sectoral-level agreements. Another indicator of resilience within the collective bargaining and social dialogue systems has been the persistence of sectoral and multi-employer agreements and the return to social dialogue after the election of left-of-centre governments in both countries. Moreover, in neither case have enterprise-based agreements become substitutes for more centralised bargaining or the dominant form of bargaining (ILO 2018;

López-Andreu, 2023). Retention of more centralised bargaining has been aided by partial reversals of austerity policies that had restricted automatic extensions of collective agreements and set temporary limits to their aftereffects. However, the effect of CBAs on pay has likely diminished or shifted since earnings floors fixed in older agreements were in practice overtaken by increases in the national minimum wage for workers in the lowest pay deciles (ILO, 2018; Malo, 2015; Visser, 2016).

The pandemic created further opportunities to reverse the most aggressive austerity policies, to re-regulate employment and to give a new central and strategic role to social dialogue (Meardi & Tassinari, 2022). This reinvigoration of social dialogue during the Covid-19 pandemic, however, further strengthened the focus on economic recovery and job creation. This followed the trend throughout Europe to use social concertation as a strategic tool to implement policies that aimed to provide firms enough flexibility to temporarily reduce the volume of work in the face of sudden downturns in economic activity but at the same time preserve jobs. These agreements continued throughout the pandemic and influenced the 2021 Labour Reform in Spain, which included a new mechanism for economic stabilisation and the internal flexibility of firms, as an alternative to redundancies and fixed-term contracts.

However, these policies during the pandemic period also had gender impacts. Real earnings among men declined more steeply in Spain, across a wide range of jobs, but including those in better-paid blue collar jobs with relatively high rates of collective bargaining coverage. Pay appears to have been exchanged for employment security both before and during the pandemic. In Portugal, real earnings in 2022 were generally higher than in 2018, in contrast to Spain, with those in lower-paid jobs the main beneficiaries.

A further change since the austerity period was the revival of both public sector employment and the recovery of pay levels. Both developments appear to have contributed towards greater gender pay equality since the austerity, particularly if we consider both that public vs. private sector earnings premiums are generally positive for women (across all qualification levels) (Couceiro de León & Dolado, 2023) and that women are more concentrated in the public sector. The rise in public sector employment has facilitated the increase in women's representation in higher level occupations in line with their rising educational levels. However, the effect on real earnings in the public sector appears to be especially concentrated among the highly skilled in Spain but among the lower skilled in Portugal (DGAEP – SIOE, 2025). The rise in legal minimum wages will have pushed up legal wage floors in relatively low-paid public sector jobs, considering that pay scales for the least qualified are directly or indirectly linked to such minimum wage levels. It appears that, in Portugal, this latter effect has been clearly dominant. Regarding middle- and higher-level jobs, the progressive restoration of pay grades, bonus payments and career progression mechanisms over this period – that characterised both countries - also had direct positive effects on gender equality considering that such pay grades are relatively compressed (compared to private sector earnings dispersion) and are, therefore, likely to disproportionately benefit women, who are less present in the top earnings brackets. Recent evidence for Spain (Couceiro de León & Dolado, 2023) does seem to suggest that pay rises for top earning public sector workers (in the highest decile) lagged those of other public sector workers in this catch-up period.

Thus, the pandemic years saw a re-emboldening of the role of the state in employment relations that also involved a continuing shift both within social dialogue and tripartite decision-making towards a focus on economic recovery and job creation. Significant pressures for fiscal conservatism and wage moderation still held throughout the whole period, particularly in Spain through concession bargaining in agreement with social partners (Cárdenas del Rey & Arribas, 2025; López-Andreu, 2019b, 2023). Consequently, the resilience of the collective bargaining and social dialogue systems was not in fact sufficient to reverse the losses in real earnings, experienced especially by higher paid men in Spain. Recognition of the weakened power of collective bargaining to increase real earnings throughout the whole period also arguably renewed interest in minimum wages as an employment and wage regulation instrument (Afonso et al., 2023). Both countries promoted real minimum wage increases in the post-austerity years, starting with Portugal (2015) and later in 2019 in Spain, an issue we cover in greater detail in the next section.

These minimum wage policies were complemented by legislative changes in both countries that, influenced by EU directives, set a new equal pay architecture which fitted with social actors' increased concerns to promote inclusion of more precarious or vulnerable workers (mainly women and young workers) in the period after austerity (see Campos Lima et al., 2021; Cruces Aguilera & De la Fuente Sanz, 2023). For example, the Portuguese government introduced legislation that provided more inclusive criteria for the extension of collective agreement clauses (including to temporary and non-standard workers). In both countries action was also taken to require organisations with over 50 employees to assess gender pay gaps and take corrective measures, including in Spain a pay audit when gaps exceeded 25%. These measures were clearly influenced by the EU's introduction of pay transparency recommendations followed by a directive. Spain also required organisations with more than 50 employees to draw up equality plans in consultation with worker representatives and to integrate pay audit results into collective bargaining.

Changes in minimum wages and the gender pay gap

As we have already noted, the partial resilience of collective bargaining systems in the post-austerity years could not reverse the previous erosion of real wages, particularly for men in high-paid jobs. Real wages for women, on the other hand, increased (mainly above the median in Spain and below the median in Portugal).

These differences in experiences by gender reflect widespread changes in both employment composition and in wage setting institutions. However, the differences between the countries in the gender effects also reflect divergences in their pay and employment structures for both genders. This is particularly reflected in the different impacts of the policy to increase the level of the minimum wage in both countries.

Trends in real minimum wages provide a clear contrast between the austerity and post-austerity periods with considerable influence on gender pay equality, particularly in Portugal. Real minimum wages decreased in both countries from 2010 to 2014 (Figure 5.5). This follows the freezing of nominal minimum wages during this period in both countries (with the exception of a small increase in Spain in 2012). In addition, minimum wages became much closer to the average wages of low-paid sectors. However, starting in 2014 in Portugal and in 2018 in Spain, real minimum wages were increased significantly until the onset and the aftereffects of the pandemic in living costs. In Portugal, the government promoted increases in the minimum nominal monthly wage from €485 to €760 between 2015 and 2023. In Spain, as a result of the coalition agreement between the Socialist Party and left-wing coalition with Unidas Podemos first, and Sumar later, the minimum monthly wage increased substantially from €735.9 in 2019 to €1,134 in 2024. Although the government coalition agreement aimed to increase it to €1,200 euros

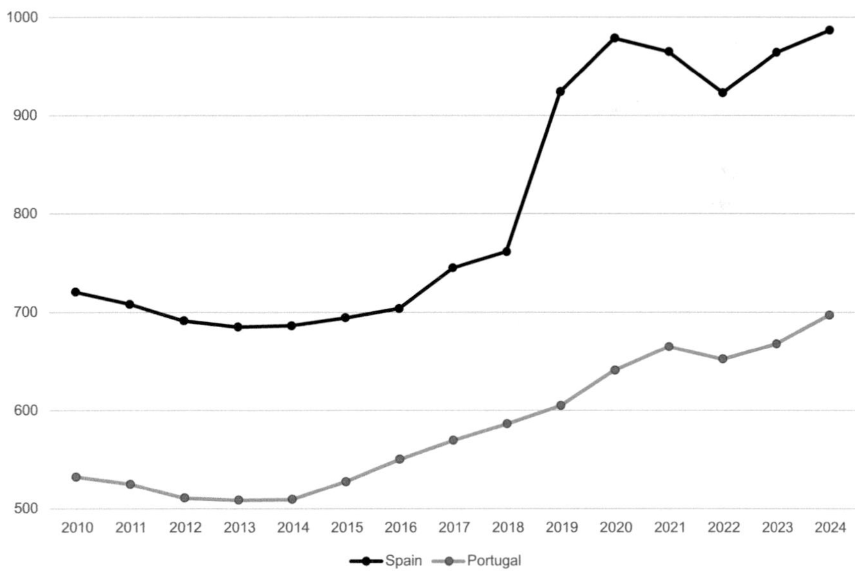

FIGURE 5.5 Real Monthly Minimum Wage, 2010–2024.

Source: Own elaboration based on data from Eurostat's Harmonised Consumer Price Index (Eurostat, n.d.).

in 2023, this was not fulfilled due to the impact it would have had on tax levels for those on the minimum wage. The resilience of social dialogue that we alluded to above then went hand in hand with a renewed focus on minimum wages as the main tool to improve pay equality in a context of eroded capacities of collective bargaining (Hansen Pedersen & Picot, 2023). Indeed, the increasing difficulties of collective agreements to underpin wage growth (López-Andreu, 2023) helped move the focus of the regulation towards such increases in the minimum wage.

Real increases in the minimum wage have evident consequences on gender pay gaps since women tend to be overrepresented in low-paid jobs. The influence of minimum wages across the left-tail of the earnings distribution is also usually stronger for women as the ratio of minimum wage to median pay is higher. That is apparent in Figure 5.6 where both Portugal and Spain witnessed such ratios increase in FTE real terms after 2014. Median wages are thus now much closer to minimum wages for both men and women in both countries.

The reach of the minimum wage increases – that is, the extent of ripple effects from these increases across the earnings distribution – appears, however, to have been very different in Portugal and Spain. It extends beyond the automatic effect of increasing the salaries of those earning less than new statutory minimum wages at

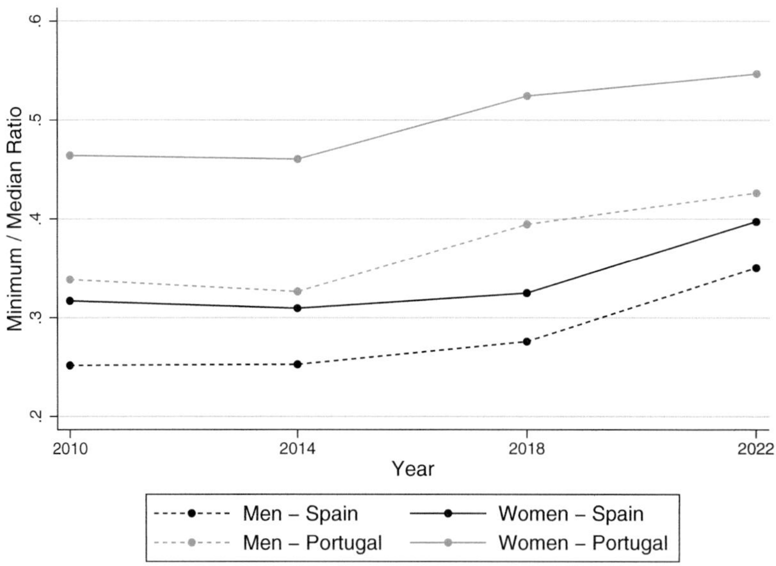

FIGURE 5.6 Ratio of Minimum to Median FTE Earnings by Gender, 2010–2022.

Source: Own elaboration based on data from Eurostat's Harmonised Consumer Price Index (Eurostat, n.d.); Median wages calculated using Gabinete de Estratégia e Planeamento (n.d.) and Instituto Nacional de Estadística (n.d.).

the time of implementation. Wages above can also be affected not least through the influence of minimum wages as a reference point for collectively bargained wage structures. However, by measuring the share of workers across the earnings distribution that in 2014 had real earnings levels below the 2022 real minimum wage, we can reach a very crude approximation of such automatic effects. In practice, we find a very stark contrast between Portugal and Spain: in Portugal, women in the first three deciles of the 2014 earnings distribution had earnings levels within the reach of the minimum wage increases that had been implemented by 2022. Only the first 15 percentiles of men were in a similar position. In Spain, however, it was only men and women in the first decile of the earnings distribution who were in reach of this change to the wage floor. So, despite the quite considerable real hikes in minimum wages in Spain, these were much less ambitious than in Portugal, measured by the share of workers that could automatically be affected.

This higher reach in Portugal appears to be consistent with the trends in real earnings across the job distribution that we already documented. In Portugal, in both these periods, real earnings increases were clearly clustered in lower-paid jobs affecting mostly women in 2014–2018 and further extending to men in 2018–2022 but within a trend of gender wage compression. In the Spanish case, the impact of the minimum wage increases from 2018 onwards seems to have stabilised pay in the low end of the occupational structure, particularly among women. Such influence from legal minimum wages is stronger in low-paid service sector jobs (e.g., retail, hospitality) which also partially compensated for the employment contraction in men's traditional areas of employment.

Conclusions

This chapter discusses the apparent successful histories of Spain and Portugal in reducing the GPG over a period of 14 years that spanned two periods of crisis and recovery, from the financial crisis and the austerity years to a recovery period interrupted by the Covid-19 pandemic. These crises were also associated with significant changes in the structure of employment and in wage setting mechanisms.

Our analysis suggests that two main factors account for such apparent success. First, the crises were moments of reinforcement of previously existing socio-demographic and labour market trends. On the one hand, occupational restructuring implied increased concentration of male workers in low-paid service sector jobs, namely as a result of the austerity hit in the construction and manufacturing sectors. On the other hand, the progressive upskilling of women led to their much greater presence in professional and knowledge-intensive jobs. Significantly, this trend coincided with a decrease in average earnings levels in such jobs. Second, such structural changes interacted with changes in wage setting mechanisms which reinforced the relative loss of men's bargaining power. During the post-austerity economic recovery and the reconstruction of collective bargaining and social dialogue institutions, pay moderation remained the norm. Such a trend seems to have had strong effects in squeezing earnings in male-dominated jobs at the middle of the earnings distribution, as well as in high-skilled occupations. This trend, together with the recovery of employment and pay levels in women-dominated, public sector related activities strongly affected by austerity cuts (López-Andreu & Rubery, 2021), and the progressive increase of real minimum wage levels reinforced the reduction of gender pay gaps. Further, our findings reveal that whereas in the Spanish case, structural transformations account for most of the reduction in the GPG, the data reveal a stronger role for the minimum wage in Portugal as the segregation of women in low-paid occupations was greater.

Overall, this chapter suggests the need to bring into interaction changes in the labour market dynamics and composition with efforts in wage setting mechanisms to foster equality. These changes in wage setting mechanisms are multi-faceted, leading through both austerity measures and a focus on wage moderation within social dialogue in Spain to declining real earnings for men particularly in higher and middle level jobs which narrowed gender pay gaps at the top of the distribution. These changes took place alongside significant rises, after the freezes in the austerity years in the real and relative level of minimum wages, especially in Portugal. These latter changes had strong positive impacts on women's pay in lower skilled segments and had beneficial impacts for those men who had entered these occupations in higher numbers post the austerity-related declines in industry and construction jobs. These divergent trends by gender and between labour market segments suggest the need for a more intersectional approach to considering progress in the aggregate gender pay gaps as the winners and losers may be different groups of women and of men within the same period. The data also reveal the potential for positive backlashes against crisis measures to retain collective bargaining and to promote more inclusive wage structures through raising the wage floor that has positive gender impacts, whether intended or unintended. Taken together, these dynamics highlight how crises reshape not just pay structures, but also the institutional configurations through which gender inequalities are reproduced or challenged.

Notes

1 Data for public sector pay in Portugal refer only to full-time workers as microdata on pay and working hours are not available.
2 Extremely low or high wages were eliminated from the dataset as outliers. These were defined as wages below the first 0.5th percentile or below the equivalent of 80% of the equivalent FTE minimum wage. Wages above three times the 99th percentile were equally eliminated.
3 We equally abstract from swings in employment and activity rates during the crisis periods, which were substantial and gender-biased. These are likely to have had a significant impact in income inequality and not simply pay inequality at work. The former analysis is, however, considered to be beyond the scope of this text.

4 We consider seven occupational groups (managers, professionals, technicians, administrative clerks, sales personnel, qualified primary and industrial workers and unqualified blue collar workers), five sectors (agriculture and industry; energy, infrastructure and construction; knowledge- and tech-intensive industries and services; public and social services; other services), two education groups (tertiary and non-tertiary), and three age/experience profiles (below 30, 30–49, 50+).

References

Addison, J. T., Portugal, P., & Vilares, H. (2017). Unions and collective bargaining in the wake of the Great Recession: Evidence from Portugal. *British Journal of Industrial Relations*, *55*(3), 551–576. https://doi.org/10.1111/bjir.12198

Afonso, A., Dorigatti, L., Molina, O., & Tassinari, A. (2023). Labor market (de)regulation and wage-setting institutions in Mediterranean capitalism. In L. Burroni, E. Pavolini, & M. Regini (Eds.), *Mediterranean capitalism revisited: One model, different trajectories* (pp. 115–148). Cornell University Press. https://doi.org/10.7591/cornell/9781501761072.003.0006

Campos Lima, M. P. (2019). Portugal: Reforms and the turn to neoliberal austerity. In T. Müller, K. Vandaele, & J. Waddington (Eds.), *Collective bargaining in Europe: Towards an endgame* (Vol. III, pp. 483–505). ETUI.

Campos Lima, M. da P., Martins, D., Costa, A. C., & Velez, A. (2021). Internal devaluation and economic inequality in Portugal: Challenges to industrial relations in times of crisis and recovery. *Transfer*, *27*(1), 47–73. https://doi.org/10.1177/1024258921995006

Cárdenas del Rey, L., & Arribas, J. (2025). Fighting "internal erosion" through social pacts? Collective bargaining in Spain from the great recession to the Covid-19 crisis. *Industrial Relations Journal*, *56*(3), 260–275. https://doi.org/10.1111/irj.12464

Couceiro de León, A., & Dolado, J. J. (2023). Revisiting the public–private wage gap in Spain: New evidence and interpretation. *SERIEs*, *14*(3), 353–377. https://doi.org/10.1177/1024258921995006

Cruces Aguilera, J., & de la Fuente Sanz, L. (2023). *Collective bargaining and inequality in Spain* (Deliverable 3.1 National report for Spain). BFORE project VS/2021/0209.

DGAEP – SIOE. (2025). *Síntese estatística do emprego público: 4º trimestre de 2024*. Direção-Geral da Administração e Emprego Público.

Eurostat. (n.d.). *Harmonised Indices of Consumer Prices (HICP)* [Dataset]. https://ec.europa.eu/eurostat/web/hicp/database

Fernandez-Rodriguez, C., & Martinez Lucio, M. (2023). *Work and employment relations in Southern Europe. The impact of de-regulation, organizational change and social fragmentation on worker representation and action.* Edward Elgar. https://doi.org/10.4337/9781789909548

Gabinete de Estratégia e Planeamento. (n.d.). *Quadros de Pessoal [Personnel Records]* [Microdata set]. Ministry of Labour, Solidarity and Social Security. https://www.gep.mtsss.gov.pt/sinteses-/-publicacoes

Hansen Pedersen, S., & Picot, G. (2023). Regulating low wages: Cross-national policy variation and outcomes. *Socio-Economic Review*, *21*(4), 2093–2116. https://doi.org/10.1093/ser/mwad019

Instituto Nacional de Estadística. (n.d.). *Encuesta de Estructura Salarial [Structure of Earnings Survey]* [Microdata set]. Instituto Nacional de Estadística. https://www.ine.es/dyngs/INEbase/operacion.htm?c=Estadistica_C&cid=1254736177025&menu=ultiDatos&idp=1254735976596

International Labour Organization. (2018). *Decent work in Portugal 2008–18: From crisis to recovery*. International Labour Office.

Karamessini, M., & Rubery, J. (Eds.). (2014). *Women and austerity: The economic crisis and the future for gender equality*. Routledge.

Las Heras, J., Risquez, M., & Messina, I. (2025). Combining union resources: The dynamics of strategic success during an automotive factory closure. *Employee Relations*, *47*(2), 380–396. https://doi.org/10.1108/ER-12-2024-0722

López-Andreu, M. (2019a). Neoliberal trends in collective bargaining and employment regulation in Spain, Italy and the UK: From institutional forms to institutional outcomes. *European Journal of Industrial Relations*, *25*(4), 309–325. https://doi.org/10.1177/0959680118810294

López-Andreu, M. (2019b). Employment institutions under liberalization pressures: Analysing the effects of regulatory change on collective bargaining in Spain. *British Journal of Industrial Relations*, *57*(2), 328–349. https://doi.org/10.1111/bjir.12418

López-Andreu, M. (2023). The political uncoupling of industrial relations and labour market change in Southern Europe. In C. J. Fernández Rodríguez & M. Martínez Lucio (Eds.), *Work and employment relations in Southern Europe* (pp. 113–136). Edward Elgar Publishing. https://doi.org/10.4337/9781789909548.00011

López-Andreu, M., & Rubery, J. (2021). Austerity and women's employment trajectories in Spain and the UK: A comparison of two flexible labour markets. *Economic and Industrial Democracy*, *42*(2), 289–313. https://doi.org/10.1177/0143831X18760988

Malo, M. Á. (2015). *Labour market measures in Spain 2008–13: The crisis and beyond*. International Labour Office.

Meardi, G., & Tassinari, A. (2022). Crisis corporatism 2.0? The role of social dialogue in the pandemic crisis in Europe. *Transfer*, *28*(1), 83–100. https://doi.org/10.1177/10242589221089785

Organisation for Economic Co-operation and Development. (2017). *Labour market reforms in Portugal 2011–15: A preliminary assessment*. OECD Publishing.

Rigby, M., & García Calavia, M. Á. (2017). Institutional resources as a source of trade union power in Southern Europe. *European Journal of Industrial Relations*, *24*(2), 129–143. https://doi.org/10.1177/0959680117708369

Sánchez-Mira, N., Serrano Olivares, R., & Carrasquer Oto, P. (2020). What slips through the cracks: The distance between regulations and practices shaping the gender pay gap. *Economic and Industrial Democracy*, *43*(2), 536–558. https://doi.org/10.1177/0143831X20924457

Távora, I. (2019). Collective bargaining in Portugal in the aftermath of the crisis: Trends and prospects. *Industrial Relations Journal*, *50*(5–6), 548–563. https://doi.org/10.1111/irj.12273

Távora, I., & González, P. (2016). Labour market regulation and collective bargaining in Portugal during the crisis: Continuity and change. *European Journal of Industrial Relations*, *22*(3), 251–265. https://doi.org/10.1177/0267323116643210

Távora, I., & Rodríguez-Modroño, P. (2018). The impact of the crisis and austerity on low educated working women: The cases of Spain and Portugal. *Gender, Work & Organization*, *25*(6), 621–636. https://doi.org/10.1111/gwao.12238

Visser, J. (2016). What happened to collective bargaining during the great recession? *IZA Journal of Labor Policy*, *5*(1), 9. https://doi.org/10.1186/s40173-016-0061-1

PART 2

The crisis of social reproduction

Households and the state

6

CRISES AS DRIVERS OF CHANGE IN COUPLES' PAID WORK ARRANGEMENTS IN EUROPE

Luana Marx, Fei Bian and Núria Sánchez-Mira

Introduction

Over the last four decades, couples' paid work patterns in Europe have undergone significant transformation. The generalised increase in women's education and the associated improvement in their employment prospects have led to sustained increases in women's integration into paid labour. By the end of the twentieth century, women were outperforming men in tertiary education in a range of high- and middle-income countries, including most of Europe (De Hauw et al., 2017). Moreover, it has been women's increased employment rates that have driven rises in overall employment rates over the past four decades across Europe, while men's employment rates have remained stable (Cipollone et al., 2014). Simultaneously, dual-earning arrangements have gradually become the norm in Europe, rising from 39% of couple households in 1983 to 73% in 2019, while male-breadwinner households decreased from 52% to 20% over this period (Paugam, 2024). Women's earnings have become increasingly essential to household economies in the context of shifting consumption standards and rising costs of living (Leonce, 2020). However, despite some convergence in these trends, significant cross-national variation remains, with different countries showing distinct levels and patterns of couples' paid work arrangements (Dotti Sani, 2018; Sánchez-Mira & O'Reilly, 2019). Moreover, studies show that progress towards equality in gender relations in the household remains uneven and non-linear, with potential signs of backlash (Dieckhoff et al., 2016). Some evidence suggests that the gender revolution might have slowed down or even stalled in recent decades (England, 2010) and in some developed countries (Hook & Paek, 2020) the effect of partnership and motherhood on women's employment may be becoming more negative.

DOI: 10.4324/9781003528210-9

Periods of crises might (re)shape long-term trends, as couples' paid work arrangements respond to the combined effects of economic needs and shifting employment opportunities (Sánchez-Mira, 2024). Economic downturns may modify and even reverse the relative weight of men's and women's earnings within households, as shown by the strong female added-worker effect observed in countries most affected by male employment destruction during the 2008 recession (Dotti Sani, 2018). However, different crises may generate distinct constraints in relation to employment opportunities, with varying impacts across labour market groups and countries (Blanton et al., 2019) and with varying consequences for couples' paid work arrangements. Women's contributions to household finances not only have important implications for inequalities in financial hardship across different household types, but also for gendered patterns of socio-economic vulnerability – two aspects often exacerbated by economic crises. In fact, dual-earner families are generally better able to absorb income shocks, as they benefit from multiple income streams, while one-earner couple households, particularly female-headed households, are more exposed to economic vulnerability (Kowalewska & Vitali, 2021).

In view of the continuing crises since 2008 and the ongoing socio-economic uncertainty, the evolution of couples' paid work arrangements across Europe is key to assessing the effects of these turbulent times on existing and emerging gendered patterns of inequality and vulnerability. Therefore, this chapter's main aim is to explore the role of crises as drivers of change in couples' long-term employment arrangements in Europe, taking into consideration differences across countries. After discussing the extant literature and presenting our data and methods, our three main empirical sections answer the following questions:

1a) How have the different types of couples' paid work arrangements evolved over the last two decades across periods of crises in Europe?
1b) How do these trends relate to the shifts in the couple's relative status in education?
2) How heterogeneous are these trajectories of change across countries?
3) Is there an association between couples' paid work arrangement and households' financial hardship, and how has this evolved over time, particularly during periods of crises, and across countries?

Together, these questions provide a multi-dimensional view of how crises interact with evolving couple-level employment dynamics – first by tracing broad structural trends, then unpacking cross-national variations and finally linking these patterns to financial vulnerability. In doing so, the chapter sets the stage for a broader understanding of how crises intersect with household configurations to shape gendered inequalities in new and underexplored ways.

The gendered effects of crises on couples' paid work arrangements

The gendered effects of crises on gender-segregated labour markets

Crises tend to have more negative repercussions on women, though these results vary by the type of crisis. Research on the consequences of financial crises in 68 countries from 1980 to 2010 found that, overall, crises undermine women's participation in employment and formal education, with long-lasting repercussions (Blanton et al., 2019). Nevertheless, the nature of each crisis has distinctive effects on couples' paid work arrangements, depending on their impact on employment reduction and patterns of recovery in gender-segregated labour markets, exposing men or women to different risks.

The 2008 financial crisis, for example, exhibited strong gendered dynamics, which have been labelled he-cession/she-austerity (Karamessini & Rubery, 2014). This is because its stronger initial phase hit traditionally male-dominated sectors, such as manufacturing, while the subsequent implementation of austerity policies had a substantial effect on women's employment (Périvier, 2018). Overall, the 2008 recession was marked by a female added-worker effect and the resulting increase in gender-atypical arrangements such as female full-time only employed couples (Dotti Sani, 2018; Vitali & Arpino, 2016). In contrast, the Covid-19 pandemic hit specific sectors in which women were overrepresented, such as hospitality, restaurants, personal services, entertainment and retail services as well as legal, social and cultural professionals – resulting in a larger decline in women's employment rates in advanced countries (Bluedorn et al., 2021; Rubery & Tavora, 2020). Women were also more likely to reduce working hours, stop working for pay or request furlough to take on the bulk of the additional childcare and housework, thereby suffering most from the blurring of boundaries across work and family life (Collins et al., 2021; Rubery & Tavora, 2020). Among women, the groups most impacted by the labour market restrictions were those with lower levels of education, migrant backgrounds, as well as those in part-time and temporary employment (Alon et al., 2020; Rubery & Tavora, 2020). These characteristics led scholars to refer to the Covid-19 pandemic as a she-cession, although evidence in this respect is still mixed (Bluedorn et al., 2021).

At the household level, short-term shocks may turn into lasting changes in couples' employment behaviour, as previous research on the mobilisation of women during the colonial wars in Portugal has illustrated (Tavora & Rubery, 2013). Thus, recent waves of crises might have contributed to fuelling long-term trends towards dual earning, given their enduring impact and the associated rising importance of women's income for household economies, particularly during the financial crisis (Sánchez-Mira, 2024). In this sense, crises may reinforce pre-existing dynamics that intersect with long-term changes in couples' internal status hierarchies, particularly shifts in women's educational and employment standing, setting the stage for new configurations of gendered couple-level dynamics.

Changes in partners' relative status and the effects of crises on couple-level dynamics

Women's rising educational attainment has occurred in a context where other structural transformations have been reshaping the gendered structuring of employment opportunities in the labour market. Up until the 1980s in Europe, it was the male partner who was often the most educated, but by the early 2000s, growing shares of women were highly educated and typically partnered with highly educated and employed men (De Hauw et al., 2017; England et al., 2012). Relatedly, the observed long-term rise in dual earning arrangements was initially led by couples with high relative educational and employment statuses, resulting in some degree of polarisation across households (Paugam, 2024). Indeed, several studies showed that the division between households with high and low work intensity arrangements in Europe tended to reflect a polarisation along educational lines, although to different extents across countries (Hook, 2015; Sánchez-Mira & O'Reilly, 2019).

However, dual-earning has also become more common among lower-skilled households over time, as processes of economic restructuring, crises and related pressures to maintain living standards have likely played a role in driving the expansion of this model (Rubery, 1988; Sánchez-Mira, 2020). Indeed, the steep increase in dual earning has occurred in parallel with the drastic reduction of the male-dominated industrial sector since the 1980s and the consequent weakening of men's labour market position, which is also reflected at the couple level. A steep rise across almost all European countries in couples with both partners working in the service sector has led to the dominance of the "dual-service-earning" couple. Even in countries with resilient male-industrial jobs, there has been a rise in "industry-services dual-earning" couples, rather than a persistence of the traditional "male-single-industry-earning" (Paugam, 2024). These compositional shifts have thus contributed to reshaping heterosexual work arrangements patterns away from the traditional male-breadwinner model. This pattern was particularly notable in the countries most affected by the financial crisis (Dotti Sani, 2018) and also primarily among working-class couples (Sánchez-Mira, 2020).

In fact, in the countries most affected by an acute male job loss in the financial crisis, the paradigmatic female breadwinner couple is found not to be a highly skilled but rather a semi-skilled woman employed in services, whose male partner was previously employed in industrial work (Sánchez-Mira, 2020). Indeed, recent evidence confirms that couples where the woman is the only earner are not only associated with higher educated women but also with male employment instability and precariousness, and not with the diffusion of gender-egalitarian attitudes (Kowalewska & Vitali, 2021). This pattern is especially evident in contexts of crises, which tend to foster female breadwinning and might have enduring effects on gender relations, with some evidence of long-lasting changes in attitudes within couples (Sánchez-Mira, 2024), possibly also fuelled by increased labour market risks and cost of living pressures, as we discuss next.

Dual earning against labour market risks and households' financial hardship in contexts of crises

The long-term rise in the dual-earner model has occurred alongside broader transformations in the structure of labour markets, most notably the spread of non-standard employment. From the 1990s to the 2010s, more than half of all jobs created in developed countries involved part-time, temporary or self-employed work. This trend was accelerated by the 2008 recession and measures of labour market deregulation that ensued, particularly in those European countries most affected by structural adjustment policies (International Labour Organization [ILO], 2012; Organisation for Economic Co-operation and Development [OECD], 2015). These jobs are generally associated with reduced employment protection, lower wages and reduced benefits (Horemans, 2018). Consequently, people in non-standard work are also more likely to be poor, especially if they live in a household with other non-standard or non-employed workers (OECD, 2015). Furthermore, while non-standard employment used to be primarily a complement to a standard (typically male) job within couples or a transitional phase for young people, it has become increasingly common for it to be a couple's sole source of labour income (Paugam, 2024). Indeed, economic vulnerability has been shifting away from dual-worklessness towards couples whose only source of labour income is from non-standard work (Horemans, 2018). This shift has a key gender bias because women are, on average, overrepresented in non-standard work in Europe, with 22% of women employed in part-time work in OECD countries compared to 9% of men, while women's temporary employment rates are above men's in about three-quarters of OECD countries (OECD, 2021). In many advanced economies, the rise in non-standard employment has become a key structural factor shaping both the vulnerability and the gendered configuration of couples' work arrangements, particularly through the widespread reliance on part-time work (Insarauto, 2021). While part-time employment can take distinct forms, as primarily a form of employer flexibility and/or strategy of work–family reconciliation, depending on the country, sector and the occupational level, it is also likely to reinforce the adoption of a dual-earner model as on its own is unlikely to generate sufficient income for a couple. More generally, research suggests that growing insecurity associated with widespread non-standard employment is favouring the adoption of the dual-earner model as a way for couples to protect against labour market risks (Gorbachev, 2016).

Alongside the restructuring of labour markets, shifting consumption standards combined with rising costs of living may also render traditional male breadwinning unviable for many households. Dual-earning arrangements are increasingly considered financially more secure than households reliant on one income

(Leonce, 2020), and crises may favour this perception. Both the 2008 recession and the Covid-19 pandemic were respectively associated with rising costs of living that extended beyond the acute crisis phase (Bengali & Duzhak, 2024). Moreover, frequent crises may heighten perceptions of economic insecurity associated with temporary and other non-standard forms of employment. In particular, reductions in working hours, non-renewal of temporary contracts and layoffs in both contexts of crisis have led to increased job insecurity and precariousness (Matysiak & Vignoli, 2024). Research also finds that income losses from unemployment are more persistent and severe when they occur during recessions (Davis & Von Wachter, 2011). Therefore, crises may have long-term consequences for couples' work arrangements. Furthermore, due to growing precarious employment, the effects are not limited to those who lose their jobs but extend to new labour market entrants (e.g., the Millennials during the Great Recession). Overall, heightened employment insecurity and prolonged labour market transitions for younger generations on the one hand, and increased costs of living, on the other, are likely to constrain the types of arrangements couples can realistically achieve and maintain, thereby amplifying their vulnerability in a context of turbulence.

Data and methods

This chapter draws on cross-sectional data from the EU Statistics on Income and Living Conditions survey (EU-Silc) which is a representative annual survey conducted across 31 European countries and includes a wide range of socio-economic and demographic information (Eurostat, n.d.). Data is collected from both co-resident partners whenever present, allowing a measure of couples' work arrangements based on the individual self-reports of each partner's employment situation. Our analysis includes the years from 2005 to 2022, covering the 2008 financial crisis as well as the Covid-19 pandemic and the ensuing cost-of-living crisis.

Our analytical sample consists of married or cohabiting women with a male partner in 23 European countries. We focus on heterosexual couples, with or without children, as they remain central for understanding household formation and dynamics of gender inequalities in employment, and represent 40%, on average, of all household types in Europe (Eurostat, n.d). Additionally, we restrict our sample to those aged 25 to 54 to minimise cross-country variations in durations of studies and retirement patterns. As we use single point in time measurement, we exclude couples where either partner is self-employed, as this often involves fluctuating work patterns throughout the year.

All couples in our sample were grouped into six categories according to both partners' employment status, defined as:

1. **Dual full-time employed**: both partners work full-time;
2. **Male full-time main employed**: the male partner works full-time, while the female partner works part-time;

3. **Male full-time only employed**: the male partner works full-time, while the female partner is either inactive or unemployed;
4. **Female full-time main/only employed**: the female partner works full-time, while the male partner works part-time, is inactive or unemployed;
5. **Part-time employed**: both partners work part-time, or one works part-time and the other is inactive or unemployed;
6. **Workless household**: both partners are either unemployed or inactive.

Our first step is a descriptive analysis: curve graphs trace the evolution of these six couple types over the past two decades, starting with aggregate European level trends and examining how they relate to changes in couples' relative status in education. Then, we explore these trends in four selected countries – Poland, Sweden, Germany and Spain – each exemplifying a distinct cluster of household work arrangements in Europe, following Sánchez-Mira and O'Reilly (2019).

1. **Poland** represents the **dual-earner full-time** country cluster, where households with both partners in full-time employment predominate. This cluster includes other Eastern and Central European countries, Portugal and Finland;
2. **Sweden** exemplifies the **dual-earner mixed** country cluster, characterised by a high prevalence of dual-earner full-time households but alongside a large share of male full-time main-employed arrangements where women are working part-time. This cluster also includes other Nordic countries (except Finland), France and the UK;
3. **Germany** illustrates the **multiple modes** country cluster, where male full-time main-employed arrangements are dominant but alongside significant yet varying shares of dual full-time and male full-time only employed arrangements. This cluster also includes the Netherlands, other Continental European countries, and Ireland;
4. **Spain** represents the **polarised** country cluster, characterised by a pronounced polarisation, often driven by educational attainment, between dual full-time and male full-time only employed arrangements. This cluster also includes Greece and, to a lesser extent, Italy.

By investigating these four representative countries, our analysis provides a nuanced understanding of how structural differences shape couples' heterogeneous responses to socio-economic disruptions across Europe and over time.

For the second step in our analytical strategy, we employ OLS regression to examine the relationship between couples' paid work arrangements and their household financial hardship over the analysed period. The outcome variable is the perceived financial hardship experienced by the household, assessed through responses to the following question: "Considering your household's total monthly or weekly income, is your household able to make ends meet and cover your usual expenses?". Responses range from: very easily, easily, fairly easily, with some difficulty, with difficulty and with great difficulty. The primary explanatory variable is household work arrangements, that is, the six couple types already outlined. We allow this couple-type variable to interact with the year to assess how the association between work arrangement and financial hardship evolves over time and during the crises. In addition, we control for the female partner's age, educational level, marital status (married vs. cohabiting) and the number of children under six years of age in the household. We include only women's characteristics – not men's – as control variables in our models, since partners' characteristics are often correlated, and prior research suggests that women's characteristics tend to have a stronger influence on household work arrangements (Klesment & Van Bavel, 2017). We also include a set of country dummies to account for cross-national differences in our model estimating at the European level. Next, we complement this regression analysis with descriptive bar graphs showing changes in financial hardship over time for three main types of arrangements in the four selected countries. EU-Silc survey weights are applied in both the descriptive analyses and the regression models to account for differential selection probabilities and ensure representativeness.

Results

Long-term trends in couples' paid work arrangements over periods of crises

Figure 6.1 shows the evolution of couples' paid work arrangements in Europe from 2005 to 2022 where we observe a steady decline in the share of male full-time only employed households and a parallel increasing share of dual full-time employed households, while the share of male full-time, female part-time households remained rather stable over most of the period. These trends are consistent with abundant literature pointing to the long-term decline of the male only breadwinner/female caregiver family model, in practice and normatively (Brewster & Padavic, 2000; Cunningham, 2008).

Also consistent with existing research (Klesment & Van Bavel, 2017), our data show that households' paid work arrangements are strongly related to women's educational attainment, which has continued to increase over the analysed period (Figure A6-1 in the online appendix). More specifically, the bar graph (Figure 6.2) uses the average values over the analysed period to show the distribution of the different paid work arrangements by educational assortative mating patterns for three types: hypergamous couples (male partner has a higher educational level than the female partner), homogamous couples (both partners have the same educational level) and hypogamous couples (the female partner has a higher educational level than the male partner). Hypergamous couples are found to align more with traditional work arrangements, because in 59% of these households the male partner is the only (31%) or main (28%) full-time employed person and

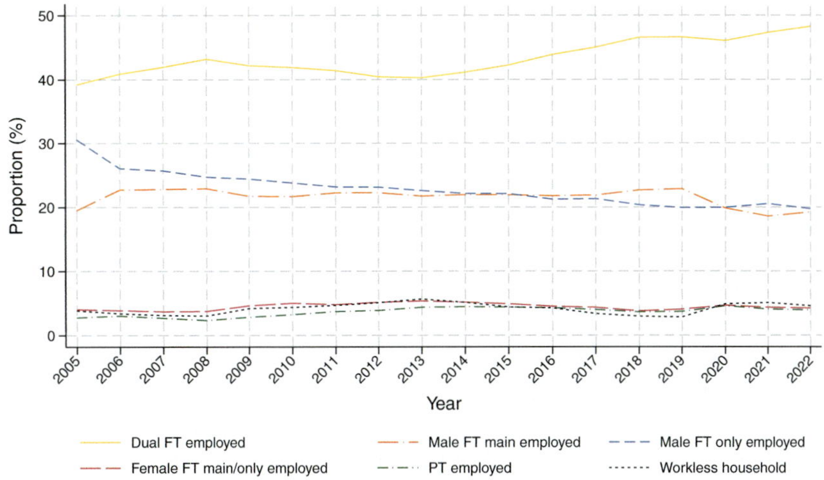

FIGURE 6.1 Trends in Couples' Paid Work Arrangements (European Average, 2005–2022).

Source: Authors' calculation based on EU-Silc cross-sectional 2005–2022.

Note: The Y-axis represents the proportion of each couple type within all couples in our sample.

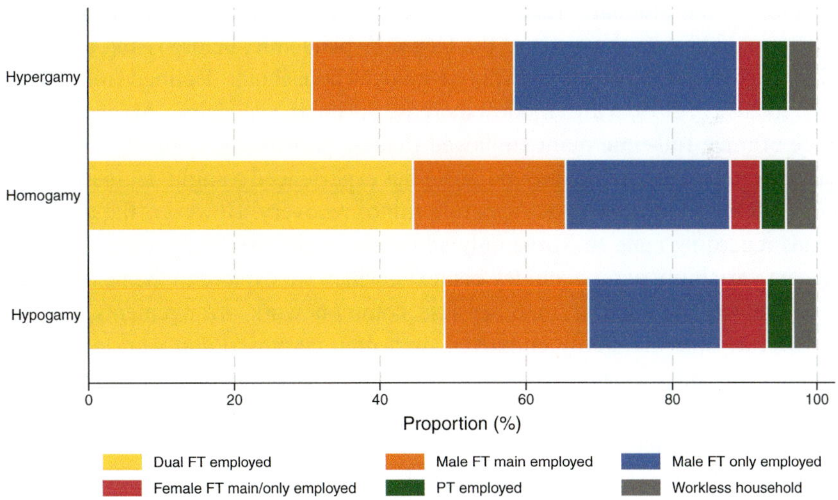

FIGURE 6.2 Couples' Paid Work Arrangements by Educational Assortative Mating Patterns (Hypergamy, Homogamy and Hypogamy).

Source: Authors' calculation based on EU-Silc cross-sectional 2005–2022.

only 31% are dual full-time employed. Homogamous couples, in contrast, have a 45% share of households where both partners work full-time, although male-dominant full-time arrangements are still quite prevalent (male only 23% and male main 21%). In contrast, almost 50% of hypogamous couples are dual full-time employed, although the gap between them and homogamous couples is smaller than between the latter and hypergamous couples. Among hypogamous couples, there is also a more noticeable share of households where the female partner is the main or only full-time employed person (6%). Thus, the move towards dual full-time employment is stronger among couples where the woman is equally or more educated. This type of household is becoming more common as there has been a decrease (Figure A6-2 in the online appendix) in hypergamous couples and a parallel increase of hypogamous couples over the last two decades, suggesting that the combination of both patterns is one of the driving forces behind rising dual-earning and female breadwinning households in Europe.

The different crises over the last two decades have also interacted with these longer-term trends, and even in these very aggregate numbers, the influence of both the 2008 financial crisis and the Covid-19 pandemic is apparent in Figure 6.1, though unequal in its intensity and duration. Indeed, despite a drop in GDP and aggregate paid working hours during the pandemic's first six months that was roughly twice that experienced during the 2008 recession's first six months, the long-term employment impact of Covid-19 was smaller (Alon et al., 2022). As shown in Figure 6.1, the upward trend in dual full-time employed households suffered a reversal over the 2008 financial crisis, reaching its lowest point (40%) in 2013. It then gradually recovered, and only wavered again, albeit to a lesser extent, in 2020 with the onset of the Covid-19 pandemic, before rising to 48% in 2022. In turn, the male full-time only employed households declined from 30% in 2005 to 20% in 2019, with a modest increase during the pandemic. Meanwhile, the share of male full-time main employed (female part-time employed) households remained relatively stable (around 20%) but experienced a slight decrease during the pandemic, followed by an apparent minor recovery. However, the aggregate trends regarding male full-time only and main employed arrangements hide significant variability across country contexts, which we explore in the next section.

There was also a rise in other less common work arrangements, such as female full-time main/only employed, part-time employed and workless households, especially during the 2008 financial crisis. Female full-time main/only employed households increased from 3.8% in 2008 to 5.4% in 2013, part-time employed households rose from 2.3% to 4.4%, and workless couples grew from 3% to 5.6%. A similar though less strong trend emerged during the Covid-19 pandemic, with female full-time main/only employed households at 4.7%, part-time employed households at 4.6% and workless households at 4.9% in 2020. These patterns indicate that the shift towards work-poor and gender-atypical household employment structures must be interpreted as an expression of the couple's vulnerable position in the labour market, which becomes particularly salient in economic downturns. Specifically, the increases in female breadwinning during the financial recession have been documented as a result of an added-worker effect related to decreased employment opportunities for men, and thus mostly a response to economic strain (Dotti Sani, 2018; Vitali & Arpino, 2016). However, while these shifts can reflect household vulnerability – especially when tied to male job loss – they may also signal longer-term adaptation to changing labour market realities, particularly where women's full-time employment is stable, and the shifting educational hierarchies within couples we have previously referred to. This evolving dynamic is further explored in our financial hardship analysis. Overall, workless households showed greater fluctuation compared to female full-time main/only employed and part-time employed households in times of economic distress, highlighting the particularly precarious nature of this household arrangement.

Trajectories in couples' paid work arrangements across European countries: convergence and divergences

The patterns observed for the European average mask significant cross-national heterogeneity in trajectories of change over the past two decades. To illustrate, Figure 6.3 presents long-term trends in couples' paid work arrangements in our four selected countries. In Poland, the dual full-time earner model has been steadily consolidated over the entire period, with the proportion of households where both partners work full-time exceeding 70% by 2022. At the same time, the share of couples where the man is the only full-time employed person has declined from 28% in 2005 to 21% in 2022, while male full-time, female part-time employed households remain relatively uncommon (around 4%). Notably, Poland did not suffer particularly large employment falls during the 2008 financial crisis or the Covid-19 pandemic compared to other eastern and central European countries (Sánchez-Mira, 2020), which could explain why couples' paid work arrangements were not significantly affected by these crises.

In Sweden, the proportion of dual full-time employed households has also increased, reaching 65% in 2022, although still below the share in Poland. This shift has been accompanied by a persistent but gradual decrease in male full-time main employed households, from 28% in 2005 to 17% in 2022. Dual full-time employed arrangements suffered a short-term decline during the Covid-19 pandemic, paralleled by an increase in male full-time only employed arrangements but still only accounting for 9% in 2022. This temporary wavering did not, however, substantially alter the country's longer-term trajectory towards dual full-time earning. While part-time work remains prevalent among mothers of preschool-aged children (Goldscheider et al., 2013), these patterns primarily reflect the country's support for work–life balance through voluntary reduced hours with earnings compensation and the right to return to full-time employment. These options help mitigate the persistence of the one-and-a-half earner

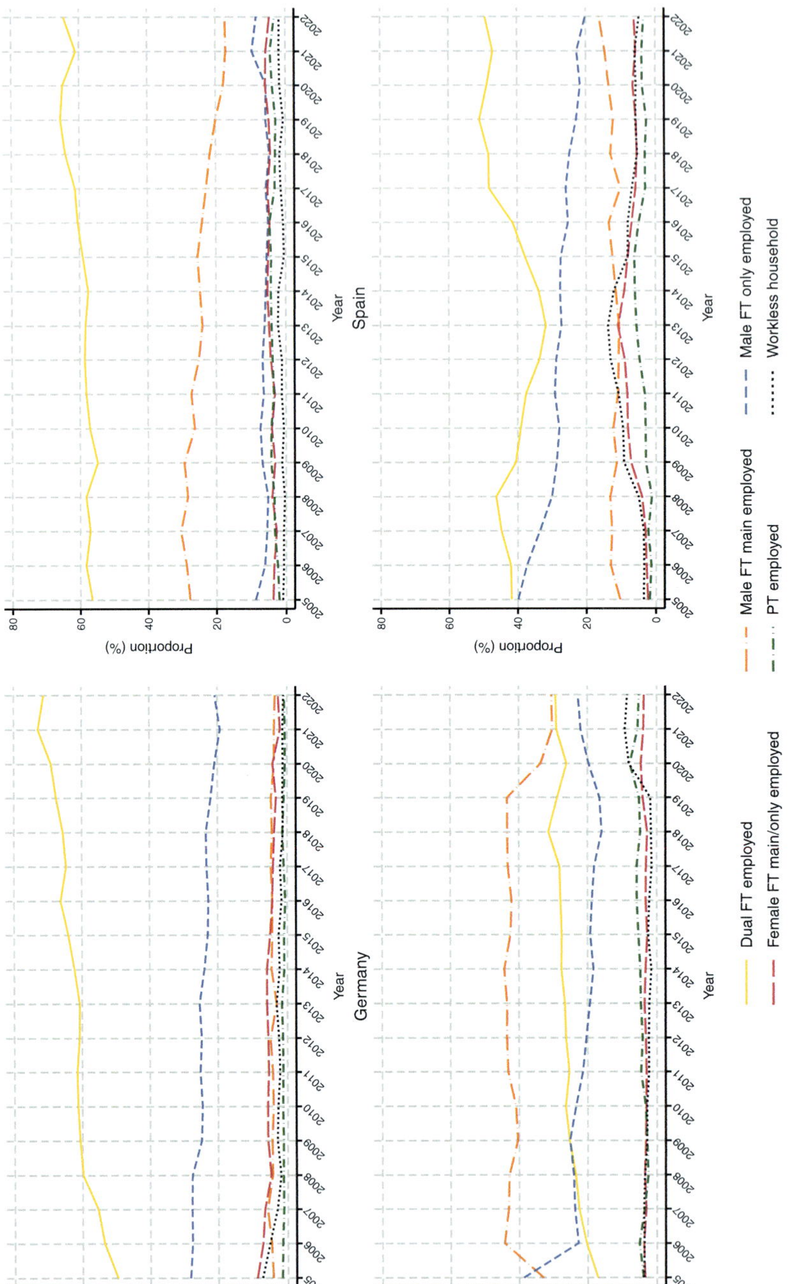

FIGURE 6.3 Trends in Couples' Paid Work Arrangements (Four European Countries, 2005–2022).

Source: Authors' calculation based on EU-Silc cross-sectional 2005–2022.

model as a long-term arrangement for couples, steering Sweden closer to a dual full-time earner model.

Germany displays some notable trends, particularly a significant decrease in male full-time main employed arrangements during the Covid-19 pandemic even though this had long been the paradigmatic arrangement in this country (Trappe et al., 2015). Meanwhile, the slight upward trend in dual full-time employed households (although this also wavered slightly during the pandemic) meant that by 2022 each of these couple types accounted for a similar 30% share of all couple households. Furthermore, while male full-time only employed households followed a downward trend for most of the period, this pattern started to reverse even before the pandemic, increasing from its lowest level of 15% in 2018 to 22% in 2022. Therefore, the country seems to be developing along an uncertain trajectory that increasingly aligns with a multiple modes pattern, where the three main types of arrangements have almost equal weight and reflect distinct patterns of socioeconomic advantage and vulnerability.

Finally, Spain is the country that experienced the most pronounced fluctuations in couples' paid work arrangements associated with the latest crises, particularly from the 2008 recession. With the steady decrease of couples based around male only full-time employed (from 40% in 2005 to 20% in 2022) and an increase in couples where both partners work full-time (from 42% in 2005 to 49% in 2022), the country seems to be moving away from polarisation towards a dual-earner full-time model. This long-term trend seems persistent, despite the decrease during the Great Recession in the share of dual full-time employed households from 46% in 2008 to 32% in 2013, only to recover in 2016. At the same time, the prevalence of less common arrangements – female main/only employed, part-time employed and workless households – increased particularly during the financial recession, potentially reflecting precarious employment within insecure labour markets. In particular, the rise in female only employed arrangements can be seen as primarily a response to the destruction of male employment (Sánchez-Mira, 2020). Moreover, the continuous even if somewhat fluctuating rise in male full-time main employed arrangements after the financial crisis may reflect the spread of part-time work as a form of flexibilisation during this period (Insarauto, 2021) and raises the possibility that Spain might move closer toward a dual-earner mixed model in the future.

Couples' paid work arrangement and households' perceived financial hardship over periods of crises

In the OLS regression analysis (see Table A6-1 in the online appendix), Model 1 assesses the relationship between couples' paid work arrangements and households' perceived financial hardship. The reference category is households where both partners are full-time employed. In Model 2, we add an interaction between couples' paid work arrangements and the year of the survey to examine how time periods moderate these relationships. To better visualize the results, we plot the predicted values in Figure 6.4, that is the expected levels of financial hardship estimated by Model 2 for each household employment type. Each line in Figure 6.4 represents the changes in the average level of financial hardship associated with a specific household work arrangement over the period from 2005 to 2022.

Looking first at differences across couple types, as expected we observe that households with both partners in full-time employment experience the lowest levels of financial hardship, as this arrangement ensures a more stable and substantial dual income. Households where the man works full-time and the woman part-time exhibit comparable levels of perceived financial hardship over the first part of the period but face greater hardship in the second part, coinciding with the post-financial crisis recovery period. Predictably, given their reliance on a single income source, male full-time only employed households faced even more difficulties. Greater financial difficulties are experienced by female main or only employed households or where employment is part-time based, especially during the first half of the period, supporting our argument that these arrangements represent some form of vulnerability and response to it, although the situation evolved over time, as discussed next. Unsurprisingly, households without any employed members are the most financially vulnerable.

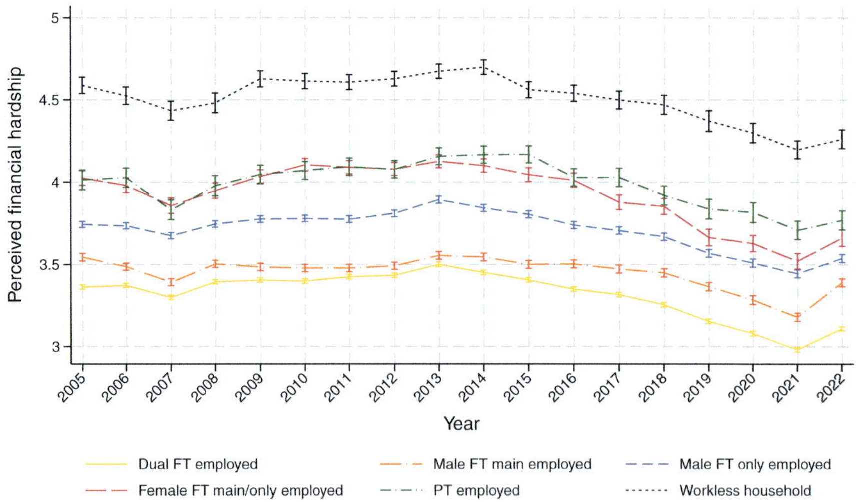

FIGURE 6.4 Perceived Financial Hardship for Each Household Work Arrangement (European Average, 2005–2022).

Source: Authors' calculation based on EU-Silc cross-sectional 2005–2022.

Note: Higher values on the Y-axis indicate greater financial harship.

Considering the evolution of financial hardship over the whole period, we see that perceived hardship rose among nearly all couple types following the 2008 crisis, though the increase was least pronounced among dual full-time employed couples, who consistently experienced the lowest level of hardship over the whole period. With the economic recovery post-recession, a decrease in perceived hardship for all couple types is observed (between 2013 and 2014). This is stronger for dual full-time employed couples than for male full-time employed, female part-time employed couples. Indeed, the lines for both couple types became distanced from each other and remained more separate thereafter, suggesting that the male main employed arrangement may be becoming less financially sustainable over time. The persistent long-term decline in hardship is also particularly pronounced for female full-time main/only employed couples, almost converging with those of male full-time only employed couples before the onset of the Covid-induced crisis. Therefore, if households with a female main/only employed partner have historically been more financially vulnerable than those with a male only employed partner, the vulnerability gap between these two couple types has significantly decreased. Nowadays, it seems that being in households with only one adult employed means more for financial vulnerability than the gender of the employed person in these particular arrangements. In this sense, and consistently with what has been shown in the first findings section, these trends may be compounded by heterogeneous situations that are hard to disentangle, with some female breadwinning households reflecting involuntary, constrained arrangements to a greater extent, while others are mostly the result of women's shifting structural position within the couple and the labour market. Figure 6.4 also suggests that the pandemic disrupted the recovery trend and is associated with another increase in perceived financial hardship, especially from 2020, when it was compounded by the ongoing cost of living crisis. Here the effect on dual full-time employed households compared to male full-time main employed households was again relatively contained, underscoring the resilience of this household work arrangement.

It is important to note that this measure of financial hardship in EU-Silc is based on respondents' perceptions, which may not always accurately reflect actual changes in the objective cost of living. These subjective assessments can be influenced by social factors that may vary across contexts, such as the country's perceived economic situation, standards of living and institutional support for given types of arrangements. For this reason, we next explore descriptively the differences in perceived financial hardship for various couples' paid work arrangements in our four selected countries. Figure 6.5 illustrates the changes in financial hardship over time for the main three types of arrangements – dual full-time, male main employed and male only employed – in Poland, Sweden, Germany and Spain. Across all four countries, dual full-time employed couples consistently face the least perceived financial hardship, followed by male main employed couples, with male only employed couples experiencing the highest financial strain. This pattern again underscores the protective effect of dual incomes (and particularly

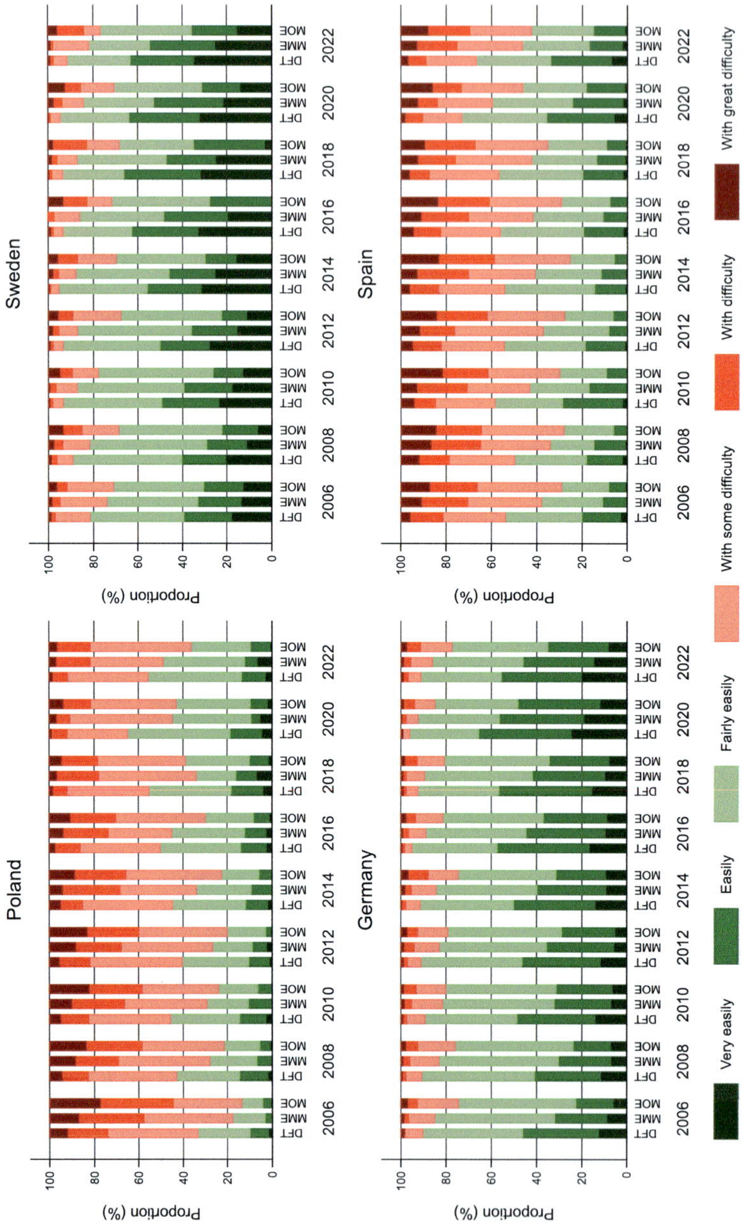

FIGURE 6.5 Perceived Financial Hardship Over Time for Dual Full-Time (DFT), Male Main Employed (MME) and Male Only Employed (MOE) Arrangements in Four European Countries.

Source: Authors' calculation based on EU-Silc cross-sectional 2005–2022.

dual full-time) in alleviating financial difficulties. However, there are notable differences across the countries in the extent of protection provided by each type. For example, the male main employed arrangement appears less protective in Spain and Poland than in Germany and Sweden, suggesting that institutional factors play a part in shaping the degree of financial protection provided by this arrangement.

There are significant differences across countries in the overall levels of financial hardship. Interestingly, Germany reports the lowest levels of financial hardship across all types of arrangements, with over 80% of couples not finding it difficult to cover their usual expenses throughout the analysed period. This points to strong economic stability (Audretsch & Lehmann, 2016) in this country that helps mitigate financial difficulties, even for male-only employed households. More generally, Germany's overall strong economic foundation has probably played a key role in reducing financial strain and cushioning the impact of recent crises, although the situation could change given the less buoyant current economic situation in the country. Sweden, with its well-established social welfare system and high levels of gender equality (Bergqvist, 2015), also shows a more balanced distribution of financial hardship, with all household work arrangements associated with relatively low levels of hardship and only moderate fluctuations during crises. The Swedish model of social support thus appears to play an important role in alleviating financial strain, regardless of household work arrangements. In contrast, Poland experiences the highest levels of financial hardship, probably reflecting the greater economic challenges and lower average wages in the Polish economy (Plomien & Schwartz, 2026, this volume). In this context, adopting a dual full-time arrangement may be the only economically viable option for most households. Similarly, in Spain, dual-earner models are often more of an imperative, as economic conditions to some extent limit the viability of other arrangements (Sánchez-Mira, 2020). More than half of couples in Poland and Spain find it difficult to cover their usual expenses and these high levels of financial hardship persist even after crises. This suggests that, in these countries, economic instability and structural labour market challenges contribute to long-term financial strain, despite variations in household employment arrangements.

Discussion and conclusions

Our chapter has investigated the main drivers of changes in couples' paid work arrangements in Europe in the context of continuing socio-economic turbulence over the last two decades. Overall, our findings are consistent with the literature (Paugam, 2024) showing a persistent long-term rise in dual full-time employed and a decline in male full-time only employed arrangements, despite key fluctuations associated with the three recent crises – financial recession/austerity, Covid-19, and cost of living. The 2008 financial recession had a negative impact on the dual full-time employed model, while the Covid-induced crisis was associated with a slight increase in male full-time only employed arrangements. However, both of these crises-related changes can be seen as temporary setbacks that have not fundamentally disturbed the underlying trends towards growing dual full-time employment in Europe.

These trends are nonetheless heterogeneous across the social groups and national contexts considered. Although over the long run the increase in dual full-time employment seems to be driven by highly educated women in increasingly common homogamous and hypogamous couples (Klesment & Van Bavel, 2017), during the financial crisis of 2008 it was lower-skilled women who showed stronger shifts in employment patterns. In contrast, although the Covid pandemic had a reportedly acute effect on working mothers, particularly those with lower educational and occupational status, the effects were not strong or long enough (Bluedorn et al., 2021) to drive up the share of male-only full-time employment in most countries except for the immediate period of the pandemic.

Our analysis further reveals that the growing importance of gender-atypical arrangements, such as female only/main employed households, is a reflection not only of the changing relative position of women in some couples but alsoof household vulnerability, in particular during crises. While in the 1980s this was a rare (nearly zero percent) couple type, it currently represents around 5%, exceeding the share of dual-workless couples' households (Paugam, 2024; our own data). The increase in this and other peripheral arrangements (such as part-time based and workless households) during economic downturns suggests that these emerge largely as responses to situations of economic strain, in line with abundant existing research in Europe and the US during the financial (Dotti Sani, 2018; Vitali & Arpino, 2016) and the Covid-19 (Brini et al., 2021; Qian & Hu, 2021) crises. However, as shown in our financial hardship analysis, this household model has recently experienced a decline in perceived vulnerability, especially in relation to male-sole earner households. This suggests there may be moves towards greater economic resilience in cases where the female partner has reached a solid employment position.

Whether the increase in frequently unwanted and temporary gender atypical arrangements is likely to favour more egalitarian attitudes and practices over the long run remains an open question. Research has shown that even involuntary experiences of female breadwinning are likely to lead to greater recognition of the importance of women's economic independence and contribution to the household (Medved, 2016); but also that couples easily revert to previous arrangements as soon as contextual conditions allow (Sánchez-Mira, 2024). In contrast, given that the dual employed model is increasingly seen as a more economically safe and viable form of couples' paid work arrangement (Sánchez-Mira, 2024), recurring economic crises, which are linked to perceptions of growing labour market insecurity, are likely to reinforce trends towards the dual full-time model.

Indeed, in line with the existing literature (Leonce, 2020), our findings confirm that households with two incomes are generally financially safer than those relying on one income, and that households with both partners in full-time employment are clearly the most financially resilient, likely reflecting the combined effects of income quantity, employment security, and in some cases, institutional support. Comparatively, over time the male main employed arrangement appears to have become less financially sustainable and this has become even more the case for male-only employed arrangements. Indeed, as financial hardship for female-only employed couple models has declined from a previous higher level, financial vulnerability is now more associated with being in a household with only one earner, whether male or female. These changes may account for some of the trend towards dual full-time employment couples, but given that levels of financial hardship vary significantly across countries, the importance of this driver is also likely to differ between contexts.

Regarding the countries' trajectories, despite a common trend of convergence towards the dual full-time model, key differences persist. Poland was the only country not to experience notable short-term changes in couples' paid work arrangements during the examined crises. Overall, the country has consolidated its position as a representative of the dual-earner full-time cluster, consistent with a low-wages model where both incomes are necessary for households. The other three all experienced some decline in dual full-time arrangements during recent crises but, except for the latest trend observed in Germany, there was no generalised reversion to more male full-time led arrangements. Instead, there was a temporary shift to even more insecure arrangements, including female main or only employed households. Across the period as a whole, Sweden, while still representing the dual-earner mixed cluster, also followed the general trend towards more dual full-time employed and fewer male full-time main employed households. Germany departed from a predominant one-and-a-half arrangement and now fits even more clearly in the multiple modes cluster: its share of dual full-time employed couples is converging towards the European average but alongside a simultaneous and apparently inconsistent rise in male full-time only employed households, particularly after the Covid-19 crisis, suggesting an uncertain future trajectory for the country. Finally, Spain, up until recently a clear representative of the polarised cluster, is also converging towards the European trend as dual full-time employed arrangements increased while male only full-time employed arrangements showed a steady decline.

In sum, while both the 2008 recession and the Covid-19 crises influenced couples' paid work arrangements, these did not reverse the pre-existing long-term trends towards a rising share of dual full-time employed households and a parallel decline in male full-time only households. If anything, the waves of crises may have reinforced these trends though more clearly in some countries than in others. How far these changes will be long lasting is not yet known but as turbulence persists, we need to continue to research how the emergent and shifting patterns of inequality and vulnerability within and across European households may act as driving forces or setbacks towards the consolidation of dual full-time earning in Europe.

By tracing how recurring crises interact with long-term shifts in gendered labour market dynamics, this chapter advances the volume's broader aim of understanding how structural inequalities are both reinforced and reshaped during turbulent times, highlighting the role of household paid work arrangements as a key lens into the evolving contours of socio-economic vulnerability and resilience.

References

Alon, T., Coskun, S., Doepke, M., Koll, D., & Tertilt, M. (2022). From mancession to shecession: Women's employment in regular and pandemic recessions. *NBER Macroeconomics Annual*, *36*(1), 83–151. https://doi.org/10.1086/718660

Alon, T., Doepke, M., Olmstead-Rumsey, J., & Tertilt, M. (2020). This time it's different: The role of women's employment in a pandemic recession. *IZA Discussion Papers*, *13562*. https://doi.org/10.3386/w27660

Audretsch, D. B., & Lehmann, E. (2016). *The seven secrets of Germany: Economic resilience in an era of global turbulence*. Oxford University Press. https://doi.org/10.1093/acprof:oso/9780190258696.001.0001

Bengali, L., & Duzhak, E. A. (2024). How do periods of inflation, recession affect real earnings? *FRBSF Economic Letter*, *2024*(09). https://www.frbsf.org/research-and-insights/publications/economic-letter/2024/04/how-do-periods-of-inflation-recession-affect-real-earnings/

Bergqvist, C. (2015). The welfare state and gender equality. In J. Pierre (Ed.), *The Oxford handbook of Swedish politics* (pp. 55–68). https://doi.org/10.1093/oxfordhb/9780199665679.013.3

Blanton, R., Blanton, S., & Peksen, D. (2019). The gendered consequences of financial crises: A cross-national analysis. *Politics & Gender*, *15*(4). https://doi.org/10.1017/S1743923X18000545

Bluedorn, J., Caselli, F. G., Hansen, M. N.-J. H., Shibata, M. I., & Tavares, M. M. M. (2021). Gender and employment in the COVID-19 recession: Evidence on "She-cessions". *International Monetary Fund Working Papers*, *21*(95). https://doi.org/10.5089/9781513575926.001

Brewster, K. L., & Padavic, I. (2000). Change in gender-ideology, 1977–1996: The contributions of intracohort change and population turnover. *Journal of Marriage and Family*, *62*(2), 477–487. https://doi.org/10.1111/j.1741-3737.2000.00477.x

Brini, E., Lenko, M., Scherer, S., & Vitali, A. (2021). Retraditionalisation? Work patterns of families with children during the pandemic in Italy. *Demographic Research*, *45*, 957–972. https://doi.org/10.4054/DemRes.2021.45.31

Cipollone, A., Patacchini, E., & Vallanti, G. (2014). Female labour market participation in Europe: Novel evidence on trends and shaping factors. *IZA Journal of European Labor Studies*, *3*, 1–40. https://doi.org/10.1186/2193-9012-3-18

Collins, C., Landivar, L. C., Ruppanner, L., & Scarborough, W. J. (2021). COVID-19 and the gender gap in work hours. *Gender, Work & Organization*, *28*, 101–112. https://doi.org/10.1111/gwao.12506

Cunningham, M. (2008). Changing attitudes toward the male breadwinner, female homemaker family model: Influences of women's employment and education over the lifecourse. *Social Forces*, *87*(1), 299–323. https://doi.org/10.1353/sof.0.0097

Davis, S. J., & Von Wachter, T. M. (2011). Recessions and the cost of job loss. *NBER Working Paper Series*, *17638*. https://doi.org/10.3386/w17638

De Hauw, Y., Grow, A., & Van Bavel, J. (2017). The reversed gender gap in education and assortative mating in Europe. *European Journal of Population*, *33*, 445–474. https://doi.org/10.1007/s10680-016-9407-z

Dieckhoff, M., Gash, V., Mertens, A., & Gordo, L. R. (2016). A stalled revolution? What can we learn from women's drop-out to part-time jobs: A comparative analysis of Germany and the UK. *Research in Social Stratification and Mobility*, *46*, 129–140. https://doi.org/10.1016/j.rssm.2016.09.001

Dotti Sani, G. M. (2018). The economic crisis and changes in work–family arrangements in six European countries. *Journal of European Social Policy*, *28*(2), 177–193. https://doi.org/10.1177/0958928717700566

England, P. (2010). The gender revolution: Uneven and stalled. *Gender & Society*, *24*(2), 149–166. https://doi.org/10.1177/0891243210361475

England, P., Gornick, J., & Shafer, E. F. (2012). Women's employment, education, and the gender gap in 17 countries. *Monthly Labor Review*, *135*(4), 1–15. https://www.bls.gov/opub/mlr/2012/04/art1full.pdf

Eurostat. (n.d.). *Income and living conditions* [Dataset]. https://ec.europa.eu/eurostat/web/income-and-living-conditions/overview

Goldscheider, F., Bernhardt, E., & Brandén, M. (2013). Domestic gender equality and childbearing in Sweden. *Demographic Research*, *29*, 1097–1126. https://doi.org/10.4054/DemRes.2013.29.40

Gorbachev, O. (2016). Has the increased attachment of women to the labor market changed a family's ability to smooth income shocks? *American Economic Review*, *106*(5), 247–251. https://doi.org/10.1257/aer.p20161119

Hook, J. L. (2015). Incorporating "class" into work-family arrangements: Insights from and for three worlds. *Journal of European Social Policy*, *25*(1), 14–31. https://doi.org/10.1177/0958928714556968

Hook, J. L., & Paek, E. (2020). A stalled revolution? Change in women's labor force participation during child-rearing years, Europe and the United States 1996–2016. *Population and Development Review*, *46*(4), 677–708. https://doi.org/10.1111/padr.12364

Horemans, J. (2018). Atypical employment and in-work poverty. In *Handbook on in-work poverty* (pp. 146–170). Edward Elgar Publishing. https://doi.org/10.4337/9781784715632.00015

International Labour Organization. (2012). *World of work report 2012: Better jobs for a better economy*. International Labour Office. https://doi.org/10.1002/wow3.7

Insarauto, V. (2021). Women's vulnerability to the economic crisis through the lens of part-time work in Spain. *Work, Employment and Society*, *35*(4), 621–639. https://doi.org/10.1177/09500170211001271

Karamessini, M., & Rubery, J. (2014). The challenge of austerity for equality: A consideration of eight European countries in the crisis. *Revue de l'OFCE*, *133*(2), 15–39. https://doi.org/10.3917/reof.133.0015

Klesment, M., & Van Bavel, J. (2017). The reversal of the gender gap in education, motherhood, and women as main earners in Europe. *European Sociological Review*, *33*(3), 465–481. https://doi.org/10.1093/esr/jcw063

Kowalewska, H., & Vitali, A. (2021). Breadwinning or on the breadline? Female breadwinners' economic characteristics across 20 welfare states. *Journal of European Social Policy*, *31*(2), 125–142. https://doi.org/10.1177/0958928720971094

Leonce, T. E. (2020). The inevitable rise in dual-income households and the intertemporal effects on labor markets. *Compensation & Benefits Review*, *52*(2), 64–76. https://doi.org/10.1177/0886368719900032

Matysiak, A., & Vignoli, D. (2024). Family life courses, uncertain futures, and the changing world of work: State-of-the-art and prospects. *European Journal of Population*, *40*(1), 19. https://doi.org/10.1007/s10680-024-09701-x

Medved, C. E. (2016). The new female breadwinner: Discursively doing and undoing gender relations. *Journal of Applied Communication Research*, *44*(3), 236–255. https://doi.org/10.1080/00909882.2016.1192286

Organisation for Economic Co-operation and Development. (2015). *In it together: Why less inequality benefits all*. OECD Publishing. https://doi.org/10.1787/9789264235120-en

Organisation for Economic Co-operation and Development. (2021). *OECD employment database*. https://www.oecd.org/en/topics/employment.html

Paugam, G. (2024). The end of polarization? Evolutions of the distribution of employment across couples in Europe over the past 40 years. *Socio-Economic Review*. https://doi.org/10.1093/ser/mwae031

Périvier, H. (2018). Recession, austerity and gender: A comparison of eight European labour markets. *International Labour Review*, *157*(1), 1–37. https://doi.org/10.1111/ilr.12032

Plomien, A., & Schwartz, G. (2026). The crisis of social reproduction provisioning: Gender, class and migration in Poland and Ukraine. In J. Rubery, N. Sánchez-Mira, & V. Insarauto (Eds.), *Women in turbulent times. Crises, transitions, and challenges for gender equality* (pp. 162–183). Routledge.

Qian, Y., & Hu, Y. (2021). Couples' changing work patterns in the United Kingdom and the United States during the COVID-19 pandemic. *Gender, Work & Organization*, *28*, 535–553. https://doi.org/10.1111/gwao.12661

Rubery, J. (Ed.). (1988). *Women and recession*. Routledge.

Rubery, J., & Tavora, I. (2020). The Covid-19 crisis and gender equality: Risks and opportunities. In B. Vanhercke, S. Spasova, & B. Fronteddu (Eds.) *Social policy in the European Union: State of play 2020* (pp. 71–96). Etui.

Sánchez-Mira, N. (2020). Work–family arrangements and the crisis in Spain: Balkanized gender contracts? *Gender, Work & Organization*, *27*(6), 944–970. https://doi.org/10.1111/gwao.12417

Sánchez-Mira, N. (2024). (Un)doing gender in female breadwinner households: Gender relations and structural change. *Gender, Work & Organization*, *31*(4), 1196–1213. https://doi.org/10.1111/gwao.12775

Sánchez-Mira, N., & O'Reilly, J. (2019). Household employment and the crisis in Europe. *Work, Employment and Society*, *33*(3), 422–443. https://doi.org/10.1177/0950017018809324

Tavora, I., & Rubery, J. (2013). Female employment, labour market institutions and gender culture in Portugal. *European Journal of Industrial Relations*, *19*(3), 221–237. https://doi.org/10.1177/0959680113493374

Trappe, H., Pollmann-Schult, M., & Schmitt, C. (2015). The rise and decline of the male breadwinner model: Institutional underpinnings and future expectations. *European Sociological Review*, *31*(2), 230–242. https://doi.org/10.1093/esr/jcv015

Vitali, A., & Arpino, B. (2016). Who brings home the bacon? The influence of context on partners' contributions to the household income. *Demographic Research*, *35*, 1213–1244. https://doi.org/10.4054/DemRes.2016.35.41

7

COVID-19 AND GENDER GAPS IN PAID AND UNPAID WORK

Janeen Baxter, Alice Campbell, Rennie Lee and Madison Lloyd

Introduction

Considerable attention has been placed on the impact of Covid-19 on gender inequalities, especially on paid and unpaid work (Collins et al., 2021; Craig & Churchill, 2020; Farré et al., 2022; Hupkau & Petrongolo, 2020; Kabeer et al., 2021; Lyttelton et al., 2021). In many countries, including Australia, there is evidence that gender inequality worsened during Covid-19 as women left paid employment to care for family members and assumed a greater share of unpaid work (Baxter et al., 2023; Craig & Churchill, 2020; Ruppanner et al., 2021). But the trends vary across countries, implying the need for careful consideration of contextual and institutional settings and caution about generalising about trends across countries, as illustrated throughout this volume.

Additionally, trends vary across different indicators of gender inequality. For example, most studies find that women shouldered the bulk of additional care work associated with school lockdowns, the provision of support for children's schoolwork, and caring for sick family members and relatives during Covid-19 (Baxter, 2021; Collins et al., 2021; Derndorfer et al., 2021). But there is also evidence that arrangements varied depending on whether the outcome under investigation was routine domestic tasks or childcare (Baxter et al., 2023; Derndorfer et al., 2021; Farré et al., 2022). Some find that lockdowns were associated with increased time spent by men caring for children but no increase in their time on domestic work (Craig & Churchill, 2020). Results indicate women spent a little more time on domestic work during Covid-19 but a lot more time on childcare (Baxter et al., 2023; Craig & Churchill, 2020). Even if men did increase their time on unpaid work, the gender gap in unpaid work may not have narrowed if women also increased their time by a similar, or possibly greater amount (Craig &

DOI: 10.4324/9781003528210-10

Churchill, 2020; Derndorfer et al., 2021). And although some studies report that women were more likely than men to experience reduced paid work hours from job losses, women in health and care occupations, such as nurses and aged care workers, experienced increased demand for employment and consequently, longer paid work hours (Wood et al., 2021; Doleman et al., 2023).

Against this background, this chapter aims to understand the short and long-term impacts of the Covid-19 pandemic on the gender division of labour in Australia. Using longitudinal data from a high-quality national household panel survey, the Household, Income and Labour Dynamics in Australia (HILDA) survey, we examine changes over time in gender gaps in paid and unpaid work, and within unpaid work (differentiating between care and routine domestic work) for mothers and fathers in Australia before, during and after the pandemic. We consider long-term trends, average trends for the country over the period of the pandemic and specific comparisons of locations where the intensity and length of pandemic lockdowns varied. Our focus is on Australia, a country with unique institutional features related to gender inequality and economic stability, which we outline in more detail in the next section.

Gender inequality in Australia

Australia is a wealthy, liberal welfare country with high living standards, universal health care, relatively low unemployment and a system of government-funded welfare safety nets (Baxter et al., 2022). Yet, gender inequality remains a critical social issue, despite areas of progress over the last few decades. Australia has a high number of women in part-time and casual employment compared to other countries, a persistent gender gap in wages, increasing rates and severity of domestic violence and a strong male breadwinner model (Australian Institute of Health and Welfare [AIHW], 2024; Baxter, 2023). This traditional gendered model continues despite increasing numbers of women entering and remaining in the labour market throughout their childbearing years, an increased focus by governments on workplace policies designed to ease the burden of work and family responsibilities and a greater proportion of women graduating with Bachelor's degrees compared to men.

Just over half of Australian families report that the main person looking after children was a woman and Australian mothers are overrepresented in the part-time/casual workforce (Baxter, 2024; OECD, 2023). Although 40% of families report equal sharing of childcare tasks, when asked "who plans/coordinates child activities" 78% of families report it was usually or always a woman (Baxter, 2024). Australian women tend to be employed full-time prior to having children, but then move to part-time employment throughout the childbearing and child-rearing years. And while there has been some progress in reducing the male breadwinner model of men as the primary family earner and women the primary caregiver, it remains the most common family-earnings arrangement in the country (Steinbring et al., 2023). In 2021, 31% of couple families had two parents working full-time compared with only 22% in 2009, indicating some changes within families (Baxter, 2023). Overall though, the most common arrangement is for one parent to be employed full-time, usually fathers, and another to be part-time, usually mothers.

Supporting women's equal access to and engagement with employment has been the key focus of most Australian policies designed to reduce gender inequality with the expectation that changes made here will flow on to greater gender equality in domestic and care tasks at home. The Australian government has introduced a number of policies designed to encourage women to remain attached to the labour market. For example, universal paid parental leave was introduced only in 2011, providing 18 weeks of paid leave at the rate of the national minimum wage to eligible primary carers, usually birth mothers. A specific Dad and Partner Pay leave (paternity leave) was introduced in 2013, providing up to two weeks' pay at the rate of the national minimum wage. Overall, the length and average payment rate of parental leave offered to Australian parents remains significantly lower than those of other OECD countries (OECD, 2024). This becomes evident when looking at full-rate equivalents, which consider both the length and payment rate and thus enable a more accurate comparison of the generosity of the leave across countries. Comparing full-rate equivalents of total paid leave available to mothers (including both maternity leave and parental leave), the 8.3 weeks offered in Australia were only higher than the 7.8 weeks of Ireland and Switzerland, and about a fourth of the 34.4 weeks available to women in Sweden (OECD, 2024). In 2023 the Australian government announced that paid parental leave would increase to 26 weeks from 2026, with 4 weeks reserved for the second parent, usually the father, which must be used or lost (Department of Social Services, 2024). Although an improvement on the original programme, the length of leave for new Australian parents is still much shorter than that of their OECD counterparts.

The provision of affordable quality childcare has long been a central plank of Australian feminist strategies for gender equality (Brennan, 2010). Childcare has been on the policy agenda in Australia since 1972 when then Prime Minister, Gough Whitlam, introduced the Child Care Act providing grants to non-profit agencies to provide childcare facilities. Since this time, Australian feminists have lobbied strongly for improving access to quality affordable childcare as key to enabling women's access to employment and improving gender equality. Australian governments have supported the affordability of childcare through a number of subsidies and benefits since the 1970s (Leahy, 2019). In 2018, the Child Care Subsidy was introduced, a means-tested payment paid directly to childcare providers and provided to families as a fee reduction (Klapdor, 2021). The subsidy varied from a maximum of 85% of the actual fee charged for families with a combined annual adjusted income of $AUD 69,390 or less, down to 20% for those with an income of $AUD 353,680 or below, and no subsidy for those with higher income (Klapdor, 2021). In 2023, the government increased the subsidy to 90% for the lowest income group (Clare & Grace, 2023). Alongside the Child Care Subsidy, the Additional Child Care Subsidy was introduced to provide extra help for families in hardship (Services Australia, 2021). This subsidy usually covers all early childhood education and care fees. Nonetheless, childcare in Australia is underfunded, and Australia does not provide universal childcare, and comparatively among OECD countries, only the Netherlands and Switzerland have higher gross childcare costs as a share of the average earnings (OECD, 2022). Consequently, inadequate and expensive childcare costs may deter families from enrolment and hold back women's employment (Grundoff, 2022).

As we will show later in this chapter, progress toward gender inequality in unpaid domestic and care tasks at home is at best slow and at worst stagnant. The gender division of labour in unpaid care and routine domestic tasks continues in Australia, as in most countries, with women undertaking the majority of this work (Altintas & Sullivan, 2016; Baxter et al., 2008; Churchill et al., 2023). For instance, the most recent data for Australia based on time use diaries indicates that women spend 4.13 hours per day on unpaid domestic and care work compared to men's 2.14 hours (Australian Bureau of Statistics [ABS], 2023).

Moreover, when change in the allocation of time to unpaid domestic and care work is observed, it is primarily due to variations in women's time rather than men's greater involvement in unpaid work. For example, Australian women's housework time increases by about six hours per week after the birth of a first child, but there is no change in men's hours on average after becoming a parent (Baxter et al., 2008). Baxter et al. (2010) and Stratton (2023) show that marital status also influences time on housework and the level of gender specialisation of tasks at home, with Australian cohabiting couples showing less gender specialisation and smaller gender gaps in unpaid hours than married couples, although gender inequality widens if they subsequently transition to marriage. The patterns observed in Australia are similar to those reported in many Western countries. Although there is some evidence of convergence over time in gender gaps in unpaid work time, there is still variation in the size of the gender gap across countries and welfare regimes, and the pace and amount of change is slow and uneven (Altintas & Sullivan, 2016; Hagqvist, 2018; Treas & Drobnič, 2010). Overall, a lack of universal and affordable childcare, limited parental leave and limited workplace opportunities for men's adjustments in employment all contribute to highly gendered childcare and housework tasks in Australia.

Pandemic effects on the gendered divison of labour: early findings

The Covid-19 pandemic had a profound impact on social and economic life in Australia and around the world. At the height of the pandemic, Australian state and territory governments imposed strict lockdowns, travel restrictions and stay-at-home orders that closed schools and businesses, led to sudden and high levels of unemployment, increased levels of social isolation and mental health concerns and placed major burdens on families to provide education for children and increased care for dependents (Schurer et al., 2023). Melbourne, Victoria, Australia's most populous city, experienced one of the longest lockdowns in the world through the pandemic with 262 days in lockdown, with over 100 consecutive days of lockdown in 2020 (Schurer et al., 2023). While other parts of Australia were also subject to periods of lockdown, none were as long or as strict as Melbourne, especially in 2020. Nonetheless, Australia's second and third largest cities, Sydney, New South Wales, and Brisbane, Queensland, experienced 181 and 84 days of lockdown respectively (Phillips et al., 2022). These variations were in part driven by the level of coronavirus cases and exposure and in part by variations in state government politics. New South Wales and Victoria adopted strict policies including stay-at-home orders, remote learning and workplace closures for extended periods (Phillips et al., 2022). Queensland on the other hand, opted for quick targeted lockdowns.

A number of studies analysed the early effects of Covid-19 on gender inequality in Australia and other countries (Baxter et al., 2021; Craig & Churchill, 2020; Ruppanner et al., 2021; Zang et al., 2024). In general, both men and women increased their time on domestic and care work during Covid-19, but women's time increased more than men's time. This means that Covid-19 likely exacerbated the double shift for women. Nonetheless, the results vary depending on whether the focus was unpaid care or housework and the country context. Craig and Churchill (2020) found that Australian men's time on household management and housework increased by 45 minutes per day and women's by one hour per day. Ruppanner and colleagues (2021) report that men stepped up to do more housework during Covid-19 in the United States, although the increase was short-lived. Farré and colleagues (2022) reported a similar trend during the Covid-19 lockdown in Spain, though men's hours in paid work fell much more than women's (14 hours relative to 2 hours) implying their total workload during this period was lower than women's. Additionally, in Singapore, Zang and collaborators (2024) found that both fathers and mothers increased their time on housework and childcare but decreased time spent on paid work. Interestingly, after the lockdown time spent on childcare and housework decreased for mothers and increased slightly for fathers though time spent on paid work increased for both (Zang et al., 2024). Overall, the literature review suggests that the Covid-19 pandemic did not have homogeneous effects across countries, and little is still known about whether its impact has been long-lasting.

In this context, our chapter examines long-term trends in time spent in paid and unpaid work in Australia. Our time trend analyses commence in 2001, enabling a long-term assessment of within-couple gender gaps in time prior to the pandemic to enable stronger conclusions about how disruptive the pandemic might be to trends already in motion. To our knowledge, we are the first to examine within-couple gender gaps in paid and unpaid work before, during and after the pandemic. We also drill down more closely to compare gender gaps in paid and unpaid work time in cities where the lockdown rules varied. This enables a more fine-grained examination of the effects of lockdowns, an unprecedented period of time in Australian history where paid and unpaid work routines were greatly disrupted and a period where, potentially, gendered rules and norms about time availability, resources and parenting norms were severely upended.

Data and methods

In this chapter, we analyse data from the first 22 waves of the Household, Income and Labour Dynamics in Australia (HILDA) Survey (2001–2022). The HILDA Survey is Australia's national household panel study. Commencing in 2001, data have been collected annually from approximately 17,000 individuals via interviews and self-completed questionnaires. The sample is largely representative of the Australian population aged 15 years and older thanks to its complex, probabilistic sampling design (Summerfield et al., 2016).

The transition to parenthood is a pivotal turning point in many women's lives and a trigger for persistent gender inequalities in unpaid domestic labour and care (Baxter et al., 2023). We therefore restricted our analyses to heterosexual (i.e., female-male) couples with at least one child who is aged under 15 or still a dependent student. Across the 22 waves of data, our analytic sample comprised 38,382 observations from 5,559 couples. Between 1,406 and 2,036 couples were observed in each wave. The mean age of mothers across observations in our sample was 39.3 years (SD = 8.5) and the mean age of fathers was 41.8 years (SD = 9.3). Most mothers (68.4%) and fathers (59.5%) were aged between 25 and 44 years, while 27.9% of mothers and 37.4% of fathers were aged 45 years or older. Only 3.6% of mothers and 2.1% of fathers were aged under 25 years.

Our two outcome variables were the within-couple gender gap in hours per week spent in (1) paid work and (2) unpaid work. Unpaid work included time spent caring for one's own children, other children, or a frail/disabled relative and time spent on housework, household errands and outdoor household tasks, but in supplementary analyses we separated the two types of unpaid work. To create the gender gap variables, we subtracted the male partner's hours per week from the female partner's hours per week. A positive value indicates more time spent by the female than the male on that task, while a negative value indicates the opposite. A value of 0 indicates no gender gap. Therefore, the closer a value is to zero – whether positive or negative – the smaller the gender gap.

We conducted two sets of analyses to address our research aims. Our first set of analyses aimed to assess the broad impact of the Covid-19 pandemic (as opposed to Covid-19 lockdowns more specifically) on gender inequalities in paid and unpaid work across Australia. To achieve this, we conducted interrupted time series analyses of the within-couple gender gaps in paid and unpaid work using Ordinary Least Squares regression. As we were using an unbalanced panel (i.e., not all couples were present in every wave), we estimated our interrupted time series analyses at the aggregated level (i.e., using the means for each year).

Our second set of analyses aimed to assess the specific impact of Covid-19 lockdowns on within-couple gender inequalities in paid and unpaid work. To achieve this, we estimated difference-in-differences models. For these models, we built on the approach that we have used previously (Baxter et al., 2023) and compared patterns across Australia's three largest cities: Sydney, Melbourne and Brisbane. As previously described in this chapter, residents of Melbourne and Sydney were exposed to the "treatment" of strict, months-long lockdowns, among the harshest in Australia and indeed the world: Melbourne in 2020 and 2021, and Sydney in 2021. In both years, lockdowns spanned July to October, which is when the HILDA Survey was in the field. Residents in Brisbane acted as the control group. While Brisbane did experience lockdowns, these were relatively brief and nothing near the duration of the aforementioned Sydney and Melbourne lockdowns. Brisbane was in lockdown from 29 July to 8 August 2021, a period of 11 days.

The results presented in this chapter are based on unadjusted models, as our primary interest lies in the associations between time period (year; pre-Covid-19 versus post-Covid-19) and average gender gaps in paid and unpaid work. We deliberately exclude potential covariates to avoid distorting these associations. Variables such as the number of children, mothers' and fathers' educational attainment and age are not confounders in this context, as they cannot temporally precede or cause the passage of time, the onset of the Covid-19 pandemic or the implementation of lockdowns. As such, adjusting for these variables would not address bias, but rather risk obscuring the trends that we aim to document. Their exclusion allows us to more accurately capture the total observed change in gendered divisions of labour over time.

Findings: gender gaps in paid and unpaid work over two decades in Australia

Paid work

Figure 7.1 shows the results of the interrupted time series analysis of the within-couple gender gap in time spent in paid work (see also Table A7-1 on the online appendix). The within-couple gender gap is plotted on the y-axis, with values ranging from −25 (mothers spending 25 hours/week *less* in paid work than fathers) to zero (no within-couple gender gap). A closing gender gap is represented by an upward sloping line. The dots in the figure show the mean gender gap in paid work for each year (observed values), and the regression lines show the predicted values. Separate regression lines are fitted for the periods before and after the onset of the pandemic, which is represented by the dashed line at year 2020. The interrupted time series analysis involves testing (1) differences in the slopes of the two regression lines (i.e., rates of change in the gender gap pre- and post-2020), and (2) differences between the gender gap observed immediately following the onset of the pandemic (2020) versus the predicted value for that year based on pre-pandemic trends.

As Figure 7.1 shows, between 2001 and 2019 the gender gap was closing slowly at a linear rate of approximately 0.31 hours/week each year. In 2001, the average within-couple gap was around −24.5 hours/week. In other words, mothers in heterosexual partnerships spent approximately 24.5 fewer hours each week in paid employment compared to their male partners. This gap closed by almost one hour every three years such that by 2019, mothers spent approximately 18.3 fewer hours each week in paid employment compared to their male partners.

The interrupted time series analyses allowed us to compare the observed within-couple gender gap in paid work during the first year of the pandemic (2020) to the expected gap based on the pre-pandemic trends just described. We found a significant difference between the expected and observed gap for 2020 in the order of 2.8 hours. Based on the previous trend, we expected a gender gap of approximately −18.6 hours/week. Instead, the observed gap was approximately −15.8 hours/week. As such, the Covid-19 pandemic appears to have had an immediate effect of narrowing the gender gap in paid work within heterosexual couples with children. Following this initial bump, the closing of the gap continued at a slower rate than it had prior to the pandemic. As outlined above, the within-couple gender gap in paid work was closing at the rate of 0.31 hours/week each year pre-Covid-19. Between 2020 and 2022, after Covid-19 had struck, the within-couple gender gap in paid work closed at a slower rate of 0.24 hours/week each year.

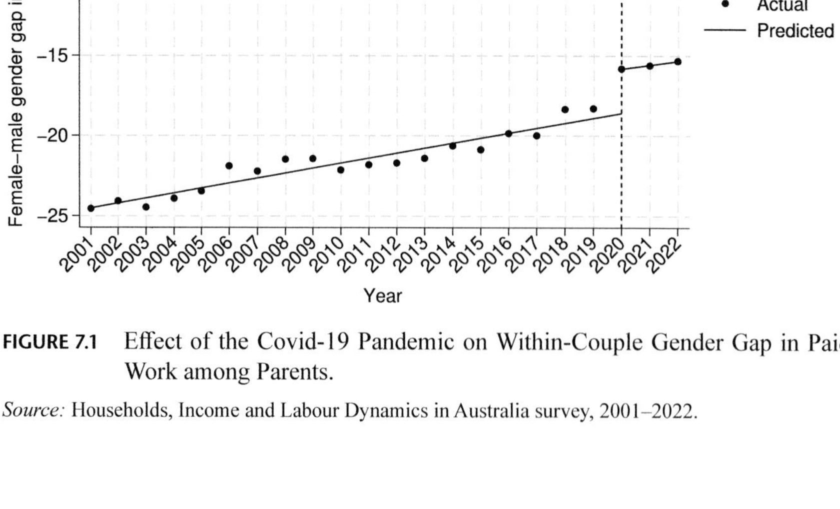

FIGURE 7.1 Effect of the Covid-19 Pandemic on Within-Couple Gender Gap in Paid Work among Parents.

Source: Households, Income and Labour Dynamics in Australia survey, 2001–2022.

Two factors could be driving changes in the gender gap in paid work: (1) changes in the proportions of mothers and/or fathers in paid work (workforce participation), and (2) changes in the number of hours worked by those in paid work (intensity of participation). We conducted descriptive analyses of mothers' and fathers' workforce participation and intensity of participation to investigate this. The first panel of Figure 7.2 shows the proportion of partnered mothers and fathers in paid work from 2001 to 2022. Both the lines for men and women show an upward trend prior to the pandemic and since around the mid-2010s, after a notable decline, possibly due to the financial recession, more pronounced for men than for women. Although Australia did not experience a large economic downturn during the financial crisis compared to other countries, the pace of economic growth did slow significantly, the unemployment rate rose sharply and there was a period of heightened uncertainty (Reserve Bank of Australia n.d.). The onset of the Covid-19 pandemic was accompanied by a small decrease in the proportion of fathers in paid work, from 93.2% in 2019 to 90.9% in 2020; the proportion of mothers in paid work increased slightly during this time from 74.4% in 2019 to 75.6% in 2020. Importantly, this does not necessarily mean that fathers were more likely than mothers to lose their job during the pandemic (although it could). Instead, our results might suggest that the flow of mothers leaving the workforce was more than compensated for by the flow of mothers (re)entering the workforce – something that prior research, to our knowledge, has not investigated in the Australian context. Approximately one in four partnered mothers in Australia were not engaged in paid work prior to the onset of the pandemic. Perhaps some of these women were prompted to (re)enter the workforce by a partner's job loss, the promise of telecommuting, or new employment opportunities that emerged during the pandemic in industries such as Social Assistance Services (Gilfillan, 2022). This is only speculation on our behalf, and further research is needed to investigate this.

The second panel of Figure 7.2 shows the intensity of workforce participation among mothers and fathers in paid work as measured by hours of work each week. Over the whole period, we observe a steady decline in men's paid work hours, along with a parallel increase in women's, although both lines are still far from converging. In the first year of the pandemic, the mean hours/week worked by fathers continued to decrease slightly, from 43.9 hours/week in 2019 to 42.7 hours/week in 2020. However, no such change was apparent in the mean paid working hours of partnered mothers, which was 30.4 hours/week in 2019 and 30.4 hours/week in 2020. Again, this does not necessarily mean that fathers were more likely than mothers to have their working hours reduced during the pandemic (although it could). Further, our findings might indicate that, while some mothers experienced reduced working hours, other mothers increased their working hours. Research from the UK found that partners' job loss was associated with increased working hours among employed mothers during the 2008-09 recession (Harkness & Evans, 2011). In some respects, it is easier for mothers than fathers to respond

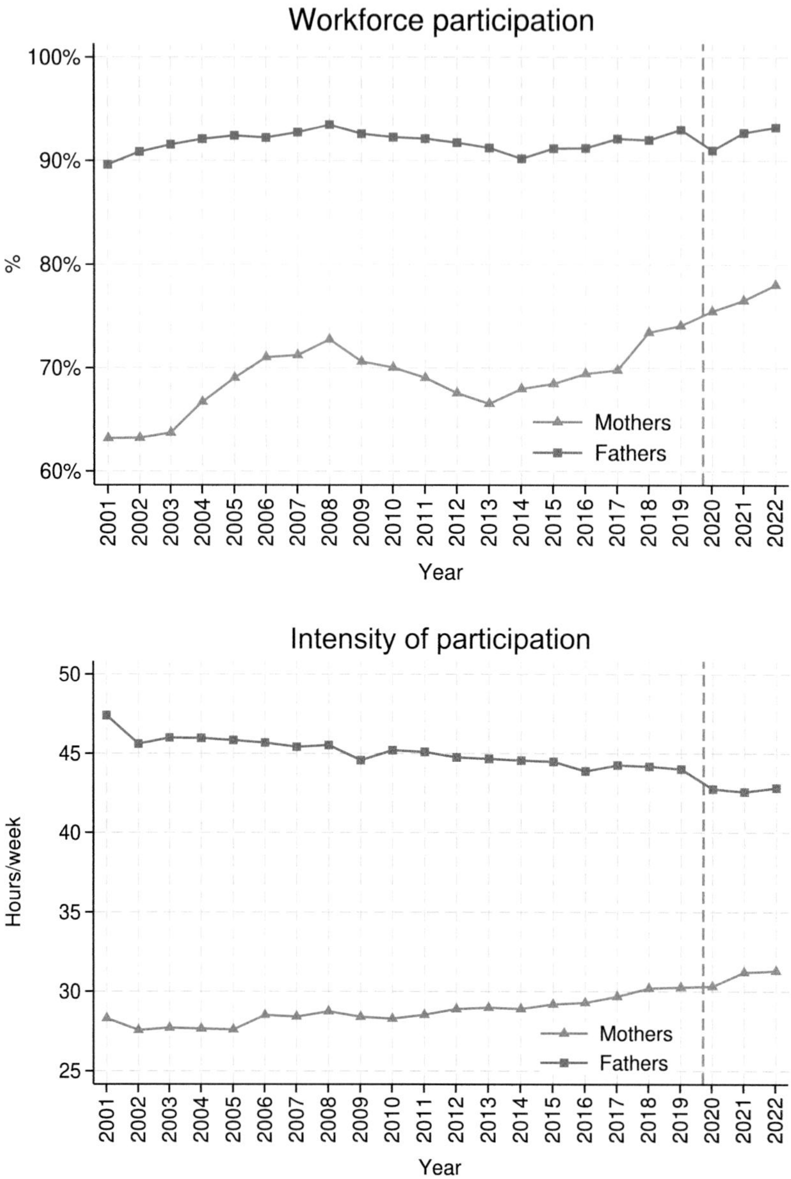

FIGURE 7.2 Gendered Trends in Parental Workforce Participation and Intensity of Participation, before and during the Covid-19 Pandemic.

Source: Households, Income and Labour Dynamics in Australia survey, 2001–2022.

to a partner's job loss in this way as they are less likely than men to already be working full time. Another explanation could be that mothers were more likely to increase their hours of paid work due to the increased demands on workers in female-dominated professions such as nursing during this time (Doleman & Bloxsome, 2023). Again, further research is needed to investigate these potential explanations.

In terms of post-pandemic trends, Figure 7.2 shows that the 2020 decrease in workforce participation among partnered fathers was a temporary phenomenon, with participation returning to pre-pandemic levels by 2022. In keeping with pre-pandemic trends, the workforce participation of mothers continued to increase post-2020, reaching a 21-year high of 78.4% in 2022. In terms of intensity of participation, hours of paid work continued to increase among mothers in 2021 and 2022, while the small decrease among fathers persisted. In 2022, partnered fathers spent on average 42.8 hours/week in paid work, compared to the 2019 average of 43.9 hours/week. The pandemic may have had lingering impacts on the way some men opt to balance paid work with other aspects of their lives, but it remains to be seen whether these effects will be long-lasting.

Unpaid work

Figure 7.3 shows the results of the interrupted time series analysis of the within-couple gender gap in time spent in unpaid work (see also Table A7-2 on the online appendix). The within-couple gender gap is plotted on the y-axis, with values in this figure ranging from zero (no gender gap) to 30 (mothers spending 30 hours/week *more* in paid work than fathers). Thus, in Figure 7.3, a closing gender gap is represented by a downward sloping line. As Figure 7.3 shows, between 2001 and 2019 the gender gap was closing slowly at a linear rate of approximately 0.26 hours/week each year. In 2001, the average within-couple gap was around 27.5 hours/week. In other words, mothers in heterosexual partnerships spent approximately 27.5 more hours each week on unpaid work compared to their male partners. From 2001 to 2019, this gap closed by approximately one hour every four years.

The results of the interrupted time series analysis of the within-couple gender gap in unpaid work indicate a significant difference between the expected and observed values for 2020 of approximately 3.3 hours. Based on pre-2020 trends, we expected a within-couple gender gap of approximately 24.2 hours, whereas we observed a significantly smaller gap of 20.9 hours. However, it should be noted that the observed gender gap for 2019 also deviated from its predicted value by approximately 2.2 hours (22.2 vs. 24.4). In other words, the gender gap in unpaid work was also smaller than expected in the year prior to the onset of the pandemic. The gender gap in unpaid work continued to close post-2020, at a faster rate than it had prior to the onset of the pandemic (−0.61 hours/week as opposed to −.26 hours/week).

In supplementary analyses, we estimated separate models for unpaid care and unpaid domestic work. The results of these analyses are shown in Tables A7-3 and A7-4 on the online appendix. We found a significant decrease in the gender gap in time spent on unpaid care in 2020 compared to what would have been expected

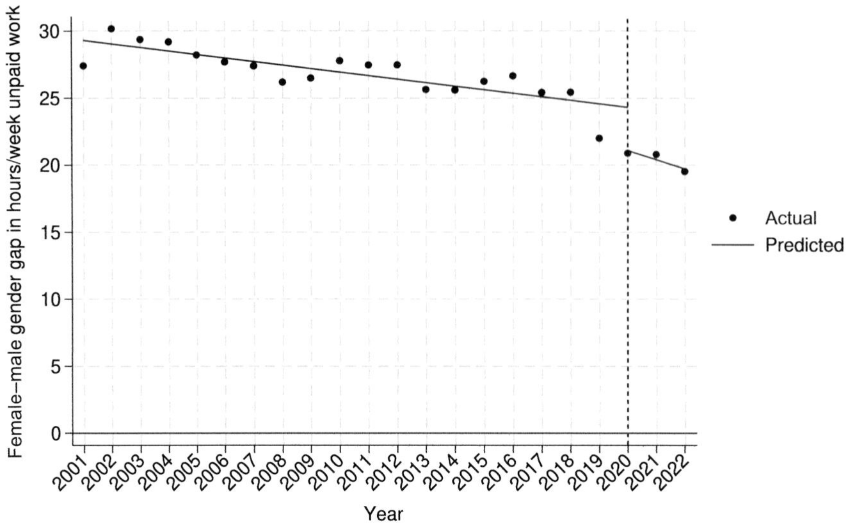

FIGURE 7.3 Effect of the Covid-19 Pandemic on Within-Couple Gender Gap in Unpaid Work among Parents.

Source: Households, Income and Labour Dynamics in Australia survey, 2001–2022.

based on pre-pandemic trends. The magnitude of this decrease was just over two hours per week. There was also a significant change in the gender gap in time spent on unpaid domestic work, albeit somewhat smaller at approximately one hour per week. This suggests that the results observed in Figure 7.3 are due to a narrowing of the gender gaps in both in unpaid care and unpaid domestic work.

The findings displayed in Figure 7.3 do not tell us anything about the amount of time women and men each spent in unpaid work across the onset of the pandemic, only the within-couple gap. To further investigate the gendered division of unpaid work, we conducted descriptive analyses of mothers' and fathers' time spent in unpaid care and domestic labour. The first panel of Figure 7.4 shows the average hours per week mothers and fathers in heterosexual couples spent doing unpaid care work for the years 2001 to 2022, while the right panel shows the same for unpaid domestic work. The most remarkable change over the whole period is the substantial and sustained decline in the time women spend in domestic labour, while there has been an imperceptible increase in men's involvement in both unpaid care and domestic labour. These trends mirror those observed internationally in several other Western countries (Sullivan et al., 2018).

However, zooming in on the pandemic, we see very little change in time spent caring or in domestic unpaid work by either fathers or mothers during the first year of the pandemic. The mean time spent by mothers in care work was 25.6 hours/week in 2019 and 25.3 hours/week in 2020. For fathers, it was 12.7 hours/week

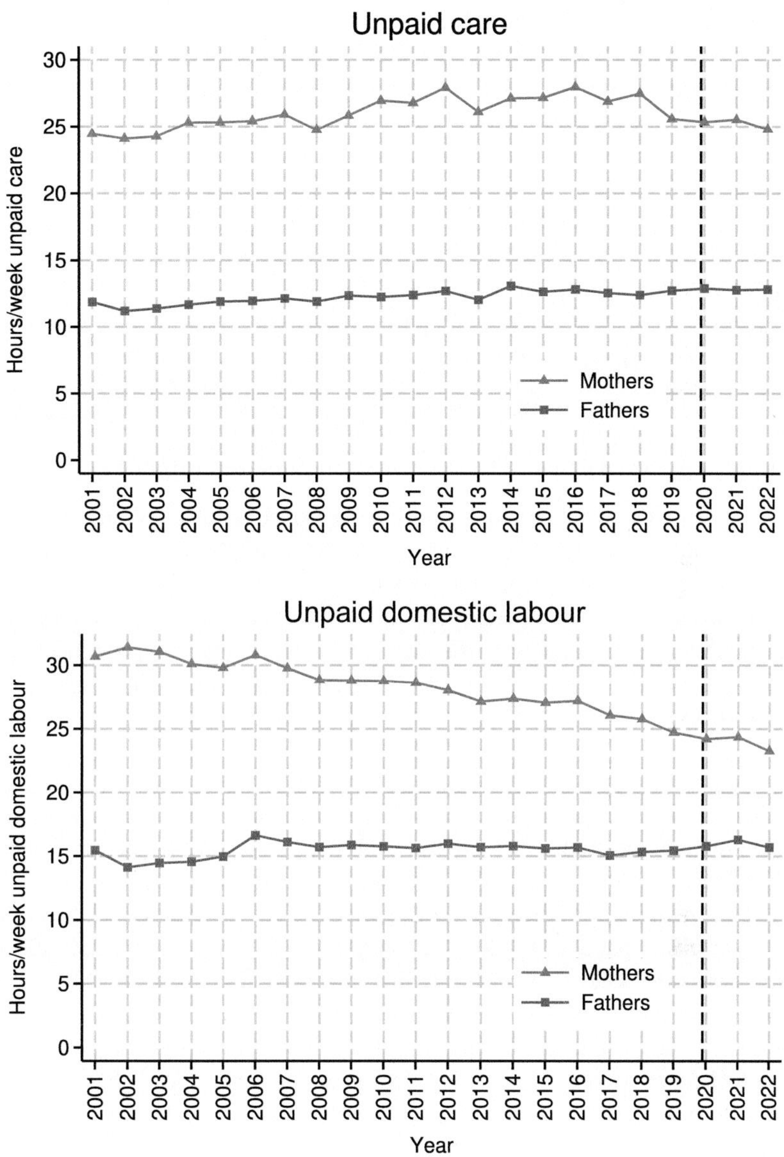

FIGURE 7.4 Gendered Trends in Unpaid Care and Domestic Labour Time before and during the Covid-19 Pandemic.

Source: Households, Income and Labour Dynamics in Australia survey, 2001–2022.

in 2019 and 12.9 hours/week in 2020, while the figures for domestic work were respectively 24.7 hours/week in 2019 and 24.2 hours/week in 2020 for mothers and 15.4 hours/week in 2019 and 15.8 hours/week in 2020 for fathers. As observed above, our analyses suggest that change over time in the allocation of unpaid work is due to longer-term trends in household arrangements rather than the impact of the pandemic specifically. But at this stage, we have only considered broad trends over the pandemic period rather than the impacts of pandemic-driven lockdowns specifically. If change in household labour allocation is to be observed, it is most likely to be evident when households were in lockdown with schools closed and women and men unable to leave the household for employment or recreation. We investigate the impacts of lockdowns using difference-in-differences models in the next section.

Findings: effects of Covid-19 lockdowns on paid and unpaid work

While the Covid-19 pandemic was a period of crisis for all Australians, the degree of interruption to people's lives varied across the nation. While residents in some cities went through extended, hard lockdowns, in other regions life carried on close to normal. This heterogeneity in experience is not well accounted for in our first set of analyses. To address this, our second set of analyses tests the specific impact of Covid-19 lockdowns on within-couple gender inequalities in paid and unpaid work.

Paid work

In our previous set of analyses, we showed that the Covid-19 pandemic had the effect of reducing the average, within-couple gender gap in time spent in paid work. The results of our difference-in-differences analysis of paid work time, visualised in the first panel of Figure 7.5, suggest that this was not a direct effect of lockdowns (see Table A7-5 on the online appendix for full results). While the gender gap in paid work does appear to have closed slightly in Melbourne in 2020 during the lockdown, it also closed slightly in Sydney and Brisbane, which were not in lockdown in 2020 at the time that data were collected. When the differences observed during lockdowns are compared to the counterfactual – that is, the differences observed in Brisbane over the same period – there is no evidence that Covid-19 lockdowns directly impacted the within-couple gender gap in paid work among parents. Impacts on paid work appear to have been felt more broadly, around the country, regardless of whether individuals were currently in a lockdown. This finding is somewhat surprising, in that the gender gap in paid work would have been driven by the pandemic's sectoral effects on employment in a gender-segregated labour market more than by situations of confinement in themselves. It is the overall share of unpaid work and its distribution that is most likely to have been affected by the latter, as we show in the next section.

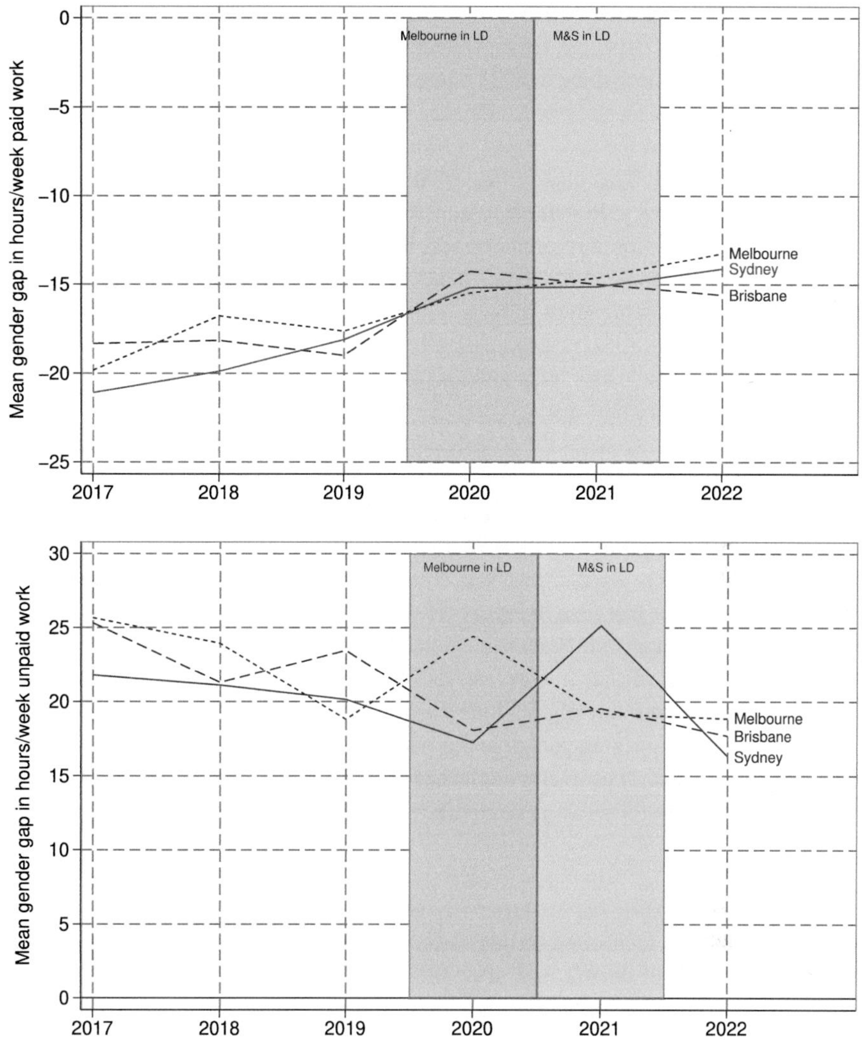

FIGURE 7.5 Effects of Covid-19 Lockdowns on Within-Couple Gender Gaps in Paid and Unpaid Work.

Source: Households, Income and Labour Dynamics in Australia survey, 2001–2022.

Unpaid work

Indeed, the results of our second difference-in-differences analysis, visualised in the second panel of Figure 7.5, suggest that being in lockdown did have an impact on the within-couple gender gap in unpaid work. We found that the gender gap in unpaid work increased during lockdowns by approximately 2.5 hours over and above what would have been expected based on the counterfactual. As Figure 7.5 shows, the gender gap increased in Melbourne in 2020 when the city was in lockdown. This spike was not evident in Sydney or Brisbane, which were not in lockdown that year. However, a similar spike is evident in Sydney in 2021 when that city was locked down. Interestingly, there is no evidence of a spike in Melbourne that year, even though the city was again locked down. Rather, the gender gap in Melbourne had almost returned to pre-pandemic levels in 2021. This could reflect that Melbournians were experiencing "pandemic fatigue" and were less likely to adhere to public health orders the second time around. Supporting this interpretation, an analysis of Australian Google Mobility Report data found some evidence of pandemic fatigue in Victoria (Melbourne) in late 2021 that was not apparent in New South Wales (Sydney) during the same time (Phillips et al., 2022). Another explanation could be adaptation: perhaps some fathers realised that they needed to "step up" and do more of the unpaid work second time round, while some mothers decided that they needed to "let go" and do less.

Next, we estimated separate difference-in-differences models for mothers and fathers with absolute time spent on unpaid work as the outcome (rather than the within-couple gap in time). The results, shown in Table A7-5 on the online appendix, indicated that both mothers and fathers increased their time on unpaid work during lockdowns. However, the increase was substantially larger for mothers, leading to the increased gender gap seen in Figure 7.5. Lockdown increased fathers' time spent on unpaid work by approximately three hours a week, on average – an effect that was not statistically significant. In contrast, lockdown increased mothers' time spent on unpaid work by approximately 5.5 hours a week, on average. Supplementary analyses found that the biggest impact of lockdowns, in terms of gender gaps, was on time spent on unpaid care. The average effect of lockdown was an additional 3.7 hours/week in unpaid care for mothers compared to 1.5 hours/week for fathers.

Conclusions

In this chapter, we examined trends in the within-couple gender gap in paid and unpaid work before, during and after the Covid-19 pandemic in Australia. Our analyses revealed three main findings. First, the within-couple gender gap in paid work has been slowly closing over time due to mothers increasing their paid work and fathers decreasing their paid work. The pandemic further narrowed this gap, with rates of workforce participation and intensity of participation dropping for fathers but not mothers in 2020. We speculated that this could reflect the (re)entry of some mothers into the workforce, perhaps prompted by a partner's job loss, the availability of telecommuting or other new employment opportunities. While the drop in fathers' workforce participation was temporary, the increase in mothers' participation was not: the proportion of partnered mothers engaged in paid work has continued to increase since 2020. The number of hours worked by participating mothers has also continued to increase since the pandemic while the number of hours worked by participating fathers has yet to return to pre-pandemic levels. Altogether, our results suggest that the pandemic did not significantly alter the long-term trend towards the closing of the gender gap in paid work. Over the whole period, the convergence in men and women's participation in paid work seems driven by women's increased participation and work hours, and to some lesser extent by men's decreasing working hours. Overall, although still far from being closed, the gap seems likely to continue to narrow into the future, albeit possibly at a slower rate than prior to the pandemic.

Second, the within-couple gender gap in unpaid work has been slowly closing since 2001 with some tentative evidence that the pandemic (in average terms) sped up that process slightly. Over the whole period analysed, we observe a notable decline in women's time spent in domestic unpaid labour, while their investment in unpaid care had started to decline in the years immediately prior to the pandemic, after a period of fluctuating but overall increasing hours. In this sense, while the closing of the gap in unpaid labour during the pandemic appears to have been driven by very small upticks in time spent on unpaid care and domestic labour by men, accompanied by very small decreases in time spent on these tasks by women, this seems to be part of a larger trend that predated the pandemic.

But when we moved beyond national averages and examined the specific impacts of lockdowns, we found different patterns than those identified in our first set of analyses. Prolonged stay-at-home lockdowns had no impact on the within-couple gender gap in paid work, but widened the within-couple gender gap in unpaid work. While both mothers and fathers spent more time on unpaid work during the lockdowns, mothers increased their time in unpaid work substantially more than fathers. This finding accords with previous research on gender and time use showing that life course events have a much larger impact on women's time in unpaid work than men's time (Baxter et al., 2008). Interestingly though, we also see some potential evidence of pandemic fatigue or adaptation during the second Melbourne lockdown, strengthening the idea that its effects were short-term.

Overall, bringing the different sets of analyses together, we conclude that the pandemic seems to have had short-term impacts, especially in terms of a widening of the gender gap in unpaid labour among families affected by prolonged stay-at-home lockdowns. However, these impacts are not reflected in the broader picture for the average of the country, which instead showed a continued closing of the gender gap as part of a broader long-term trend. The effects of the pandemic in paid work also seem restricted and did not reverse the trends towards a closing of the gender gap, although there is some evidence of slowing down in the aftermath of the pandemic. Future analyses with additional longitudinal data will be necessary to examine how the delineated trends continue to develop. Our current results suggest that although the pandemic upended lives momentarily, most trends in gendered time use returned remarkably quickly to pre-pandemic arrangements. As a historical event, the impact of the pandemic on gendered time use within couples appears to have been targeted and fleeting. This points to the ingrained and systemic nature of gendered time use and the need for sustained intervention to realise gender equality in time use arrangements.

Our work also points to the multi-faceted and divergent nature of gender divisions and the ways in which changes towards equality in one area – such as women's increased access to higher education and paid work – are counterbalanced by a lack of change in other areas – such as women's continued responsibility for most domestic and care work. Further moves towards greater equality in paid and unpaid work will require a stronger focus on fathering roles, men's attitudes and behaviours and workplace cultures and support for fathering. Current paid and unpaid work arrangements point to a deficit for men in their time spent with children and in domestic labour. Addressing this deficit will require not just a focus on policies to support women to balance paid and unpaid work demands, but a recognition and corresponding action focused on ways to encourage and support men to participate more equally in family work and care.

Acknowledgements

We are grateful for feedback on earlier versions of this chapter from the editors and volume contributors. This paper uses data from the Household, Income and Labour Dynamics in Australia (HILDA) Survey. The HILDA Project was initiated and is funded by the Commonwealth Department of Family, Housing, Community Services and Indigenous Affairs and is managed by the Melbourne Institute: Applied Economic & Social Research. This research was supported by the Australian Government through the Australian Research Council's Centre of Excellence for Children and Families over the Life Course (Project ID CE200100025) and the Australian Research Council Kathleen Fitzpatrick Laureate Fellowship (FL230100104).

References

Altintas, E., & Sullivan, O. (2016). Fifty years of change updated: Cross-national convergence in housework. *Demographic Research*, *35*(16), 455–470. https://doi.org/10.4054/DemRes.2016.35.16

Australian Bureau of Statistics. (2023). *Education and work, Australia*. https://www.abs.gov.au/statistics/people/education/education-and-work-australia/latest-release

Australian Institute of Health and Welfare. (2024). *Family, domestic and sexual violence*. FDSV summary - Australian Institute of Health and Welfare.

Baxter, J., Haynes, M., & Hewitt, B. (2010). Pathways into marriage: Cohabitation and the domestic division of labor. *Journal of Family Issues*, *31*(11), 1507–1529. https://doi.org/10.1177/0192513X10365817

Baxter, J. (2021). *Towards COVID normal: Sharing of housework in couple families in 2020*. Australian Institute of Family Studies. https://aifs.gov.au/research/research-reports/towards-covid-normal-sharing-housework-couple-families

Baxter, J. (2023). *Employment patterns and trends for families with children*. Australian Institute of Family Studies. https://aifs.gov.au/research/research-reports/employment-patterns-and-trends-families-children

Baxter, J. (2024). *How mothers and fathers share child care in Australia.* Australian Institute of Family Studies. https://aifs.gov.au/research/research-reports/how-mothers-and-fathers-share-child-care-australia

Baxter, J., Campbell, A., & Lee, R. (2023). Gender gaps in unpaid domestic and care work: Putting the pandemic in (a life course) perspective. *Australian Economic Review, 56*(4), 502–515. https://doi.org/10.1111/1467-8462.12538

Baxter, J., Cobb-Clark, D., Cornish, A., Ho, T., Kalb, G., Mazerolle, L., Parsell, C., Pawson, H., Thorpe, K., De Silva, L., & Zubrick, S. (2021). Never let a crisis go to waste: Opportunities to reduce social disadvantage from COVID-19. *Australian Economic Review, 54*(3), 343–358. https://doi.org/10.1111/1467-8462.12428

Baxter, J., Hewitt, B., & Haynes, M. (2008). Life course transitions and housework: Marriage, parenthood and time on housework. *Journal of Marriage and Family, 70*, 259–272. https://doi.org/10.1111/j.1741-3737.2008.00479.x

Baxter, J., Lam, J., Povey, J., Lee, R., & Zubrick, S. R. (Eds.). (2022). *Family dynamics over the life course. Foundations, turning points and outcomes.* Springer.

Brennan, D. (2010). *The politics of Australian childcare: Philanthropy to feminism and beyond.* Cambridge University Press.

Churchill, B., Ruppanner, L., & Kornrich, S. (2023). Children of the revolution? The continued unevenness of the gender revolution in housework, sleep, leisure, childcare and work time across cohorts. *Social Science Research, 111*, 102868. https://doi.org/10.1016/j.ssresearch.2023.102868

Clare, J., & Grace, G. (2023, June 28). Cheaper child care and free kindy for Queensland families [Press release]. Department of Education. https://ministers.education.gov.au/clare/cheaper-child-care-and-free-kindy-queensland-families

Collins, C., Landivar, L. C., Ruppanner, L., & Scarborough, W. J. (2021). COVID-19 and the gender gap in work hours. *Gender, Work and Organization, 28*, 101–112. https://doi.org/10.1111/gwao.12506

Craig, L., & Churchill, B. (2020). Working and caring at home: Gender differences in the effects of Covid-19 on paid and unpaid labor in Australia. *Feminist Economics, 27*(1–2), 310–326. https://doi.org/10.1080/13545701.2020.1831039

Department of Social Services. (2024, July 8). *Paid parental leave scheme.* Families and Children. https://www.dss.gov.au/our-responsibilities/families-and-children/programs-services/paid-parental-leave-scheme

Derndorfer, J., Disslbacher, F., Lechinger, V., Mader, K., & Six, E. (2021). Home, sweet home? The impact of working from home on the division of unpaid work during the COVID-19 lockdown. *PLOS ONE, 16*(11), e0259580. https://doi.org/10.1371/journal.pone.0259580

Doleman, G., De Leo, A., & Bloxsome, D. (2023). The impact of pandemics on healthcare providers' workloads: A scoping review. *Journal of Advanced Nursing, 79*(12), 4434–4454. https://doi.org/10.1111/jan.15690

Farré, L., Fawaz, Y., González, L., & Graves, J. (2022). Gender inequality in paid and unpaid work during Covid-19 times. *Review of Income and Wealth, 68*(2), 323–347. https://doi.org/10.1111/roiw.12563

Gilfillan, G. (2022). *Impact of COVID-19 on the Australian labour market.* Briefing Book: Key Issues for the 47th Parliament. https://www.aph.gov.au/About_Parliament/Parliamentary_departments/Parliamentary_Library/pubs/BriefingBook47p

Grundoff, M. (2022). *The economic benefits of high-quality universal early child education.* The Australia Institute. https://futurework.org.au/wp-content/uploads/sites/2/2022/11/Economic_Aspects_of_ECEC_in_Australia_FINAL.pdf

Hagqvist, E. (2018). Toward gender equality in practice? Cross-national patterns of change in the gendered division of housework over two decades. *Journal of Comparative Family Studies*, *49*(3), 355–377. https://doi.org/10.3138/jcfs.49.3.355

Harkness, S., & Evans, M. (2011). The employment effects of recession on couples in the UK: Women's and household employment prospects and partners' job loss. *Journal of Social Policy*, *40*(4), 675–693. https://doi.org/10.1017/S0047279411000201

Hupkau, C., & Petrongolo, B. (2020). Work, care and gender during the COVID-19 crisis. *Fiscal Studies*, *41*(3), 623–651. https://doi.org/10.1111/1475-5890.12245

Kabeer, N., Razavi, S., & van der Meulen Rodgers, Y. (2021). Feminist economic perspectives on the COVID-19 pandemic. *Feminist Economics*, *27*(1–2), 1–29. https://doi.org/10.1080/13545701.2021.1876906

Klapdor, M. (2021). *Child care subsidy changes*. Parliament of Australia. https://www.aph.gov.au/About_Parliament/Parliamentary_Departments/Parliamentary_Library/pubs/rp/BudgetReview202122/ChildCareSubsidy

Leahy, C. P. (2019, May 27). Mothers explain how they navigated work and childcare, from the 1970s to today. *The Conversation*. https://theconversation.com/mothers-explain-how-they-navigated-work-and-childcare-from-the-1970s-to-today-117617

Lyttelton, T., Zang, E., & Musick, K. (2021). Telecommuting and gender inequalities in parents' paid and unpaid work before and during the COVID-19 pandemic. *Journal of Marriage and Family*, *84*(1), 230–249. https://doi.org/10.1111/jomf.12810

Organisation for Economic Co-operation and Development. (2022). *Family database. PF3.4: Childcare support*. https://webfs.oecd.org/els-com/Family_Database/PF3-4-Childcare-support.pdf

Organisation for Economic Co-operation and Development. (2023). *Family database. LMF1.2. Maternal employment rates*. https://www.oecd.org/content/dam/oecd/en/data/datasets/family-database/lmf1_2_maternal_employment.pdf

Organisation for Economic Co-operation and Development. (2024). *Family database. PF2.1. Parental leave systems*. https://www.oecd.org/en/data/datasets/oecd-family-database.html

Phillips, T., Edwards, B., Barnes, R., Rehill, P., Ellen, L., Zhong, F., Killigrew, A., Gonzalez, P. R., Sheard, E., & Zhu, R. (2022). Variation in policy response to COVID-19 across Australian states and territories. *Blavatnik School Working Paper Series*. https://www.bsg.ox.ac.uk/research/publications/variation-policy-response-covid-19-across-australian-states-and-territories

Reserve Bank of Australia. (n.d.). *The global financial crisis*. https://www.rba.gov.au/education

Ruppanner, L., Collins, C., Landivar, L. C., Scarborough, W., & Tan, X. (2021, February 12). COVID forced Australian fathers to do more at home, but at the same cost mothers have long endured. *The Conversation*. https://theconversation.com/covid-forced-australian-fathers-to-do-more-at-home-but-at-the-same-cost-mothers-have-long-endured-154834

Schurer, S., Atalay, K., Glozier, N., Vera-Toscano, E., & Wooden, M. (2023). Quantifying the human impact of Melbourne's 111-day hard lockdown experiment on the adult population. *Nature Human Behaviour*, *7*(10), 1652–1666. https://doi.org/10.1038/s41562-023-01638-1

Services Australia. (2021). *Additional child care subsidy*. https://www.servicesaustralia.gov.au/additional-child-care-subsidy

Steinbring, R., Perales, F., Lam, J., & Baxter, J. (2023). Taking the long view: Long-term couple earnings arrangements across the transition to parenthood. *Australian Journal of Social Issues*, *59*(1), 4–19. https://doi.org/10.1002/ajs4.264

Stratton, L. (2023). Marriage versus cohabitation: How specialization and time use differ by relationship type. *Life Course Centre Working Paper*. https://doi.org/10.14264/50a1772

Sullivan, O., Gershuny, J., & Robinson, J. P. (2018). Stalled or uneven gender revolution? A long-term processual framework for understanding why change is slow. *Journal of Family Theory & Review*, *10*(1), 263–279. https://doi.org/10.1111/jftr.12248

Summerfield, M., Freidin, S., Hahn, M., La, N., Li, N., Macalalad, N., O'Shea, M., Watson, N., Wilkins, R., & Wooden, M. (2016). *HILDA user manual – Release 15*. Melbourne Institute of Applied Economic and Social Research, University of Melbourne. https://melbourneinstitute.unimelb.edu.au/__data/assets/pdf_file/0007/2194342/HILDA_User_Manual_Release_15.0.pdf

Treas, J., & Drobnič, S. (2010). *Dividing the domestic: Men, women and household work in cross-national perspective*. Stanford University Press. https://doi.org/10.11126/stanford/9780804763578.001.0001

Wood, D., Griffiths, K., & Foley, T. (2021). *Women's work: The impact of the COVID crisis on Australian women*. Grattan Institute. https://apo.org.au/node/311282

Zang, E., Tan, P. L., Lyttelton, T., & Guo, A. (2024). Impacts of the COVID-19 lockdown on gender inequalities in time spent on paid and unpaid work in Singapore. *Population and Development Review*, *50*, 303–337. https://doi.org/10.1111/padr.12554

8

THE CRISIS OF SOCIAL REPRODUCTION PROVISIONING

Gender, class and migration in Poland and Ukraine

Ania Plomien and Gregory Schwartz

Introduction

Recent global economic shocks, including the great recession, austerity, Covid-19 and armed conflicts, have undermined livelihoods, decent work and social protection, affecting different populations and gender and class relations. Poland and Ukraine have undergone significant transformations as part of post-socialist European integration. Initial factory closures triggered job losses and deindustrialisation, followed by an expansion of service jobs. The deterioration of state-socialist welfare and underdevelopment of public support to address new economic risks have eroded many households' ability to meet changing social needs. Labour migration stimulated by these developments has been notable, with Poles moving primarily to the UK and Germany since the 2004 EU accession, and Ukrainians relocating mainly to Russia since the 2008 economic crisis and Poland since the 2014 war in eastern Ukraine. While men and women adjusted their local or transnational labour market activities, gender division in unpaid and paid labour has persisted, shaping gender relations adaptation rather than transformation.

This chapter aims to show that such developments represent not only an outcome of socioeconomic policies, but societal adaptations to the crisis of *social reproduction provisioning*. With market wages becoming the main source sustaining households in the absence of adequate social wages, labour markets, migration processes and the gender order, reinforced by new class-based politics, have re-articulated relations of (re)production. In managing successive crises, states have changed the parameters of social reproduction provisioning, making material well-being and structures of production and consumption increasingly subject to marketisation (Plomien and Schwartz, 2024a). Reforms aimed at generating a workforce ready to participate in competitive economic processes, compelling households

DOI: 10.4324/9781003528210-11

and communities to navigate deregulated labour markets and market-disciplining public assistance. One objective of this chapter is to delineate how neoliberal macroeconomic, labour market and social policies have precipitated a secular crisis of social reproduction provisioning in Poland and Ukraine. Another is to explore how this crisis has influenced the gender order and class relations in these countries.

Understanding crises and social reproduction provisioning

The crisis of social reproduction (Fraser, 2022), the care crisis from the exhaustion of social capacities and resources (Dowling, 2021) and the costs of caring revealed through such depletion (Rai, 2024), have been interlocked with state management of various politico-economic crises (Bakker, 2007; Brenner et al., 2010; Karamessini, 2026, this volume). Crises stem from the contradictory relationship between the social forces and relations of production (Marx, 1977, pp. 20–21), between the potential of knowledge, technology and social development enhancing human flourishing and the limits imposed by the social form of value appropriation as private property and market-based wealth distribution. Table 8.1 outlines types of nested crises and responses. First, cyclical disequilibria (crisis tendencies) drive refinements in production and distribution through pro- or

TABLE 8.1 Nested Crises and Crises-Responses

Crises/Crises Tendencies	*Crises-Responses/Outcomes*
Within regime of accumulation • e.g. 1973 oil crisis, 1997 Asian financial crisis, 2007-09 global financial & economic crisis	Reforms consistent with the prevailing political economy paradigm when self-correcting mechanisms fail • *e.g. countercyclical macroeconomic policy via public sector investment and wage-led growth* • *e.g. procyclical macroeconomic policy via public sector austerity and deregulation, wage-restraint*
Of regime of accumulation • e.g. breakdown of the Keynesian ideological, institutional and economic infrastructure	Search for fundamentally new political economy approaches generating an alternative regime of accumulation • *e.g. emergence of neoliberalism*
Systemic • e.g. fall of socialism in PL (1989) and in UA (1991)	Collapse across economic, political and cultural domains leading to the establishment of a new mode of production • *e.g. integration into global capitalism*

Source: Authors' own elaboration.

counter-cyclical macroeconomic policies, managerial or technological changes, or industrial relations and social policy reforms. These visible and frequent crises are central to the analysis in this chapter. Second, when tendencies overwhelm core politico-economic arrangements, they instigate a broader crisis of a "regime of accumulation", precipitating sustained efforts to find a new regulatory infrastructure (e.g. from Keynesianism to neoliberalism) (Boyer, 1990). Third, a systemic crisis leads to a radical transformation of the mode of production and distribution, encompassing property relations and the material basis of society (e.g. from feudalism to capitalism). The systemic crisis of state-socialism in Eastern Europe based on deep economic and political contradictions (Ticktin, 1992) resulted in a transition towards capitalism. Eastern Europe's transformations coincided with the consolidation of neoliberalism in capitalist societies, structuring their political economies and cyclical crisis management in line with this ascendant policy framework.

Within the political economy, the state is a point of conjunction of multiple contradictions, compelled to contain crises within its class character (Clarke, 1991; Holloway & Picciotto, 1978), shaping social reproduction as demands to counter effects of overaccumulation (e.g. unemployment and poverty) require commensurate policies (Clarke, 1991). Social reproduction, understood as daily and intergenerational effort to reproduce life, material well-being and the social relations sustaining production and consumption, is an 'indispensable background condition' (Fraser, 2016, p. 102) in the production and appropriation of surplus value in capitalism (Ferguson, 1999). The "conflictive relationship between the imperatives of capitalism and the necessities of material life" (Bakker, 2007, p. 543) delineates the tension between spheres of *provisioning*, including markets, states, households and communities (Elson, 1998; Razavi, 2007). Social reproduction provisioning (see Figure 8.1) involves institutionally-distinct arrangements and resources across spheres, interweaving gendered and racialised forms of paid and unpaid work that are linked, multi-directional and increasingly transnational (Bezanson & Luxton, 2006; Glenn, 1992; Humphries & Rubery, 1984; Kofman & Raghuram, 2015; Truong, 1996). This interdependence implies that political-economic restructuring reverberates across all spheres, necessitating communities and households to realign with markets and states, and vice versa.

The neoliberalisation of the state confronted cyclical crises by meeting economic globalisation's downward pressure on wages and working conditions with labour market deregulation, privatisation of public assets and disinvestment from social services. States have aligned material security with work-readiness and wages with market rewards (Brenner et al., 2010; Hay, 2004), breaking with regulation protecting "society" from the "economy" (Polanyi, 1944/2001; Fraser, 2014) in favour of economic efficiency. However, elevating markets as the primary means of stability and prosperity has detracted from other spheres and sources of provisioning. With policies encouraging market-reliance by minimising social support and pushing households towards income generation (Bakker, 2007; Fraser, 2014;

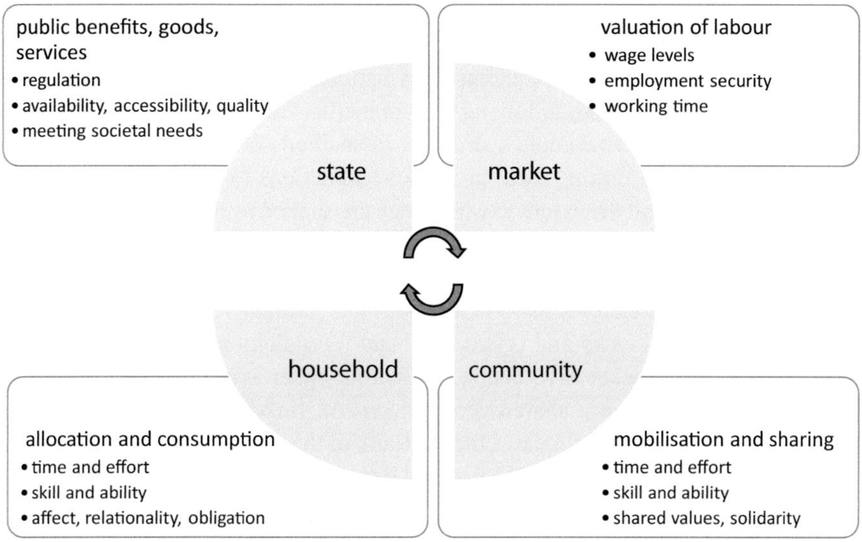

FIGURE 8.1 Social Reproduction Provisioning.

Source: Authors' own elaboration.

Plomien & Schwartz, 2024a), adequate wages simultaneously have become scarce amid labour market restructuring and feminisation of standard employment (i.e. erosion of its security that approximate feminised non-standard employment) (Fudge & Vosko, 2001; Standing, 1999). As markets have reached deeper into social reproduction, the depletion of individual, household, community and public resources has intensified gendered social harms (Plomien & Schwartz, 2020; Rai et al., 2014). This has tended to erode labour's relative class power and limit the transformation of the gender division of labour (England, 2010), undermining women's economic security despite promises of greater economic freedom.

Below we assess how cyclical neoliberal crises and crises-management in post-socialist Poland and Ukraine have exacerbated pressures on social reproduction provisioning, highlighting adaptations in gender order and class. Conceptualising social reproduction in crisis does not mean it ceases, as efforts to sustain life and social relations continue, ranging from flourishing to withering depending on the political economy of surplus value distribution (Plomien & Schwartz, 2024b). However, healthcare access difficulties, poor health, food insecurity, housing exclusion and homelessness, low birthrates, household indebtedness, and high labour migration suggest that social reproduction is not only variegated (Bakker & Gill, 2019) but far from flourishing for many in Europe.[1]

This is the point of departure for our analysis. Methodologically employing a genealogical and transnational approach, we examine Poland's and Ukraine's historically-contingent governance of macroeconomic, labour market and social policies in the three decades following the dissolution of state-socialism and European integration. In this analysis, genealogy entails tracing processes and actions that have given rise to contemporary patterns of gender and class relations, including labour migration, following their immediate and long-term effects, since policy outputs may have complex, stifled or intensified outcomes. A transnational perspective involves linking local processes and actions to external phenomena, seeking to understand the extent to which they are shaped by, manifest in, and contribute to developments occurring beyond the nation-state. Interpreting countries' management of discrete politico-economic events as operating within European and global relations enables us to detect both the cumulative and interdependent effects of periodic shocks and crises on social reproduction provisioning across Europe. Analysing successive changes affecting spheres of social reproduction provisioning throughout a shared economic space, linked by high rates of east-to-west labour mobility, delineates the contours of the intensification of a crisis of social reproduction in Poland, Ukraine and Europe as a whole.

Neoliberal crisis management and the erosion of social reproduction provisioning

Since the fall of state-socialism, social transformations across political, economic, and cultural spheres have been more decisively determined by the state's neoliberalisation. Poland and Ukraine began from similar levels of economic development, human capital and social infrastructure, but their subsequent divergence has been affected by each country's distinct management of instability and crisis, institutional consolidation, and regional integration (see Figure 8.2). With notable differences in the triggers, and the respective macroeconomic, labour market and social policy responses, the resultant crisis in social reproduction provisioning underscores the shared logic underlying these developments.

Poland's neoliberalisation by design

In 1990 Poland implemented the "shock therapy" market liberalisation policies, representing a radical path of transformation towards capitalism. This followed the slow disintegration of the planned economy (Poznanski, 1996), reliance on foreign creditors (Pluciński, 2020), and efforts throughout the 1980s to formulate a new socioeconomic system (Shields, 2003). Institution-building occurred under fiscal and monetary restraint, trade and price liberalisation, privatisation, and EU integration (Kołodko & Nuti, 1997). The first decade faced multiple crises: a systemic crisis transitioning from planning to free markets, a financial crisis driven by high foreign debt and budget deficit, falling tax revenues and rising social expenditures, and a structural adjustment crisis moving from heavy industry to consumer goods and services. Social reproduction was rearticulated through ending price controls and subsidies (e.g., food, housing, transportation), falling

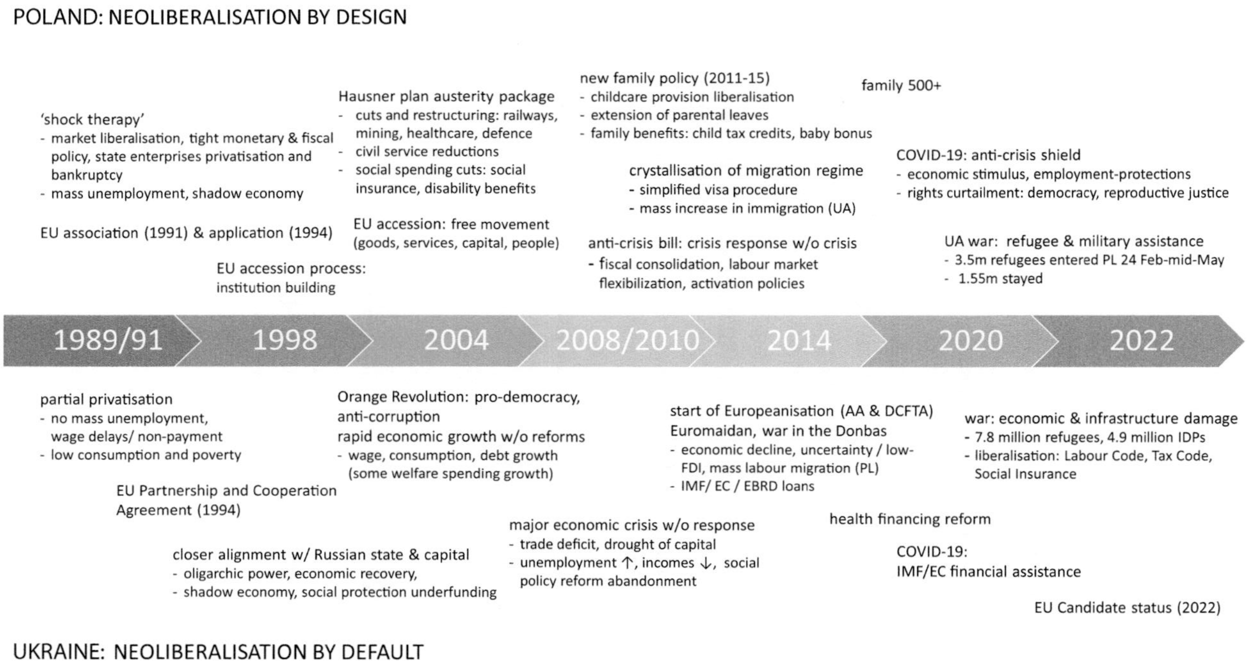

FIGURE 8.2 Synthesis of Major Politico-Economic Events in Poland and Ukraine.

Source: Authors' own elaboration.

public-to-private employment ratios, soaring unemployment, and the spread of early retirement and informal work.

Reforms undermined counter-cyclical redistributive policies. Fiscal policy reduced public expenditure from 32-34% in 1993 to below 30% in 1996 to curb inflation, while tax cuts were justified to formalise the "shadow economy" (Kołodko & Nuti, 1997). Corporate income tax dropped from 40% in 1992 to 19% by 2004, and personal income tax rates fell from three brackets (20%, 30%, 40%) to two (18%, 32%) by 2009 (Kołodko & Nuti, 1997; Tomkiewicz, 2016). A flat 19% tax for entrepreneurs encouraged self-employment among high earners with management contracts and dividend payments while lower income workers could not avail themselves of the same advantages. Companies saved on social security contributions with both genuine and bogus self-employment arrangements (Tomkiewicz, 2016). The VAT, introduced in 1993 at 20% for standard goods and services, reached 23% in 2011 as a deficit-management measure following the global economic crisis (Ministerstwo Finansów, 2012). Consequently, the decreasing tax burden relative to rising income has favoured households with the highest earnings and assets (Tomkiewicz, 2016).

Economic restructuring has had major gendered implications for employment by type of ownership (see Table 8.2). Public sector employment, still crucial for women (27.9% of whom worked in it in 2020), rapidly declined. Its transformation from being economy-wide to a *public service* has feminised it, contributing to the rearticulation of Poland's gender order.

Two major problems pervaded the Polish labour market over the last three decades: mass unemployment (exceeding 20% by 2004), workforce flexibilisation (over 3.5 million workers in temporary jobs in 2015) and the proliferation of "junk contracts" (2.4 million people with civil law contracts in 2023) (Czarzasty et al., 2014; Drahokoupil & Piasna, 2018; Główny Urząd Statystyczny [GUS], 2024b). Unemployment system reforms throughout the 1990s decreased its coverage and

TABLE 8.2 The Gendered Character of Private and Public Employment Restructuring in Poland

Category	*1990*	*1995*	*2000*	*2010*	*2020*
Public sector employment as % of total employment	52.0	38.6	27.8	25.3	21.2
Women's employment public: private sector ratio	50.3 : 49.6	41.1 : 58.8	31.6 : 68.4	31.7 : 68.3	27.9 : 72.1
Feminisation of public sector employment	43.8	49.2	53.6	57.8	61.5

Source: Authors' calculations based on Główny Urząd Statystyczny [GUS], 2024a (archives accessed November 2024).

generosity, as the share of unemployed workers receiving benefits fell from 79% in 1991 to 24% in 1999 and wage replacement rates declined (Vodopivec at al., 2005). Although unemployment fell from the mid-2000s, flexible and precarious employment expanded, through temporary employment (fixed-term and agency work) and especially through civil law contracts. Regulated by civil law, rather than labour code, such contracts entail inferior rights regarding protection against dismissal, paid leave, social security coverage and pensions, and are mostly used in the private sector (9 out of 10), particularly in administration and supporting activities (19%) and health and social care (12%), the most feminised sectors of the economy (GUS, 2024b). Their normalisation also occurred in the public sector, where rationalisation of administration and outsourcing of cleaning, security and other low-wage and high-workload jobs tripled between 2001 and 2014 (Lewandowski & Magda, 2017). The state has thus "contributed to the weakening of employment standards, the proliferation in the use of non-standard jobs and the evolution of their perception" (Lewandowski & Magda, 2017, p. 160).

The implications of these changes are reflected in living standards inequality rising to levels of the most unequal European countries (Brzeziński et al., 2022; Bukowski & Novokmet, 2021). Although absolute income growth has been positive, unequal growth set in from the early 1990s (Bukowski & Novokmet, 2021; Kołodko & Nuti, 1997). Cumulative (1989-2015) pre-tax income growth of 458% for the top percentile compared with 31% for the bottom half (Bukowski & Novokmet, 2021) and cumulative (1994-2015) real disposable income growth of up to 167% for the top percentile compared with 57% for the bottom decile (Brzeziński et al., 2022) demonstrate the disproportionate benefits enjoyed by high-income earners.

Such rising inequality and falling redistribution encouraged the emergence of populism (Brzeziński et al., 2022), spearheaded by the Law and Justice party (*Prawo i Sprawiedliwość* – PiS) governing between 2015 and 2023. One of its flagship policies is the Family 500+ benefit – a monthly cash transfer of 500 złoty to every second and subsequent child, extended to all children from 2019. The programme, costing 1-1.5% of GDP annually and the benefit reaching 37% of net minimum wage, raised household consumption and lowered child poverty (Magda et al., 2019; Myck & Trzciński, 2019). However, it has neglected the greater needs of lone mothers and children with disabilities, disincentivised employment of low-income mothers, redistributed income to higher earners, and, due to high costs, impeded adequate social infrastructure development, such as childcare services, education, or healthcare (Magda et al., 2019; Myck & Trzciński, 2019; Plomien, 2019) capable of alleviating social reproduction pressures. Although childcare provision has increased gradually since the 2000s, deregulation of standards and forms of care services has made it popular among market providers (Plomien, 2019; Plomien & Schwartz, 2024a). With the regressive tax system, deficient redistribution, and restriction of resources for public measures to benefit those with greater needs, Family 500+ is a "neoliberal social innovation" subordinate to the pursuit of economic liberalism (Shields, 2021 p. 3). The benefit offers families greater freedom by enlarging their scope of consumption. Yet, by directing their needs to the market rather than to quality public goods and services, it limits options for households with complex needs, diverting resources to those with no such requirements or with already sufficient means, deepening class fragmentation. In contrast to the reactive and stagnant social policies of the 1990s, Family 500+ continues the "accelerated merger of conservative, pronatalist ideologies with a neoliberal emphasis on individual rights" (Inglot et al., 2012 p. 41) initiated in the 2000s, binding populist politics with neoliberal pragmatism (Korolczuk & Graff, 2018; Shields, 2021).

Ukraine's neoliberalisation by default

Emerging from the Soviet economy without independent institutions or coherent national policies, Ukraine pursued partial, contradictory reforms that deterred foreign direct investment. The 1990s saw economic shocks, industrial decline, unemployment, informality, and insecurity (International Labour Organization - Central and Eastern European Team [ILO-CEET], 1995; Mykhnenko & Swain, 2010; Yurchenko, 2018). GDP contracted sharply (9.7–22.7% annually, 1991–1996), fixed assets deteriorated, and labour productivity fell (Bojcun, 2020). Hyperinflation and a budget deficit (14.4% of GDP) exacerbated instability (Sutella, 2012). The fragmented economy comprised state-owned enterprises, emerging private SMEs, and subsistence food production (ILO-CEET, 1995), while soaring "shadow" activities undermined taxation and decimated social security funding (Bojcun, 2020).

The 1994-1996 reforms targeted monetary stabilisation, inflation control and privatisation (Kholod, 2012) but failed to achieve growth. Weak legal frameworks and absent national accounts reforms diverted public resources to private businesses within state-owned enterprises benefiting their *de facto* owners (senior managers and their business associates). Public sector workers often laboured in private firms, while industrial and service employment shifted to subsistence farming (Bojcun, 2020). Barter, surrogate currencies and the shadow economy offset widespread wage arrears, while safety nets, offering broad rather than targeted benefits (ILO-CEET, 1995), were ineffective amidst labour market changes. Tax evasion and corruption undermined funding for education, family support, healthcare, and unemployment benefits.

From 1998 Ukraine's GDP grew by an average of 9% annually before plummeting to minus 14.0% in 2009 (Mykhnenko & Swain, 2010, pp. 142–143). Growth stemmed from privatising profitable firms to foster a domestic capitalist class and technological upgrading as a prelude to EU membership. Investments from Russia and the EU capitalised on low wages and exports of primary goods and semi-finished products in agriculture, energy, chemicals and minerals (Bojcun, 2020). However, productivity gains were uneven, with profits rising while the wage share fell, disproportionately affecting low- and medium-skilled workers (ILO, 2013). Although wages increased and absolute poverty dropped from 32% in 2001 to 8% in 2005 (ILO, 2013), income inequality widened, with the top 10% earning 35% of national income (Blanchet et al., 2019, 2021). Labour force participation, especially among women, remained low despite service sector growth, with increased family cash transfers potentially contributing to this trend (Anastasia et al., 2022). Western European banks facilitated domestic consumption and helped to alleviate household deprivation through low-interest consumer credit. Mass migration, largely to Russia between 2004 and 2013, also mitigated declining living standards. This combination of factors underpinned short-term economic stability but reinforced structural inequalities and labour market imbalances. In the end, ownership changes, profit increases and economic improvements did not enhance weak institutional foundations of labour markets and social policies. Minimum wage, working time and social protection regulations and enforcement remained deficient (Czaplinski & Dzhaman, 2019; Lehmann & Pignatti, 2018). Informal employment in low value sectors persisted, with an estimated 35-40% of the population deriving incomes from the shadow economy (Adamczyk, 2016; Muzychenko, 2018), undermining social insurance funding (Williams et al., 2011) thus rendering pensions, unemployment, disability and other protections insufficient.

The 2008 global economic crisis hit Ukraine's heavily indebted economy hard, causing unemployment and real incomes to decline, partly compensated by a limited increase in social transfers and a promise to institute reforms that would align Ukraine with the EU. However, as the 2012 reform programme, based on the Association Agreement (AA) and the Deep and Comprehensive Free Trade Area (DCFTA), stalled, wages and living standards declined under the dual pressure of Russia's economic blackmail and European banks' consumer loan repayments being called in. The IMF judged the government's attempted mitigation of hardship through minimum wage and pension increases as a breach of conditions and suspended its stand-by programme (Bojcun, 2020). Failure to sign the AA in November 2013 was the linchpin turning social pressures into months-long country-wide protests (known as Euromaidan), with Russia exploiting the unrest to occupy Crimea and launch a military operation in eastern Ukraine.

Lacking strategic labour market and social policies, Ukraine's macroeconomic foundations favoured integrating its elites into global markets, neoliberalising by default, shifting, since 2014, to a more systematic programme by its and the EU's cadre of reformers. However, expected economic and legal changes proved difficult for Ukraine fighting a low-intensity war and losing Russia as a major trading partner. The consequent 2014-2015 economic crisis influenced the conditions of macro-financial assistance (from the EU, IMF and World Bank) and triggered structural adjustments and fiscal consolidation reforms to improve the functioning of markets, protect property rights, sever oligarchic interests and reduce "regulatory burdens" (European Commission [EC], 2020, p. 25; World Health Organization Europe [WHO-Europe], 2021). Fiscal austerity brought cuts to environmental protection (-49.1%), health care (-36.3%), education (-36.2%) and the civil service (-30.6%) in comparison to 2013 (Bogdan et al., 2017). Reforms reduced public services by 30%, cutting employees' benefits, rationalising state agencies, and diminishing capacity to assist the Internally Displaced Persons (Adamczyk, 2016; EC, 2015). The gendered consequences of these were formidable. First, public sector employees saw their real wages decline significantly by 2016, dropping to 70.4% of 2013 levels for education workers and 74% for health care workers (Bogdan et al., 2017). Low wages in the healthcare sector (83% employees are women) were a major factor in protests by nurses in 2019 (Dutchak, 2020) and in healthcare workers leaving their jobs (Office of the High Commissioner for Human Rights, 2021). Second, as spending on public goods declined, both access and quality were affected, exacerbating class inequalities. For instance, in 2019 Ukraine's domestic general government health expenditure was 3.2% of GDP and household out-of-pocket payments reached 3.6% of GDP - public spending being lower and private expenses higher than in Poland (4.6% and 1.3%, respectively) (World Health Organization [WHO], 2024). High costs of medical care entailed forgoing treatment and financial barriers to healthcare are experienced particularly acutely by women, 18% of whom had to reduce medicine dosage, compared with 9% of men (Cabinet of Ministers of Ukraine, 2022).

Despite real wage growth in 2016-2019, the deficit of decent work, unemployment, wage poverty, workplace inequality and poor public services (European Trade Union Confederation, 2021) meant that many (27.6% in 2018) still earned below subsistence minimum incomes (World Bank, 2020). By the end of 2021, with increased financial needs to counter the Covid-19 pandemic requiring more borrowing (WHO-Europe, 2021) and further fraying social provisioning and security, Ukraine had launched major macroeconomic, labour market and social policy reforms. Following Russia's full-scale invasion on 24 February 2022, parliamentarians began discussing changes that would limit trade union freedoms and coverage and normalise the use of civil law contracts in employment, providing minimal grounds for dismissal, limiting severance pay, legalising zero-hours contracts, while merging the Social Insurance Fund with the heavily indebted Pension Fund would strip workers of many benefits (Rowley & Guz, 2022). Developing labour market and social policies during wartime has been stunted by the simultaneous requirement of establishing social partnerships, democratisation and bureaucratic capacity, and the pursuit of growth and fiscal responsibility as the criterion of EU integration and the IMF and the EBRD loans.

Effects of neoliberalisation of the state on gender and class relations

As we have outlined, markets in Poland and Ukraine have become more determining in social reproduction, compelling households to manage with inadequate direct state involvement. By 2018 social protection expenditure as a percentage of GDP was cut in Poland to 19.7 (from 21 in 2016) and in Ukraine to 17.5 (from 31.2 in 2012) (Eurostat, 2022). These developments have had the subsequent three-fold effect. First, households have needed to transfer more time and effort to paid employment. Their adjustment has taken the form of women's greater participation in paid work at a time when downward pressures of labour market liberalisation have also eroded men's pay and conditions. The resultant change in gender relations has been partial, as women have been held back by the persistence of the gender division of unpaid and paid labour – men have not filled the shortfall of state provisioning, while the necessity of unpaid labour sustaining social reproduction has disqualified women from the care-free masculine model of employment. For example, by 2019 Polish women's (aged 20-64) employment rate increased to 65.7% (from 51.1% in 2004) and continued to rise to 72% in 2023. Unlike in many western European countries, this is predominantly full-time (in 2019 only 9% of this was part-time, compared with 38% in the UK and 47% in Germany), but remains lower than men's employment rate at 85% (Eurostat, 2024b; Marx et al., 2026, this volume). During the same two decades in Ukraine, women's employment, also largely full-time, oscillated around 62-63%, dipping to 59% in the 2014-17 period (Eurostat, 2024c). Ukrainian women spend twice as much time on household work as men (257 minutes in urban and 382 minutes in rural areas per day), and given limited childcare facilities for under three-years-old (15% in 2020), 30% of women outside the labour force are not employed due to family responsibilities (State Statistics Service of Ukraine – United Nations Women [SSSU/UN Women], 2022). For employed women, these patterns underlie the 20% gender pay gap and the 30% gender pension gap, borne out by women's lower pay and discontinuous employment (SSSU/UN Women, 2022).

The persistence of the inegalitarian gender order interacts with the second effect – the deepening of within-class inequalities. The same state policies that have shifted the burden of provisioning to households' own efforts to navigate competitive markets for goods, services and jobs have affected the class structure in Poland and Ukraine. Household gendered adaptation to markets to make up for the fall of state support is an individualised response, rather than socialised and potentially more egalitarian, permitting some to obtain market-based security, while others experience downward pressure on wages and working conditions. Thus, while some women have been able to realise financial improvements offered by the labour market, becoming part of the new property-owning class, the managerial cadre, or the professions serving business, others have either been excluded from formal employment or have taken on insecure and exploitative service sector or domestic jobs catering to the reproduction of the middle class. Class transformation does not represent a linear worsening of gender inequality; rather, it has provided the basis for the reconstitution of the gender order.

Third, the relative re-weighting of state provisioning towards markets has been associated not only with households' material ability to survive, but also with the changing social expectations of what constitutes a good life, thus comprising a major factor in labour migration. Integration into the EU single market brought with it visa liberalisation (Plomien & Schwartz 2020). As Poles and Ukrainians have sought to augment deficient social protection and public services, given inadequate opportunities in local labour markets, they have looked to migration to make up for provisioning shortfalls, often taking jobs below their skill or education levels, and seen in the destination labour markets as specifically "migrant jobs". The interconnected flow of migrants has been an especially distinctive feature of contemporary Polish and Ukrainian societies. Nearly 1.8 million Poles moved to Germany and the UK alone, while over 2 million Ukrainians at the same time

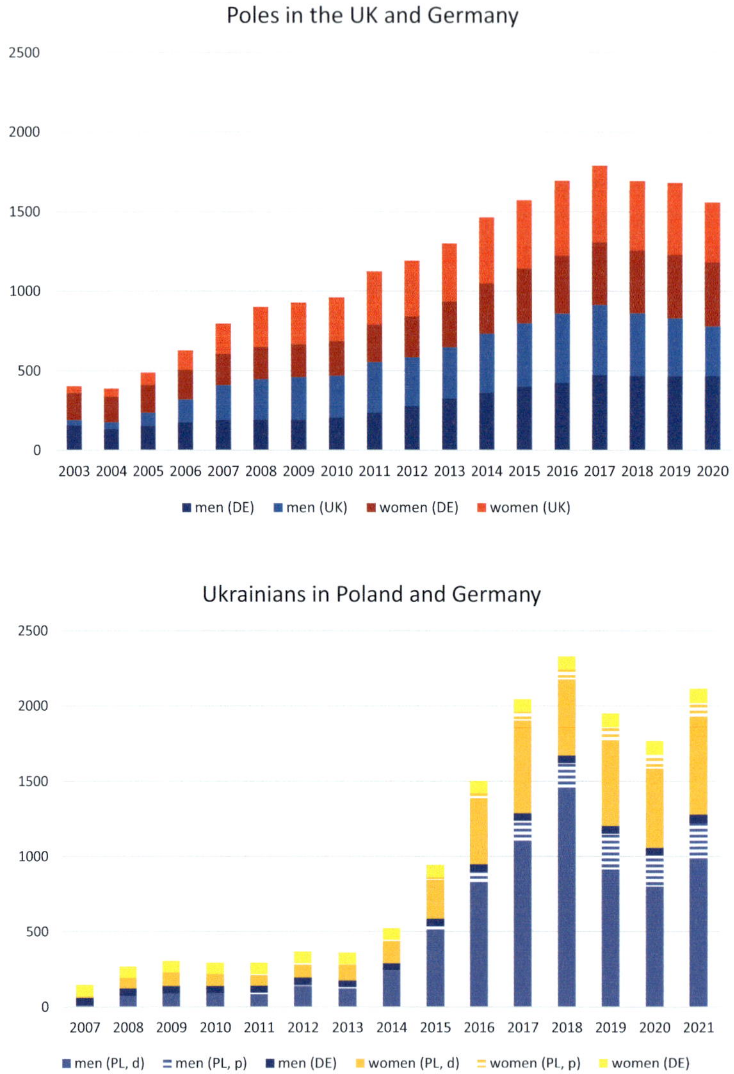

FIGURE 8.3 Migration of Poles to Germany and the UK and Ukrainians to Poland and Germany, in Thousands.

Source: Based on Federal Statistical Office (2024), Ministerstwo Rodziny, Pracy i Polityki Społecznej (2024), and Office for National Statistics, (2021) databases (accessed November 2024).

Note: "d" registered declarations of intent to employ (until 2017) and having employed (from 2018) a Ukrainian worker, "'p" work permits issued.

worked in Poland and some in Germany (see Figure 8.3). Migrating at different rates and periods, and working in different sectors, these patterns change both with the migrants' circumstances and the opportunities arising from migration regulations or employment options.

Migration processes interact with gender, positioning Polish and Ukrainian migrant women as *workers* (their employment rates tend to be higher than non-migrant women in the countries of origin and destination alike), as *migrant* workers (they are over-represented in "migrant" niches), and as *women* migrant workers (they tend to be employed in feminised sectors and occupations) (Aziz, 2015; Górny & Van der Zwan, 2024; Kaczmarczyk & Górny, 2017). Among Polish migrants in the UK, women tend to work full-time, are concentrated in gender-balanced wholesale and retail trade as well as in male-dominated manufacturing and in female-dominated accommodation and food service, with the widest gender gaps occurring in human health and social work (where women dominate) and construction (where men dominate) (Aziz, 2015). The experiences of Ukrainians in Poland are similarly shaped by migration and gender. Their key sectors of employment are agriculture, construction, trade and food service and domestic services. Two gendered migrant niches concentrate women in domestic services and men in construction, while a newer hospitality and catering sector attracts more women (Górny & Van der Zwan, 2024). A survey conducted in the Warsaw region established that among Ukrainian migrants, feminised sectors are characterised by longer weekly hours and lower monthly pay than masculinised sectors. Specifically, women in domestic service worked nearly 76 hours to earn 1,519 złoty, while men in construction worked 57 hours for 2,375 złoty (Kaczmarczyk & Górny, 2017) – effectively, women in domestic service earned half of men's earnings in construction.

Conclusion

In this chapter we have examined the contours and implications of successive crises in Poland and Ukraine, their management through macroeconomic, labour market and social policies, and how these have precipitated a social reproduction crisis in the European political economy, with profound implications for gender relations, economic inequality and labour mobility. Four substantive takeaways derive from our analysis. First, the neoliberalisation of state policies in Poland and Ukraine has transformed social reproduction. By transferring provisioning responsibilities from the public to the private sphere, reforms have intensified the burden on paid employment as the main source of meeting needs. Simultaneously, greater dependence on markets and wages has often been based on low-wage, low-skill, insecure jobs with limited protections. Consequently, households have faced heightened pressures to secure adequate resources. Second, such policies have led to the adaptation of gender relations, particularly in paid labour. Polish and Ukrainian women have increasingly faced employment as an immediate necessity in offsetting the declining state support for childcare, healthcare, and to afford goods and services necessary for participating in social and economic life. However, labour market participation has not delivered gender equality, as women have continued to bear the brunt of unpaid care work, limiting their economic security and reinforcing gender roles in both paid and unpaid labour. Third, neoliberalisation of the state has increased economic inequality, exacerbating class fragmentation, while wealth concentration and income inequality surges have been detrimental to the majority. Regressive taxes and the erosion of public services have advanced demands for populist responses, which have come in the form of Poland's Family 500+ or Ukraine's stimulation of consumption through cheap credit, providing some immediate relief but maintaining market-reliance over robust social support. Fourth, migration has emerged as a critical strategy for households grappling with the pressures of provisioning. Many Polish and Ukrainian workers have obtained employment in low-skilled and gendered jobs abroad. At such scale, migration has not only disrupted families and communities, deepening demographic, health and care crises experienced in origin countries, but has also reinforced the dependency on incomes earned abroad and limited the development of adequate local economic opportunities and social reproduction provisioning across Europe. In Ukraine this has been fuelled by economic instability and poor employment prospects, in Poland there has been some compensation through the rapid inflow of Ukrainian workers filling vacancies left by migrating Poles, and in the UK and Germany social reproduction has been shored up by the low-value labour of eastern European workers.

The transnational and genealogical lens has allowed us to analyse aspects of post-socialist transformations in the wider context of "uneven and combined" Europe, bringing into view how crises and adversities in social reproduction in one country are mitigated by the preponderance of a European market and labour mobility, facilitating the improvement of wages for some and the purchase of adequate necessities for others, though sharpening class and gender inequalities. The unfolding, and the mitigations, of crises at different scales, degrees, and frequencies have cumulative implications for social relations, which depend on both the existing class and gender arrangements and the struggles involved in adaptations. Thus, both aspirations and pressures to adapt to markets lead actors to devise policies and practices within the neoliberal framing of the EU's political economy. Such framing resists the deterministic construction of state neoliberalisation, seeing it instead as emerging from the relative command of resources in resolving local crises by permitting actors to integrate economic interests within globally hegemonic projects.

Finally, policies aimed at tackling specific problems through the advancement of neoliberal policies have been wearing down the foundations of social reproduction provisioning, creating a wider crisis of social reproduction and undermining the basis for flourishing. The continuum of provisioning – across its different spheres and with varying levels of resourcing – suggests that there is scope for either deterioration or improvement. Because it is achieved through both gender and class struggles over the division and conditions of work, social security, taxation, and redistribution, the management of discrete and successive crises offers wide-ranging political opportunities.

Note

1 For example, 18% of Europeans report unmet health needs (49% in the 18–24 age group) (Eurofound, 2022). A high proportion of households (9.5% overall, and 17.5% single parents with children) cannot afford a meal with meat, chicken, fish or a vegetarian equivalent every other day (Eurostat, 2024a). Distressingly, 7.2 million people (11% of the population) in the UK in 2022-23 lived in households experiencing food poverty and foodbanks distributed a record 3.12 million emergency food parcels (House of Commons Library, 2024), while the European Food Banks Federation assisted 12.8 million in 2023 (European Food Banks Federation, 2024). Housing costs have increased by 8% for homeowners and by 23% for tenants within a decade; overcrowding and severe housing deprivation rates are particularly high in eastern Europe (e.g. in Poland over 30% and 5%, respectively) (Eurofound, 2023), and the estimates of homeless people in the EU exceeded 890,000 in 2023 (Fondation Abbé Pierre & FEANTSA, 2023). Between 1990 and 2020, total fertility rates fell in Poland (2.1 versus 1.4), Ukraine (1.9 versus 1.2), the UK (1.8 versus 1.6), and remained low in Germany (1.4 versus 1.5) (World Bank, 2024). The stock of household loans and debt securities as a share of GDP rose by 2008 before falling by 2020 in many countries, including Ukraine (29.4 versus 4.9), Germany (59.74 versus 57.07), the UK (94.74 versus 91.01), while continuing to grow in Poland (30.05 versus 34.62) (International Monetary Fund, 2024). In 2017 working age (20–64) Polish migrants in the EU exceeded 1.7 million (734,000 in the UK and 559,000 in Germany) (EC, 2019), whereas of the 2.3 million Ukrainian labour migrants, 900,000 worked in Poland (Pieńkowski, 2020), rising to 1.3 million before the Covid-19 pandemic (Górny & Van der Zwan, 2024).

References

Adamczyk, A. (2016, November). *Labour market rules in the European Union and Ukraine: Common features and differences. Bringing Ukrainian labour law into line with EU legislation.* EU-Ukraine Civil Society Platform. Kyiv, 8–9 November. https://eu-ua-csp.org.ua/media/uploads/3d_CSP_EESC_Labour_report_eng.PDF

Anastasia, G., Boeri, T., Kudlyak, M., & Zholud, O. (2022). The labour market in Ukraine: Rebuild better. In Y. Gorodnichenko, I. Sologoub, & B. Weder di Mauro (Eds.), *Rebuilding Ukraine: Principles and policies* (pp. 283–321). CEPR Press.

Aziz, K. (2015). Female migrants' work trajectories: Polish women in the UK labour market. *Central and Eastern European Migration Review, 4*(2), 87–105.

Bakker, I. (2007). Social reproduction and the constitution of a gendered political economy. *New Political Economy, 12*(4), 541–556. https://doi.org/10.1080/13563460701661561

Bakker, I., & Gill, S. (2019). Rethinking power, production, and social reproduction: Toward variegated social reproduction. *Capital & Class, 43*(4), 503–523. https://doi.org/10.1177/0309816819880783

Bezanson, K., & Luxton, M. (2006). *Social reproduction: Feminist political economy challenges neo-liberalism.* McGill-Queen's University Press. https://doi.org/10.1515/9780773576902

Blanchet, T., Chancel, L., & Gethin, A. (2019). *How unequal is Europe? Evidence from distributional national accounts, 1980–2017* (Working Paper No. 2019/06). World Inequality Lab. https://wid.world/document/bcg2019-full-paper/

Blanchet, T., Chancel, L., & Gethin, A. (2021). *Why is Europe more equal than the United States?* (Working Paper No. 2020/19). World Inequality Lab. https://wid.world/document/why-is-europe-more-equal-than-the-united-states-world-inequality-lab-wp-2020-19/

Bogdan, T., Gligorov, V., Havlik, P., & Landesmann, M. (2017). *From fiscal austerity towards growth-enhancing fiscal policy in Ukraine* (Research Report No. 417). Vienna Institute for International Economic Studies. https://wiiw.ac.at/from-fiscal-austerity-towards-growth-enhancing-fiscal-policy-in-ukraine-p-4189.html

Bojcun, M. (2020). *Towards a political economy of Ukraine: Selected essays 1990–2015.* Ibidem Verlag.

Boyer, R. (1990). *The regulation school: A critical introduction.* Columbia University Press.

Brenner, N., Peck, J., & Theodore, N. (2010). After neoliberalization? *Globalizations, 7*(3), 327–345. https://doi.org/10.1080/14747731003669669

Brzeziński, M., Myck, M., & Najsztub, M. (2022). Sharing the gains of transition: Evaluating changes in income inequality and redistribution in Poland using combined survey and tax return data. *European Journal of Political Economy, 73*, Article 102121. https://doi.org/10.1016/j.ejpoleco.2021.102121

Bukowski, P., & Novokmet, F. (2021). Between communism and capitalism: Long-term inequality in Poland, 1892–2015. *Journal of Economic Growth, 26*(2), 187–239. https://doi.org/10.1007/s10887-021-09190-1

Cabinet of Ministers of Ukraine. (2022). *State strategy for ensuring equal rights and opportunities for women and men until 2030.* https://www.kmu.gov.ua/news/uriadom-skhvaleno-derzhavnu-stratehiiu-zabezpechennia-rivnykh-prav-ta-mozhlyvostei-zhinok-i-cholovikiv-na-period-do-2030-roku

Clarke, S. (1991). State, class struggle, and the reproduction of capital. In S. Clarke (Ed.), *The state debate* (pp. 183–203). Palgrave Macmillan. https://doi.org/10.1007/978-1-349-21464-8_6

Czaplinski, P., & Dzhaman, V. (2019). Problems of the Ukrainian labor market. *Journal of Geography, Politics and Society, 9*(4), 24–34. https://doi.org/10.26881/jpgs.2019.4.03

Czarzasty, J., Gajewska, K., & Mrozowicki, A. (2014). Institutions and strategies: Trends and obstacles to recruiting workers into trade unions in Poland. *British Journal of Industrial Relations, 52*(1), 112–135. https://doi.org/10.1111/j.1467-8543.2012.00919.x

Dowling, E. (2021). *The care crisis: What caused it and how can we end it?* Verso.

Drahokoupil, J., & Piasna, A. (2018). What is behind low wages in Central and Eastern Europe? *Post-Communist Economies, 30*(4), 421–439. https://doi.org/10.1080/14631377.2018.1442037

Dutchak, O. (2020). *Mission impossible: Achieving gender equality within neoliberal austerity.* Rosa Luxemburg Stiftung. http://www.rosalux.org.ua/de/ausgewaehltes/203-mission-impossible-achieving-gender-equality-within-neoliberal-austerity

Elson, D. (1998). The economic, the political and the domestic: Businesses, states and households in the organisation of production. *New Political Economy, 3*(2), 189–208. https://doi.org/10.1080/13563469808406349

England, P. (2010). The gender revolution: Uneven and stalled. *Gender & Society, 24*(2), 149–166. https://doi.org/10.1177/0891243210361475

European Commission. (2015). *Implementation of the European Neighbourhood Policy in Ukraine: Progress in 2014 and recommendations for actions* (SWD(2015)74). https://eur-lex.europa.eu/legal-content/EN/TXT/PDF/?uri=CELEX:52015SC0074

European Commission. (2019). *2018 annual report on intra-EU labour mobility*. https://data.europa.eu/doi/10.2767/25927

European Commission. (2020). *Background analysis accompanying the report from the Commission to the European Parliament and the Council on the implementation of macro-financial assistance to third countries in 2019* (SWD(2020)125 final). https://eur-lex.europa.eu/legal-content/EN/TXT/?uri=CELEX%3A52020SC0125

European Food Banks Federation. (2024). *Annual reports 2017–2023*. https://www.eurofoodbank.org/annual-reports/

European Trade Union Confederation. (2021). *European trade unions urge EU to implement Ukraine commitments*. https://www.etuc.org/en/document/european-trade-unions-urge-eu-implement-ukraine-commitments

Eurofound. (2022). *High risk of depression persists following COVID-19 pandemic: Data behind the mental health crisis*. https://www.eurofound.europa.eu/en/blog/2022/high-risk-depression-persists-following-covid-19-pandemic-data-behind-mental-health

Eurofound. (2023). *Unaffordable and inadequate housing in Europe*. Publications Office of the European Union. https://doi.org/10.2806/715002

Eurostat. (2022). *Population and social conditions database*. https://ec.europa.eu/eurostat/web/main/data/database

Eurostat. (2024a). *Living conditions and welfare, income and living conditions, material deprivation, economic strain* [Data set]. https://doi.org/10.2908/ILC_MDES03

Eurostat. (2024b). *Population and social conditions database* [Data set]. https://doi.org/10.2908/LFSA_EPPGA

Eurostat. (2024c). *East European Neighbourhood Policy Countries ENP-East database* [Data set]. https://doi.org/10.2908/ENPE_LFSA_ERGAN

Federal Statistical Office (2024). *Migration and integration database*. https://www.destatis.de/EN/Themes/Society-Environment/Population/Migration-Integration/database-teaser.html

Ferguson, S. (1999). Building on the strengths of the socialist feminist tradition. *Critical Sociology, 25*(1), 1–15. https://doi.org/10.1177/08969205990250010201

Fondation Abbé Pierre, & FEANTSA. (2023). *Eighth overview of housing exclusion in Europe*. https://www.feantsa.org/public/user/Resources/reports/2023/OVERVIEW/Rapport_EN.pdf

Fraser, N. (2014). Can society be commodities all the way down? Post-Polanyian reflections on capitalist crisis. *Economy and Society, 43*(4), 541–558. https://doi.org/10.1080/03085147.2014.898822

Fraser, N. (2016). Contradictions of capital and care. *New Left Review, 100*, 99–117.

Fraser, N. (2022). *Cannibal capitalism: How our system is devouring democracy, care, and the planet and what we can do about it*. Verso.

Fudge, J., & Vosko, L. F. (2001). Gender, segmentation and the standard employment relationship in Canadian labour law, legislation and policy. *Economic and Industrial Democracy, 22*(2), 271–310. https://doi.org/10.1177/0143831X01222005

Glenn, E. N. (1992). From servitude to service work: Historical continuities in the racial division of paid reproductive labor. *Signs: Journal of Women in Culture and Society, 18*(1), 1–43. https://doi.org/10.1086/494777

Główny Urząd Statystyczny. (2024a). *Roczniki Statystyczne Rzeczypospolitej Polskiej*. https://stat.gov.pl/obszary-tematyczne/roczniki-statystyczne/roczniki-statystyczne/rocznik-statystyczny-rzeczypospolitej-polskiej-2024,2,24.html

Główny Urząd Statystyczny. (2024b). *Wykonujący pracę na podstawie umów zlecenia i pokrewnych w Polsce w grudniu 2023 r.* https://stat.gov.pl/statystyki-eksperymentalne

/kapital-ludzki/wykonujacy-prace-na-podstawie-umow-zlecenia-i-pokrewnych-w-polsce-w-grudniu-2023-r-,16,4.html
Górny, A., & Van der Zwan, R. (2024). Mobility and labor market trajectories of Ukrainian migrants to Poland in the context of the 2014 Russian invasion of Ukraine. *European Societies, 26*(2), 438–468. https://doi.org/10.1080/14616696.2023.2298425
Hay, C. (2004). Re-stating politics, re-politicising the state: Neo-liberalism, economic imperatives and the rise of the competition state. *The Political Quarterly, 75*(1), 38–50. https://doi.org/10.1111/j.1467-923X.2004.621_1.x
Holloway, J., & Picciotto, S. (Eds.). (1978). *State and capital: A Marxist debate*. Edward Arnold.
House of Commons Library. (2024). *Food poverty: Households, food banks and free school meals* [Research Briefing]. https://researchbriefings.files.parliament.uk/documents/CBP-9209/CBP-9209.pdf
Humphries, J., & Rubery, J. (1984). The reconstruction of the supply side of the labour market: The relative autonomy of social reproduction. *Cambridge Journal of Economics, 8*(4), 331–346. https://doi.org/10.1093/oxfordjournals.cje.a035554
Inglot, T., Szikra, D., & Raţ, C. (2012). Reforming post-communist welfare states. *Problems of Post-Communism, 59*(6), 27–49. https://doi.org/10.2753/PPC1075-8216590603
International Labour Organization. (2013). *Decent work country profile: Ukraine*. https://www.ilo.org/sites/default/files/wcmsp5/groups/public/@dgreports/@integration/documents/publication/wcms_221717.pdf
International Labour Organization - Central and Eastern European Team (ILO-CEET). (1995). *The Ukrainian challenge: Reforming labour market and social policy*. CEU Press.
International Monetary Fund. (2024). *Global Debt Database*. https://www.imf.org/external/datamapper/datasets/GDD
Kaczmarczyk, P., & Górny, A. (2017). A temporary solution with structural consequences? Ukrainian workers on the Polish labor market (Paper No. 149). *mBank – CASE Seminar Proceedings*, *149*, 1–22. https://ssrn.com/abstract=3076870
Karamessini, M. (2026). The "care transition" in turbulent times. In J. Rubery, N. Sánchez-Mira, & V. Insarauto (Eds.), *Women in turbulent times. Crises, transitions, and challenges for gender equality* (pp. 207–228). Routledge.
Kholod, N. (2012, April 2). Reforming the Ukrainian economy under Yanukovych: The first two years. *Carnegie Endowment for International Peace*. https://carnegieendowment.org/research/2012/04/reforming-the-ukrainian-economy-under-yanukovych-the-first-two-years
Kofman, E., & Raghuram, P. (2015). *Gendered migrations and global social reproduction*. Palgrave Macmillan. https://doi.org/10.1057/9781137510143
Kołodko, G. W., & Nuti, D. M. (1997). *The Polish alternative: Old myths, hard facts and new strategies in the successful transformation of the Polish economy*. UNU-WIDER. https://collections.unu.edu/view/UNU:5198
Korolczuk, E., & Graff, A. (2018). Gender as "Ebola from Brussels": The anti-colonial frame and the rise of illiberal populism. *Signs: Journal of Women in Culture and Society*, *43*(4), 797–821. https://doi.org/10.1086/696691
Lehmann, H., & Pignatti, N. (2018). Informal employment relationships and the labor market: Is there segmentation in Ukraine? *Journal of Comparative Economics*, *46*(3), 838–857. https://doi.org/10.1016/j.jce.2018.07.011
Lewandowski, P., & Magda, I. (2017). Temporary employment, unemployment and employment protection legislation in Poland. In A. Piasna & M. Myant (Eds.), *Myths*

of employment deregulation: How it neither creates jobs nor reduces labour market segmentation (pp. 143–163). ETUI.

Magda, I., Brzeziński, M., Chłoń-Dominczak, A., Kotowska, I., Myck, M., Najsztub, M., & Tyrowicz, J. (2019). *"Rodzina 500+" – ocena programu i propozycje zmian*. IBS. http://ibs.org.pl//app/uploads/2019/05/Raport_500plus.pdf

Marx, K. (1977). *A contribution to the critique of political economy*. Progress Publishers.

Marx, L., Bian, F., & Sánchez-Mira, N. (2026). Crises as drivers of change in couples' paid work arrangements in Europe. In J. Rubery, N. Sánchez-Mira, & V. Insarauto (Eds.), *Women in turbulent times. Crises, transitions, and challenges for gender equality* (pp. 119–140). Routledge.

Ministerstwo Finansów. (2012). *Preferencje podatkowe w Polsce Nr 3*. https://www.podatki.gov.pl/abc-podatkow/podatki-w-polsce/preferencje-podatkowe-w-polsce/

Ministerstwo Rodziny, Pracy i Polityki Społecznej. (2024). *Zatrudnianie cudzoziemców w Polsce Wortal*. https://psz.praca.gov.pl/rynek-pracy/statystyki-i-analizy/zatrudnianie-cudzoziemcow-w-polsce

Muzychenko, V. (2018, February 19–22). Reform of the program of housing and utilities subsidies in conditions of increase energy prices. In *South-South Learning Forum 2018: Building resilience through adaptive social protection*. Frankfurt, Germany. https://pubdocs.worldbank.org/en/721741520534548015/SSLF18-Economic-Shocks-Ukraine.pdf

Myck, M., & Trzciński, K. (2019). From partial to full universality: The family 500+ programme in Poland and its labor supply implications. *ifo DICE Report, 17*(3), 36–44. https://hdl.handle.net/10419/216278

Mykhnenko, V., & Swain, A. (2010). Ukraine's diverging space-economy: The Orange Revolution, post-soviet development models and regional trajectories. *European Urban and Regional Studies, 17*(2), 141–165. https://doi.org/10.1177/0969776409357363

Office for National Statistics. (2021). *Population by country of birth and nationality dataset*. https://www.ons.gov.uk/peoplepopulationandcommunity/populationandmigration/internationalmigration/datasets/populationoftheunitedkingdombycountryofbirthandnationality

Office of the High Commissioner for Human Rights. (2021). *Impact of the COVID-19 pandemic on healthcare workers in Ukraine*. https://ukraine.un.org/en/124052-briefing-note-impact-covid-19pandemic-healthcare-workers-ukraine

Pieńkowski, J. (2020). The impact of labour migration on the Ukrainian economy. *European Commission Discussion Paper, 123*. https://economy-finance.ec.europa.eu/publications/impact-labour-migration-ukrainian-economy_en

Plomien, A. (2019). Gender inequality by design: Does successful implementation of childcare policy deliver gender-just outcomes? *Policy and Society, 38*(4), 643–662. https://doi.org/10.1080/14494035.2019.1617513

Plomien, A., & Schwartz, G. (2020). Labour mobility in transnational Europe: Between depletion, mitigation and citizenship entitlements harm. *European Journal of Politics and Gender, 3*(2), 237–256. https://doi.org/10.1332/251510820X15850652538936

Plomien, A., & Schwartz, G. (2024a). Market-reach into social reproduction and transnational labour mobility in Europe. *New Political Economy, 29*(2), 288–304. https://doi.org/10.1080/13563467.2023.2244448

Plomien, A., & Schwartz, G. (2024b). Welfare as flourishing social reproduction: Polish and Ukrainian migrant workers in a market-participation society. *Global Social Policy, 24*(2), 282–301. https://doi.org/10.1177/14680181231178895

Pluciński, P. (2020). Debt and crisis: Socio-economic critique of neoliberal transformation in Poland. *Economic and Labour Relations Review*, *31*(2), 211–229. https://doi.org/10.1177/1035304620911120
Polanyi, K. (2001). *The great transformation: The political and economic origins of our time*. Beacon Press. (Original work published 1944).
Poznanski, K. Z. (1996). *Poland's protracted transition*. Cambridge University Press. https://doi.org/10.1017/CBO9780511549458
Rai, S. (2024). *Depletion: The human costs of caring*. Oxford University Press. https://doi.org/10.1093/oso/9780197535547.001.0001
Rai, S. M., Hoskyns, C., & Thomas, D. (2014). Depletion: The cost of social reproduction. *International Feminist Journal of Politics*, *16*(1), 86–105. https://doi.org/10.1080/14616742.2013.789641
Razavi, S. (2007). *The political and social economy of care in a development context: Conceptual issues, research questions and policy options* (Paper No. 3). UNRISD Gender and Development Programme.
Rowley, T., & Guz, S. (2022, August 9). Ukraine could abandon key labour principle as part of EU drive. *OpenDemocracy*. https://www.opendemocracy.net/en/odr/ukraine-new-labour-law-social-dialogue/
Shields, S. (2003). The "charge of the right brigade": Transnational social forces and the neoliberal configuration of Poland's transition. *New Political Economy*, *8*(2), 225–244. https://doi.org/10.1080/13563460307174
Shields, S. (2021). Domesticating neoliberalism: "Domification" and the contradictions of the populist countermovement in Poland. *Europe-Asia Studies*, *73*(9), 1622–1640. https://doi.org/10.1080/09668136.2021.1972937
Standing, G. (1999). Global feminization through flexible labor: A theme revisited. *World Development, 27*(3), 582–602. https://doi.org/10.1016/0305-750X(89)90170-8
State Statistics Service of Ukraine – United Nations Women. (2022). *Indicators for the monitoring of gender equality in Ukraine*. https://www.ukrstat.gov.ua/druk/publicat/kat_e/2021/2021_GEIndicators-MonitoringRepor_ENG.pdf
Sutella, P. (2012). *The underachiever: Ukraine's economy since 1991*. The Carnegie Papers. https://coilink.org/20.500.12592/vqbg7g
Ticktin, H. (1992). *Origins of the crisis in the USSR: Essays on the political economy of a disintegrating system*. Routledge.
Tomkiewicz, J. (2016). Tax system in Poland – progressive or regressive? *Journal of Management and Business Administration. Central Europe*, *24*(2), 107–122. https://doi.org/10.7206/jmba.ce.2450-7814.172
Truong, T. D. (1996). Gender, international migration and social reproduction: Implications for theory, policy, research and networking. *Asian and Pacific Migration Journal*, *5*(1), 27–52. https://doi.org/10.1177/011719689600500103
Vodopivec, M., Worgotter, A., & Raju, D. (2005). Unemployment benefit systems in Central and Eastern Europe: A review of the 1990s. *Comparative Economic Studies*, *47*(4), 615–651. https://doi.org/10.1057/palgrave.ces.8100062
Williams, C. C., Round, J., & Rodgers, P. (2011). Explaining the normality of informal employment in Ukraine: A product of exit or exclusion? *American Journal of Economics and Sociology*, *70*(3), 729–755. https://doi.org/10.1111/j.1536-7150.2011.00789.x
World Bank. (2020). *Ukraine–Poverty and equity brief*. World Bank Group. https://databankfiles.worldbank.org/public/ddpext_download/poverty/33EF03BB-9722-4AE2-ABC7-AA2972D68AFE/Global_POVEQ_UKR.pdf

World Bank. (2024). *Database*. https://data.worldbank.org/indicator/SP.DYN.TFRT.IN
World Health Organization. (2024). *Global health expenditure database*. https://apps.who.int/nha/database/ViewData/Indicators/en
World Health Organization Europe. (2021). *Budgetary space for health in Ukraine: Policy document to support budget preparation dialogue for 2021* (Paper No. 20/01). Health Policy Paper Series. https://iris.who.int/handle/10665/350215
Yurchenko, Y. (2018). *Ukraine and the empire of capital: From marketisation to armed conflict*. Pluto Press. https://doi.org/10.2307/j.ctv7h0tq7

9

ENHANCING DIGNITY AND EQUITY

Homecare workforce challenges amidst the cost-of-living crisis, with a focus on California

Enrique Lopezlira and Savannah Hunter

Introduction

Homecare workers play a vital role in supporting older adults and individuals with disabilities, enabling them to live safely and with dignity in their homes and communities. By assisting with activities of daily living (ADLs) such as bathing, dressing, meal preparation, medication management and transportation, homecare workers provide essential care that is both physically and emotionally demanding. This labour-intensive work, often performed by women of colour and immigrants, has historically been undervalued and excluded from basic labour protections due to systemic racism and sexism (Boris & Klein, 2012). Homecare is a preferred and cost-effective alternative to institutional care (Kitchener et al., 2006). Despite being in high demand and facing job shortages, homecare in the United States remains at the bottom of the occupational hierarchy, marked by low wages and high turnover. Even within the homecare workforce, systemic underinvestment in long-term care and fragmented governance have led to significant disparities in job quality among homecare workers across the United States and California (Milkman, 2023).

This chapter is concerned with job quality among homecare workers during two recent turbulences, the Covid-19 pandemic and the cost-of-living crisis. We primarily focus on homecare workers in California's In-Home Supportive Services (IHSS) programme, the largest publicly-funded homecare system in the United States. The IHSS programme is a "consumer-directed" model where over 795,000 low-income care recipients independently hire and supervise their homecare workers, most of them relatives of the recipients (Rhee et al., 2024).[1] While a statewide programme, county governments operate IHSS and bargain locally with homecare workers, resulting in notable geographical differences in wages

DOI: 10.4324/9781003528210-12

and benefits. We situate California's publicly-funded homecare programme as a case study of the broader challenges facing a stratified and fragmented homecare workforce during economic crises.

A first section sets the scene of how homecare came to be structured as a devalued and low-wage occupation in the United States and California, underscoring how welfare policy, fragmented governance and union organising have contributed to heterogeneity in job quality. We then examine the demographic and economic realities of the IHSS workforce and show how the Covid-19 pandemic and the ongoing cost-of-living crisis have further exposed and exacerbated long-standing inequities faced by the homecare workforce, with a focus on the differing impact high inflation and local cost of living have had on workers' wages. We highlight the successes of union organising and collective bargaining in improving wages, benefits and job security, but show how these gains remain unevenly distributed across the state. We end with calls for sustained investment in homecare jobs and policies that revalue the essential labour provided by homecare workers to improve job quality and ensure equitable treatment for a workforce that provides essential care.

The structure of homecare as a low-wage occupation in the United States and California

Homecare, an occupation that disproportionately employs women, workers of colour and immigrants, has been shaped by crises and government policy. During the economic crisis of the Great Depression in the 1930s the United States' Works Progress Administration (WPA) created new publicly-funded homecare occupations as a form of work relief for poor unemployed women, particularly Black women who had prior experience as domestic workers (Boris & Klein, 2012). These women worked to help poor families, the elderly and those with medical conditions live at home with dignity and avoid institutionalisation or foster care. The occupation became part of the welfare state and marketed as a job for low-income women, still considered unskilled and separate from the prestige of the nursing or medical profession (Boris & Klein, 2012). A result of the Great Depression was the United States' foundational wage and hours laws that set a minimum wage and rights to overtime (Lichtenstein, 2003); however, the legacy of slavery and homecare's association with unpaid women's work excluded the occupation from basic protections (Boris & Klein, 2012). The devaluing of care jobs was reinforced again in 1975 when homecare workers (along with babysitters) were again carved out from the country's foundational minimum wage and hour laws under the guise that these women were friendly elder companions, visitors or sitters and not workers (Boris & Klein, 2012).

The government played a central role in shaping the homecare labour market, both relying on the devaluation of women and women of colour's labour as well as perpetuating homecare as a low-wage occupation. The act of funneling poor women of colour into low-wage homecare jobs as a form of work relief would for decades continue to shape the demographic make-up of the occupation (Boris & Klein, 2012). In the 1960s, the United States' War on Poverty policies reinforced racial and gender segregation by expanding homecare and encouraging poor women receiving cash assistance through a welfare programme called Aid to Families with Dependent Children (AFDC) into the low-wage profession (Boris & Klein, 2012). Racism and cultural ideas that the undeserving poor abuse welfare systems fuelled approaches to fill needed homecare jobs with poor women on welfare who could be "rehabilitated" through employment (Katz, 2013). These practices continued into the 1990s when President Bill Clinton's welfare reform eliminated AFDC and replaced it with the more limited Temporary Assistance for Needy Families (TANF) programme which set a five-year limit on receiving welfare benefits and required poor, often single, mothers to work in exchange for benefits after two years. Welfare reform in the United States pushed many women into low-wage jobs including in homecare (Edin & Shaefer, 2016).

Over the last several decades, periods of high inflation like in the 1970s and economic recessions have fuelled concerns over public sector budget deficits. Homecare jobs continued to grow in demand but in response to these crises they also became casualised (Boris & Klein, 2012). For state governments, classifying homecare workers as independent contractors became a strategy to avoid employer responsibility to follow labour and employment laws (Smith, 2008). Additionally, the structure of federalism allowed governments to search for levers to off-load the costs of homecare to other levels of government or contract out the work to non-governmental organisations, thereby creating different forms of work arrangements for homecare workers across the United States. These differing forms of work arrangements, payment systems and the lack of clarity about how to interpret workers' employment status have created a complicated and confusing system to navigate and further cemented homecare jobs as low wage (Boris & Klein, 2012).

California was not immune to these broader national trends. In the 1970s, public resistance to high taxes, referred to as the Tax Revolt, created financial instability and made it harder to raise local revenues in response to economic changes or growth in population (Boris & Klein, 2012). California's publicly-funded homecare programme called In-Home Supportive Services (IHSS) operates as an entitlement programme – in which any person with a need for care and a low enough income is eligible to receive care – but it has often been viewed as a convenient programme to put on the budget chopping block (Boris & Klein, 2012). For example, during the Great Recession in the 2010s, IHSS programme funding was cut by hundreds of millions of dollars and homecare workers' hours decreased, impacting both the amount of care recipients could receive and the earnings of homecare workers (California Budget Project, 2012; Murphy et al., 2019). The amount of service hours recipients could receive was not restored until the 2015–2016 fiscal year (Legislative Analyst's Office [LAO], 2015).

These dynamics have shaped a complex homecare industry with different employment relations. Individuals who need care and have low enough income may be able to access publicly-funded care, which is contracted out and run by private agencies in some states but run by state or local governments in others (Milkman, 2023). However, many who need care will have to purchase it through private sector agencies or hire self-employed homecare workers in an unregulated "grey market" (Milkman, 2023). In some states, homecare workers have unionised, contributing to stratification in wages between union and non-union workers (Milkman, 2023; Rhee et al., 2025).

In California, the In-Home Supportive Services programme operates under an "independent provider" model supported by federal, state and local county funds, whereby the care recipient has the autonomy to hire, supervise and fire the homecare worker. State law shapes the complex arrangement between the recipient, the state and local governments, shaping both the experiences of care recipients and workers. The state sets overall programme policy, such as determining recipients' eligibility for services and setting the level of care provided and issues workers' paychecks (Rhee et al., 2025). Each of California's 58 counties administers the IHSS programme locally by handling recipient eligibility determinations, worker enrolment and ensuring quality control. Workers, through their unions, negotiate with local county government public authorities over wages and benefits (Boris & Klein, 2007; Delp & Quan, 2002). While negotiations take place at the local level, state policy on cost-sharing sets a limit on what the state will finance with counties covering the rest. Counties' local budgetary resources vary and thus union agreements, including wage rates, differ across counties. Though many homecare workers are paid through public funds, they are not considered public employees, highlighting again the unique structure of homecare work within the broader labour market (Boris & Klein, 2007).

The IHSS programme allows family members to serve as homecare workers for relatives, as is also the case in other states, including Washington, Oregon and Illinois (Edwards, 2023). Seven out of ten homecare workers (72%) are relatives of the care recipient and 59% of all homecare workers live with their client (Rhee et al., 2025). This creates an opportunity for IHSS to serve as a form of income support for work that otherwise would have been performed unpaid (Boris & Klein, 2012). This is in line with a recent report calling for such unpaid care time to be converted into paid work time across the United States due to it leading to increasing economic insecurity for poor women in old age (Forden et al., 2023). Low job quality and poor compensation contribute to high turnover in homecare, impacting the health of the recipient and creating a cycle of recruitment, training and relationship building between the homecare worker and recipient (Rhee et al., 2025). Overall 16.8% left the IHSS programme in 2023, but the rate of turnover was twice as high for non-family homecare workers compared to family homecare workers (28.1% compared to 12.7%) (Rhee et al., 2025). The latter group may be less likely to turnover even with poor job quality, given significant personal commitment to care for their own family members (Howes, 2004). However, publicly-funded homecare programmes will not be able to rely only on family members to care for programme recipients as the population ages and fewer family members are available to care for older adults (Rhee et al., 2025).

Throughout each crisis, the government has been the primary funder of homecare services but has at times perpetuated the devaluation of care work and cultural ideas that those who relied on state-funded social benefits programmes were undeserving, abusing the system and needed rehabilitation through employment. Low wages in homecare continued to be justified due to its association with unpaid and "unskilled" work that women and women of colour were traditionally expected to perform for free (Smith, 2008). Low wages, wage theft and poor treatment of homecare workers have also been justified morally by an "ethics of care" which demands that the homecare worker sacrifice themselves to care for those who need it (Boris & Klein, 2012).

Demographics of homecare workers

These structural forces combined have shaped the occupation as one at the bottom of the occupational hierarchy. Estimates of the exact size of the workforce are challenging to obtain due to imprecise survey measurement, differing definitions of the workforce and undercounting of informal workers, immigrant workers or multiple-job holders (Banerjee et al., 2022; Hunt et al., 2023). Estimates for homecare workers nationally are around 1.4 million (Banerjee et al., 2022), but in California alone, the IHSS programme employs over half a million workers (CDSS, 2024) which does not include workers providing private or informal care. Previous research has identified that homecare workers are predominantly women and women of colour, include higher shares of immigrant workers and tend to be older (Banerjee et al., 2022; Campbell, 2017; Paraprofessional Healthcare Institute [PHI], 2022). In addition, studies have shown that intersecting identities likely shape experiences in the homecare workforce. Workers of different racial/ethnic groups report differences in having children at home, levels of education, wages, income, full-time employment and experiences with poverty and public assistance usage (PHI, 2022).

Figure 9.1 shows major demographic characteristics of homecare workers who serve through the publicly-funded In-Home Supportive Services (IHSS) programme in California. These data come from administrative records and represent the entire universe of state-funded homecare workers; however, limited demographic characteristics are collected. IHSS homecare workers are predominantly female (74.3%), the majority are over the age of 45 (median age is 51) and about a quarter (26.4%) report primarily speaking a language other than English. The consumer-directed nature of the programme likely shapes the make-up of the IHSS workforce. IHSS homecare workers predominately care for one programme recipient (79.6%) and most of the recipients are relatives (72.1%). The

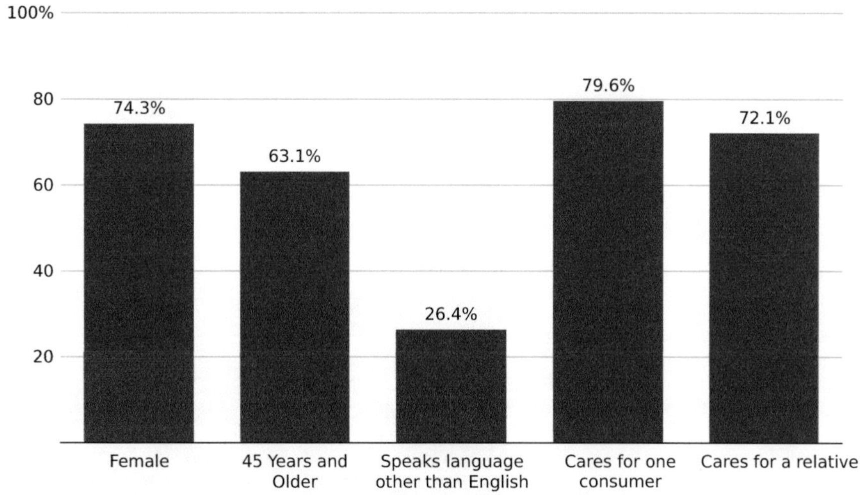

FIGURE 9.1 Demographic Characteristics of Homecare Workers in California's In-Home Supportive Services Programme, 2024.

Source: Own elaboration based on data from the California Department of Social Services Case Management Information System Data (CDSS, 2024). Created with Datawrapper.

amount of hours worked depends on how much care recipients are authorised for by the programme. On average, most recipients are allowed 117 hours of care per month, which enables the average homecare worker to work around 29 hours per week (Rhee et al., 2025). Median annual earnings for IHSS homecare workers employed year-round is only $23,006.

Figure 9.2 shows the demographics of homecare workers in California using data from the United States Census' American Community Survey 2018–2022 (ACS). Table A9-1 in the online appendix provides complete demographic characteristics for the homecare workforce in California and the United States. ACS data likely include workers in the IHSS programme as well as homecare workers more broadly who are employed in other arrangements. Estimates suggest 75% of all homecare workers work in the IHSS programme (Kerstein, 2024) but it is not possible to distinguish between the two groups in the ACS data. ACS data undercount the number of homecare workers in the state but offer a broader picture of this workforce including race/ethnicity, educational attainment and other key characteristics. Homecare workers in California are disproportionately female (79.3%), non-white (74.7%) and foreign-born (48.3%) with respect to the overall workforce in the state. Non-Hispanic Black, Non-Hispanic Asian American or Pacific Islander, Hispanic and foreign-born workers disproportionately serve as homecare workers compared to their make-up in the workforce both in California and in the United States overall (Table A9-1, online appendix). This diversity is reflected in the primary languages spoken by homecare workers with over half

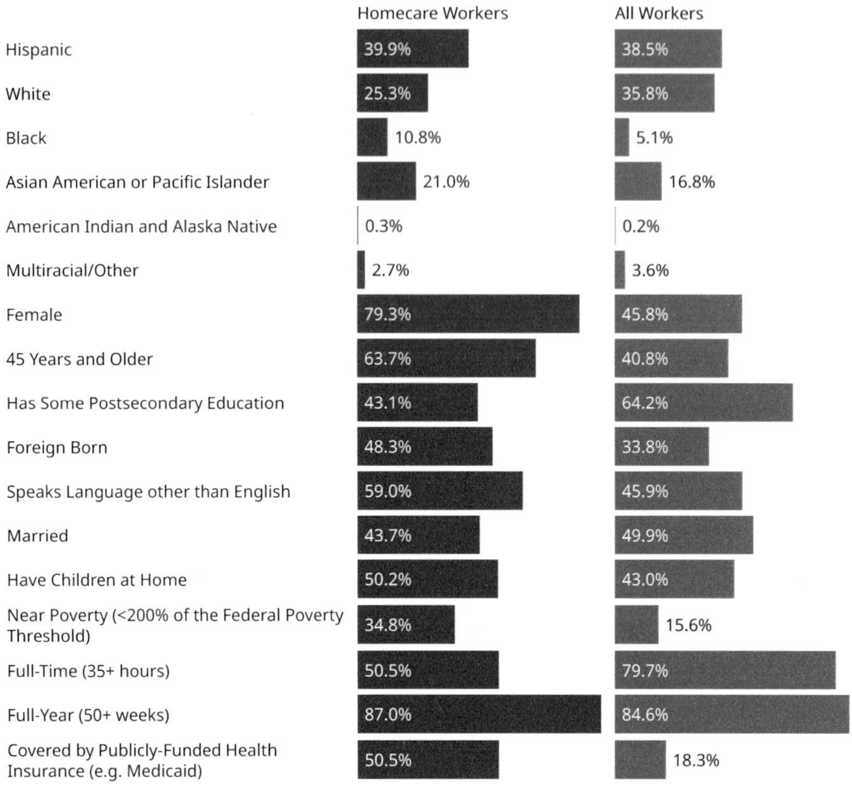

FIGURE 9.2 Demographic Characteristics of all Homecare Workers in California, 2018–2022.

Source: Own elaboration based on data from the American Community Survey 2018–2022 obtained from IPUMS USA (Ruggles et al., 2024). Sample includes employed workers (including self-employed) over the age of 18 with non-zero earnings who were not unpaid family members. Created with Datawrapper.

(59.0%) speaking a language other than English at home.[2] Homecare workers in California and the United States tend to have lower levels of education than the workforce more broadly and are less likely to have achieved a bachelor's or graduate degree. However, about four out of ten have experienced some type of post-secondary education.

In California and the United States, most homecare workers are employed year-round, but only around half work full-time. Working time is complex in the home-care industry in the United States as in other countries. Workers' pay is tied to the number of hours the recipient is eligible to receive, the schedule they are assigned in the case of agency workers, and whether they are compensated for travel time, breaks and training (Rubery et al., 2015). Inadequate hours, involuntary part-time employment and unpaid time all shape insufficient pay. Heterogeneity in work hours is common across and within employment relations both in the United States and abroad (Macdonald et al., 2018; Milkman, 2023; Rubery et al., 2015). A survey of homecare workers employed in the private market in California found that more than a third worked less than 25 hours a week, about half worked full-time and one in ten worked more than 65 hours a week (UCLA Labor Center, 2022), with agency workers more likely to work greater numbers of hours than those hired directly by the recipient (UCLA Labor Center, 2022). Additionally, while many worked overtime, half said they never received compensation, suggesting significant unpaid time and wage theft in the industry.

For many homecare workers, part-time work is involuntary. A study in New York among homecare agency workers found that work schedules fluctuated often as workers shifted between clients who might be allocated different amounts of hours of care (Milkman, 2023). Nationally, a survey of union and non-union homecare workers found that eight out of ten desired to work more hours, a third worked a second job and half were seeking additional employment (Christman, 2017). For some workers, not getting enough hours, along with low pay, leads to inconsistent and inadequate earnings. Others face significant overwork, with a majority of the survey respondents reporting they put in extra time before or after their shift "off the clock" (Christman, 2017). These factors, combined with the emotional labour that goes beyond their formal duties, highlight the economic strain homecare workers face, making it difficult for them to achieve financial stability (Christman, 2017).

Low wages in combination with part-time employment contribute to lower earnings. In California and the United States, homecare workers' median annual earnings were less than half what the median worker earned in the workforce overall ($23,951 in California and $24,386 in the United States). The share of homecare workers at or "near" poverty is double that of the workforce overall. In California, a third (34.8%) of homecare workers make 200% or less than the Federal Poverty Threshold (i.e., "near" poverty) compared to 15.6% of the workforce overall. And half are enrolled in publicly-funded low-income health insurance programmes (e.g., Medicaid).

Impact of the Covid-19 pandemic

The Covid-19 pandemic brought to light and intensified existing challenges within the homecare workforce, at both the state and the national levels. The Covid-19 pandemic profoundly affected direct care workers (including homecare workers), who had been widely categorised as "essential" since the beginning of the health crisis. According to True et al. (2020), 29% of direct care workers contracted Covid-19 during the pandemic. Despite their crucial role on the frontlines, many of these workers had to operate without adequate protection or proper compensation and benefits to ensure their economic security. A qualitative study of home healthcare workers in New York City, an early epicentre of the pandemic, revealed that these workers often felt invisible. They received inconsistent information and support from their employers, frequently had to source their own supplies and resources and faced an increased risk of Covid-19 transmission (Sterling et al., 2020). A national survey conducted in November 2020, which included responses from over 9,000 direct support professionals showed: 47% reported being exposed to Covid-19 at work, with higher transmission rates in congregate settings such as nursing homes or residential facilities (Hewitt et al., 2021). Although 97% were designated as "essential", 54% noted a decline in their work conditions and only 30% reported receiving a salary increase (Hewitt et al., 2021).

One significant shift during the Covid-19 pandemic was the increased preference for care at home, as opposed to facility-based care, due to the heightened risk of virus transmission to vulnerable populations in nursing homes (UCLA Labor Center, 2022). Workers were faced with difficult trade-offs between continuing to work, thereby risking their personal safety and that of their families, or quitting and facing deep financial instability (Allison et al., 2020; Sterling et al., 2020). Those who chose to continue providing care often felt invisible, dispensable, undervalued and disregarded as essential members of healthcare teams (Allison et al., 2020; Milkman, 2023; Sterling et al., 2020). This sentiment was exacerbated by the inconsistent classification of these workers as "essential", which varied by state and had significant implications. For instance, essential classification typically granted access to support systems, testing, vaccines and personal protective equipment (PPE). However, many direct care workers were expected to perform new duties, prevent virus transmission and care for patients without adequate resources (Allison et al., 2020; Milkman, 2023; Sterling et al., 2020; Tyler et al., 2021).

The pandemic's impact on women, who predominantly perform homecare work, and the industry itself was profound. There was a surge in unemployment, as demand for homecare services declined due both to those in need of care avoiding seeking care out of fear of infection, as well as to recipients getting sick and requiring hospitalisation rather than in-home care. Additionally, many homecare workers voluntarily separated from employment due to concerns about exposure to the virus or because the closure of schools and childcare centres required them to stay home to care for their families (Rowe et al., 2020; Tyler et al., 2021). Homecare job shortages persisted due to the industry's low wages, lack of benefits, inconsistent training and the inherent risks associated with the work (Tyler et al., 2021).

In California, the state took measures to mitigate the impact on homecare workers, particularly those in the IHSS programme, implementing hazard pay and one-time bonus payments. There was also an effort to secure PPE for workers, but access to PPE was uneven, with rural areas receiving less support (Myles, 2020).

Nationally, the pandemic highlighted the need for systemic reforms in how homecare workers are compensated and protected. Worker shortages have not disappeared. The demand for homecare services is rebounding and is expected to continue growing. As the world continues to recover from the Covid-19 pandemic, both those in need of care and workers face ongoing challenges. The former struggle to afford care, while workers contend with low wages in the face of record inflation and a persistent cost-of-living crisis, particularly in California.

IHSS homecare workers' earnings in the context of the cost-of-living crisis

Federalism, the fractured structure of government-funded homecare and cultural devaluation of homecare work have led to differing employment relations and levels of wages and benefits across the United States and within California (Boris & Klein, 2012; Milkman, 2023). In the 1990s, California engaged in a policy strategy called realignment, shifting the administration of social welfare programmes including IHSS, from the state to local governments. The IHSS programme is funded with federal, state and local dollars and counties administer the programme locally and share in the programme costs. Because of the localised operations of homecare, homecare workers' collective bargaining also occurs at the county level. The local county public authority is considered the employer of record (Boris & Klein, 2012), which means that counties have different levels of local general funding available, differing political environments and resultantly IHSS workers have organised at different times and have different collective bargaining agreements with different levels of wages and benefits. While homecare workers perform similar types of work state-wide, they are not all paid the same and are differently affected by differing levels of cost of living between counties across the state.

California's state minimum wage sets the baseline for homecare workers, with unions negotiating an additional wage supplement at the county level that rises as the state minimum wage increases annually. The Fight for $15 movement, a campaign led by low-wage workers including fast food and homecare workers, advocated for a $15 minimum wage to combat income inequality and improve living standards. Although the Fight for $15 was a national campaign, California became the first state to adopt a $15 minimum wage in 2016. As a result, the state-wide minimum wage increased by $1 each year from 2018 to 2022, leading to wage growth for IHSS homecare workers and gradual increases in the wage supplement above the state minimum. Figure 9.3 shows wage growth in the average IHSS homecare worker's wage during this period. Lighter grey bars show the evolution of the levels of the state minimum wage and darker grey bars show the amount of the average supplement unions and counties negotiated above the state minimum. Importantly, these averages mask the underlying variation in IHSS homecare workers' wages by county, which is illustrated in Figure 9.4. As of July 2024, IHSS wages in California ranged from the state-wide minimum of $16 to $21.50 in San Francisco, with a weighted average wage of $18.13 and a weighted

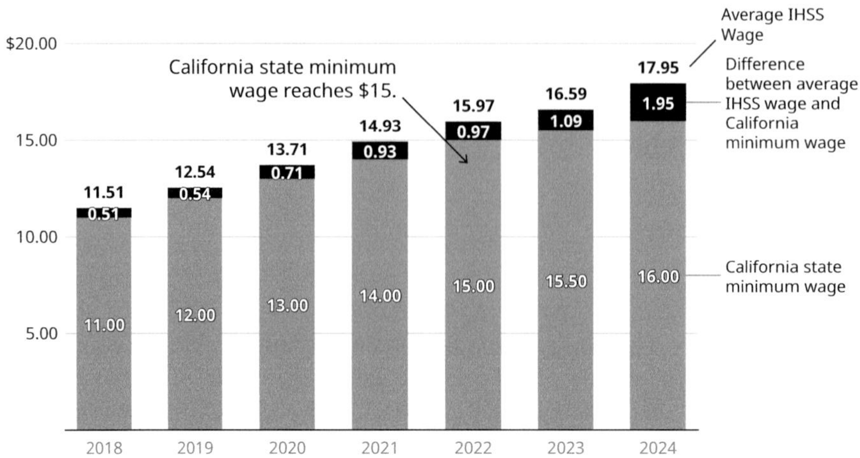

FIGURE 9.3 Average IHSS Worker Wage vs. the California State Minimum Wage, 2018–2024.

Source: Own elaboration based on data from the California Department of Social Services Case Management Information System Data (CDSS, 2024). Average IHSS worker wage is weighted by the share of hours paid out in each county (counties employ different numbers of IHSS workers and pay different rates). Created with Datawrapper.

median of $18.00. This wage variation across counties is due to factors such as differences in the cost of living and how each county administers the programme, including union negotiations and wage agreements. Wages are generally highest in the San Francisco Bay area, coastal and southern counties, while northern and central California counties, which have higher rural populations (Johnson & Cuellar Mejia, 2024), tend to offer lower wages.

Despite growth in IHSS homecare workers' wages between 2018 and 2024, high inflation caused mainly by supply chain disruptions associated with the Covid-19 pandemic resulted in a decline in their real value (Ball et al., 2022). In 2022, the United States experienced the highest year-on-year inflation since 1980. Figure 9.5 shows year-to-year changes in the inflation-adjusted weighted average homecare worker wage. The average homecare worker wage grew by at least 6% each year between January 2019 and January 2021. Much of this growth was due to rises in the California state minimum wage. However, as the cost of living increased rapidly, homecare worker wages did not keep up. Between January 2021 and January 2022, the value of homecare worker wages fell by a little more than half a percentage point and fell again by 1% between January 2022 and January 2023. As inflation began to slow, the average inflation-adjusted homecare wage grew by 4.8%. While growth in workers' wages was trending positive again, high inflation left a toll. The average workers' wage was only $0.54 above where it had been in January 2021.

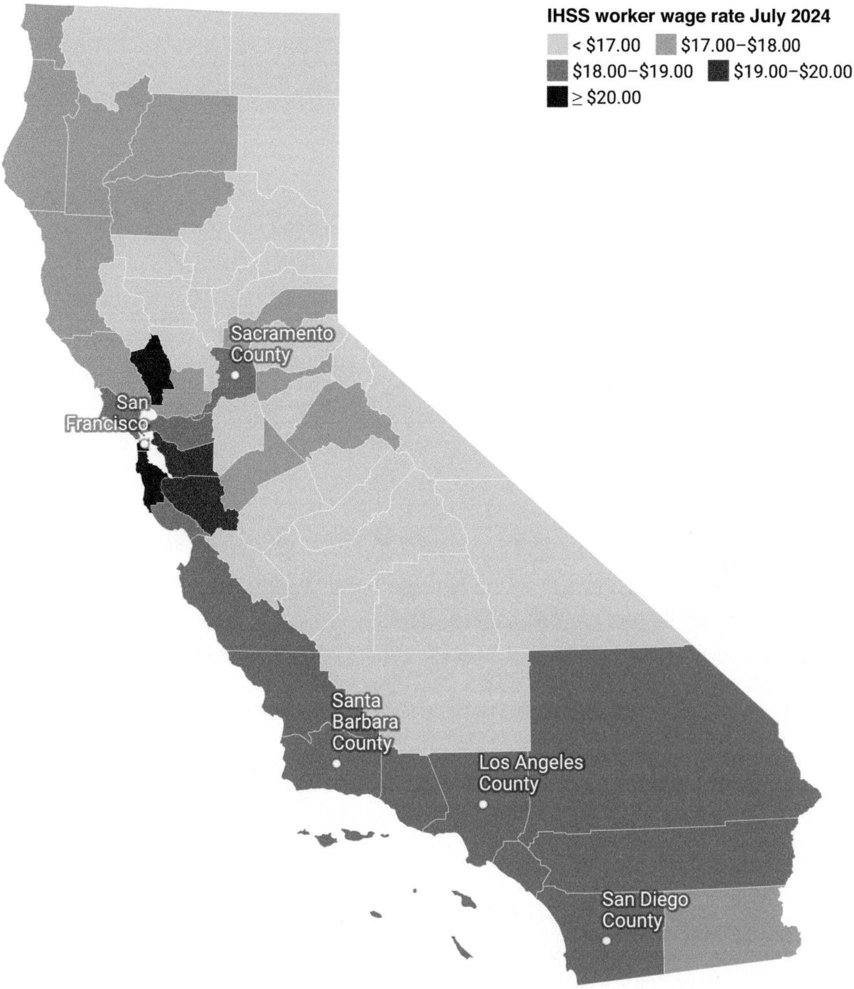

FIGURE 9.4 IHSS Worker Wage Rates by California County, 2024.

Source: Own elaboration based on data from the California Department of Social Services Case Management Information System Data (CDSS, 2024). Hourly wage rates in 2024 dollars. The weighted average IHSS worker wage statewide was $18.13 and the median was $18.00. Created with Datawrapper.

However, not all homecare workers experienced positive wage growth by January 2024. Figure 9.6 shows homecare worker wage levels between 2018 and 2024 and demonstrates both how wages vary by county but also how recovery occurred unevenly. For example, homecare workers' wages in Santa Clara County lost value between 2021 and 2022 but experienced real wage growth in the following two years, while other counties recovered more slowly if at all. Overall, 34 counties had lower wages in real terms in January 2024 than they did in either 2021

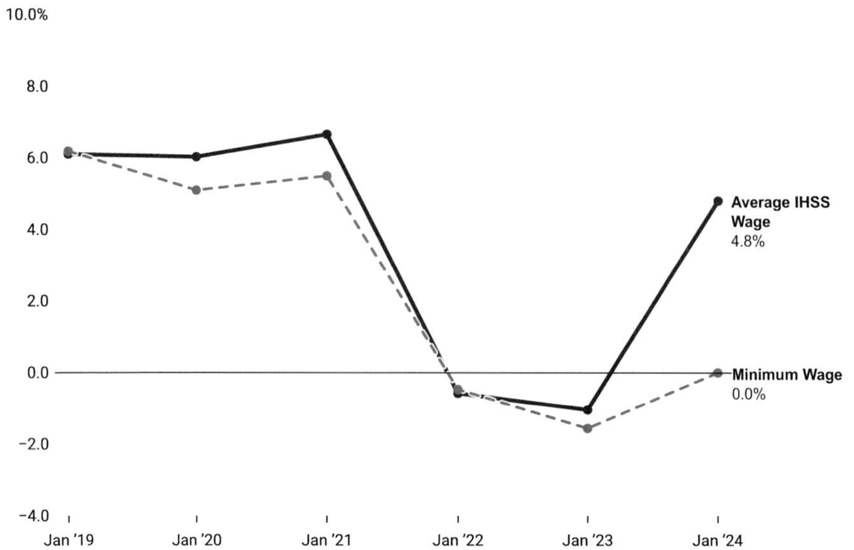

FIGURE 9.5 Real Wage Growth of the Average IHSS Worker Wage and the California State Minimum Wage, 2018–2024.

Source: Own elaboration based on data from the California Department of Social Services Case Management Information System Data (CDSS, 2024). The average IHSS worker wage is weighted by county paid hours and is inflation-adjusted using the California Consumer Price Index for Urban Wage Earners and Clerical Workers (CPI-W). Created with Datawrapper.

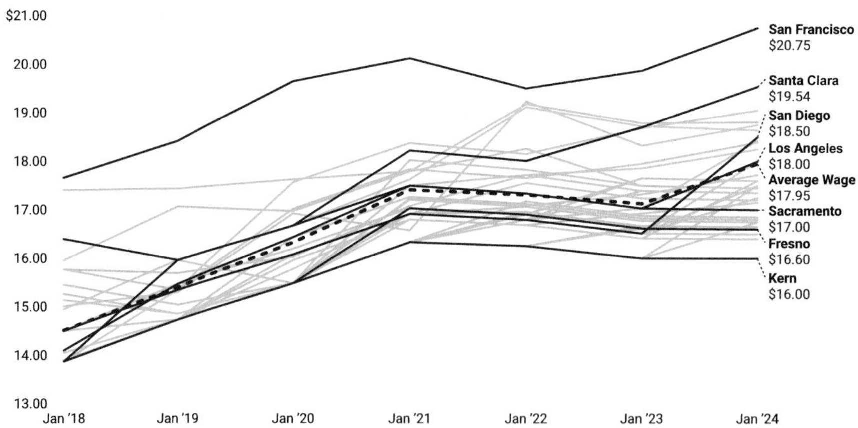

FIGURE 9.6 Inflation-Adjusted IHSS Worker Wages by County, 2018–2024.

Source: Own elaboration based on data from the California Department of Social Services Case Management Information System Data (CDSS, 2024). Average IHSS worker wage is weighted by county paid hours. Wages are in 2024 dollars and were inflation-adjusted using the California Consumer Price Index for Urban Wage Earners and Clerical Workers (CPI-W). Created with Datawrapper.

or 2022. These counties tended to employ a smaller share of homecare workers and represent about 20% of the total homecare worker population. Six of the 34 counties had reversed this trend and reported higher wages in real terms by July 2024.

While the San Francisco Bay area, coastal and southern counties tend to offer higher wages than northern and central valley California counties, when factoring in the cost of living, no IHSS homecare workers in any county are offered a wage high enough for a worker to support their basic needs according to the Massachusetts Institute for Technology (MIT) Living Wage Calculator (Glasmeier & Massachusetts Institute of Technology [MIT], 2024) (See Figure 9.7).[3] For California as a whole, the hourly wage needed to meet basic living expenses was $27.32 for a single adult with no children, $33.26 for two working adults with two children and $47.96 for a single adult with one child (Glasmeier & MIT, 2024). Living wage estimates vary by county depending on cost of living. Figure 9.7 shows IHSS homecare workers' wage rates as a share of MIT living wage estimates for each county. No county currently offers a wage great enough for a single adult without children to meet their basic needs. Workers' wages in Los Angeles County, which hosts the largest population of IHSS homecare workers in the state, only cover 75% of basic needs for a single-adult.[4] While Bay Area counties offer higher wages, higher costs of living mean that a single adult working full-time would only be able to cover between 51–75% of their basic needs. Rural, northern and central valley counties tend to offer lower wages and have slightly lower costs of living. However, even factoring in lower costs of living, these counties also do not offer living wages.

The fractured structure of homecare work, even within the same government-funded programme, provides a case study to understand how homecare workers are impacted by crises. Homecare is a low-wage job across the United States and California, but differing employment relations (employee versus independent contractor), unionisation status, political environments and government funding availability can translate into heterogeneity in earnings within the occupation, suggesting that workers do not all experience economic crisis identically. For example, IHSS homecare workers in some counties started to see positive wage growth more quickly than others, and by January 2024, some counties had not recovered at all. This included Kern County, where the union had been without a contract for seven years and only recently struck a deal for a hard-fought one-dollar wage increase spread out over the course of three years (Donegan, 2024).

Gains from union organizing

The intimate relationship between the homecare sector and the state has prompted long-standing efforts to achieve dignity and recognition for homecare workers. Through organising campaigns, workers have focused on increasing public funding for homecare in order to improve workers' wages (Delp & Quan, 2002). A central focus of homecare organising has been to grant care workers visibility and dignity by framing their labour as a public good (Boris & Klein, 2007).

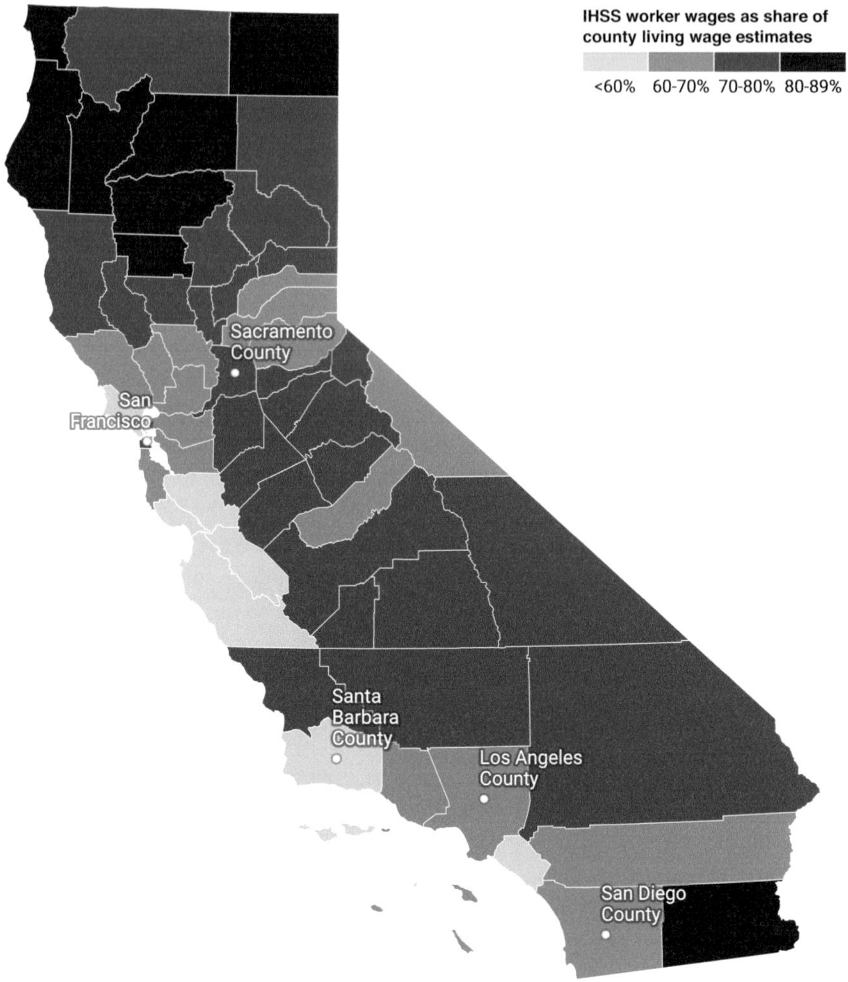

FIGURE 9.7 IHSS Workers' Wages Relative to County-Level Living Wage Estimates, 2024.

Source: Own elaboration based on data from the California Department of Social Services Case Management Information System Data (CDSS, 2024). Living wage estimates are based on expenses for a single full-time working adult with no children and are sourced from the Massachusetts Institute for Technology (MIT, 2024). Created with Datawrapper.

Collective bargaining has significantly improved the wages, benefits and working conditions for IHSS homecare workers in California. Over the years, IHSS workers, represented by two unions, the United Domestic Workers (UDW) and Service Employees International Union (SEIU), have fought for and won substantial gains, transforming an underpaid workforce into one with improved protections and compensation.

Historic legislative wins

The collective power of IHSS workers and their unions resulted in landmark legislative achievements.

- In 1999, IHSS homecare workers won the right to collective bargaining, marking a pivotal moment in their fight for better working conditions.
- Overtime pay was another major victory in 2013, ending a 75-year exclusion from these protections. This victory was followed by a successful campaign in 2014 that prevented restrictions on overtime that would have limited workers to 40 hours per week and disrupted care provision.
- Paid travel time between clients and compensation for medical accompaniment were won in 2014, addressing gaps in compensation that disproportionately affected caregivers providing services to multiple care recipients.

Fighting cuts and defending services

Over the years, IHSS workers have also successfully fought back against attempts to reduce services and pay. In 2009, California faced significant budget deficits, prompting proposals to reduce IHSS workers' wages to the state minimum of $8 per hour, while severely cutting services to some and entirely eliminating service to other care recipients. Advocacy from unions prevented politicians from implementing these proposals that would have reduced care to about 87% of IHSS care recipients. One year later, unions thwarted efforts to completely eliminate the IHSS programme under Governor Schwarzenegger, protecting tens of thousands of vulnerable care recipients from losing essential care, and tens of thousands of care workers.

Union efforts were also instrumental in 2012 in blocking within court a 20% cut to IHSS hours. This legal win was followed by efforts to stop an additional 7% cut to hours in 2015, 2016, 2019 and finally in 2020, during the Covid-19 pandemic, when unions prevented the reinstatement of these cuts despite massive budget deficits. In 2021, unions pushed back on the 7% cut to hours once and for all, a significant victory for both workers and care recipients.

Protecting workers and strengthening the programme

In addition to protecting wages and benefits, collective bargaining has led to systemic improvements in the IHSS programme. For example, in 2007, unions successfully pushed for legislation allowing IHSS workers to receive their pay directly into their bank account (direct deposit), making payments more reliable than with the previous paper cheque-based system which led many workers to financial stability due to delayed, lost or stolen cheques. In 2011, unions helped end burdensome bureaucratic requirements, such as multiple background checks for workers in different counties and the fingerprinting of IHSS clients and home-care workers, which unnecessarily complicated care provision.

Wage increases

One of the most tangible benefits of collective bargaining has been increases in wages for many IHSS workers. For example, in San Bernardino County, a recent contract resulted in a nearly 10% wage increase, raising hourly wages from $16 to $17.60 by January 2024. Moreover, unions have secured local wage supplements in many counties, which ensure that IHSS wages are always set above the state minimum wage by a predetermined amount.

Improved benefits and resources

In addition to wage increases, IHSS workers have gained access to a variety of other critical benefits through collective bargaining.

- Personal Protective Equipment (PPE): recent IHSS contracts allocated new funding, such as $10,000 specifically for PPE, addressing the workers' needs during the Covid-19 pandemic and beyond.
- Training: funding for essential training has also been secured. For example, $50,000 set aside in San Bernardino County for upskilling workers to provide better care and improve job security.
- Paid Sick Leave: in 2016, IHSS workers won the right to paid sick leave, which was a significant victory for a workforce that historically lacked such basic protections.

Most recently, unions have fought to ensure that counties bargain in good faith with IHSS workers. In 2021, they won legislation that financially penalises counties for refusing to engage in fair negotiations, ensuring a more just and equitable bargaining process. These victories demonstrate the power of organised labour in protecting and advancing the rights of essential workers.

Conclusion and implications for policy

Working at the bottom of the labour market and primarily funded by public dollars, homecare workers are vulnerable to economic crises. The structure of federalism, cultural devaluation of an occupation performed by predominantly racial/ethnic minorities, immigrants and women, differing political environments and levels of unionisation among other forces have shaped homecare as a low-wage job while also creating stratification within the occupation. As such, homecare workers may not all experience crises equally. This chapter has analysed California's In-Home Supportive Services programme as a case of the broader phenomenon.

Local county-level administration of the IHSS programme results in workers performing the same jobs but receiving different wages and benefits, and the recovery from inflation-induced wage devaluation due to Covid-19 supply chain disruptions has occurred at varying times and rates. While no IHSS homecare worker earns a wage high enough to cover basic expenses, stratification within the state results in disparities in pay and benefits. How homecare workers – both under the IHSS programme and more broadly – will navigate future crises will depend on whether workers, unions, care recipients and policymakers address the underlying differences in homecare employment relations and secure stable funding for long-term care. We next outline key policy strategies that could be implemented to achieve these aims.

The devaluation of homecare work and the women, workers of colour and immigrants who perform it, is central to the structure of homecare as a low-wage job in California and the United States as it is the case in other advanced economies. Revaluing care labour as important, essential and productive is critical to address gender and racial/ethnic inequality, enhance worker dignity and attract and retain a workforce to care for our ageing population (Boris & Klein, 2012; Smith, 2008). The public sector finances around 80% of homecare occupations in the United States through publicly-funded healthcare programmes (Medicaid and Medicare) and should be the prime target for revaluing care work and improving homecare worker job quality (Howes, 2014; Leberstein et al., 2015).

Policy strategies to improve homecare in California and the United States more broadly should address the structures maintaining homecare as a low-wage job. Central to policy recommendations is significant and sustained public investment in long-term care and homecare to raise wages and benefits, fund training and education and support public agencies' operating budgets. In addition to higher wages and addressing stratification in the workforce, homecare workers should have portable benefit options for healthcare, paid time off and retirement savings, which could be funded through a social insurance programme for long-term care (UCLA Labor Center, 2022). In California, one pathway to address wage inequality within the IHSS programme that is under consideration by workers and their unions, programme recipients, counties and the state, is the implementation of a state-wide collective bargaining strategy as an alternative to local bargaining with county public authorities, which may ease disparities in worker pay across the state (California Legislative Information, 2023; Rhee et al., 2025). Sectoral bargaining, much more common in Europe, can limit fragmentation of working conditions by setting a floor across an entire industry (Jacobs et al., 2021; Sánchez-Mira et al., 2021). Addressing low pay and lack of benefits is critical for attracting and retaining homecare workers and improving the quality of care for recipients.

Additionally, policy-makers should set and enforce labour standards in homecare to foster high-road jobs. This requires first removing all homecare exemptions from state wage and hour laws, workers' compensation, unemployment insurance and health and safety laws (Leberstein et al., 2015) and second, fostering high-road jobs by raising labour standards and enforcing compliance with labour law (UCLA Labor Center, 2022). California provides publicly-funded homecare through an independent provider model managed by counties but other states contract with private agencies to provide care. In these cases, states should award contracts to the companies providing living wages and benefits, cap how much profit private companies can absorb from Medicaid reimbursements and require reporting on workers' pay and hours (Leberstein et al., 2015). Third, fostering high-road jobs requires engagement in strategic enforcement of labour law and proactively providing clear rules and guidance on employer responsibilities especially considering contracting and subcontracting models (Leberstein et al., 2015; UCLA Labor Center, 2022). Fourth, increases in federal and state funding for long-term care are needed to ensure that job quality standards are tied to the use of government funds (Leberstein et al., 2015). Fifth, support is needed for worker organising through unions and other workers' organisations (Leberstein et al., 2015).

A final set of policy recommendations concerns providing training for homecare workers and the care recipients. Training and education programmes for homecare workers, culturally appropriate and available in multiple languages, could go a long way to valuing the skills of the workforce and creating an occupation with development and career opportunities (Hunt et al., 2023; Osterman, 2017; UCLA Labor Center, 2022). Additionally, training those receiving care is critical so they understand their responsibilities to workers under labour law (UCLA Labor Center, 2022). Moreover, given that the association of homecare with the welfare system is linked to the devaluation of the occupation (Boris & Klein, 2012), another route for revaluing their work is to integrate homecare workers into healthcare teams. This could improve the prestige of the profession and workers could also have their roles expanded through training on caring for wounds, health coaching, basic physical therapy, which some, but not all, already perform (Osterman, 2017). Upskilling homecare workers' jobs has the potential to bolster care, reduce healthcare costs and improve homecare worker job quality (Osterman, 2017). Ultimately, transforming homecare into dignified, stable and well-compensated work will require not only sustained public investment and stronger labour protections, but also a cultural and political reckoning with the gendered and racialised devaluation of care labour that has long undermined both the workforce and the quality of care itself.

Notes

1 Almost 80% of California's IHSS workers are employed to care for a single recipient – often a family member, setting it apart from other care systems where workers typically serve multiple clients. Thus, there are roughly the same number of IHSS workers as care recipients.

2 The IHSS administrative programme data and the nationally representative data from the American Community Survey (ACS) show markedly different shares of homecare workers who speak a language other than English (26.4% versus 59.0%), which may

be due to disparities in the underlying data and measurement. The ACS data include IHSS workers but our comparison to administrative data shows the ACS is significantly undercounting the workforce. Additionally, the ACS asks respondents about the primary language they speak at home, which may differ from the language workers report speaking to the IHSS program.

3 The MIT Living Wage calculator (Glasmeier & MIT, 2024) estimates how much workers and their families would need to earn to meet minimum standards of living in counties, metros, and states across the United States. It is an alternative to US federal poverty thresholds which underestimate the true cost of living in communities. The estimates factor in costs of a basic needs budget for food, healthcare, housing, childcare, transportation, other necessities and taxes (but do not include savings for retirement, vacations or even eating out at a restaurant). The estimates are available for 12 different family types and assume that either one or two adults are working full-time and year-round.

4 MIT Living Wage estimates assume that a single adult lives in a studio apartment. However, most IHSS workers (70.2%) care for family members, some of whom they may live with. These dynamics can complicate the picture as the workers and recipients may share expenses. However, to be eligible for an IHSS worker, the recipient must be low income and eligible for Medi-Cal (the state's Medicaid programme), suggesting that recipients likely do not have significant resources available to them. Additionally, for non-family workers who do not live with the recipient, wage rates are not adequate for self-sufficiency.

References

Allison, T. A., Oh, A., & Harrison, K. L. (2020). Extreme vulnerability of home care workers during the COVID-19 pandemic—A call to action. *JAMA Internal Medicine, 180*(11), 1459–1460. https://doi.org/10.1001/jamainternmed.2020.3937

Ball, L., Leigh, D., & Mishra, P. (2022). *Understanding U.S. inflation during the COVID era* (IMF Working Paper). International Monetary Fund. https://www.imf.org/en/Publications/WP/Issues/2022/10/28/Understanding-U-S-525200

Banerjee, A., deCourcy, K., Moore, K. K., & Wolfe, J. (2022). *Domestic workers chartbook 2022.* Economic Policy Institute. https://www.epi.org/publication/domestic-workers-chartbook-2022/

Boris, E., & Klein, J. (2007). "We were the invisible workforce" unionizing home care. In D. S. Cobble (Ed.), *The sex of class: Women transforming American labor* (pp. 177–193). Cornell University Press.

Boris, E., & Klein, J. (2012). *Caring for America: Home health workers in the shadow of the welfare state.* Oxford University Press. https://doi.org/10.1093/acprof:oso/9780195329117.001.0001

California Budget Project. (2012). *Falling behind: The impact of the Great Recession and the budget crisis on California's women and their families.* https://calbudgetcenter.org/app/uploads/120201_Falling_Behind.pdf

Rhee, N., Jacobs, K., Lucia, L., Lopezlira, E., Manzanilla, A., Hunter, S., & Quinn, K. (2024). Analysis of the potential impacts of statewide or regional collective bargaining for in-home supportive services providers.UC Berkeley Labor Center. https://laborcenter.berkeley.edu/ihss-statewide-bargaining/.

California Legislative Information (2023). *AB 102. Budget Act of 2023.* https://leginfo.legislature.ca.gov/faces/billNavClient.xhtml?bill_id=202320240AB102

Campbell, S. (2017). *U.S. home care workers: Key facts.* PHI. http://phinational.org/sites/phinational.org/files/phi-home-care-workers-key-facts.pdf

Christman, A. (2017). *Surveying the home care workforce*. National Employment Law Project. https://www.nelp.org/insights-research/surveying-the-home-care-workforce/

Delp, L., & Quan, K. (2002). Homecare worker organizing in California: An analysis of a successful strategy. *Labor Studies Journal*, *27*(1), 1–23. https://doi.org/10.1177/0160449X0202700102

Donegan, J. (2024, April 23). Kern reaches tentative deal with United Domestic Workers union. *The Bakersfield Californian*. https://www.bakersfield.com/news/kern-reaches-tentative-deal-with-united-domestic-workers-union/article_9266bacc-01ce-11ef-a8dc-2b0c5994286a.html

Edin, K. J., & Shaefer, L. H. (2016). *$2.00 a day: Living on almost nothing in America*. Mariner Books. https://www.harpercollins.com/products/200-a-day-kathryn-j-edinh-luke-shaefer

Edwards, E. (2023). *Paying family caregivers: State options, limitations, and policy considerations*. National Health Law Program. https://healthlaw.org/wp-content/uploads/2023/12/Paid-Family-Caregivers-NHeLP-2023.pdf

Forden, J., Radpour, S., Conway, E., & Ghilarducci, T. (2023). *Reducing the unequal burden of unpaid eldercare work*. Schwartz Center for Economic Policy Analysis. https://www.economicpolicyresearch.org/who-we-are

Glasmeier, A. K., & Massachusetts Institute of Technology. (2024). *Living wage calculator*. https://livingwage.mit.edu/

Hewitt, A., Pettingell, S., Smith, J., Dean, K., Kleist, B., Sanders, M., & Bershadsky, J. (2021). *Direct support workforce and COVID-19 national report: Six-month follow-up*. Institute on Community Integration, University of Minnesota. https://publications.ici.umn.edu/community-living/covid19-survey-6-month-followup/main

Howes, C. (2004). Upgrading California's home care workforce: The impact of political action and unionization. *State of California Labor*, *2004*(1), 71–105. https://doi.org/10.1525/scl.2004.2004.1.71

Howes, Candace. Raising Wages for Home Care Workers: Paths and Impediments. Fair Labor Standards Act (FLSA) Working Paper Series. Department of Labor (DOL) | Institute for Research on Labor and Employment, 2014.

Hunt, L., Yeh, J., & Fix, M. (2023). *California's direct care workforce: Who they are, the work they do, and why it matters*. California Health Care Foundation.

Jacobs, K., Smith, R., & McBride, J. (2021). State and local policies and sectoral labor standards: From individual rights to collective power. *ILR Review, 74*(5), 1132–1154. https://doi.org/10.1177/00197939211020706

Johnson, H., & Cuellar Mejia, M. (2024). *Rural California*. Public Policy Institute of California. https://www.ppic.org/publication/rural-california/

Katz, M. B. (2013). *The undeserving poor: America's enduring confrontation with poverty* (2nd ed.). Oxford University Press.

Kerstein, S. (2024). *California's low-wage workers and minimum wage: Who are California's low-wage workers?* Legislative Analyst's Office. https://lao.ca.gov/Publications/Report/4878/1

Kitchener, M., Ng, T., Miller, N., & Harrington, C. (2006). Institutional and community-based long-term care: A comparative estimate of public costs. *Journal of Health & Social Policy, 22*(2), 31–50. https://doi.org/10.1300/J045v22n02_03

Legislative Analyst's Office. (2015). *The 2015–16 budget: Analysis of the human services budget*. https://lao.ca.gov/reports/2015/budget/human-services/hs-analysis-021215.aspx

Leberstein, S., Tung, I., & Connolly, C. (2015). *Upholding labor standards in home care: How to build employer accountability into America's fastest-growing jobs*. National Employment Law Project.

Lichtenstein, N. (2003). *State of the union: A century of American labor*. Princeton University Press.

Macdonald, F., Bentham, E., & Malone, J. (2018). Wage theft, underpayment and unpaid work in marketised social care. *The Economic and Labour Relations Review, 29*(1), 80–96. https://doi.org/10.1177/1035304618758252

Milkman, R. (2023). Stratification among in-home care workers in the United States. *Critical Sociology, 49*(1), 11–22. https://doi.org/10.1177/08969205221123034

MIT. (2024). *Living Wage Calculator*. https://livingwage.mit.edu/

Myles, M. (2020). *COVID-19 crisis presents especially tough challenges for home care workers*. AFSCME. https://www.afscme.org/blog/covid-19-crisis-presents-especially-tough-challenges-for-home-care-workers

Murphy, P., Danielson, C., McConville, S., Paluch, J., & Thoman, T. (2019). *Balancing budgets and need during recessions: California's safety net programs*. Public Policy Institute of California

Osterman, P. (2017). *Who will care for us? Long-term care and the long-term workforce*. Russell Sage Foundation. https://doi.org/10.7758/9781610448673

Paraprofessional Healthcare Institute. (2022). *Direct care worker disparities: Key trends and challenges*. https://www.phinational.org/resource/direct-care-worker-disparities-key-trends-and-challenges/

Rhee, N., Jacobs, K., Lucia, L., Lopezlira, E., Manzanilla, A., Hunter, S., & Quinn, K. (2025). *Analysis of the potential impacts of statewide or regional collective bargaining for In-Home Supportive Services providers*. UC Berkeley Labor Center. https://laborcenter.berkeley.edu/ihss-statewide-bargaining/

Rowe, T. A., Patel, M., O'Conor, R., McMackin, S., Hoak, V., & Lindquist, L. A. (2020). COVID-19 exposures and infection control among home care agencies. *Archives of Gerontology and Geriatrics, 91*, 104214. https://doi.org/10.1016/j.archger.2020.104214

Rubery, J., Grimshaw, D., Hebson, G., & Ugarte, S. M. (2015). "It's all about time": Time as contested terrain in the management and experience of domiciliary care work in England. *Human Resource Management, 54*(5), 753–772. https://doi.org/10.1002/hrm.21685

Ruggles, S., Flood, S., Sobek, M., Backman, D., Cooper, G., Rivera Drew, J. A., Richards, S., Rodgers, R., Schroeder, J., & Williams, K. C. W. (2024). *IPUMS USA: Version 16.0* [dataset]. IPUMS. https://doi.org/10.18128/D010.V16.0

Sánchez-Mira, N., Serrano Olivares, R., & Carrasquer Oto, P. (2021). A matter of fragmentation? Challenges for collective bargaining and employment conditions in the Spanish long-term care sector. *Transfer, 27*(3), 319–335. https://doi.org/10.1177/10242589211028098

Smith, P. R. (2008). The publicization of home-based care work in state labor law. *Minnesota Law Review, 601*. https://scholarship.law.umn.edu/mlr/601/

Sterling, M. R., Tseng, E., Poon, A., Cho, J., Avgar, A. C., Kern, L. M., Ankuda, C. K., & Dell, N. (2020). Experiences of home health care workers in New York City during the coronavirus disease 2019 pandemic: A qualitative analysis. *JAMA Internal Medicine, 180*(11), 1453–1459. https://doi.org/10.1001/jamainternmed.2020.3930

True, S., Cubanski, J., Garfield, R., Rae, M., Claxton, G., Chidambaram, P., & Orgera, K. (2020, April 23). COVID-19 and workers at risk: Examining the long-term care workforce. *Paid and Unpaid Care Work*. https://digitalcommons.wcl.american.edu/wlpcarework/1

Tyler, D., Hunter, M., Mulmule, N., & Porter, K. (2021). *COVID-19 intensifies home care workforce challenges*. Assistant Secretary for Planning and Evaluation. https://aspe.hhs.gov/reports/covid-19-intensifies-home-care-workforce-challenges

UCLA Labor Center. (2022). *Lives and livelihoods: California's private homecare industry in crisis*. https://labor.ucla.edu/wp-content/uploads/2022/03/Lives-and-Livelihood-Report-1.pdf

10

THE "CARE TRANSITION" IN TURBULENT TIMES

Maria Karamessini

Introduction

Notwithstanding the great variety of national care regimes, from the 1980s onwards there has been a general trend in all advanced OECD economies and EU Member States towards the "defamilialisation" of care, which means that a growing share of the care for dependent persons in the family-state-market mix comes from the welfare state and market provision. This trend has been accompanied by an equally general but much slower and limited move towards the "degenderisation" of care, i.e., towards a more equal sharing between women and men of unpaid/informal care work for dependent family members. We call the above common trends across all care regimes the "care transition". The term denotes a long-term transformation in the social organisation of care. It is an ongoing and uneven process, influenced by policies aimed at multiple goals, characterised by both continuity and contradictions and affected by economic crises.

Undoubtedly, the de-familialisation trend applies more to childcare than elderly care. State support for working mothers and parents through publicly-funded care services has accompanied and enabled women's spectacular integration into paid work and their more continuous activity patterns. This has led to a decisive shift away from the male-breadwinner towards a dual-earner family model, which is nevertheless still associated with varying degrees of gender inequality in paid and unpaid work (see Marx et al., 2026, this volume). However, long-term care (LTC) for the elderly still remains an overwhelmingly family-based responsibility. Out of 27 EU countries, 17 states still make only a limited intervention in this field (Pavolini, 2022) with reforms mainly focusing on supporting family caregivers.

Evidence indicates that the austerity phase of the Great Recession and the Covid-19 pandemic temporarily interrupted and/or reversed the care transition in

DOI: 10.4324/9781003528210-13

the EU (Blaskó & Sanjuán-Belda, 2022; Karamessini & Rubery, 2014). However, these disruptions in the social cohesion of EU Member States, produced by the harsh austerity policies during 2011-2015, also gave rise to the revival of EU social policy, starting with the 2017 adoption of the European Pillar of Social Rights (EPSR) (European Union, 2017). Similarly, the Covid-19 pandemic made visible the importance of care for social reproduction and the resilience of European societies against shocks. Such visibility, along with EU policymakers' increased awareness of the urgent need to mitigate and counter the negative economic and social effects of rapid population ageing, pushed work–life balance and care policy towards the top of the EU's social policy priorities post-Covid. Furthermore, the European Care Strategy, adopted in 2022, extended the scope of EU policy intervention from its previous childcare focus into the field of LTC.

In this chapter, we examine whether and to what extent the successive crises of the past fifteen years have derailed the transition of EU Member States' care regimes from familial care for children and other dependants towards publicly funded or provided formal care. We also study recent EU social policy developments in the fields of care, work–life balance, and gender equality and discuss the conditions for their success in accelerating the care transition.

The next section introduces the notion of the care transition in relation to the multiple goals of the different care policies and takes stock of where we stand today. This is followed by an exploration of the damages to the care transition caused by the Great Recession and the Covid-19 pandemic and the subsequent EU social policy initiatives as a corrective reaction and way forward. The last section expands on the latest initiative, the new EU Care Strategy, by examining its scope for promoting the care transition across EU Member States in turbulent times.

The "care transition": where do we stand, where do we go?

From the 1980s onwards, all care regimes of economically-advanced countries have been in continuous transformation involving two general trends: the defamilialisation of care and the narrowing of gender gaps in unpaid care work. The defamilialisation of care through state support has been associated with multiple goals, with child-care support used both to facilitate women's mass mobilisation into paid work and to prevent the collapse of fertility rates. Likewise, deficiencies in elderly care began to be addressed due to ageing societies. Although the primary goal has been the mobilisation of the large unexploited female pool of low-wage and flexible labour to meet the needs of the economy, both care agendas have also been advanced as promoting gender equality. However, the narrowing of gender gaps in unpaid care work has advanced at a slower pace. Changes are the result of both women's demands and struggles for a gender-equal division of domestic labour and changes in male identities and attitudes towards paternity and stereotypical gender roles. In the recent literature, the latter trend has been called the "degenderisation" of care.

Feminist theory on care, gender relations and the welfare state: defining the "care transition"

The concept of defamilialisation originated from the feminist critique of Esping-Andersen's (1990) initial regime typology of welfare capitalism, for ignoring gender relations and women's relationship to the labour market and the welfare state. "Defamilialisation" was proposed as a gendered parallel to his concept of "decommodification" of wage labour by the welfare state (Esping-Andersen, 1990, p. 86), which presupposed that all individuals participate in the labour force, ignoring the reality of women with respect to paid work. Orloff (1993) was the first to suggest extending Esping-Andersen's welfare regime typology to recognise that welfare is not only provided through states and markets but also through families, while Lister (1994) was the first to introduce and define defamilialisation as "the degree to which individuals are able to uphold a socially acceptable standard of living independently of family relationships, either through paid work or social security provision" (p. 37).

Taking on board the feminist critique, Esping-Andersen (1999) integrated the familialism-defamilialisation axis with the commodification-decommodification axis to enrich his welfare regimes analysis by recognising that welfare is not only produced through labour market participation and the welfare state but also through the household economy in which women's unpaid family labour and care work constitute the cornerstones. To defamilialise care for children, the elderly and the disabled, some part of its provision must be transferred to the welfare state and/or the market, depending on the "care regime" prevailing in a country at a given period.

The 1990s also saw a great intellectual effort among feminist scholars to conceptualise "care", a defining characteristic of women's life condition, as a unique activity and form of work and as distinct from unpaid work. This provided the basis for theorising the relationship of care to the welfare state and the processes of restructuring occurring in all advanced economies at that time (Daly & Lewis, 2000; Folbre, 1994; Fraser, 1994; Leira, 1992; Orloff, 1993). By the 2000s, individual countries' policies had produced distinct "care regimes" characterised by different family-state-market mixes in care provision (Bettio & Plantenga, 2004; Simonazzi, 2008). As a result of women's growing employment, the defamilialisation of care and the individualisation of insurance rights, the male breadwinner-female caregiver family model became gradually outdated and by the 2000s the "adult-worker family model" predominated (Crompton, 1999; Lewis & Giullari, 2006), although this model did not entail either equal participation of men and women in employment or the degenderisation of care.

The adult-worker family model implicitly attached a low value to care. Gornick and Meyers (2009) instead proposed that the gender equality ideal should be a "dual earner/dual carer" family model in which men and women share unpaid care work equally while paid carers are highly qualified, well-paid and deliver high-quality care. This has resonances with Nancy Fraser's (1994) "universal caregiver model" that recognised that women's disadvantage would continue unless men shared equally the care work that could not be outsourced. Fraser (1994) sought to change societal norms towards women's life patterns – both earners and caregivers – by reducing working hours and leaving room for publicly-supported informal care work by parents, relatives, friends and civil society institutions. However, neither critique focused on how to reshape wage work organisation to facilitate everyone being a carer (Rubery, 2015). Furthermore, the term dual presupposes a couple, while more inclusive terms such as "earner-carer" or "worker-carer" better reflect the reality of lone parents and indeed all adults irrespective of sexual orientation or identity (Ellingsæter, 2024). We consider this family model the implicit goal of the "care transition".

The 1990s and 2000s witnessed the impressive development of work–family balance and care policies in all economically-advanced countries, motivated by their common challenge to increase women's employment but shaped by different rationales depending on the national context. This gave rise to a feminist debate on the character of work–life balance and care policies and to the construction of typologies (Leitner, 2003; Saraceno, 2016; Saraceno & Keck, 2011). Leitner (2003) classified policies that encourage the provision of childcare or elder care by the family as familialistic and policies that foster care outside the family through state intervention as defamilialising. Elaborating on Leitner's framework, Saraceno (2016) advanced the concept of "supported familialism" where policies enable family members to keep up both their financial and caring responsibilities and women to combine care and work. She also distinguished between two types of defamilialisation policies: (i) through-the-market policies, when the state provides cash benefits to care users and families with which they can buy care services on the market, and (ii) through-public-provision policies, when the state directly provides public care to those in need of care. Finally, Saraceno and Keck (2011) examined the variety of familialistic/defamilialising care policy approaches in EU Member States and their gender equality implications and found that countries do not always follow consistent policy approaches in that they may internally diverge between support for a dual earner or a modified form of a male breadwinner/female carer family model.

However, to go further and capture the impact of these care policies on the sharing of informal care between women and men, Saxonberg (2013) introduced a further distinction: policies promoting different gender roles for men and women were labelled "genderizing" and policies promoting the elimination of gender roles "degenderizing". These notions (genderizing, degenderising and hybrid) were used to analyse the gender impact of parental leaves and childcare services in the EU, clustering countries according to their care model.

The policy-based typologies of (de)familialisation and (de)genderisation allow us to understand differences in the goals, rationale and gendered implications of state intervention in different national contexts and the crucial policy fields where much policy innovation is taking place (e.g. parental leave, long-term care etc.). However, the goal here is not to analyse the variety of work–life balance and care policies across advanced economies over the past thirty years but to capture their outcomes and assess the progress of the care transition. In the following two sections we show where Europe stands today with respect to the two main trends shaping the care transition, i.e., the defamilialisation and the degenderisation of informal care, by making use of comparative data on common indicators and the findings of empirical research and large surveys carried out by the EU, the OECD and the ILO.

The defamilialisation of care in Europe: an incomplete transition

The defamilialisation of care provision in Europe has its origins in the Swedish work–family life reconciliation policy introduced in the early 1970s under the new "gender contract", the "equality contract" between women and men (Hirdman, 1998). Working mothers were offered day care, insured parental leave, and individual taxation as compensation for their "double role" as workers and carers. The goal was to encourage the mass engagement of married women and mothers in paid work to cover the economy's workforce needs while avoiding a childcare deficit and a decline in fertility. The other Nordic countries quickly followed the Swedish course, but the other European countries did so only much later.

Policy to reconcile or balance work and family found its way unobtrusively into the EU equality policy from the late 1980s onwards (Karamessini, 2023). A 1992 Council Recommendation on childcare provided the first EU-level official definition and suggested to EU-15 Member States four initiatives, including providing care services and entitlements to a special care leave for employed parents. Later, following the adoption of the European Employment Strategy within the EU's Amsterdam Treaty, the strategy's Equal Opportunities pillar included "Reconciling Work and Family Life" among its 1998 guidelines. This recommended Member States to raise access to good quality care for children and other dependants as a priority, among other measures such as enabling career breaks, facilitating parental leave and promoting part-time work. Finally, at the 2002 Barcelona European Council, common targets were set for all Member States for formal childcare services, namely for 33% of children aged under three and 90% of those aged three to compulsory school age to be in formal childcare or pre-school education. By 2021 these Barcelona targets were surpassed for children under three (37.9% up from 24.5% in 2005) and nearly met for those over three (87.8%) and were revised upwards by the Council Recommendation on Early Childhood Education and Care, adopted in 2022 under the European Care Strategy.

The above EU policy initiatives fostered sizeable social investment in childcare services. Since the mid-1990s, the share of children in formal childcare has expanded significantly in all EU Member States, but at a different pace and from different starting points. Today, after 30 years of progress, the transition to the defamilialisation of care remains incomplete, especially for children aged less than three years. Figure 10.1 shows wide variation in the formal childcare or education coverage rates across EU Member States plus Norway, Switzerland and the UK in 2023. Many states still record very low coverage for children under three, with the greatest deficiencies found in Eastern Europe, the UK, Germany, Austria, Switzerland, Croatia, Greece and Ireland.

Significant progress has, however, been made over these thirty years in working parents' rights to care leaves. These have operated as employment policy tools to help mothers remain in employment i.e., "commodified". Such care leaves correspond to "supported familialism" (Saraceno & Keck, 2011) as they potentially increase the share of the very young children cared for only by their parents. Within

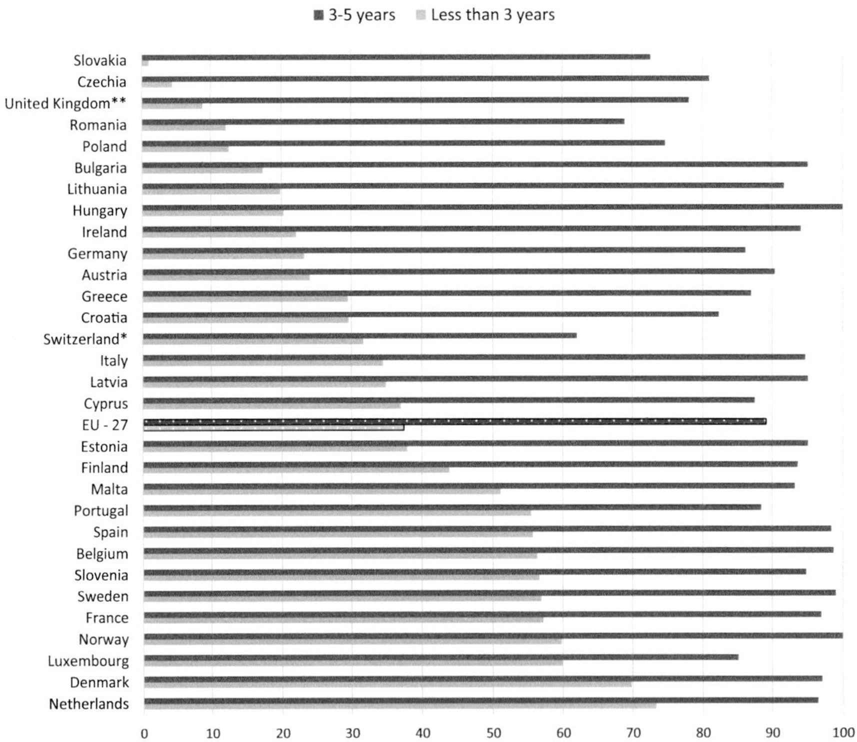

FIGURE 10.1 Children in Formal Care or Education, EU Member States, Norway, the UK and Switzerland in 2023. Percentage of the population of each age group.

Source: Eurostat, EU-SILC data (accessed on 15-6-2024).

Note: *Data refer to 2018 for less than 3, 2022 for 3–5 years. **Data refer to 2022.

the EU, Czechia, Slovakia, Hungary, Bulgaria, Romania, Estonia and Lithuania have opted for long and paid parental leaves, followed by Sweden, Germany and Austria (Dobrotić et al., 2024). All these countries, except Sweden and recently Germany, have invested very little in formal childcare and display low coverage rates for children aged under three (see Figure 10.1).

Elderly care also followed a trend towards defamilialisation over recent decades, although taking diverse forms depending on the pre-existing elderly care regime (Bettio & Plantenga, 2004; Simonazzi, 2008). After World War II up until the 1980s, according to Pavolini and Ranci (2013) "elder care" policies in Europe were directed to older people with limited means, with residential institutions for the poor or lone older people being the primary policy instrument. Until the 1990s only the Scandinavian countries and the UK had developed a generous supply of home and residential long-term care (LTC) services for older people with chronic diseases and heavy dependence under a universal principle of social rights (universalistic LTC regime) while continental and Southern European countries retained family-based residual LTC regimes.

From the mid-1990s all countries have reformed their LTC policies to cope with socio-demographic, cultural and cost-containment pressures. Those with universalistic regimes introduced some market provision of services and rationalised residential care, while those with family-based residual regimes expanded LTC coverage and generosity by providing in-cash care benefits to the elderly or to their family caregivers but according to a principle of "restricted universalism" (Ranci & Pavolini, 2015). The above reforms have created in several countries of continental Europe (e.g. Austria, Germany) a sizeable private market for LTC services in which migrants play a significant role as live-in domestic carers (Da Roit & Moreno-Fuentes, 2019), thus extending the scope of the "migrant-in-the family" model, first identified in Southern Europe in the mid-2000s (Bettio et al., 2006).

Although there are no macro-level indicators of the impact of different types of elderly care policies on familialisation-defamilialisation, it can be deduced from the nature of the reforms that these have not led to defamilialisation through extended public service provision. Instead, following Saraceno (2016), the reform directions have induced supported defamilialisation through the market, namely care allowances that can only be used by the elderly to buy formal care services and supported familialism, namely financial transfers untied to formal care provision, either directly granted to family caregivers or that elderly beneficiaries can use to pay the latter.

These widespread reforms of the European LTC systems have occurred despite the EU's lack of policy initiative in this field until 2022, when a Council Recommendation on LTC was adopted as part of the European Care Strategy. As a result, as shown in Table 10.1, not only is there inadequate defamilialisation of elder care, but also great national variation across Europe. In Eastern European countries, Greece and Italy, a significant share (35% to 43%) of the people aged 65+ years with severe limitations on their daily living activities receive care

TABLE 10.1 Share of the Population 65+ with at Least Three ADL* or IADL** Limitations by Type of Care Received, 2021

	Formal Care Only (%)	*Both Formal and Family Care (%)*	*Only Family Care (%)*	*No Care at All (%)*
Lithuania	11	9	38	41
Poland	11	10	42	37
Latvia	14	8	39	39
Estonia	16	9	43	32
Hungary	21	12	36	31
Italy	25	9	31	34
Slovenia	20	15	34	31
Greece	19	19	33	29
Slovak Republic	15	25	27	34
Czech Republic	12	28	35	25
OECD-21	28	24	22	26
Spain	34	25	19	22
Germany	33	29	14	24
Austria	36	29	17	18
Sweden	38	30	8	25
France	36	37	7	20
Switzerland	45	29	6	21
Denmark	37	37	8	18
Belgium	44	35	7	14
Netherlands	40	40	6	14
Luxembourg	49	31	5	15

Source: OECD (2023), Figure 5.2, data based on SHARE data (Survey on the Health, Ageing and Retirement in Europe) (wave 8), p. 158.

Note: Family care is received from family and friends; formal care is delivered by paid carers. *ADL Activities of Daily Living; **IADL Instrumental Activities of Daily Living.

only from their family, while only a small share (11% to 25%) receives only formal care. Defamilialisation of elderly care is more advanced in Northern and Western European countries and Spain. In these countries, only a small minority (5% to 19%) of those aged 65+ years with severe limitations in daily living activities receives care only from their family, while 34% to 49% receive only formal care.

By considering developments in child and elderly care together, we can conclude that the defamilialisation of care is inadequate in most European countries. This is the first manifestation of the incomplete care transition in Europe.

The degenderisation of unpaid and the genderisation of paid care

The second manifestation of the incomplete care transition in Europe, according to our definition of the concept, is the slow degendering of informal/unpaid care in parallel to a long-standing gender division of formal/paid care.

One of the central demands of the second wave of the feminist movements in the Western world was for an equal gender division of domestic labour, considered as key for advancing gender equality in both private and public spheres. Yet, although the dual-earner family model is now dominant in all advanced economies (Marx et al., 2026, this volume), there is abundant evidence that we are still very far from the universal earner-caregiver model. Closing gender gaps in unpaid work is thus the main policy challenge of what is sometimes called the "second half/phase" of the gender revolution (Engeman & Burman, 2023).

Care leaves for workers with care responsibilities correspond to "supported familialism" (Saraceno, 2016). However, since all care cannot and should not be outsourced, given that informal care is an essential element of intimate and loving relationships and a prerequisite for the emotional development of children, what matters most from a care transition perspective is whether and to what extent care leaves are equally taken up and shared by women and men, thus contributing to the degenderisation of unpaid care.

Since the 1990s, working mothers have undoubtedly been the primary target of work–life balance policies and the main care leave-takers in economically-advanced countries. Times are now changing and several countries have adopted policies to strengthen fathers' roles as family carers. Engeman and Burman's (2023) study of fathers' leave provisions from 1965 to 2015 in 23 countries identified five leave types that send different messages about fatherhood and gender roles, i.e., mothers' transferable leave, transferable parental leave, paternity leave, non-transferable parental leave and bonus leave. Their main finding is that welfare states have increasingly established well-paid and non-transferable leave provisions, but such provisions remain underfunded, while transferable parental leave entitlements, when offered, are typically more generous. A special report on care leaves in 51 countries (Dobrotić et al., 2024) found a recent increase in "father's quotas" in many countries, particularly in EU countries, to align with the EU's 2019 Directive on Work–Life Balance for Parents and Carers that asks for two non-transferable paid parental leave months. However, all measures have a long way to go before the take-up and sharing of care leaves become gender balanced.

Turning from policies to outcomes, recent studies in advanced economies using time-use data on long-term trends in unpaid work point to a gender convergence in unpaid work over time; albeit slow and incomplete (Baxter et al., 2026, this volume; Kan et al., 2011; Pailhé et al., 2021; Sullivan et al., 2018). These studies indicate a closing of the gender gap in unpaid work but mainly through a reduction of the time women spend on housework, while men, from a considerably lower starting point, have increased more than women their time spent on childcare. Moreover, segregation in domestic chores persists, with women still doing the bulk of routine housework and caring for family members, and men having increased their contributions more to non-routine domestic work. The first wave of the recent CARE survey by the European Institute for Gender Equality (EIGE) covering all EU Member States in 2022 found a much smaller childcare and eldercare gap compared to routine housework: thus among those aged 18–74, 33.5% of women against 24.6% of men cared for and educated their children or grandchildren, elderly or disabled people every day in the EU on average; while the female and male shares doing cooking and/or housework every day were 63.1% and 35.7%, respectively (EIGE, 2022). There is a debate about whether these patterns reflect a stalling (Kan et al., 2022) or rather slowing down (Sullivan et al., 2018) of the trend towards closing domestic work gender gaps and its determinants: namely institutional and cultural obstacles that (partly) offset the positive effect of generational change.

However, to take stock of where we stand today regarding the degenderising of unpaid housework and care work, we need to also consider the gender distribution of total time spent on it. Figure 10.2, based on OECD Time Use for 25 selected countries, shows that the female share of the average daily time spent on unpaid

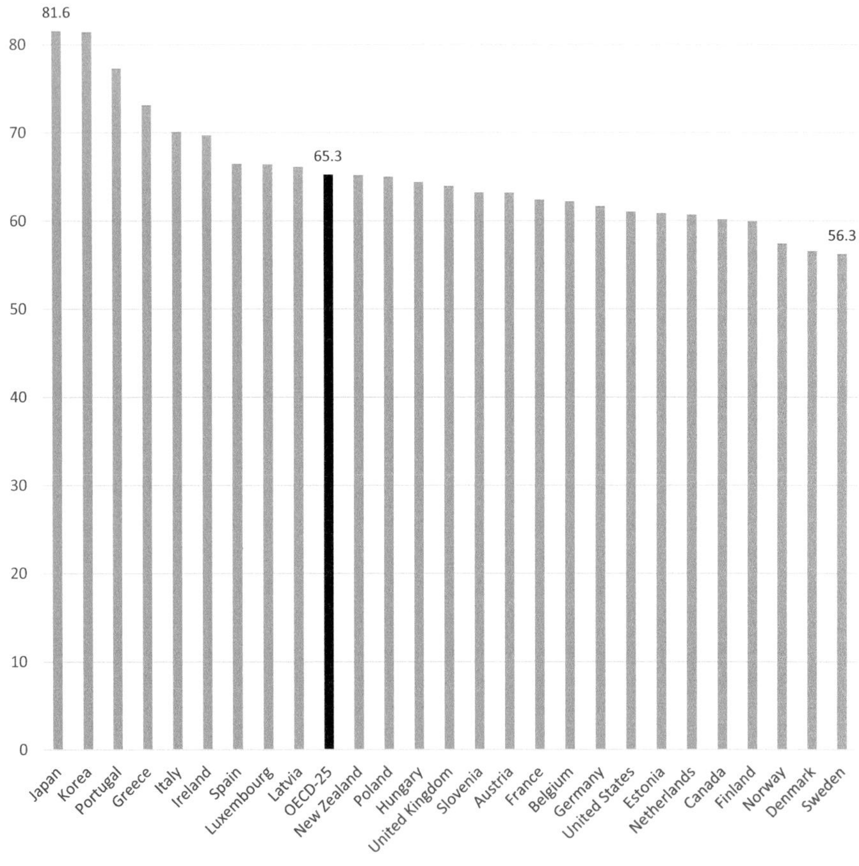

FIGURE 10.2 Female Share (%) of Unpaid Work (Latest Year Available).

Source: Author's calculation on the basis of data from the most recent Time Use Survey of each country – OECD Time Use database (online).

Note: Time spent on unpaid work includes time spent on housework and caregiving to dependent family members and is measured in minutes per day.

care work was the smallest in Sweden (56.3%) and the largest in Japan (81.6%) with the OECD average standing at 65.3%. Therefore, the aim of degenderising unpaid work still has a long way to go, before the "second phase" of the gender revolution is done.

Any degenderising of unpaid (care) work has gone hand in hand with the genderising of paid care work. Given that the female share of paid care workers has always been high, genderisation here implies a great increase in the total number of employed women, thereby adding to gender segregation in paid work, as well as the feminisation of higher-level care jobs, especially in healthcare. Eurostat data coming from the EU Labour Force Survey and EU Education Statistics indicate that in the EU women accounted for 93% of all childcare workers and teachers' aides in 2020 (Eurostat, 2021) and for 95.5 % of all early childhood education teachers in 2021 (Eurostat, n.d.). A recent Organisation for Economic Co-operation and Development (OECD) study (2023) found that women accounted for 87.4% of all LTC workers in 25 OECD Member States, with shares among European countries ranging from 81.3% in Sweden to 94.2% in Czechia (Figure 10.3). In turn, the EIGE Gender Statistics Database shows that in 2023, the vast majority (76.2%)

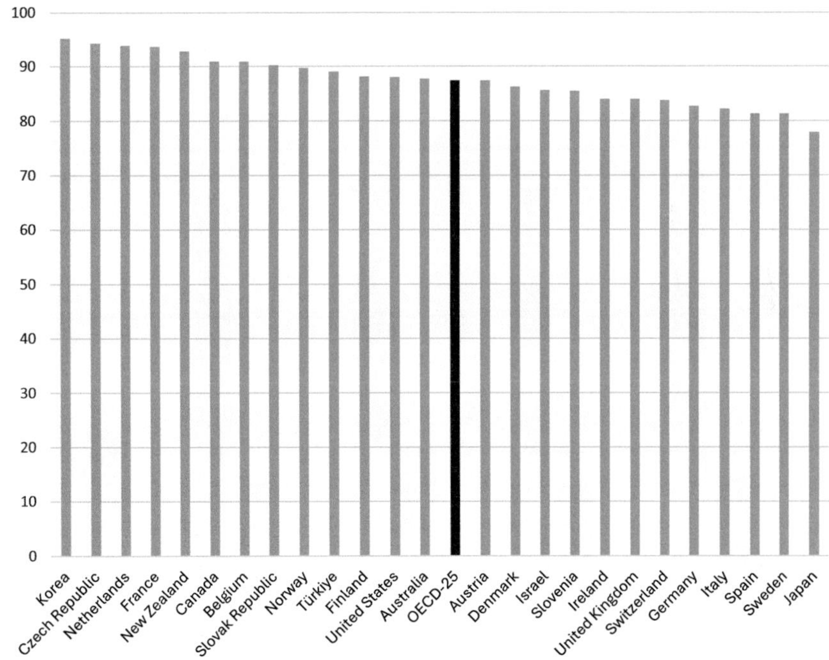

FIGURE 10.3 Female Share (%) of Long-Term Care (LTC) Workers, 2021.

Source: OECD (2023), Figure 4.1, p. 133.

Note: *2019: New Zealand; **2020: Sweden, Korea, Austria; ***2016: USA, Canada, Australia, Japan.

of health care workers in the EU were women including medical doctors, nurses, midwives and their associates, personal care workers and other health professionals and associates (EIGE, n.d.).

The effects of the Great Recession and the Covid-19 pandemic on the care transition and post-crises policy developments

The 2008 Great Recession and the Covid-19 pandemic have had negative effects on the care transition though in each case the negative effects have operated through different channels. At the same time, both crises have stimulated the revival of care policy in their aftermath, by making evident the risks of reversing or stalling the care transition.

Temporary refamilialisation and ambiguous (de)genderisation of care in the EU: coping with austerity and lockdowns

Both the Great Recession and the Covid-19 pandemic had negative impacts on the coverage of children by formal childcare services, particularly for children aged 3 years to compulsory school age, albeit for different reasons (Figure 10.4).

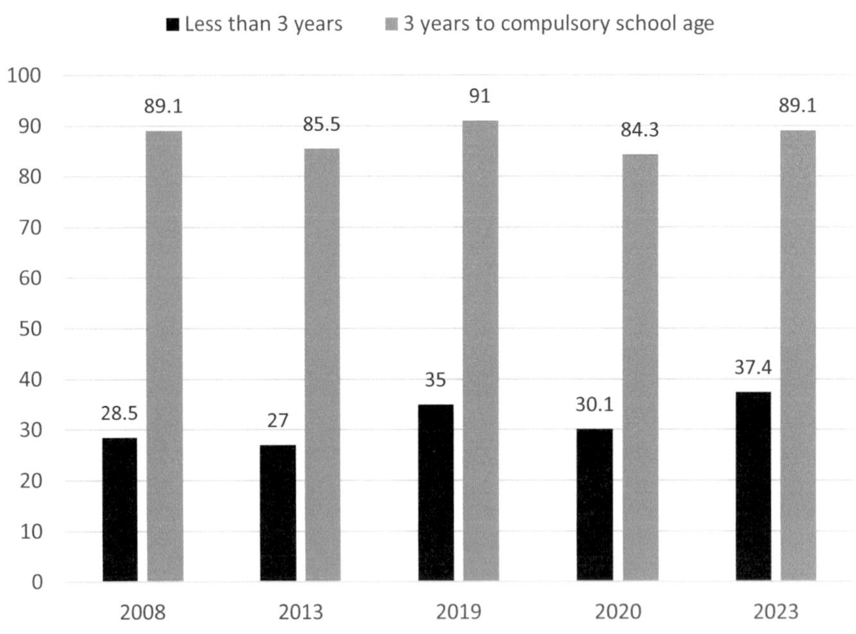

FIGURE 10.4 Children (%) in Formal Childcare in the EU, 2008–2023.

Source: Eurostat, EU-SILC data online (accessed 15.6.2024).

During the austerity phase of the Great Recession, family allowances, child benefits and family tax credits were frozen, cut or abolished, while childcare services were reduced due to underfunding and understaffing, especially in those countries implementing the most severe austerity policies; budgetary cuts also reduced care allowances and elder care domiciliary provision by municipalities (Karamessini & Rubery, 2014). Moreover, rising male and female unemployment deprived some middle-class households of their capacity to buy domestic care services; the burden was thus transferred to the informal carers, among whom women dominate.

Although Szelewa and Polakowski's (2023) study of childcare policy in nine EU countries during 2005-2015 found that in these countries, despite austerity measures, childcare policies largely remained stable during the Great Recession and that most policy shifts were more often degenderising than genderizing following policies to increase accessibility to childcare services and improved fathers' entitlements and generosity of care leaves, these results are not confirmed for the EU as a whole. The formal childcare coverage rate dropped between 2008 and 2013 for children under three and to an even larger extent for those aged three to compulsory school age (Figure 10.4). The drop in 2020 in Figure 10.4 also reflects the refamilialisation of care that occurred during the Covid-19 pandemic, as the direct outcome of school and daycare centre closures during lockdowns. In most EU countries, formal childcare was only guaranteed for workers in health care and other essential services and in a few countries also to families where both parents needed to work outside home (Rubery & Tavora, 2021). Refamilialisation also occurred in elderly care, evidenced by an increase in time spent on informal LTC by both sexes in the EU on average during the pandemic (EIGE, 2022).

The refamilialisation of care was further encouraged by measures of "supported familialism", such as the promotion of teleworking in all countries and the introduction of special parental leave schemes in 20 EU Member States. While Bulgaria, the Netherlands and Sweden already allowed access to emergency leaves pre-pandemic, most of the remaining EU countries enacted new temporary emergency leave measures to provide job protection and (mostly partial) wage replacement for parents impacted by day care closures and unable to work from home. However, not all forms of leave were paid and most were short-term and had eligibility restrictions (Koslowski et al., 2020). In 10 of the 20 EU Member States introducing such special measures, the leave pay was lower than for job retention schemes while in Spain the leave was unpaid (Rubery & Tavora, 2021). It follows that in these 11 countries, this measure has indirectly contributed to the genderisation of care through the take-up of leaves mostly by mothers.

All in all, it seems that the refamilialisation of care during the lockdown phases of the Covid-19 pandemic was accompanied by a massive burden on working parents, especially mothers. Blaskó and Sanjuán-Belda's (2022) systematic review of studies reporting online surveys on how men and women organised their lives during the first lockdowns suggests that, compared to pre-lockdown measurements, women increased their time spent on childcare and housework by 7–20 hours per week, corresponding to a change of 23–56% for childcare and an increase of around two hours for housework. Over the same period, the time men spent on childcare and housework increased by 30–91%. Although this represents a higher relative increase than was the case for women, this finding reflects the fact that men originally did fewer unpaid work hours than their female partners. Moreover, a Eurofound (2022) research report allows the impact of the lockdowns on unpaid work and its gender division to be measured for the EU-27 as a whole (Table 10.2). These estimates indicate that the time spent on unpaid work during these lockdown phases increased more among all employed men and all male full-timers than among their female counterparts, thus reducing the gender gap in unpaid work. The opposite occurred among parents working full-time. During the 2020 and 2021 lockdowns time spent on unpaid work increased among full-time working mothers much more than among working fathers (9.6 against 7 hours per week) and the gender gap in unpaid work reached 19.6 hours, up from 17 pre-pandemic.[1] However, as pre-pandemic working fathers spent only 60% of the time that working mothers spent on unpaid work, the proportional increase in unpaid working time was higher among fathers, pushing the male share of unpaid work up from 35.8% to 38.4% between 2016 and 2020-2021. Finally, the lockdown experience seems not to have left a mark on the gender division of unpaid work, since time spent on childcare returned to normal after the schools and nurseries reopened (Eurofound, 2022).

TABLE 10.2 Mean Total Working Time Spent on Unpaid Work in the EU27 (Hours per Week)

	2016[a]	*2020–2021*[b]	*Difference*
All employed women	28.1	29.9	1.8
All employed men	14.9	18.9	4.0
Gender gap	13.2	11.0	-2.2
Women employed full-time	26.1	27.7	1.6
Men employed full-time	14.8	18.7	3.9
Gender gap	11.3	9.0	-2.3
Women employed full-time with children	42.3	51.9	9.6
Men employed full-time with children	25.3	32.3	7.0
Gender gap	17.0	19.6	2.6

Source: Author's calculations based on data from Eurofound (2022), Figure 9, p. 14 (2016) and Figure 32, p. 41 (2020–2021).

Notes: [a]Data from the Eurofound's European Quality of Life Survey 2016.

[b]Aggregate data from the Eurofound's Living, working and Covid-19 e-survey, rounds 2 (June to July 2020) and 3 (February to March 2021).

The above analysis suggests that the evidence on the (de)genderisation of unpaid care work during the Covid-19 pandemic is ambiguous, depending on whether working parents are examined separately, whether the focus is on changes in the absolute or relative gender gap, and if the study is limited to lockdown periods.

To conclude, the refamilialisation of care that occurred during the Great Recession and the Covid-19 pandemic was a temporary phenomenon. After both crises were over, the coverage of children by formal childcare services quickly recovered its pre-crisis level and upward trend (Figure 10.4). Nor was maternal employment affected at all by the refamilialisation of care during the two crises. Figure 10.5 shows that, between 2008 and 2013, the employment rate of mothers aged 25–49 with one child under six years remained stable, that of mothers with 2 children less than six years even increased, while that for childless women fell. In 2020 there was no change compared to 2019 in the employment rate of mothers aged 25–49 with two children under six while that for mothers with one child

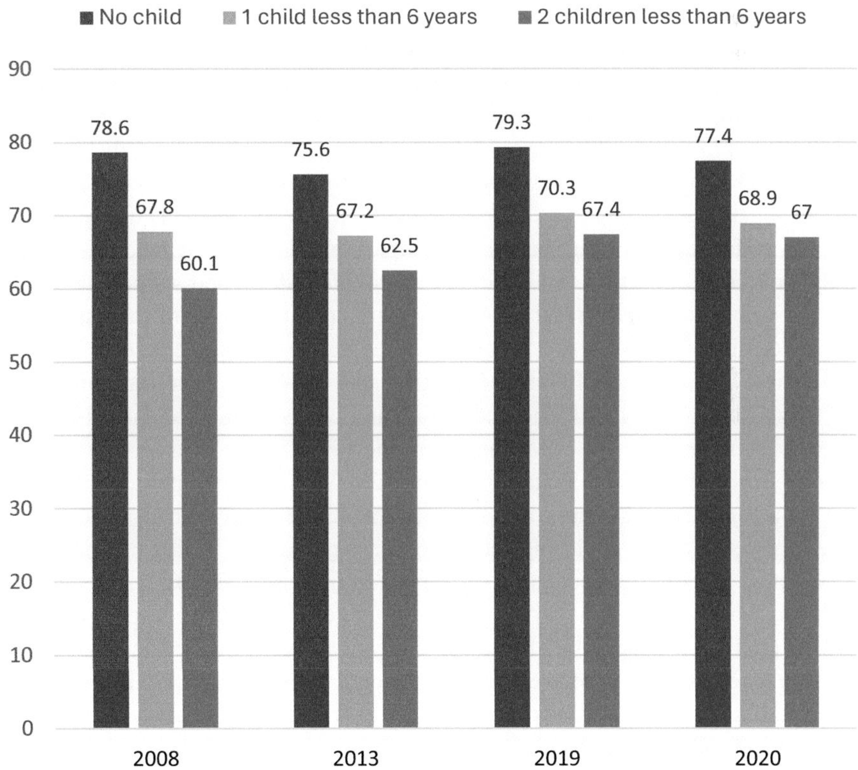

FIGURE 10.5 Employment Rate (%) of Women Aged 25–49 Years with and without Children.

Source: Eurostat, ELFS online data (accessed 15-6-2024).

under six reduced less than that for childless women. Of course, childless women may on average be younger than mothers and therefore more affected in lockdowns regarding their access to employment.

EU policy post-crises and the care transition

The two crises have been crucial for EU policy promoting the care transition. A move from the prevailing work–life balance approach to a rights-based defamilialising care policy and a degenderising of informal care and unpaid care work started in the aftermath of the Great Recession and was consolidated after the Covid-19 crisis.

The Great Recession and the austerity response to the sovereign debt crisis that ensued severely affected the living standards and working conditions of the European population and the social cohesion of the EU by amplifying inequalities within and between Member States. The result of the referendum on Brexit and the menace it represented for the disintegration of the EU, shortly after the eurozone crisis, reinforced the idea that a revival of EU social policy was needed in order to restore the appeal of the European unification project. The EPSR approved in 2017 epitomises such a revival and constitutes a turning point for the enhancement of minimum employee and social rights in the EU.

Three out of the 20 EPSR principles concern care, establishing: a) the right of parents and people with caring responsibilities to suitable leave, flexible working arrangements and access to care services, linked to gender equality in the take-up of leaves (work–life balance principle); b) children's right to affordable early childhood education and good quality care (childcare and support for children principle); and c) the right to affordable and quality long-term care services, in particular home-care and community-based services (long-term care principle). The EU Work–Life Balance Directive and the Council Recommendation on "High-quality early childhood education and care systems", adopted in 2019, constitute the first initiatives to implement the EPSR in the field of care policy. Moreover, the EU Gender Equality Strategy 2020-2025 proclaimed, for the first time in a comparable EU programmatic document, the equal sharing of domestic care responsibilities and closing the gender care gap as key policy priorities for achieving a gender-equal economy (European Commission, 2020).

It was, however, the Covid-19 crisis that triggered a qualitative leap forward in EU policy. By bringing public health, social care and informal care at home into focus, it acted as a driver of social awareness on the importance of care for social reproduction, even if such awareness was not generalised or enduring. It has also increased the social and political influence of the feminist debate on six main issues (Karamessini, 2023): 1) The centrality of care-giving/work to sustaining life, the key role of the welfare state for public health and in universally meeting the basic care needs of the population, and women's invaluable contribution as unpaid and paid carers to social reproduction; 2) The scope and continuity of care and its gendered nature; it includes not only social and personal care for children, the elderly, and the disabled, but also early childhood education, health care, and long-term care – all female-dominated sectors – and the provision of assistance to all persons and groups in a state of dependency; 3) The large gender inequalities in unpaid care work, the need for its more equal sharing between women and men, and the important role of the welfare state in defamilialising and degendering care work as a prerequisite for gender equality in paid work; 4) The undervaluation of care work, predominantly female, as reflected in the low pay, poor working conditions, and low status of care workers, who experience a wage penalty relative to other essential workers with comparable personal and work characteristics (Folbre et al., 2021); 5) The contribution that many women with precarious immigration status and intersectional disadvantages make to basic and frontline services; 6) The large inequalities in access to adequate care among large populations: poor elderly and people with disabilities, the homeless, refugees, or people living in remote areas.

Although not responding to all these issues raised by feminists, the European Care Strategy adopted in 2022 constitutes the EU's post-pandemic response to the main challenges in the field of care brought to the fore by the 2020-2021 health crisis (European Commission, 2022). Based on the EPSR principles and the EU's Gender Equality Strategy priorities, the European Care Strategy revised upwards the Barcelona targets for formal childcare coverage and proposed a Council Recommendation on access to affordable high-quality long-term care. It also called for national level policy measures to promote a gender-equal sharing of unpaid care work and to improve working conditions and career progression in the care sector as both a recognition of the social value of care work and a prerequisite to tackle the great labour shortages in the sector across the EU.

Nevertheless, the European Care Strategy displays serious deficiencies. In the field of LTC, it fails to develop a rights-based approach to care and largely accepts the status quo in regard to social protection (no discussion on social insurance or a dedicated social protection branch) and the deep systemic reliance on informal care and unpaid carers (Daly, 2025). Moreover, it remains silent on the issue of migrant care labour, displacing the EU's LTC care deficit and cost of social reproduction to poorer EU Member States, as well as beyond the bloc's borders (Zacharenko, 2024).

Last but not least, a recent gender-assessment study of the EU recovery response to the Covid-19 pandemic (EIGE, 2023) found that the Recovery and Resilience Facility, the EU instrument put in place to support reforms and investments in the Member States and enhance their recovery from the coronavirus crisis, has not prompted a cross-cutting approach to gender equality in the national plans submitted by national governments. Moreover, only thirteen out of 27 Member States have included public investment in child and long-term care services in their plans. This is a disappointing figure, which indicates that most governments do not recognise the seriousness of the care crisis and also reveals the major obstacle to achieving the goals of the European Care Strategy. In the end, the care transition in the EU depends (a) on the political will of national governments and the political trends in the Member States, which are not all supportive of the care transition, and (b) on the fiscal space of governments under the new EU fiscal framework and the availability of earmarked EU transfers and financial tools. We turn next to these and other political risks in the chapter's concluding section.

Epilogue: the care transition (in Europe) in turbulent times

The Great Recession and the coronavirus crisis, examined above, have been followed by the energy and cost-of-living crises, in a context of wars in Europe and the Middle East and aggravation of the climate crisis. What are the prospects of the care transition in turbulent times?

The care transition in Europe, and more specifically in the EU, faces a number of political risks at the current juncture of polycrisis. First of all, social investment in the care sector and the degenderisation of care may be hampered by

a) The new Fiscal Framework, which dictates a return to austerity at the national level;
b) The EU turn towards military spending as a matter of strategic priority, restricting the fiscal space at national level and precluding EU borrowing for social investment;
c) A return to conservative ideas of the family and gender and the rise of far-right political forces in government.

Second, the restrictive EU migration/refugee policy will hinder the coverage of the already important and increasing labour shortages in the care sector, especially long-term care, and encourage illegal migration, informal work, and exploitation of migrant care workers.

To make a forecast about future trends, the above risks should be set against the recent progress in EU social and care policy as described above. Under such contradictory influences, the care transition will probably not be permanently stalled but could be seriously delayed.

Note

1 The figures in Table 10.2 underestimate the impact of the Covid-19 pandemic on unpaid work and the gender gaps since the period when the second round of the Eurofound e-survey was carried out excluded the initial lockdown period of spring 2020, when additional childcare hours would have been higher.

References

Baxter, J., Campbell, A., Lee, R., & Lloyd, M. (2026). Covid-19 and gender gaps in paid and unpaid work. In J. Rubery, N. Sánchez-Mira, & V. Insarauto (Eds.), *Women in turbulent times. Crises, transitions, and challenges for gender equality* (pp. 141–161). Routledge.

Bettio, F., & Plantenga, J. (2004). Comparing care regimes in Europe. *Feminist Economics, 10*(1), 85–113. https://doi.org/10.1080/1354570042000198245

Bettio, F., Simonazzi, A., & Villa, P. (2006). The care drain in the Mediterranean: Notes on the Italian experience. *Journal of European Social Policy, 16*(3), 271–285. https://doi.org/10.1177/0958928706065 5

Blaskó, Z., & Sanjuán-Belda, J. (2022). *Division of childcare and housework among men and women during COVID-19 lockdowns.* European Commission. https://publications.jrc.ec.europa.eu/repository/handle/JRC128157

Crompton, R. (1999). Discussion and conclusions. In R. Crompton (Ed.), *Restructuring gender relations and employment: The decline of the male breadwinner* (pp. 201–214). Oxford University Press. https://doi.org/10.1093/oso/9780198294696.001.0001

Da Roit, B., & Moreno-Fuentes, F. J. (2019). Cash for care and care employment: (Missing) debates and realities. *Social Policy and Administration, 53*(4), 596–611. https://doi.org/10.1111/spol.12503

Daly, M. (2025). Long-term care as a policy issue for the European Union and United Nations organisations. *International Journal of Care and Caring, 9*(1), 9–24. https://doi.org/10.1332/239788221X16887213701095

Daly, M., & Lewis, J. (2000). The concept of social care and the analysis of contemporary welfare states. *British Journal of Sociology, 51*(2), 281–298. https://doi.org/10.1111/j.1468-4446.2000.00281.x

Dobrotić, I., Blum, S., Kaufmann, G., Koslowski, A., Moss, P., & Valentova, M. (Eds.). (2024). *International review of leave policies and research 2024.* https://doi.org/10.31219/osf.io/2frts

Ellingsæter, A.-L. (2024). Introduction: Placing the Nordic earner-carer politics in time. In A.-L. Ellingsæter (Ed.), *Nordic earner-carer politics: A comparative and historical analysis* (pp. 2–22). Edward Elgar Publishing. https://doi.org/10.4337/9781802207088

Engeman, C., & Burman, S. (2023). Signs of the gender revolution's second phase? Historical and cross-national development of fathers' leave provisions. *Social Policy & Administration, 57*(5), 626–641. https://doi.org/10.1111/spol.12882

Esping-Andersen, G. (1990). *The three worlds of welfare capitalism.* Polity Press.

Esping-Andersen, G. (1999). *Social foundations of postindustrial economies.* Oxford University Press. https://doi.org/10.1093/0198742002.001.0001

Eurofound. (2022). *The Covid-19 pandemic and the gender divide at home and work.* https://doi.org/10.2806/015588

European Commission. (2020). *A union of equality: Gender equality strategy 2020-2025 (COM(2020) 152 final).*

European Commission. (2022). *European care strategy (COM(2022) 440 final).*

European Institute for Gender Equality [EIGE]. (n.d.). *Employment in the health care sector by sex* [Data set]. Retrieved April 14, 2025, from https://eige.europa.eu/gender-statistics/dgs/browse/ta/ta_wrklab/ta_wrklab_lab/ta_wrklab_lab_employ/ta_wrklab_lab_employ_selected/ta_wrklab_lab_employ_selected_healthcare

European Institute for Gender Equality [EIGE]. (2022). *Gender Equality Index 2022: The COVID-19 pandemic and care.* Publications Office of the European Union. https://doi.org/10.2839/035888

European Institute for Gender Equality [EIGE]. (2023). *Evidence to action: Gender equality and gender mainstreaming in the COVID-19 recovery*. Publications Office of the European Union. https://doi.org/10.2839/05678

European Union. (2017). *European pillar of social rights: Proclamation of the European parliament, the council and the commission*. https://ec.europa.eu/info/sites/default/files/social-summit-european-pillar-social-rights-booklet_en.pdf

Eurostat. (n.d.). *Classroom teachers and academic staff by education level, programme orientation, sex and age groups [educ_uoe_perp02]* [Data set]. Retrieved April 14, 2025, from https://ec.europa.eu/eurostat/databrowser/view/educ_uoe_perp02__custom_15899704/default/table?lang=en

Eurostat. (2021, September 3). *2 million childcare workers and teachers' aides in the EU in 2020*. https://ec.europa.eu/eurostat/web/products-eurostat-news/-/ddn-20210903-2

Folbre, N. (1994). *Who pays for the kids? Gender and the structures of constraints*. Routledge. https://doi.org/10.4324/9780203168295

Folbre, N., Gautham, L., & Smith, K. (2021). Essential workers and care penalties in the United States. *Feminist Economics*, *27*(1–2), 173–187. https://doi.org/10.1080/13545701.2020.1828602

Fraser, N. (1994). After the family wage. *Political Theory*, *22*(4), 591–618. https://doi.org/10.1177/0090591794022004001

Gornick, J., & Meyers, M. (2009). Institutions that support gender equality in parenthood and employment. In O. Wright, J. Gornick, & M. Meyers (Eds.), *Gender equality, transforming family divisions of labor: The real Utopias project* (Vol. VI, pp. 3–64). Verso Press.

Hirdman, Y. (1998). Social policy and gender contracts: The Swedish experience. In E. Drew, R. Emerek, & E. Mahon (Eds.), *Women, work and the family in Europe* (pp. 36–46). Routledge. https://doi.org/10.4324/9780203442845

Kan, M. Y., Sullivan, O., & Gershuny, J. (2011). Gender convergence in domestic work: Discerning the effect of interactional and institutional barriers from large-scale data. *Sociology*, *45*(2), 234–251. https://doi.org/10.1177/003803851039401

Kan, M.-Y., Zhou, M., Kolpashnikova, K., Hertog, E., Yoda, S., & Jun, J. (2022). Revisiting the gender revolution: Time on paid work, domestic work, and total work in East Asian and Western societies 1985–2016. *Gender and Society*, *36*(3), 368–396. https://doi.org/10.1177/08912432221079664

Karamessini, M. (2023). *From work-life balance policy to the European care strategy: Mainstreaming care and gender in the EU policy agenda* (Document de travail No 213). Le Cnam, Centre d'études de l'emploi et du travail. https://cnam.hal.science/CEET/hal-03993871v1

Karamessini, M., & Rubery, J. (2014). Economic crisis and austerity: Challenges to gender equality. In M. Karamessini & J. Rubery (Eds.), *Women and austerity: The future for gender equality* (pp. 314–351). Routledge. https://doi.org/10.4324/9780203066294

Koslowski, A., Blum, S., Dobrotić, I., Kaufman, G., & Moss, P. (2020). Leave policy responses to COVID-19: A cross-country comparison. In A. Koslowski, S. Blum, I. Dobrotić, G. Kaufman & P. Moss (Eds.), *16th International Review of Leave Policies and Related Research 2020: COVID-19 supplement* (pp. 1–10). International Network on Leave Policies & Research. https://www.leavenetwork.org/fileadmin/user_upload/k_leavenetwork/annual_reviews/2020/Covid_19_policy_responses_summary.pdf

Leira, A. (1992). *Welfare states and working mothers*. Cambridge University Press. https://doi.org/10.1017/CBO9780511898259

Leitner, S. (2003). Varieties of familialism: The caring function of the family in comparative perspective. *European Societies*, *5*(4), 353–375. https://doi.org/10.1080/1461669032000127642

Lewis, J., & Giullari, S. (2006). The adult-worker-model family and gender equality: Principles to enable the valuing and sharing of care. In S. Razavi & S. Hassim (Eds.), *Gender and social policy in a global context: Uncovering the gendered structure of the "social"* (pp. 80–101). Palgrave Macmillan. https://doi.org/10.1057/9780230625280_8

Lister, R. (1994). She has other duties: Women, citizenship and social security. In S. Baldwin & J. Falkinham (Eds.), *Social security and social change: New challenges to the beveridge model* (pp. 31–44). Harvester Wheatsheaf.

Marx, L., Bian, F., & Sánchez-Mira, N. (2026). Crises as drivers of change in couples' paid work arrangements in Europe. In J. Rubery, N. Sánchez-Mira, & V. Insarauto (Eds.), *Women in turbulent times. Crises, transitions, and challenges for gender equality* (pp. 119–140). Routledge.

Organisation for Economic Co-operation and Development [OECD]. (2023). *Beyond applause? Improving working conditions in long term care*. OECD Publishing. https://doi.org/10.1787/27d33ab3-en

Orloff, A. (1993). Gender and the social rights of citizenship. *American Sociological Review*, *58*, 303–328. https://doi.org/10.2307/2095903

Pailhé, A., Solaz, A., & Stanfors, M. (2021). The great convergence: Gender and unpaid work in Europe and the United States. *Population and Development Review*, *47*(1), 181–217. https://doi.org/10.1111/padr.12385

Pavolini, E. (2022). Long-term care social protection models in the EU, 2021. *European Social Policy Network (ESPN)*. Publications Office of the European Union. https://doi.org/10.2767/5178

Pavolini, E., & Ranci, C. (2013). Reforms in long-term care policies in Europe: An introduction. In C. Ranci & E. Pavolini (Eds.), *Reforms in long-term care policies in Europe: Investigating institutional change and social impacts* (pp. 3–22). Springer. https://doi.org/10.1007/978-1-4614-4502-9

Ranci, C., & Pavolini, E. (2015). Not all that glitters is gold: Long-term care reforms in the last two decades in Europe. *Journal of European Social Policy*, *25*(3), 270–285. https://doi.org/10.1177/0958928715588

Rubery, J. (2015). Regulating for gender equality: A policy framework to support the universal caregiver vision. *Social Politics*, *22*(4), 513–538. https://doi.org/10.1093/sp/jxv036

Rubery, J., & Tavora, I. (2021). The Covid-19 crisis and gender equality: Risks and opportunities. In B. Vanhercke, S. Spasova, & B. Fronteddu (Eds.), *Social policy in the European Union: State of play 2020. Facing the pandemic* (pp. 71–96). European Trade Union Institute (ETUI) & European Social Observatory (OSE). https://www.etui.org/publications/social-policy-european-union-state-play-2020

Saraceno, C. (2016). Varieties of familialism: Comparing four southern European and East Asian welfare regimes. *Journal of European Social Policy, 26*(4), 314–326. https://doi.org/10.1177/095892871665727

Saraceno, C., & Keck, W. (2011). Towards an integrated approach for the analysis of gender equity in policies supporting paid work and care responsibilities. *Demographic Research, 25*(11), 371–406. https://doi.org/10.4054/DemRes.2011.25.11

Saxonberg, S. (2013). From defamilialization to degenderization: Toward a new welfare typology. *Social Policy & Administration*, *47*(1), 26–49. https://doi.org/10.1111/j.1467-9515.2012.00836.x

Simonazzi, A. (2008). Care regimes and national employment models. *Cambridge Journal of Economics*, *33*(2), 211–232. https://doi.org/10.1093/cje/ben043

Sullivan, O., Gershuny, J., & Robinson, J. P. (2018). Stalled or uneven gender revolution? A long-term processual framework for understanding why change is slow. *Journal of Family Theory and Review*, *10*(1), 263–279. https://doi.org/10.1111/jftr.12248

Szelewa, D., & Polakowski, M. (2023). Who cares, too? Degenderization of childcare policies in Europe: A dynamic fuzzy-set analysis. *Feminist Economics*, *29*(3), 153–177. https://doi.org/10.1080/13545701.2023.2230239

Zacharenko, E. (2024). Long-term care in EU policy 1999-2022: Women's responsibility, migrants' work? *Journal of Common Market Studies*, *62*(1), 38–54. https://doi.org/10.1111/jcms.13476

11

UNEMPLOYMENT AND CARE RISKS IN TIMES OF CRISIS

Gender (in)equalities at the intersection of unemployment benefits, childcare and leave policies

Trine P. Larsen, Janine Leschke and Sonja Bekker

Introduction

Comparative literature on (un)employment and care often omits differences in labour market characteristics and employment opportunities between countries (Sánchez-Mira & O'Reilly, 2019), although these are key to understanding the labour market transitions available to women while combining work and care. Women, particularly mothers, are more likely than men to be found in non-standard employment; that is, other than the standard full-time, open-ended employment contract. This not only increases their risks of becoming unemployed, but also affects their access to and the adequacy of unemployment benefits (Leschke & Finn, 2019). Moreover, for parents, and especially mothers, who still do the bulk of care work, transitions to unemployment may restrict access to childcare and future paid parental leave entitlements. These dynamics become even more salient in times of crisis when employment opportunities decrease and unemployment rises.

While international institutions have become concerned by the insufficiency of unemployment insurance benefits (UIB), particularly during recent crises, including the 2008 economic and financial crisis and the Covid-19 pandemic, they often focus on non-standard workers and the self-employed in general (for example, European Commission, 2017; Organisation for Economic Co-operation and Development [OECD], 2018a; International Labour Organization [ILO], 2021). Largely neglected are the particular challenges women face as carers, for instance, if job loss also entails losing their childcare entitlements. Similarly, in the academic literature, the focus is typically on coverage and UIB adequacy (for example, Grimshaw & Rubery, 1997; Bekker et al., 2025), while the interface between unemployment insurance benefits and care obligations is usually neglected. This

DOI: 10.4324/9781003528210-14

chapter tackles this omission and scrutinises parents', notably mothers', eligibility when unemployed for family support, including childcare and paid leave. This perspective is particularly important in times of crisis, as women are often disproportionately affected not only by job losses but also by cuts in services. This impact can be delayed, as seen in the austerity measures that followed the financial crisis (Karamessini & Rubery, 2014). For example, Adema and Ali (2015) found that in the 2008 crisis expenditure on family support initially increased, particularly in countries where it is means-tested, but was reduced under austerity. Inspired by the transitional labour markets and flexicurity approaches and explicitly combining the literature on gender, entitlement to unemployment insurance benefits and the gendered implications of caregiving, we argue that unemployment insurance benefits should be genuinely inclusive in every employment and family situation.

The chapter considers the specific challenges faced by women with care responsibilities and proposes a novel analytical framework that combines the ideal-type unemployment welfare regime typology of Gallie and Paugam (2000) with the concepts of (de)genderisation and (de)familialisation of care (Saxonberg, 2013). We take Denmark, Germany, the Netherlands and the United Kingdom as illustrative cases, with a variety of UIB characteristics and their interlinkages with childcare and parental leave policies, and examine whether these are accessible to mothers, who are particularly vulnerable to unemployment in times of crisis, given their overrepresentation in non-standard employment.

Literature review

Labour market transitions, gender and unemployment insurance benefits

Studies have found that eligibility criteria for unemployment insurance benefits can raise access barriers for workers that do not conform to the male breadwinner norm (Atkinson & Micklewright, 1991; Kvist, 1998). A number of these, now dated, studies focus specifically on gendered labour market participation and UIB coverage (Grimshaw & Rubery, 1997; Jepsen & Meulders, 1997; Mooi-Reci & Mills, 2012). Most UIB schemes punish part-time or temporary work when using a minimum hours' criteria or earnings' thresholds or calculating the contribution period with reference to working hours or days (Grimshaw & Rubery, 1997; Bekker et al., 2025). Likewise, career breaks can pose barriers to unemployment insurance benefit coverage if caring periods are not or only partially accounted for (Grimshaw & Rubery, 1997; Jepsen & Meulders, 1997). Restricted access to UIB may also imply potential loss of other social rights, including health care, pension contributions, access to active labour market policies (ALMPs) or to subsidised childcare and leave entitlements (Oehrli et al., 2024). Moreover, access to second- and third-tier benefit systems[1] usually implies less generous flat-rate and means-tested benefits.

Recent academic literature has paid limited attention to these issues or offered only a cursory overview (Avlijaš, 2023). For example, accounts of changing labour markets and UIB systems often disregard gender disparities in coverage or generosity (for example, Clegg & Nenning, 2023). Likewise, discussions of the role of work–life balance policies in female labour market participation rarely examine social protection from a gendered perspective (for example, Taylor-Gooby, 2004; Gallie & Paugam, 2000). Those concerned with precarious work and non-standard employment, however, have considered different policies to mitigate these effects (Rubery et al., 2018) especially for some part-time workers (Rubery et al., 2024). Also the crisis literature rarely engages with the gendered implications of social protection and income, with a few exceptions (Rubery & Tavora, 2021; ILO, 2021). Even more scarce are studies on social protection for mothers transitioning from work to unemployment in times of crisis. The neglect starts with the very definition of "unemployment". Gautié (2023) notes that female labour market participation, and especially involuntary part-time work, calls into question the appropriateness of both unemployment as an indicator and the institutions surrounding unemployment, which are frequently geared to the male-breadwinner and full-time employment model. However, the 2008 financial crisis and the Covid-19 pandemic (see detailed literature review by Bekker et al., 2025) stimulated interest in inclusive unemployment benefits, especially among policy bodies with the OECD, the ILO and EU institutions, which all commissioned new studies (European Commission, 2017; Matsaganis et al., 2016; OECD, 2018a; ILO, 2021). Gender coverage gaps received less attention, however. Instead, the focus in the wake of the financial crisis was more on young people, non-standard workers and commonly also the self-employed (Larsen & Ilsøe, 2022; Leschke & Finn, 2019; Spasova & Regazzoni, 2022).

While Matsaganis et al. (2016, table p. 21) do provide analyses of unemployment benefit entitlements by gender, the EU LFS data they used do not allow them to distinguish between unemployment insurance benefits and unemployment assistance benefits. Men are found to be particularly disadvantaged in countries with high self-employment shares, while permanent part-timers are not necessarily disadvantaged, except in a few countries, such as Denmark. Although the ILO (2021) explicitly provides some gendered reflections on adequate social protection, OECD country studies (2018a) put limited emphasis on gender differences overall, although they offer some relevant recommendations for more inclusive social protection, including from a gendered perspective. Notably, the OECD (2018a) chapter focused on potential deficiencies in social protection for varieties of non-standard workers, including UIB coverage, but excludes part-time work for the perverse reason that the very high rate of part-time employment means that part-time work is not considered non-standard in the Dutch context, being moreover mostly voluntary and fully covered by labour law (de Graaf-Zijl et al., 2018).

The interface between unemployment and family/care regimes

Care-giving has been subject to much welfare research, but only a few studies focus on the design features that might impede comprehensive access to unemployment insurance benefits for women (Gottschall, 2023; Walby, 2020). The focus is often on the link between care-giving and female labour market participation, along with national policies on care provision, leave rights, social transfers and take-up rates. Less attention is paid to women's transition from paid work to unemployment or broader welfare policies and their implications for gender inequalities within and beyond the family (Esping-Andersen, 1999; Gottschall, 2023). While much of the welfare literature has focused on the (de)familialisation of care (that is, the extent of alternative provision via the market or the state), more recent approaches have added the concepts of "(de)genderising" and "gender regimes" (see also Karamessini, 2026, this volume). These concepts better illuminate the embedded gender biases present in social protection systems (Gottschall, 2023; Szelewa & Polakowski, 2023; Walby, 2020). Following Saxonberg (2013), genderising policies embrace traditional gender roles such as the male breadwinner/female caregiver, while degenderising policies aim to equalise participation in productive and reproductive tasks by both sexes. This distinction helps to capture inequalities embedded within social protection systems beyond just family and care policies (Saxonberg, 2013). In this sense, gender equality is often assumed to be greater in social democratic welfare regimes because of their more extensive equality regulations (Esping-Andersen, 1999; Gottschall, 2023). Nevertheless, the complexity and idiosyncrasy of gender inequality challenge the welfare state regime typologies as all seem to have their shortcomings (Kowalewska, 2023). Our four-country analysis considers whether the social democratic regime is indeed always the best performer on all aspects of gender equality or may also display biases and limitations in terms of its analytical lens, policy focus and target groups.

Mothers transitioning from work to unemployment: an analytical framework

Both the transitional labour markets approach and the flexicurity approach have stressed how increasing flexibility over the life course and associated labour market transitions should be buffered by social security and other policies fostering sustainable transitions, for instance, between unemployment and jobs (Bekker & Leschke, 2023; Larsen & Ilsøe, 2022; Schmid & Gazier, 2002). However, despite the clear relationship with genderlabour market divisions, few empirical studies engage with what has been termed combination security, which captures an individual's work and care combinations (Larsen, 2010 is an exception but does not explore transitions to unemployment).

This chapter proposes a framework for scrutinising the complexities of contemporary unemployment insurance benefits through a gender lens by combining

Gallie and Paugam's (2000) unemployment welfare regimes with Saxonberg's (2013) (de)-genderisation concept. Gallie and Paugam's (2000) original fourfold typology considered UIB coverage, benefit generosity, benefit duration and use of active labour market policies. We add degenderisation policies to these considerations (see Table 11.1). This chapter focuses on country examples from three out of the four regime types:[2] liberal/minimal (UK), employment-centred (Germany, the Netherlands) and universalist regimes (Denmark). The universalist regime is held to perform best by offering comprehensive coverage, higher and longer benefits, extensive active employment policy and degenderisation policies. The liberal/minimal regime is characterised as incomplete in terms of coverage and weak with regard to the other dimensions. The employment-centred regime has variable coverage and unequal levels and durations of benefits, extensive active employment policies and limited (de)genderisation beyond just family and care policies.

After providing some contextual labour market information, we draw on this framework to interlink unemployment insurance benefits, childcare and leave entitlements of mothers who transition to unemployment in our case study countries.

Comparing the four countries: key contextual information

Key labour market indicators

Figure 11.1 shows that all the selected countries, compared with the EU27 average, have high employment, low unemployment and relatively low gender gaps in both indicators. Weekly working hours are lower than the EU average across all four countries, particularly for women.

Gender and country differences in working hours are also evident: female part-time shares are highest in the Netherlands (52%), followed by Germany (35%), the UK (32%) and Denmark (22%) (Figure 11.2). In the first three cases, female part-time employment is still strongly driven by care needs as indicated in the reasons for part-time work, but Danish women are much less likely to emphasise care as their main reason for part-time working (see Figure A11-1, Online appendix). The gender differences are less pronounced for other forms of non-standard work, but visible for temporary employment with higher shares for women (except for Germany) and own account self-employed with higher shares for men (Figure 11.2).

Unemployment benefits, childcare and leave: public spending and take-up rates

Figure 11.3 compares the resources countries deploy to create security. Expenditure on passive and active unemployment benefits (PLMP and ALMP)

TABLE 11.1 Unemployment Welfare Regimes and (De)genderisation Policies

Welfare Regimes	*Country Examples*	*UIB Coverage*	*UIB Level and Duration*	*Active Labour Market Policy*	*(De) genderisation Policies*
Sub-protective	Spain, Poland	Very incomplete	Very weak	Almost non-existent	Weak
Liberal/minimal	UK, US	Incomplete	Weak	Weak	Weak
Employment-centred	Germany, France, Netherlands	Variable	Unequal	Extensive	Unequal
Universalistic	Denmark, Sweden	Comprehensive	High	Very extensive	Extensive

Source: Author's extension of Gallie and Paugam (2000, p. 5) drawing on Saxonberg (2013).

Note: UIB = unemployment insurance benefits.

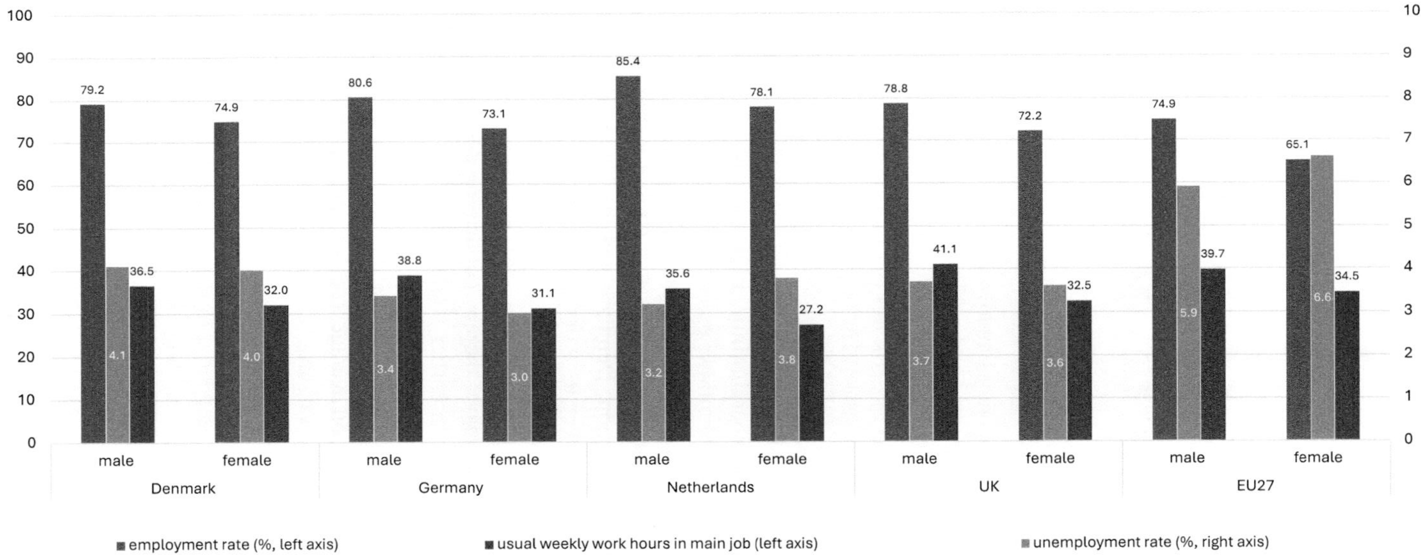

FIGURE 11.1 Unemployment Rates, Employment Rates and Weekly Working Hours by Gender across Four Countries, 2022 (or Latest Available Year).

Source: Own elaboration based on data from the OECD (n.d.).

Note: Data referring to population 15–64 years of age. UK data on usual weekly hours of work refer to 2019.

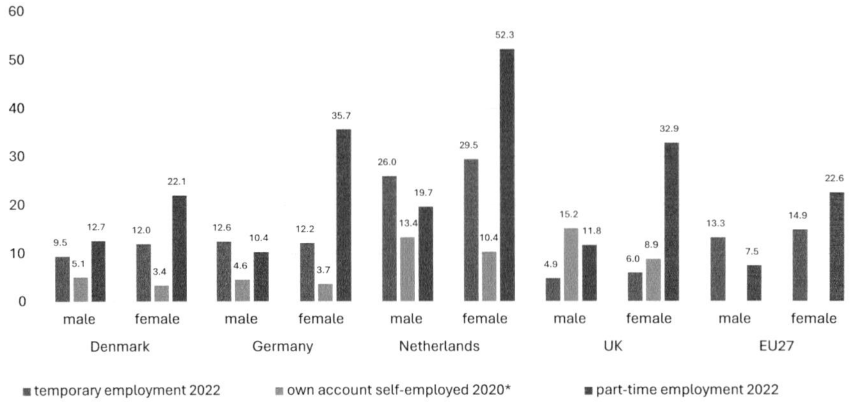

FIGURE 11.2 Part-Time Employment, Temporary Employment and Own Account Self-Employment across Countries and Gender, 2022 (or Latest Available Year).

Source: Own elaboration based on data from the OECD (n.d.).

Note: Data referring to population 15–64 years of age; *UK data on own account self employment refers to 2019; no information for own account self employed for EU27.

is in line with Gallie and Paugam's typology for the universalist example Denmark (high PLMP and ALMP) and for the liberal/minimal UK example. Among the employment-centred examples, Germany follows expectations (high PLMP, moderate ALMP), but the Netherlands is closer to Denmark. Using public expenditure figures on early childhood education and care (ECEC) and maternity and parental leave to capture (de)genderisation, Denmark and the United Kingdom also conform to expectations of best versus worst performers with Germany in a mid-way position. The Netherlands is a more peculiar case; although just below Germany in ECEC expenditure, it is by far the worst performer in terms of expenditure on maternity and parental leave, thereby confirming the designation of the Netherlands as a hybrid regime in earlier studies (Ferragina & Seeleib-Kaiser, 2011).

The picture regarding benefit coverage appears bleaker. Fewer than one in three unemployed and one in four jobseekers, on average, received unemployment benefits in the OECD (2018b). Using Eurostat figures on unemployed persons receiving unemployment insurance benefits and/or unemployment assistance, marked cross-country variations are found (highest in Germany and lowest in the United Kingdom for short-term benefits), but gender differences are strongest in the United Kingdom for short-term benefits, although around a comparatively low coverage rate for both men and women (Table 11.2). Importantly, the Eurostat indicator includes means-tested unemployment benefits such as ALG II for Germany or income-based jobseeker's allowance (JSA) for the United Kingdom, which are generally low. Unemployed women are more likely to live in households with incomes that exceed the threshold for benefit eligibility. For all four countries, the

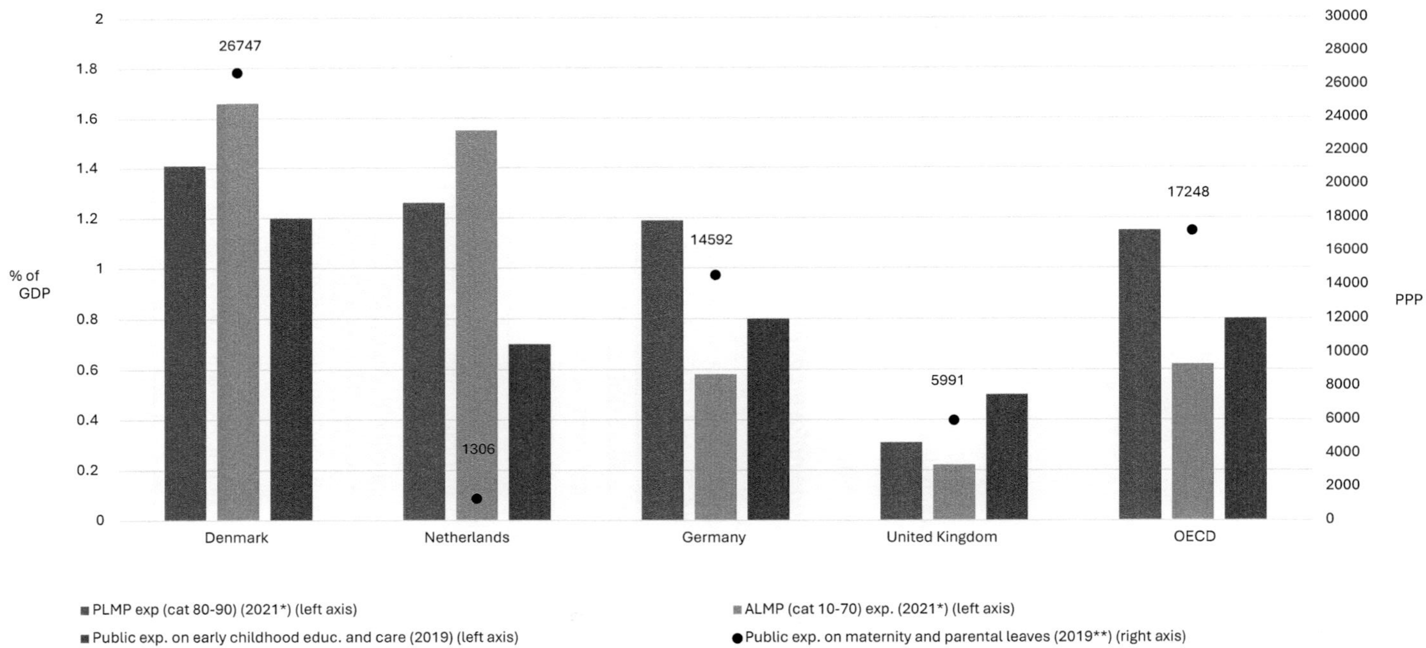

FIGURE 11.3 Public Expenditure on Passive and Active Unemployment Benefits and Early Childhood Education (ECEC) as a Percentage of GDP and on Maternity and Parental Leave in Purchasing Power Parity, 2021 (or Latest Available Year).

Source: Own elaboration based on data from the OECD (n.d.). (Public expenditure and participant stocks and LFS, extracted 22.4.2024); OECD Family Data Base (2024, indicator PF3.1 & PF2.1).

Notes: *UK PLMP and ALMP data for 2011. This potentially biases the comparison as they had not yet recovered from the Great Recession, with unemployment at 8.4% in 2011. **Public expenditure on maternity, paternity, parental and home care leaves per live birth, in USD PPP.

TABLE 11.2 Unemployed Receiving Benefits and Assistance (% of All Registered Unemployed) by Duration of Unemployment, 2023 (2019 for UK)

	Denmark		*Germany*		*Netherlands*		*United Kingdom*		*EU27*	
	M	*F*	*M*	*F*	*M*	*F*	*M*	*F*	*M*	*F*
3–5 months	42	45	67	60	40	40	35	20	41	39
<12 months	33	33	58	52	27	25	28	17	36	35
>12 months	48	43[a]	78	70	66	44	48	42	31	24

Source: Eurostat (2024).
Note: [a]Low reliability.

share of unemployed receiving benefits for over 12 months is generally higher than for those receiving benefits for less than 12 months, but there is a more pronounced gender gap in the Netherlands, where length of eligibility is related to job tenure.

Analysing UIB, paid leave and childcare

Genderising design features of unemployment insurance benefits

The UIB systems across our four countries are designed mainly around standard employment, particularly with regard to the various qualifying conditions, benefit levels and duration (Table 11.3 and Table A11-1, online appendix). Access to UIB is often restricted for non-standard workers, thus making regime-type classifications redundant in this respect and to some degree calling into question Gallie and Paugam's original typology. Here, a genderisation lens is more helpful. Access is typically conditional on minimum accrued hours (United Kingdom, Denmark) and/or minimum earnings (Denmark, United Kingdom), or a minimum loss of working hours (Netherlands). These are problematic qualifying conditions, given the overrepresentation of women in (low hours and low-wage) part-time work. Women are also overrepresented among temporary workers, a category that usually struggles to qualify for unemployment insurance benefits because of their shorter tenure within the reference period. Non-standard work may also influence the amount of benefits received, particularly if duration of benefits depends on the contribution period. Likewise, career breaks may impact on access or benefit levels, unless these are counted towards contribution periods. The same criticism applies to schemes excluding certain categories of workers, such as mini-jobbers with short weekly working hours, who are disproportionally married women (Germany) or household workers, commonly women (Netherlands) (de Kort & Bekker, 2024). Regarding self-employment (in which women are underrepresented, Figure 11.2), some countries provide no access, while others at most grant voluntary or partial access (Denk & Königs, 2022). Denmark operates

TABLE 11.3 Elements of Unemployment (Insurance) Benefits and Gendered Implications

Main Institutional Features of UIB	*Possible Design Features*	*Gendered Implications*	*Country Examples*
Qualifying conditions	Contribution record: contribution period within a specific reference period	Women likely to have shorter contribution record than men due to periods of leave or temporary employment	DK, DE, NL, UK
	Contribution record: minimum hours or earnings thresholds	Women more likely to be on short hours	DK, UK
	Formal employment relationship (self-employed often excluded, some exclude professions with short hours)	Men more likely to be self-employed, women more likely to have short hours	DE (mini-jobbers, mostly self-employed), NL (domestic workers, self-employed), UK (self-employed)
	Requirement to be a member of an unemployment insurance fund	Women and non-standard workers less likely to join	DK
Level of benefits	Earnings-related with upper ceiling vs uniform (flat rate)	Lower benefits for women in earnings-related systems where there is a gender pay gap (though may be moderated by upper ceiling)	UK (flat rate[a]) DK, DE, NL (DK with comparatively low earnings ceilings)
	Uniform (flat rate)	Could potentially benefit women with commonly lower median earnings, but usually very low benefit level	UK (flat rate[a]), DE (ALG II[b])
	Adjusted according to family situation	Could be beneficial for women but if there are in-built mechanisms penalising second-income household earners – typically women – they may be under pressure to keep earnings low or leave paid work	DE, UK

(*Continued*)

TABLE 11.3 *(Continued)*

Main Institutional Features of UIB	*Possible Design Features*	*Gendered Implications*	*Country Examples*
	Means-testing	Often but not always applies to second-tier systems in which women are over-represented	UK (flat rate[a]), DE (ALG II[b])
	Private top-ups	Usually geared to more "standard" workers, too expensive for low wage workers so likely to disadvantage women	DK
Duration of benefits	Contribution record	Women have more frequent career breaks and overrepresentation in temporary employment; sometimes offset by credits for periods outside the labour market, or the assessment period is prolonged (e.g., parental leave)	DE (the reference period includes period of official parental leave), NL
	Duration co-determined by age/family situation/regional labour market situation	UIB duration that takes into account family situation can be beneficial to women	DE (older workers receive benefits for a longer duration)

Source: Authors' elaboration drawing on Bekker et al. (2025) and Spasova and Regazzoni (2022).

Note: [a]Flat rate payable to full- and part-timers; short hours part-timers unlikely to be eligible because not allowed to pay contributions. [b]Means-tested basic income support for those not eligible for unemployment insurance benefits.

with voluntary unemployment insurance, and many non-standard workers are less likely to join an unemployment fund (Larsen & Ilsøe, 2022).

Nonetheless, some features of unemployment insurance benefit systems can be beneficial to parents. Some countries provide higher net replacement rates for recipients with children (for instance, Germany: 60% without, 67% with children). Other countries have relatively low earnings ceilings, resulting in higher replacement rates for recipients formerly on low earnings (Denmark and the United Kingdom's flat rate). Both aspects are beneficial for women, who are more likely to be single mothers and low earners. In the United Kingdom, there is now an integrated benefit system – Universal Credit[3] – for those with and without access to contributory unemployment benefits, as means-tested top-up benefits are very important for all unemployed given the low flat-rate unemployment insurance benefits. This means-tested social assistance via Universal Credit is based on individual assessments, taking into account family circumstances (Chaudhuri & Waters, 2024) and also provides means-tested additional family-related benefits but subject to a cap of up to two children, which has detrimental effects on child poverty in larger families (Andersen et al., 2024). Private insurance schemes that top up collective unemployment insurance benefits address the hollowing-out of ordinary UIB and are increasingly popular, including in countries belonging to the universalist unemployment welfare regime (Denmark) (Lindellee, 2021; Denderski & Stoltenberg, 2023). These schemes tend to exclude the self-employed and restrict access mainly to full-time workers with open-ended contracts and coverage by the ordinary UIB scheme. These schemes' insurance fees also usually render them inaccessible to low-wage workers. Combined with their various qualifying conditions, they contribute to increased gender inequalities because of women's overrepresentation in low-wage non-standard jobs (except for self-employment).

Genderising paid leave policies

Across countries, entitlements to paid maternity, paternity and parental leave vary, but everywhere mothers take by far the majority of paid leave (OECD, 2024). Access is often contingent on gender, parents' employment status, past employment record (tenure, minimum earnings, minimum weekly working hours) and sometimes social insurance contributions (Table 11.4). In the United Kingdom, fathers' rights to paid parental leave are contingent on their partners' employment status and their willingness to share the leave period (O'Brian et al., 2023). In the other countries, paid parental leave is partially reserved with the option of sharing it equally. However, unlike Denmark, the German and Dutch leave schemes favour mothers by granting them additional weeks of paid maternity leave (den Dulk & Yerkes, 2023; Table 11.4). The Dutch, German and especially the United Kingdom's leave schemes thus embrace genderising policies with their inherited gender bias. In contrast, the Danish leave system promotes a more equal division

TABLE 11.4 Paid Leave Entitlements and Qualifying Conditions

		Denmark	*Germany*	*Netherlands*	*United Kingdom*
Paid leave	Maternity	4 weeks pre-leave = 11 weeks	14 weeks[a]	16 weeks	39 weeks
	Paternity	11 weeks	–	6 weeks	2 weeks
	Parental	13 weeks each	10(+2) months	9 weeks per parent	–
Qualifying conditions	Employment status	Yes	No	Yes	Yes
	Min. income ceiling	Yes	No	No	No
	Min. accrued working hours	Yes	No	No	No
	Past employment record	Yes	Yes	Yes	No
	Social insurance contribution	Yes	No	No	No
Level of benefit	Maternity leave	UIB rate (CA 100% pay)	100% pay (flat rate if no prev. earnings)	100% pay	6 weeks at 90% pay, 33 weeks: flat rate[b] (company specific: 50–100% pay)
	Paternity leave	UIB rate (CA 100% pay)	–	100% pay (1 week)	Flat rate[b]
	Parental leave	UIB rate (CA 100% pay)	65–67% pay	70% pay	Unpaid

Source: OECD (2024, Indicators PF2.2. & PF2.1), Mutual Information System on Social Protection (MISSOC), 2023.

Note: CA = Collective agreement coverage.

[a]4 to 6 before, 8 to 10 weeks after birth.

[b]£184.03 a week 2024 or 90% pay whichever is lowest (only affects part-timers).

of leave between parents, exclusively comparing paid leave entitlements, echoing expectations from the gender regime literature.

The qualifying conditions and benefit levels also reveal institutionally embedded gender inequalities and thus different levels of (de)genderised policies, but sometimes in different ways than expected. For example, in Denmark's universalist regime, access to paid leave and payment levels are contingent on employment status, a minimum income and working-time threshold, social insurance contributions and collective agreement coverage. This leaves unemployed and non-standard working mothers less protected than standard workers after childbirth, and disadvantages women, who are more likely to have shorter tenure or reduced hours (Borger.dk, n.d.; Rostgaard & Ejersnaes, 2023). Moreover, paid leave rights and compensation levels are partly tied to the Danish unemployment insurance benefit system, in which different rules apply depending on the parent's employment situation. Those that comply with the minimum earnings and working hours threshold are guaranteed paid leave equal to unemployment insurance benefits regardless of UIB-scheme membership, while full wage compensation applies only to parents working under a collective agreement for a certain period. In contrast, unemployed mothers' or fathers' rights to paid leave depend on UIB scheme membership, which grants only UIB-insured paid leave entitlements (Borger.dk, n.d.). This aligns only partly with expectations that degenderising policies would flourish in the universalist unemployment regime. These expectations seem jeopardised at the intersection with the Danish UIB system as uninsured unemployed parents or ineligible parents (i.e., those struggling to meet the minimum thresholds for income or working hours) are left without any paid leave rights but may qualify for social assistance. From a gender perspective, this exacerbates inequalities and points to genderising policies within a system that on the surface appears degenderising with its equal division of paid leave rights.

The United Kingdom has paid maternity leave of 90% of average weekly earnings for the first six weeks, followed by a very low rate (£184.03 per week or 90% of past earnings, whichever is lowest) for the next 33 weeks. Many companies also provide between 50 and 100% of average weekly earnings during paid maternity leave, but typically for varying lengths of time (Churchill, 2021). The United Kingdom also stands out for offering only unpaid parental leave. The low reimbursement rate after six weeks makes it difficult for women to be a significant breadwinner in the family if they intend to have children as they effectively have to survive without the mother's earnings. Those in non-standard employment or unemployed also risk lower levels of income security during maternity or paternity leave, but the income loss is greater for those in full-time employment after the first six weeks or for those on company-based paid leave schemes because of the flat rate or upper income cap. This is in line with the expected weak degenderising and even genderising leave policies in the liberal/minimalist regime, even if most parents have some form of paid leave entitlement. However, in the case of sudden job loss, unemployed prospective mothers retain their rights to statutory maternity pay or maternity allowance (even if very low paid), if they qualify for paid leave prior to their unemployment. This is more generous than in the universalist Danish regime, under which they risk losing their entitlement (O'Brian et al., 2023; Table 11.4).

The employment-centred regimes of the Netherlands and Germany appear rather inclusive compared with Denmark and the United Kingdom. The Netherlands guarantees paid maternity leave to most groups, including self-employed/freelancers, temporary workers, employees with open-ended contracts, the unemployed and persons on sick leave (den Dulk & Yerkes, 2023). The Dutch reimbursement rate is also comparatively generous (maternity is 100 % paid, but only the first week of paternity leave is 100% paid). But the lower parental leave rates at 70% (with a daily maximum) provide an incentive to fathers to go back to work, even though the paid leave is nine weeks. This obstructs more equal participation (Table 11.4). Sometimes collective agreements award (additional) paid leave to fathers or mothers (up to 26 weeks per parent). Germany also guarantees access to paid maternity leave at full wage compensation to employees, including those on regular part-time or fixed-term contracts, but requires 12 months of continuous employment at the same employer. Insured self-employed persons can obtain a flat-rate maternity benefit through their health insurance and uninsured or ineligible mothers may be covered by their partners' health care insurance as the employment-centred regime in Germany offers derived rights (Schober et al., 2023), for example to mini-jobbers. From a gender perspective, this may increase dependence on the claimant's partner, along with the inherited risks of disincentives to work more hours. This situation applies especially to women because they are more likely to benefit from derived health care insurance. The fact that parents independent of their former employment status have access to parental leave benefits (sometimes flat-rate) stands in contrast to the typical insurance features of the German welfare regime. Instead, the Dutch system, although fairly inclusive for maternity leave, links extended paternity leave and parental leave to employment status. This aligns with our expectations of highly genderising leave policies, which are further reinforced by the associated benefit levels.

Access to affordable childcare

Access to affordable childcare seems pivotal in enabling parents to continue in or return to paid work during or after periods of childrearing. Across regime types, governments have increasingly invested in national childcare infrastructure to accompany the different statutory childcare guarantees offered to parents with children below the age of compulsory schooling. However, take-up rates of full-time day care remain low, especially among 0- to 2-year-olds (Table 11.5). Nevertheless, research has scarcely explored what happens to these childcare rights when one or both parents become unemployed, which may happen more frequently in times of crisis.

TABLE 11.5 Rules on Access to Childcare

		Denmark	*Germany*	*Netherlands*	*United Kingdom (England)*
Key characteristics	Childcare rights – eligibility	All children aged 6 months to age of compulsory schooling	All children aged 1 year to age of compulsory schooling	All children aged 0 to 4 years, whereafter school may start	All children aged 9 months to 4 years
Qualifying conditions	Day-care hours guaranteed	30+ hours	20 hours typically guaranteed	No guaranteed (full-time) place – dependent on availability	15 weekly hours free 30 weekly hours (only working parents – children aged 3–4 years)
	Enrolment rate (%) 0–2 years	54.3	38.6	72.8	41.3
	Average usual weekly hours (0–2 years)	34.4	30.3	18.5	19.5
	Age of the child	Yes	Yes	Yes	Yes
	Parent's employment situation	No	No	No	Yes[a]
	Minimum weekly working hours	No	No	No	Yes
	Minimum earnings	No	No	No	Yes

TABLE 11.5 *(Continued)*

		Denmark	*Germany*	*Netherlands*	*United Kingdom (England)*
Childcare fees	Free	No	Yes (depends on state and age)	No	Yes (38 weeks only)
	Subsidised (earnings-related)	Yes (up to 75%)	Yes (75–80%)	Yes (33–96%)	Yes (85%)
	Parent's employment status	No	No	Yes[b]	Yes[c]

Sources: OECD, 2024 (PF3.2); Schober et al., 2023.

Notes: [a]Both parents for 15 hours for under 3s and for extra 15 hours 3- to 4- year-olds; [b]unemployed lose child-care benefits after 3 months; [c]for under 3s and for extra 15 hours 3- to 4 -year-olds.

In the liberal/minimalist regime in the United Kingdom (referring here explicitly to England) childcare support is being expanded, but primarily to help working parents; that is, where both parents are working more than 16 hours per week and earn above the minimum income ceiling (£183 per week). The only unconditional support is a universal childcare guarantee of 15 hours of free childcare to all children aged 3–4 years (aged 2 years if in receipt of benefits), but only during school terms. New rights for 15 hours for children from 9 months to 2 years of age (soon to be raised to 30 hours) and for a top-up to 30 hours for 3- to 4-year-olds apply only to working parents as defined (HM Government, 2025). The United Kingdom's government also offers tax relief on childcare costs that tends to help middle-income families. However, there is no upper limit to childcare fees, which enables providers to increase care prices for hours not covered by the free childcare hours (De Henau, 2022; HM Government, 2025; West et al., 2020). The United Kingdom's childcare infrastructure also remains underdeveloped and underfunded even though the government provides public funding. It is thus struggling to deliver on its different childcare offers, leaving parents with care rights, but unable to utilise them (De Henau, 2022).

In addition, parents risk changes to or even loss of their childcare rights if they or their partner become unemployed or lose income or working hours. However, the unemployed may be able to access 15 hours of free childcare for children aged 2 years or less, if claiming benefits. They also have a universal right to 15 free hours for 3- to 4-year-olds, although not the full 30 hours for 3- to 4-year-olds. Those claiming Universal Credit (and therefore on low household income) may also be able to claim up to 85% of childcare fees, though again only if both parents are working. These regulatory restrictions point to different levels of (de)gendering childcare policies that promote gender (in)equalities at the intersection with unemployment insurance benefits or the broader UK benefit system, despite some inbuilt mechanisms to protect low-income groups, non-standard workers on short hours and the unemployed. However, our findings may call into question the classification of the United Kingdom as a weak degenderising regime regarding its childcare policies, not least its recently expanded free childcare offer, which appears more comprehensive (in terms of care hours covered) than the employment-centred German and Dutch regimes. Conversely, the underdeveloped UK care infrastructure with its inadequate and variegated top-up care fees would seem to indicate a system that continues to reflect a weak degenderising regime, not least due to benefit traps for second-income earners under Universal Credit and the high unregulated childcare fees for non-free hours (De Henau, 2022).

The employment-centred regimes in the Netherlands and Germany in principle have no restrictions on access to childcare, but rights to a childcare placement may only be for part-time care (Schober et al., 2023). In the Netherlands, childcare allowances depend not only on parents' earnings but also on their employment situation, in line with expectations of an employment-centred regime. To receive childcare allowance, parents need to work, study or follow a re-integration trajectory, increasing the risks often associated with unemployment as parents lose their rights to childcare allowance after three months of unemployment and no re-integration activities ("Ik heb geen werk meer…", 2024). In Germany, childcare costs are heavily subsidised, though usually dependent on parents' earnings, but in some federal states, childcare is free for all children or children from a specific age onwards. Unlike the Netherlands and the United Kingdom, access to subsidised childcare is not contingent on parents' employment status, which minimises the associated risks of unemployment and potential gender inequalities, at least from a childcare perspective. Germany thus appears to be putting a stronger emphasis on degenderising policies and decommodification. This goes for both childcare and parental leave policies.

Denmark's universalistic regime makes it the only one of the four countries in which all children from the age of six months have the right to full-time subsidised childcare (30 hours per week) until the age of compulsory schooling, without any restrictions related to parents' employment status. Childcare usually takes place in publicly provided childcare facilities, but parents can also use private, but publicly funded childminders covered by the public authorities or cash-for-care/home-based care. Moreover, the childcare guarantee also applies to the unemployed and additional means-tested childcare fee reductions or even waivers are available for low-income families, including the unemployed (Larsen & de la Porte, 2022; Rostgaard, 2014). This is very much in line with expectations of the universalist regime, with degenderising policies aimed at reducing the gendered implications often associated with unemployment and low-paid non-standard work.

These different national childcare facilities, especially the consideration given to low-wage workers and the unemployed, point towards both degenderising and genderising policies. On the one hand, universal childcare rights, with additional incentives for low-income families to take up paid work, encourage dual-earner households. On the other hand, the few guaranteed hours of childcare echo genderising policies as they rarely match full-time work and consequently force parents to find alternative care solutions. The latter often involves mothers working reduced hours, combining multiple jobs or leaving paid work. Many parents may thus use non-standard work as a work–life balance strategy, with its associated negative consequences for their access to adequate social protection.

Conclusions

In times of economic crisis, there is an exacerbated risk of job or income loss. Access to social protection thus takes on greater importance. Women thus face multiple risks, including, in some crises, being in sectors in the eye of the storm or employed in non-standard jobs that could be the first to be affected and offer limited access to unemployment insurance benefits. While women in general may have more limited protection from unemployment insurance benefits due to lower earnings and interrupted labour market participation, for mothers of young children a transition to unemployment may involve additional risks vis-à-vis leave and child-care entitlements. Furthermore, in times of crisis, family policies may be restricted because of budget cuts (Adema & Ali, 2015). In order to trace such often hidden gendered implications, this chapter applies a novel analytical framework based on applying a genderisation/degenderisation lens (Saxonberg, 2013) to an established typology of unemployment welfare regimes (Gallie & Paugam, 2000) in order to illustrate how UIB design features intersect with childcare and leave policies and at times foster institutionally embedded gender inequalities. A comparison of Denmark, Germany, the Netherlands and the United Kingdom shows differences in entitlements for women who become unemployed. This indicates a need to review the ideal-type unemployment welfare regime typology proposed by Gallie and Paugam (2000).

This chapter shows that in all four countries, non-standard workers face challenges in accessing unemployment insurance benefits. The two employment-centred regimes exclude particular employment categories such as mini-jobbers (Germany) and domestic workers (Netherlands), while in all four cases eligibility requirements that take into account past employment records (tenure, minimum earnings, minimum weekly working hours) or insurance contributions also tend to disadvantage women. Moreover, paid leave entitlements are commonly related to employment status, particularly when it comes to more extended parental leave. Regarding childcare, availability and accessibility vary considerably across the four countries, but rarely match full-time working hours, with few exceptions (Denmark). Such care services are commonly combined with high childcare fees, which may hinder women taking up (full-time) jobs. Gender inequalities are exacerbated further by the fact that women take longer leave periods than men (even though recent studies point towards increased uptake among fathers due to recent rule changes with regard to earmarked leave).

Thus, between- and within-country variations across distinct claimant groups point to institutionally embedded gender inequalities and genderising policies, which are not always in line with expectations associated with the (unemployment) welfare regime or degenderisation literature. On some dimensions, Germany and the United Kingdom grant broader accessibility than might be expected: for example, in Germany, parental leave is independent of employment status, and the United Kingdom (England) offers free childcare for large groups of parents and for significant numbers of hours per week. The inverse is true for Denmark, where, on some dimensions, provision is less universal than expected (for example, private top-ups for unemployment insurance benefits, paid parental leave not universal). Germany is particularly noteworthy because some institutions – most notably parental leave – have changed from a system that typically supports the male-breadwinner model to one that aims to incentivise more equal participation of mothers and fathers. Future research should also expand this analysis to so-called sub-protective regimes, which have faired particularly poorly according to Gallie and Paugam (2000) but have improved their general position over time.

They now figure before the liberal/minimalist regime, but their gendered implications are still unknown (Bekker et al., 2025).

This chapter highlights the importance of looking at social security subsystems not in isolation, but in combination. Every welfare system typically has positive or negative consequences for workers' eligibility to access different forms of social protection – in our case unemployment insurance benefits, childcare and paid leave – that may exacerbate gender inequalities. This is particularly relevant to workers whose labour market transitions are combined with care responsibilities. Systems that successfully combine care and leave with unemployment compensation would be better able to cope with periods of crisis, turbulence and transition.

Notes

1 Unemployment benefit systems are typically structured in two tiers: a first tier comprising contribution-based unemployment insurance, offering earnings-related benefits to individuals with sufficient employment history; and a second tier encompassing means-tested support, which may include unemployment assistance or general social assistance, for those not eligible for insurance benefits or whose entitlements have expired. In some countries, the United Kingdom being an example, first and second tier systems are more similar to one another than in other countries.

2 For practical reasons we could not include a country example for the sub-protective regime. We focused instead on the other three regime types where we have strong language skills and a thorough understanding of the institutional configurations. For a contemporary assessment of the sub-protective regime, which is not covered in our country sample, see Bekker et al. (2025), though not for a gender perspective.

3 In the United Kingdom, Universal Credit protects people without contributory unemployment benefits, which is an integrated means-tested benefit, based on an individual assessment taking into account family circumstances (Chaudhuri & Waters, 2024).

References

Adema, W., & Ali, N. (2015). Recent changes in family outcomes and policies in OECD countries: The impact of the economic crisis. *Community, Work and Family*, *18*(2), 145–166. https://doi.org/10.1080/13668803.2015.1013020

Andersen, K., Redman, J., Stewart, K., & Patrick, R. (2024). "It's the kids that suffer": Exploring how the UK's benefit cap and two-child limit harm children. *Social Policy and Administration*, *59*(1), 57–72. https://doi.org/10.1111/spol.13034

Atkinson, A. B., & Micklewright, J. (1991). Unemployment compensation and labour market transitions: A critical review. *Journal of Economic Literature*, *29*(4), 1679–1727. http://www.jstor.org/stable/2727794

Avlijaš, S. (2023). Women, work, and labour market policy. In D. Clegg & N. Durazzi (Eds.), *Handbook of labour market policy in advanced democracies* (pp. 103–115). Edward Elgar.

Bekker, S., Larsen, T., & Leschke, J. (2025). Unemployment protection in changing labour markets. In J. Heyes, J. Leschke, K. Newsome, M. Reich, & A. Wilkinson (Eds.), *Research handbook on decent work in a post-Covid 19 world* (pp. 221–241). Edward Elgar Publishing. https://doi.org/10.4337/9781800882751.00015

Bekker, S., & Leschke, J. (2023). The academic and policy roots of flexicurity and its pathways. In D. Clegg & N. Durazzi (Eds.), *Handbook of labour market policy in advanced democracies* (pp. 127–148). Edward Elgar. https://doi.org/10.4337/9781800880887.00011

Borger.dk. (n.d.). *Barsel og orlov – Barselsdagpenge*. https://www.borger.dk/familie-og-boern/barsel-oversigt

Chaudhuri, S. R., & Waters, T. (2024). *Universal credit: Incomes, incentives and the remaining roll-out*. Institute for Fiscal Studies.

Churchill, F. (2021, May 24). Two-thirds of businesses now provide enhanced maternity pay, poll finds. *People Management*. https://www.peoplemanagement.co.uk/article/1747219/two-thirds-of-businesses-now-provide-enhanced-maternity-pay

Clegg, D., & Nenning, L. (2023). The parabola of unemployment insurance in advanced democracies. In D. Clegg & N. Durazzi (Eds.), *Handbook of labour market policy in advanced democracies* (pp. 315–342). Edward Elgar Publishing. https://doi.org/10.4337/9781800880887.00028

de Graaf-Zijl, M., Scheer, B., & Bolhaar, J. (2018). Netherlands: Non-standard work and social protection. In *The future of social protection: What works for non-standard workers?* OECD. https://doi.org/10.1787/9789264306943-en

de Henau, J. (2022). Simulating employment and fiscal effects of public investment in high-quality universal childcare in the UK. *International Journal of Child Care and Education Policy*, *16*(1), Article 3. https://doi.org/10.1186/s40723-022-00096-y

de Kort, D., & Bekker, S. (2024). Excluded workers and exempted employers: A qualitative study on domestic workers' access to social protection in the Netherlands. *Social Policy and Administration*, *58*(4), 658–671. https://doi.org/10.1111/spol.12989

den Dulk, L., & Yerkes, M. A. (2023). Netherlands country note. In S. Blum, I. Dobrotić, G. Kaufman, A. Koslowski, & P. Moss (Eds.), *International review of leave policies and research* (pp. 415–425). International Network on Leave Policies & Research. https://www.leavenetwork.org/annual-review-reports/

Denderski, P., & Stoltenberg, C. (2023). On the existence of private unemployment insurance with advance information on future job losses. *Journal of Public Economics*, *224*, Article 104946. https://doi.org/10.1016/j.jpubeco.2023.104946

Denk, O., & Königs, S. (2022). Supporting jobs and incomes: An update on the policy response to the COVID-19 crisis. In OECD (Ed.), *OECD employment outlook 2022*. OECD Publishing. https://doi.org/10.1787/06cfa2e6-en

Esping-Andersen, G. (1999). *Social foundations of postindustrial economies*. Oxford University Press. https://doi.org/10.1093/0198742002.001.0001

European Commission. (2017). *Access to social protection for people working on non-standard contracts and as self-employed in Europe – A study of national policies 2017*. https://data.europa.eu/doi/10.2767/700791

Eurostat. (2024). *EU labour force survey*. https://ec.europa.eu/eurostat/web/microdata/european-union-labour-force-survey

Ferragina, E., & Seeleib-Kaiser, M. (2011). Thematic review - Welfare regime debate: Past, present, future? *Policy & Politics*, *39*(4), 583–611. https://doi.org/10.1332/030557311X603592

Gallie, D., & Paugam, S. (2000). The experience of unemployment. In D. Gallie & S. Paugam (Eds.), *The welfare regimes and the experience of unemployment in Europe*. Oxford University Press. https://doi.org/10.1093/oso/9780198280392.001.0001

Gautié, J. (2023). The rise and demise of unemployment. In D. Clegg & N. Durazzi (Eds.), *Handbook of labour market policy in advanced democracies* (pp. 14–260). Edward Elgar Publishing. https://doi.org/10.4337/9781800880887.00008

Gottschall, K. (2023). The interaction of gender regimes and long-term care provision across Europe: Ambivalent intersections of gender, class and ethnicity. *Women's Studies International Forum*, *98*, Article 102745, 1–9. https://doi.org/10.1016/j.wsif.2023.102745
Grimshaw, D., & Rubery, J. (1997). Workforce heterogeneity and unemployment benefits: The need for policy reassessment in the European Union. *Journal of European Social Policy*, *7*(4), 291–318. https://doi.org/10.1177/095892879700700402
HM Government. (2025). *Check if you're eligible for free childcare if you're working.* GOV.UK. https://www.gov.uk/check-eligible-free-childcare-if-youre-working
Ik heb geen werk meer – wat betekent dit voor de kinderopvangtoeslag? (2024, augustus 29). *Belastingdienst.* https://www.belastingdienst.nl/wps/wcm/connect/nl/kinderopvangtoeslag/content/ik-raak-werkloos
International Labour Organization. (2021). *World social protection report 2020–22: Social protection at the crossroads – In pursuit of a better future.* https://www.ilo.org/publications/flagship-reports/world-social-protection-report-2020-22-social-protection-crossroads-pursuit
Jepsen, M., & Meulders, D. (1997). Gender inequalities in European unemployment benefit systems. *International Social Security Review, 50*(4), 43–61. https://doi.org/10.1111/j.1468-246X.1997.tb01083.x
Karamessini, M. (2026). The "care transition" in turbulent times. In J. Rubery, N. Sánchez-Mira, & V. Insarauto (Eds.), *Women in turbulent times. Crises, transitions, and challenges for gender equality* (pp. 207–228). Routledge.
Karamessini, M., & Rubery, J. (Eds.). (2014). *Women and austerity: The economic crisis and the future for gender equality.* Routledge. https://doi.org/10.4324/9780203066294
Kowalewska, H. (2023). Gendered employment patterns: Women's labour market outcomes across 24 countries. *Journal of European Social Policy*, *33*(2), 151–168. https://doi.org/10.1177/09589287221148336
Kvist, J. (1998). Complexities in assessing unemployment benefits and policies. *International Social Security Review*, *51*(4), 33–55. https://doi.org/10.1111/1468-246X.00023
Larsen, T. P. (2010). Flexicurity from the individual's work-life balance perspective: Coping with the flaws in European child- and eldercare provision. *Journal of Industrial Relations*, *52*(5), 575–593. https://doi.org/10.1177/0022185610381562
Larsen, T. P., & de la Porte, C. (2022). Early childhood education and care in Denmark: A social investment success. In C. de la Porte, G. B. Eydal, J. Kauko, D. Nohrstedt, P. Hart, & B. S. Tranøy (Eds.), *Successful public policy in the Nordic countries: Cases, lessons, challenges* (pp. 66–87). Oxford University Press. https://doi.org/10.1093/oso/9780192856296.003.0004
Larsen, T. P., & Ilsøe, A. (2022). Nordic relief packages and non-standard workers: Towards expanded universalism and institutional inequalities. *Nordic Journal of Working Life Studies*, *13*(S10). https://doi.org/10.18291/njwls.135099
Leschke, J., & Finn, M. (2019). Labor market flexibility and income security: Changes for European youth during the Great Recession. In A. J. O'Reilly, J. Leschke, R. Ortlieb, M. Seeleib-Kaiser, & P. Villa (Eds.), *Youth labor in transition: Inequalities, mobility and policies in Europe* (pp. 132–162). Oxford University Press. https://doi.org/10.1093/oso/9780190864798.003.0005
Lindellee, J. (2021). Transformation of the Ghent system in Sweden: Silent institutionalization of complementary unemployment benefits. *Nordic Journal of Working Life Studies*, *11*(3). https://doi.org/10.18291/njwls.123605
Matsaganis, M., Ozdemir, E., Ward, T., & Zvakou, A. (2016). *Non-standard employment and access to social security benefits* (Research Note 8/2015). European Commission.

Mutual Information System on Social Protection. (2023). *Comparative tables – MISSOC (Version 01.07.2023).* https://www.missoc.org/missoc-database/comparative-tables/?y=1061&y=1062

Mooi-Reci, I., & Mills, M. (2012). The gendered consequences of unemployment insurance reforms. *Social Forces*, *91*(2), 583–608. https://doi.org/10.1093/sf/sos111

O'Brian, M., Atkinson, J., & Koslowski, A. (2023). United Kingdom country note. In S. Blum, I. Dobrotić, G. Kaufman, A. Koslowski, & P. Moss (Eds.), *International review of leave policies and research* (pp. 527–538). International Network on Leave Policies & Research. https://www.leavenetwork.org/annual-review-reports/

Organisation for Economic Co-operation and Development. (n.d.). OECD Data Explorer [Database]. Retrieved March 22, 2024, from https://data-explorer.oecd.org/

Organisation for Economic Co-operation and Development. (2002). *Benefits and wages 2002: OECD indicators. Comparative tables*. OECD Publishing. https://doi.org/10.1787/ben_wages-2002-en

Organisation for Economic Co-operation and Development. (2018a). *The future of social protection: What works for non-standard workers?* OECD Publishing. https://doi.org/10.1787/9789264306943-en

Organisation for Economic Co-operation and Development. (2018b). Unemployment benefit coverage: Recent trends and their drivers. In *OECD employment outlook 2018* (pp. 185–210). OECD Publishing. https://doi.org/10.1787/empl_outlook-2018-9-en

Organisation for Economic Co-operation and Development. (2024). *OECD family database*. https://www.oecd.org/en/data/datasets/oecd-family-database.html

Oehrli, D., Stadelmann-Steffen, I., & Lütolf, M. (2024). How does the provision of childcare services affect mothers' employment intentions? Empirical evidence from a conjoint experiment. *Journal of Social Policy*, *53*(2), 450–469. https://doi.org/10.1017/S0047279422000423

Rostgaard, T. (2014). *Family policy in Scandinavia*. Friedrich-Ebert-Stiftung.

Rostgaard, T., & Ejrnæs, A. (2023). Denmark country note. In S. Blum, I. Dobrotić, G. Kaufman, A. Koslowski, & P. Moss (Eds.), *International review of leave policies and research 2023* (pp. 195–206). International Network on Leave Policies & Research. https://www.leavenetwork.org/annual-review-reports/

Rubery, J., Grimshaw, D., Keizer, A., & Johnson, M. (2018). Challenges and contradictions in the "normalising" of precarious work. *Work, Employment and Society*, *32*(3), 509–527. https://doi.org/10.1177/0950017017751790

Rubery, J., Grimshaw, D., Méhaut, P., & Weinkopf, C. (2024). Dualisation and part-time work in France, Germany and the UK: Accounting for within and between country differences in precarious work. *European Journal of Industrial Relations*, *30*(4), 363–381. https://doi.org/10.1177/09596801221120468

Rubery, J., & Tavora, I. (2021). The COVID-19 crisis and gender equality: Risks and opportunities. In B. Vanhercke, S. Spasova, & B. Fronteddu (Eds.), *Social policy in the European Union: State of play 2020: Facing the pandemic* (pp. 71–96). European Trade Union Institute (ETUI) & European Social Observatory (OSE). https://www.etui.org/sites/default/files/2021-01/06-Chapter4-The%20Covid%E2%80%9119%20crisis%20and%20gender%20equality.pdf

Sánchez-Mira, N., & O'Reilly, J. (2019). Household employment and the crisis in Europe. *Work, Employment and Society*, *33*(3), 422–443. https://doi.org/10.1177/0950017018809324

Saxonberg, S. (2013). From defamilialization to degenderization: Toward a new welfare typology. *Social Policy and Administration*, *47*(1), 26–49. https://doi.org/10.1111/j.1467-9515.2012.00836.x

Schmid, G., & Gazier, B. (Eds.). (2002). *The dynamics of full employment: Social integration through transitional labour markets*. Edward Elgar Publishing.

Schober, P., Blum, S., Reimer, T., Son, K., & Stertz, A. M. (2023). Germany country note. In S. Blum, I. Dobrotić, G. Kaufman, A. Koslowski, & P. Moss (Eds.), *International review of leave policies and research 2023* (pp. 239–249). International Network on Leave Policies & Research https://www.leavenetwork.org/annual-review-reports/

Spasova, S., Ghailani, D., Bouget, D., & Vanhercke, B. (2017). *Access to social protection for people working on non-standard contracts and as self-employed in Europe: A study of national policies 2017*. European Commission, Directorate-General for Employment, Social Affairs and Inclusion. https://data.europa.eu/doi/10.2767/700791

Spasova, S., & Regazzoni, P. (2022). Income protection for self-employed and non-standard workers during the COVID-19 pandemic. *International Social Security Review*, *75*(2), 3–24. https://doi.org/10.1111/issr.12292

Szelewa, D., & Polakowski, M. (2023). Who cares, too? Degenderization of childcare policies in Europe: A dynamic fuzzy-set analysis. *Feminist Economics*, *29*(3), 153–177. https://doi.org/10.1080/13545701.2023.2230239

Taylor-Gooby, P. (Ed.). (2004). *New risks, new welfare: The transformation of the European welfare state*. Oxford University Press. https://doi.org/10.1093/019926726X.001.0001

Walby, S. (2020). Varieties of gender regimes. *Social Politics: International Studies in Gender, State and Society*, *27*(3), 414–431. https://doi.org/10.1093/sp/jxaa018

West, A., Blome, A., & Lewis, J. (2020). What characteristics of funding, provision and regulation are associated with effective social investment in ECEC in England, France and Germany? *Journal of Social Policy*, *49*(4), 681–704.

PART 3

Gendering the digital and net-zero transitions

12

DIGITALISATION AND REMOTE WORK

Gendered outcomes in job quality and the role of persistent gender inequalities in paid and unpaid work

Agnieszka Piasna

Introduction

The digital transition is having powerful transformative and disruptive effects on labour markets and employment relations (Kalleberg, 2009; Prassl, 2018; Valenduc & Vendramin, 2016). Digital technologies are being implemented in traditional workplaces for algorithm-based management of employees as well as in scaled-up models of outsourcing and subcontracting. These technologies also substitute for human labour and enable remote work (Countouris et al., 2023). Debate and research on the digital economy tend to focus on the novelty of the technological solutions it offers for the organisation and performance of work. However, to understand fully the impact of digitalisation on work and employment, it is vital to recognise that these developments do not unfold in a (social) vacuum. Indeed, digitalisation is embedded in current social structures and shaped by social relations, including those related to gender (Estévez-Abe, 2005; Piasna & Drahokoupil, 2017; Rubery, 2015). Drawing on postulates put forward in particular by feminist scholars, this chapter focuses on how changes in employment, focusing on those related to technological developments, interact with persistent gender inequalities in paid and unpaid work (Feldberg & Glenn, 1979; Gornick et al., 2009; Pateman, 1988; Vosko, 2000).

While the potential challenges related to the digital economy span many areas, this contribution focuses on remote work performed in the European context, including both telework arrangements in standard employment and gig work performed online through digital labour platforms. The key feature of these arrangements is that the workplace is generally brought into the private sphere of the household (Arabadjieva & Franklin, 2023; Sewell & Taskin, 2015). In such contexts, the gendered division of labour in the household and the gendered roles

DOI: 10.4324/9781003528210-16

associated with employment have direct implications for engagement in paid work. This means that gender is central to the study of remote work.

In this chapter, remote work from home is considered in terms of the opportunities and risks for progress towards gender equality in paid and unpaid work, with a focus on its interaction with the household division of labour. Gendered roles and expectations in the private sphere affect the uptake of remote work and its impact on the quality of working life, in particular the ability to reconcile paid work performed from home with private life. Women are still more likely than men to work remotely, and they do so for different reasons, more often related to work–life balance strategies (Eurofound, 2023). This can potentially lead to increased gender segregation, with men working in the office and women at home, making women less visible in organisations and with a negative impact on promotion opportunities or access to skills development (Arabadjieva & Franklin, 2023; Yerkes et al., 2022). This can breed risks of self-exploitation, with remote workers compelled to be always available and responsive as a way of demonstrating their productivity and work commitment (Chung, 2022), and of blurring the boundaries between life domains with an inability to disconnect from work. On the other hand, opportunities for enhanced gender equality may arise from the reduction in commuting time associated with working from home, while allowing paid and unpaid tasks to be intertwined as they are located in the same physical space and often arise synchronously (Adams-Prassl et al., 2023). Therefore, workers who do relatively more tasks at home, such as housework or caring for children and relatives, may find working from home a viable work–life balance solution (Eurofound, 2023). It may enable mothers with young children or other caring obligations to participate in the labour market, albeit at the cost of the risks outlined above. Finally, the proliferation of remote work may positively influence employer attitudes and strategies – for instance, by challenging a corporate culture of "presenteeism" (Chung, 2022).

Advances in digitally-mediated work, including remote work, therefore require a better understanding of their impact on the quality of working life and the implications for gender equality at work and at home. This chapter aims to identify gender differences related to remote work: firstly in terms of its incidence, and secondly in terms of job quality outcomes. The analysis thus sheds new light on how the temporal, spatial and contractual flexibility associated with remote work interacts with existing social inequalities. In particular, the chapter explores the extent to which men's and women's experiences of remote work differ, even when they have similar characteristics and positions in the labour market, by identifying the gender gaps that persist after controlling for compositional effects. The empirical part adopts a gendered lens for analysing digitalisation, which is summarised in the next section. The analysis first examines gender differences in the uptake of work from home and its relationship with parental status. It then examines gender differences in job quality, starting with working time quality and proceeding to career prospects and opportunities. The chapter concludes with a summary of the findings and policy lessons, highlighting the importance of considering remote work in the context of gendered roles in the household.

Gender inequality in digitally-mediated work from home

The workplace has long been designated as central to the formation and evolution of gender inequalities (Acker, 2006; Bettio & Verashchagina, 2009; Rubery, 2011). Much of this stems from stereotypes and attitudes held by managers, colleagues and society at large about what types of tasks are appropriate for women and how their work should be valued in comparison to their male counterparts. The consequences include a vicious circle between persistent sectoral and occupational gender segmentation, gender pay gaps and a glass ceiling that limits women's upward career progression (Birkelund et al., 2022; Murphy & Oesch, 2016; Rubery, 2015). In fact, the roots of inequality as it materialises in paid employment reach deep into the structure of power in a society and in the family (Pateman, 1988). The impact of digitalisation on gender inequality should then be considered against entrenched power imbalances and the unequal positions of men and women (Wajcman, 2004). The key question is whether technological change, and in particular the new ways of organising or performing work associated with digitalisation, targets and overcomes barriers and vulnerabilities, or rather potentially reinforces and exacerbates existing inequalities.

Remote work is a particular case of the use of digital technology to mediate the performance of work because it relocates paid labour from the public sphere of the employer's premises into the private sphere of the worker's home. The division of social space into public and private spheres has had strong gender connotations throughout the history of European civilisation. Its modern iteration can be linked to the growth of the factory system of production from the eighteenth century onwards (Basham, 2021; Pateman, 1988). The separation of home and workplace made it more difficult for women to combine paid work and childcare and contributed to their push into the private sphere – usually as domestic workers in their own family or for the wealthy, or as industrial homeworkers, generally doing lower paid and less skilled work than (male) factory-based workers (Nilsson et al., 2022). This gendered public–private divide has also defined the scope of labour law, which is not concerned with protecting unpaid labour and which treats workers performing paid work in the household less favourably (Arabadjieva & Franklin, 2023; Fudge, 2014). Consequently, emerging labour regulation and collective interest representation have consistently overlooked paid work performed in the private sphere of the home, resulting in generally poorer working and employment conditions for this female-dominated workforce (International Labour Organization [ILO], 2021).

In the European context, work from home is now practically equivalent to telework in terms of relying on the use of computers and ICT for work. It thus contrasts with a significant proportion of the craft work and industrial work that is done from home in low-income countries (ILO, 2021) and can be expected to have some positive outcomes for gender equality through the levelling effect resulting from some technological developments being assumed to be free of stereotypes and attitudes (Organisation for Economic Co-operation and Development [OECD], 2017). In particular, online labour markets, where paid work is accessed through digital labour platforms, have some potential to address gender inequality in employment (Piasna & Drahokoupil, 2017). Unequal treatment based on the gender stereotypes held by managers, clients or employers should be less likely to surface in work environments that remove workers from their sight, thus hiding their gender and other demographic characteristics that underlie discriminatory practices. If access to and the allocation of tasks, remuneration and rewards are determined by an algorithm rather than by potentially biased humans, the outcomes might indeed be more equal, or at least more gender-blind, than in traditional employment settings.

Such optimistic expectations, however, have been tempered by research on the platform economy which has found that many of the existing inequalities are reproduced in online labour markets (Piasna & Drahokoupil, 2021). Firstly, digitally-mediated work is not free from a gender-segmented occupational distribution, with women performing different types of tasks than men. There is also emerging evidence that algorithms, being trained on biased data, are prone to reproducing existing gender segregation and gender pay gaps in their recruitment or pay-setting decisions (Cook et al., 2021; Imana et al., 2021). Secondly, workers experience platform work differently depending, among other things, on their socio-economic characteristics (Goods et al., 2019; Piasna & Drahokoupil, 2021; Wood et al., 2019).

Moreover, previous studies have pointed to the risk of an erosion of the temporal boundary between paid and unpaid work when working from home (Berg, 2022; Yerkes et al., 2022). The lack of real spatial separation between "office" and "home" makes it more likely that work will be done in free time to catch up with workload. This permeability has been found to work in the other direction too – care and domestic obligations hamper the efficient and productive performance of paid work (Adams-Prassl et al., 2023). The flexibility offered by working from home generates different outcomes depending on the extent of these two-directional interferences (Chung, 2022). With women shouldering unequal shares of unpaid work at home, the quality of their (working) life is likely to be worse in such conditions compared to that of men. The development of digitally-enabled remote work thus needs to be analysed through the lens of the entrenched gendering of social space and gender inequalities in the division of paid and unpaid work.

Virtual workplaces have also been linked to a host of specific challenges in terms of lower workers' visibility. A reduced presence in a shared workplace leads to fewer opportunities to interact with colleagues, worker representatives and trade unions (Vandaele & Piasna, 2023). This hampers the formation of collective identity and solidarity among workers and makes it more difficult for unions to organise. As a result, employers may face less resistance to changes or arrangements that are unfavourable to workers, and the bargaining power of remote workers may be relatively lower. Moreover, the lower visibility of workers to supervisors may have a negative impact on promotion and training opportunities (Sewell & Taskin, 2015). Physical presence at the workplace is generally given a premium by management if it is considered necessary for the performance of certain tasks or because it remains an important prerequisite for monitoring and managing workforces (Countouris et al., 2023). All this may lead to a lower quality of work for remote workers, or an increased vulnerability to unfavourable arrangements. Coupled with gender segmentation and inequality, it could be expected to pose particular risks for women through the accumulation of disadvantage. Thus, in addition to being more often exposed to remote work and the potential risks associated with it, women may also experience remote work less favourably in terms of quality of work and well-being.

In the empirical analysis presented in this chapter, remote work includes both work conducted from home in the context of traditional employment and remote platform work in online labour markets. There is a certain selection into these groups, linked to the teleworkability of occupations (Eurofound, 2023). This may obscure a comparison of the differences related directly to remote work, with the more substantial ones arising rather from gendered variations in skills, occupational class and contractual arrangements. For this reason, the analysis introduces a series of control variables to account for compositional differences between remote and non-remote workers.

Digitally-mediated remote work is analysed here at a particular time. The data explored in the following sections were collected across the EU in 2021, which was a period of heightened public health emergency measures that importantly included strong incentives, or even obligations, to work from home. The incidence of remote work has remained at similarly high levels thereafter (falling from 24.1% in 2021 to 22.6% in 2024 in the EU27 among all employed, and with some reduction in its intensity, according to Eurostat [dataset lfsa_ehomp]), but the pandemic period was coupled with special circumstances created by school and day care closures. As a result, unpaid work carried out in the household increased, accentuating rather than reducing, gender divides in care responsibilities and domestic tasks (Nivakoski & Mascherini, 2021; Sevilla & Smith, 2020). Taken together with literature pointing to the generally more vulnerable position of women in recent crises (Karamessini & Rubery, 2013; Rubery & Rafferty, 2013), this underscores the importance of developing our understanding of digitally-mediated work against the background of gendered roles and power relations at home and in the workplace.

Data and methods

The analysis presented in the chapter is based on two large-scale European surveys. The first is the Internet and Platform Work Survey (IPWS) carried out by the ETUI in spring and autumn 2021 (Piasna et al., 2022). It is based on a random sample representative of the working-age population, with at least 1,750 interviews per country. The sample for the analysis includes 35,440 respondents aged 18–65 from 14 EU countries. The second is the European Working Conditions Telephone Survey (EWCTS), conducted by Eurofound in 2021. It is based on a random sample of workers, and the analysis includes 58,216 workers aged 16 and over from EU27 countries (Eurofound, 2026).

These two data sources provide complementary information on remote work, covering its different types and reference periods. The IPWS includes questions on remote work in the traditional labour market, defined as telework and working from home in the main paid job, and allows a distinction to be made between those workers who were working from home before the pandemic and those who started doing so because of it. It also provides information on remote platform work, which includes tasks that are commissioned and delivered online in a freelance capacity through digital labour platforms, typically performed from the private homes of workers (Eurofound, 2021; Piasna et al., 2022). It measures two types of platform work based on the skill requirements and complexity of tasks: remote clickwork (microtasks such as data entry or sorting, transcription, paid online surveys); and remote professional work (creative, IT or other professional work). Remote platform work remains a rare form of gainful activity, reported by 3.5% of respondents in the IPWS. The EWCTS provides information on work from home, without making a distinction between telework in traditional employment and platform or gig work. Based on the reported frequency, we distinguish between no work from home (respondents who "never" work from home), occasional ("rarely" or "sometimes") and usual ("often" or "always") work from home. The EWCTS is used for its rich information on job quality and unpaid care and domestic work.

The empirical analysis is aimed at revealing gender differences related to remote work both in terms of its incidence and its job quality outcomes.

Firstly, the IPWS is used to assess the gendered incidence of remote work, with respect to telework (started before or during the pandemic) and platform work. To compare the share of women across types of remote work, logistic regression is performed with gender as the dependent variable. A series of control variables (age, occupation, educational attainment and main employment status in the traditional economy) are included to distinguish the gender differences linked directly to remote work from other types of segmentation. Results are presented in terms of the predicted share of women.

Secondly, the EWCTS is used to examine gender differences in job quality related to remote work. Two dimensions of job quality are examined: working time, and career prospects and opportunities. Each is expressed as a 0–100 index with higher values indicating a better quality of work. Working time quality is an index created from three items: the frequency with which workers are asked to come to work at short notice; the frequency of working in one's free time to meet work demands; and the ease of taking an hour or two off during normal working hours to attend to personal or family matters. The calculation of the index (Cronbach's alpha 0.36) is premised on the summed contribution of these three characteristics to develop an overall concept of working time quality, intended to reflect individual autonomy over scheduling and the extent to which work extends beyond the boundaries of usual working hours. The quality of career prospects and opportunities is also an index based on three items (Cronbach's alpha 0.45): the extent to which respondents perceive that their job offers good prospects for career advancement; having sufficient opportunities to use their knowledge and skills; and training received in the last 12 months, either provided by the employer or as on-the-job training provided by colleagues or supervisors.

In addition, the analysis examines the link between working from home and family-to-work conflict (FWC); that is, the extent to which workers find it difficult to concentrate on their job because of family responsibilities (expressed on a scale of 0–100 with higher values indicating more conflict), as well as the amount of time spent on unpaid care and domestic work (measured in hours).

OLS regression analyses are carried out on the job quality indexes, as well as FWC and unpaid work as dependent variables. Models are built in several steps: firstly, only gender and work from home, with their interaction, are included as predictors, controlling for country fixed effects; the second step adds a set of control variables (age, main employment status, occupation, educational attainment and the presence of children aged up to 12 years in the household); the third, final, step additionally includes a three-way interaction term between gender, work from home and the presence of young children. The results obtained in the third step reflect the main focus of this chapter and reveal the gender differences related directly to the performance of remote work which are unexplained by compositional differences. They serve to provide evidence about the gender inequality that arises in remote work performed from home, in addition to other, already better understood, aspects of gender-related divides. These results are presented as predicted outcomes, in graphical format. More details of the previous two steps (models with a two-way interaction, without and with control variables) are reported in the online appendix (Table A12-1) and show the gender differences related directly to remote work but also reflect the effects of various layers of disadvantage and segmentation, including occupational gender segregation.

Gendered patterns in telework and remote platform work

In the EU27, working from home mainly involves telework. According to the EWCTS data, among workers who usually work from home, 93% of men and 95% of women always or often use a computer for work purposes. Relatedly, working from home is heavily segmented by occupational class, being dominated by white-collar workers (92.2% of women who usually work from home, 88.7% of men), with around half in professional occupations (52% of women, 51% of men). Additionally, previous research revealed that, in the European context, women are more likely than men to work from home (Eurofound, 2023), but this difference is smaller compared to other global regions (ILO, 2021).

Given the highly segmented nature of remote work, the question then arises as to whether there are gender differences in the use of telework within similar types of jobs. This question is addressed here by analysing gender patterns in the prevalence of telework, taking into account individual and occupational differences between men and women. The results displayed in Figure 12.1 (left panel) show that, before the Covid-19 pandemic, men were significantly more likely to telework than women in similar positions in the labour market. During the course of the pandemic, this pattern changed, with more women taking up work from home (Countouris et al., 2023). This change is partly due to the exceptional circumstances in which large groups of workers were assigned to work from home in occupations that had not experienced this before, such as teaching professionals in education and skilled clerks in public administration (Vandaele & Piasna, 2023). As these occupational groups are dominated by women, the proportion of women teleworkers has increased, but our results suggest that, beyond these structural changes, even in similar jobs, women were more likely to start teleworking than men. Finally, parenthood has a discernible impact, with the share of women in telework being highest among parents of young children who started telework in the pandemic, and much higher compared to those who teleworked beforehand. All this suggests that women bore the brunt of the increased childcare work during the pandemic by working more often from home.

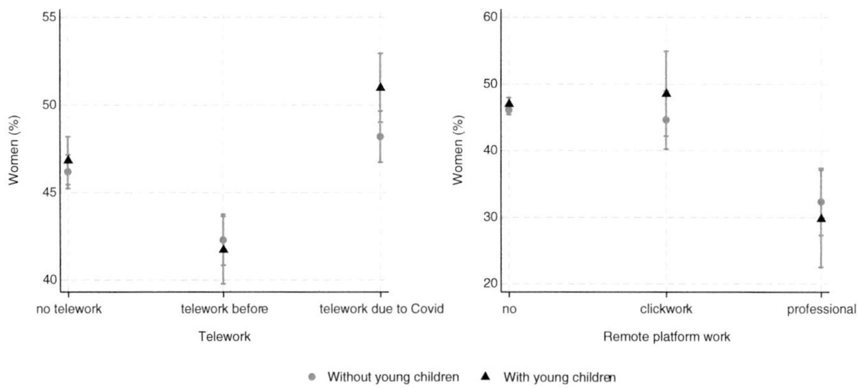

FIGURE 12.1 Prevalence of Women in Telework (Left) and Remote Platform Work (Right). Predicted Shares by Presence of Young Children in the Household.

Source: Own elaboration based on data from the IPWS (2021).

Note: Logistic regression estimates with 95% confidence intervals, controlling for age, employment status, occupational group, education and country. Interaction: a young child (up to 12 years) living in the household.

A particular subset of remote work considered here is platform work. In Europe, there is a relative gender balance in overall engagement in platform work, but with a considerable degree of gender segmentation depending on the type of activity, mirroring that found in traditional labour markets (Piasna et al., 2022). In particular, men are reported to dominate remote professional activities (68%), while women to some extent outnumber men in clickwork (52%) (IPWS data). The more detailed analysis, using logistic regression to account for socio-economic differences, reveals a similar gender pattern with the predicted share of women being higher in clickwork (46%) compared to professional remote platform work (31.6%) (Figure 12.1, right panel). Overall, even when workers are matched on a number of supply-side characteristics, women are less likely to engage in the highest-paid types of work available in the platform economy, such as professional remote work.

Moreover, parenthood has some impact – having young children increases the relative share of women in clickwork and further diminishes it in professional work, although this is not statistically significant at the 5% level due to the small sample size of remote platform workers. Nevertheless, this could lend credence to earlier findings about difficultes engaging in more complex tasks among women working from home who also have childcare responsibilities (Adams-Prassl et al., 2023). Short and simple tasks available on clickwork platforms, which require less mental focus to perform and can be completed even when only very short spells of uninterrupted time are available, are more easily reconcilable with care and housework, but come at the cost of the very low earnings and lack of any career prospects attached to this type of work (Berg, 2016).

Inequality in working time quality: autonomy and work–life conflict

In the context of remote work performed from home, the quality of working time is central to understanding how existing social inequalities and patterns of gender segregation in the labour market interact with digitalisation. Working time quality is determined not only by how long and when people work, but also, and especially in the context of remote work, by the degree of autonomy and control over scheduling (Piasna, 2024; Piasna & Drahokoupil, 2021). In general, women tend to be subject to more forms of control and find themselves in a more subordinate position compared to men, with relatively less authority even within similar jobs (Fana et al., 2023; Stojmenovska et al., 2021). The question is whether digitally-mediated work performed from home reproduces these outcomes in a "virtual" workplace.

All analyses from this point forward rely on data from the EWCTS and thus use a concept of telework which centres mainly on traditional employment and not platform work. A comparison is made between various patterns of frequency in working from home and the quality of working time. The results shown in Figure 12.2 indicate that, once individual and job characteristics are taken into account, telework is generally associated with less favourable conditions in terms

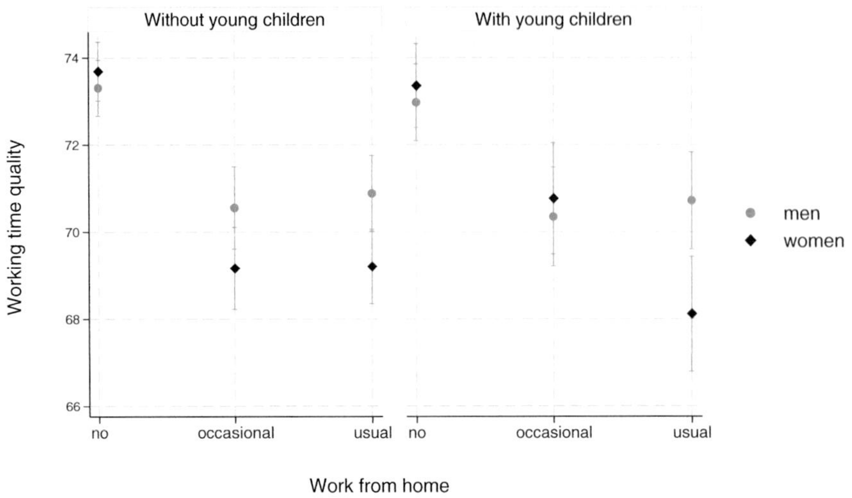

FIGURE 12.2 Gender Differences in Working Time Quality Linked to Working from Home. Predicted Outcomes by Presence of a Young Child in the Household.

Source: Own elaboration based on data from the EWCTS (2021).

Note: OLS regression estimates with 95% confidence intervals, controlling for age, employment status, occupational group, education and country.

of working time quality compared to workplace-based work. These findings are in line with the literature which warns of the erosion of the boundary between paid and unpaid work for people who work from home (Berg, 2022; Yerkes et al., 2022). Taking an hour or two off for personal reasons appears to be more difficult for teleworkers than for those who never work from home, which challenges the expectation that telework is associated with greater scope for control over one's work schedule, especially when workers face heightened work demands. Finally, the higher frequency with which teleworkers are required to come to work at short notice may be due to a general lack of physical presence at the workplace. The latter may be considered necessary by management for the performance of certain tasks or in terms of monitoring and managing workforces (Countouris et al., 2023).

Previous job quality research has revealed better outcomes for women in terms of overall working time quality (Leschke & Watt, 2014; Piasna, 2023), largely driven by shorter hours of work and, relatedly, a lesser occurrence of work during unsocial hours. However, when focusing, as we do here, on individual autonomy and the predictability of working time – that is aspects of working time quality that are more related to workers' control over their schedules – the gender gap takes a different form. Firstly, when comparing similar workers in similar jobs who do not telework, we find no gender difference in working time quality (Figure 12.2). It is only in the context of working from home that significant gender differences emerge, and to the disadvantage of women. Among workers without young children at home, women who telework have a worse quality of working time than men. Among parents with young children, the disadvantage for women only emerges for usual teleworkers. Thus, women who usually work from home, and who are likely to face the greatest demands on their time from young children, have the least scope to organise their time around private commitments, and their working time is most likely to spill over into their "free" time. This shows that the impact of digital technologies such as telework that have the potential to increase temporal and spatial flexibility for workers are firmly embedded in pre-existing gendered roles and the unequal division of labour in the household. If the latter are not addressed at the outset, the digitalisation of work, as in the form of teleworking, risks exacerbating such inequalities.

The fact that women who work from home, especially those with young children, may be forced to carry out work tasks beyond their normal working hours could in turn be related to childcare responsibilities spilling over into paid work time to a larger extent than for their male counterparts. This is supported by the following analysis of family-to-work conflict, measured by how often workers find it difficult to concentrate on their work because of family responsibilities (Figure 12.3). Overall, FWC is higher for women and for teleworkers. Moreover, parental status plays an important role here and its effect is gender specific. For men

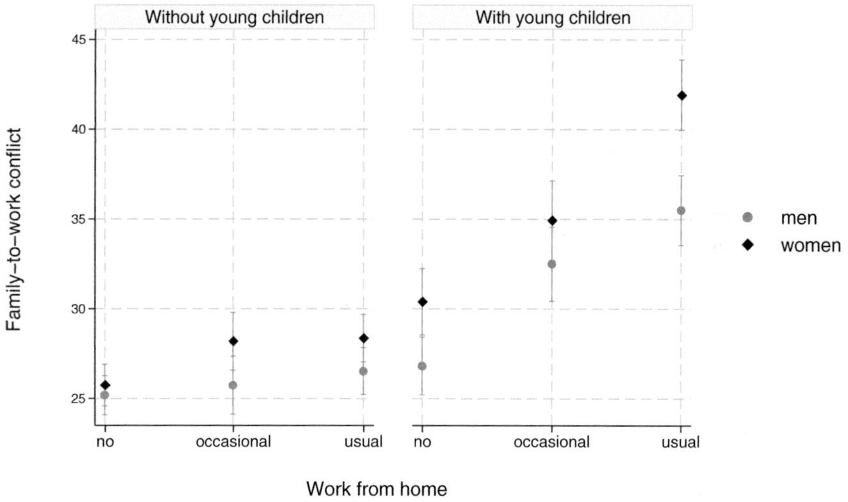

FIGURE 12.3 Gender Differences in Family-to-Work Conflict Linked to Working from Home. Predicted Outcomes by Presence of a Young Child in the Household.

Source: Own elaboration based on data from the EWCTS (2021).

Note: OLS regression estimates with 95% confidence intervals, controlling for age, employment status, occupational group, education and country.

without young children in the household, working from home does not make much difference in terms of FWC, and they are generally the least negatively affected group. In contrast, for women with young children, teleworking is associated with particularly strong conflict between family and work which increases with the frequency of working from home. Thus, women who usually work from home are by far the most affected. This finding is most likely due to the fact that women with children (who telework) assume a disproportionate share of unpaid labour, as the next analysis shows.

Indeed, remote work puts women at a disadvantage in terms of the extent to which family responsibilities interfere with paid work: for women, especially those with young children, working from home means even more hours spent on unpaid care and domestic work, regardless of the type of job they have and the number of hours they work each week. As illustrated in Figure 12.4, work done usually from home imposes a particularly high burden, in terms of hours of unpaid work, on mothers with young children, but has little effect on fathers' involvement in care and housework compared to workplace-based workers. For workers without young children, working from home also makes little difference to their load of unpaid work. This further highlights the interplay between family context, the gendered division of unpaid work and digitally-mediated work in the form of telework.

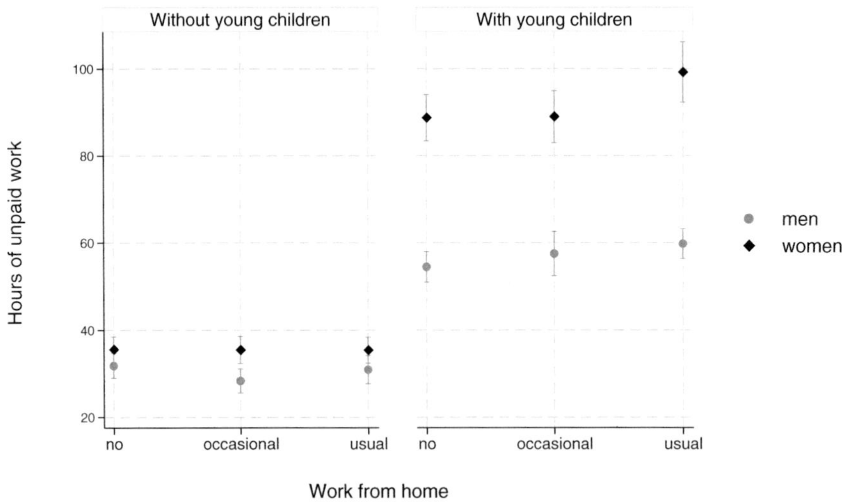

FIGURE 12.4 Gender Differences in the Average Number of Hours of Unpaid Work per Week. Predicted Outcomes by Telework Arrangements and Presence of a Young Child in the Household.

Source: Own elaboration based on data from the EWCTS (2021).

Note: OLS regression estimates with 95% confidence intervals, controlling for number of weekly hours of paid work, age, employ.ment status, occupational group, education and country.

The role of work from home in career prospects and opportunities

Working from home may help address some childcare issues but, as demonstrated in the previous section, it comes at a cost, especially for women, in terms of working time quality. Moreover, it does not seem to foster gender equality at home (see also Tomei, 2021), as measured by a particularly heavy burden of unpaid care and domestic work among teleworking women. Previous studies have also drawn attention to the specific challenges of virtual workplaces in terms of the lower visibility of workers vis-à-vis the employer, which can have a negative impact on promotion and training opportunities, as well as with regard to collective interest representation. This section investigates whether gender differences surface also in this respect.

Figure 12.5 shows gender differences in terms of prospects and opportunities for career progression across different telework arrangements. It reveals that a hybrid arrangement with occasional work from home is generally associated with better prospects compared to work that is exclusively workplace-based, once various socio-economic differences between workers are accounted for. This may reflect some positive effects of telework, such as the development of the digital skills needed to perform the job, but it may also confound unobserved differences between firms in the application of more developed HR policies that promote both

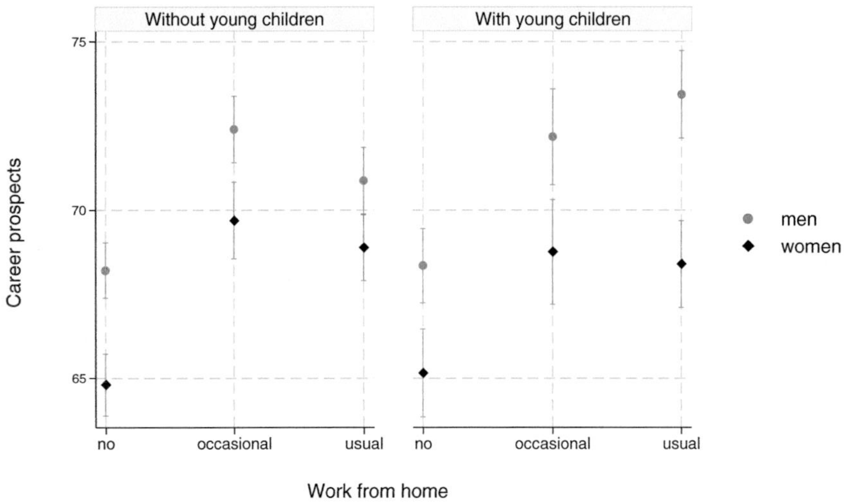

FIGURE 12.5 Gender Differences in Career Prospects and Opportunities Linked to Working from Home. Predicted Outcomes by Presence of a Young Child in the Household.

Source: Own elaboration based on data from the EWCTS (2021).

Note: OLS regression estimates with 95% confidence intervals, controlling for age, employment status, occupational group, education and country.

telework and workforce upskilling. Selection bias into remote work is also conceivable, with workers who are more trusted by their employer (and who hence have better prospects) being offered the flexibility to work remotely. More committed employees who want to improve their career prospects may also work remotely to catch up on work after normal office hours.

In terms of gender differences, women have worse career prospects and opportunities than men, with the widest gender gap among parents of young children who usually work from home. While this arrangement is associated with a substantial premium for fathers in terms of career prospects and opportunities, it has a much weaker effect for mothers. This pattern mirrors the fatherhood premium and the motherhood penalty in gender wage gaps (Budig & England, 2001). In the EU context, where remote work is mostly accessible to highly skilled and relatively better paid occupations, our finding of a significant motherhood penalty in the career prospects of this group is consistent with previous studies showing that highly skilled and highly paid women suffer the highest motherhood wage penalty (England et al., 2016).

Taken together with the results on working time quality presented in the previous section, this finding suggests a particularly vulnerable and disadvantaged position for working mothers with young children who usually telework from home. Not only does a "virtual" workplace not eliminate traditional gender inequalities, but it accentuates the intersection of persistent inequalities related to gender and life course.

Discussion and conclusions

In contrast to some optimistic expectations that digitally-mediated work and "virtual" workplaces would disrupt entrenched gender inequalities (OECD, 2017), this chapter identifies significant gendered constraints on the quality of working time and career opportunities linked to remote work. The investigation of gendered patterns in telework and remote platform work in Europe shows that the impact of digitalisation, which increases temporal and spatial work flexibility, is shaped by various persistent forms of gender inequality and vulnerability across society. In particular, mothers of young children working from home are found to suffer the most in terms of job quality relative to men. An arrangement based on telework, that may be supposed to facilitate the more flexible management of work and family life, comes at a significant cost in terms of poorer career prospects and opportunities; neither does it in reality increase the scope for control over working time. This lends support to claims that digitalisation in the world of work does not unfold in a social vacuum (Piasna & Drahokoupil, 2017; Tomei, 2021). It may be creating a workplace that is to a certain extent "virtual", but it remains deeply rooted in a social reality which features gendered roles and an unequal position of men and women in public and private spheres. The job quality outcomes of remote work are not solely technical but socially determined (Fana et al., 2023).

These findings should be considered in view of the data limitations. Both data sources used in the analysis, the EWCTS and the IPWS, reflect the situation in 2021, thus in the midst of the Covid-19 pandemic with some compulsory working from home and limitations in access to day care services across the countries surveyed. Furthermore, for many of the analysed workers, working from home is a relatively recent experience. It is therefore difficult to determine the extent to which the gender gaps identified are related to the effects of remote work itself or to the underlying gender segregation and stereotyping that predate remote work. Nevertheless, the aim of the analysis was to compare gender differences in the conditions associated specifically with remote work by controlling for a number of other characteristics. Thus, there is a need to continue research beyond the exceptional period of the pandemic to allow the impact of remote work to materialise over a longer time horizon, as well as across various institutional frameworks.

Digitally-mediated work, whether in the platform economy or as telework within regular employment, is bound to continue to grow since it appeals to certain needs of both companies and workers. And yet, as this chapter makes abundantly clear, digitalisation interacts with gender-related inequality and segmentation and reproduces them in new contexts. This raises the need not only for a better understanding of these effects across a spectrum of intersecting inequalities, but also for appropriate policy and regulatory responses. On the one hand, measures aimed at improving the quality of work from home and supporting the articulation of a boundary between paid work and private life are crucial. A right to disconnect, limits on the granularity and unpredictability of working hours, and a correct classification of the employment status of remote workers to guarantee full access to labour rights and protections should all be policy priorities (Piasna, 2024; Tomei, 2021). The principle of equal treatment between home-based and workplace-based workers should also be based on dissociating remote work from a specific work-life balance solution for parents of young children, unless its take-up is ensured to the same extent for both fathers and mothers. At the same time, the persistent gendered division of unpaid work in the household remains to be addressed. Extensions of parental leave provisions should be accompanied by stronger incentives for fathers to take advantage of them, while the promotion of work cultures and management styles must also be generally supportive not only of labour productivity but also of reproductive labour.

References

Acker, J. (2006). Inequality regimes: Gender, class, and race in organizations. *Gender & Society*, *20*(4), 441–464. https://doi.org/10.1177/0891243206289499

Adams-Prassl, A., Hara, K., Milland, K., & Callison-Burch, C. (2023) The gender wage gap in an online labor market: The cost of interruptions. *The Review of Economics and Statistics*, *107*(1), 55–64. https://doi.org/10.1162/rest_a_01282

Arabadjieva, K., & Franklin, P. (2023). Home-based telework, gender and the public-private divide. In N. Countouris, V. De Stefano, A. Piasna, & S. Rainone (Eds.), *The future of remote work* (pp. 61–81). ETUI.

Basham, V. M. (2021). A necessarily historical materialist moment? Feminist reflections on the need for grounded critique in an age of crises. *International Relations*, *35*(1), 178–182. https://doi.org/10.1177/0047117821992408

Berg, J. (2016). *Income security in the on-demand economy: Findings and policy lessons from a survey of crowdworkers* (Conditions of Work and Employment, Series No. 74). International Labour Office.

Berg, J. (2022). Contemporary digital home work: Old challenges, different solutions? In M. Nilsson, I. Mazumdar, & S. Neunsinger (Eds.), *Home-based work and home-based workers (1800–2021)* (pp. 288–307). Brill.

Bettio, F., & Verashchagina, A. (2009). *Gender segregation in the labour market: Root causes, implications and policy responses in the EU.* Publications Office of the European Union.

Birkelund, G. E., Lancee, B., Larsen, E. N., Polavieja, J. G., Radl, J., & Yemane, R. (2022). Gender discrimination in hiring: Evidence from a cross-national harmonized field experiment. *European Sociological Review*, *38*(3), 337–354. https://doi.org/10.1093/esr/jcab043

Budig, M. J., & England, P. (2001). The wage penalty for motherhood. *American Sociological Review*, *66*(2), 204–225. https://doi.org/10.1177/000312240106600203

Chung, H. (2022). *The flexibility paradox: Why flexible working leads to (self-) exploitation.* Bristol University Press. https://doi.org/10.1332/policypress/9781447354772.001.0001

Cook, C., Diamond, R., Hall, J. V., List, J. A., & Oyer, P. (2021). The gender earnings gap in the gig economy: Evidence from over a million rideshare drivers. *The Review of Economic Studies*, *88*(5), 2210–2238. https://doi.org/10.1093/restud/rdaa081

Countouris, N., De Stefano, V., Piasna, A., & Rainone, S. (Eds.). (2023). *The future of remote work.* ETUI.

England, P., Bearak, J., Budig, M. J., & Hodges, M. J. (2016). Do highly paid, highly skilled women experience the largest motherhood penalty? *American Sociological Review*, *81*(6), 1161–1189. https://doi.org/10.1177/0003122416673598

Estévez-Abe, M. (2005). Gender bias in skills and social policies: The varieties of capitalism perspective on sex segregation. *Social Politics*, *12*(2), 180–215. https://doi.org/10.1093/sp/jxi011

Eurofound. (2021). *The digital age: Implications of automation, digitisation and platforms for work and employment* (Challenges and prospects in the EU series). Publications Office of the European Union.

Eurofound. (2023). *Working conditions in the time of COVID-19: Implications for the future* (European Working Conditions Telephone Survey 2021 series). Publications Office of the European Union.

Eurofound (2026) *European Working Conditions Telephone Survey, 2021.* [data collection]. *3rd Edition.* UK Data Service. SN: 9026: http://doi.org/10.5255/UKDA-SN-9026-3

Fana, M., Villani, D., & Bisello, M. (2023). Gender gaps in power and control within jobs. *Socio-Economic Review*, *21*(3), 1343–1367. https://doi.org/10.1093/ser/mwac062

Feldberg, R. L., & Glenn, E. N. (1979). Male and female: Job versus gender models in the sociology of work. *Social Problems*, *26*(5), 524–538. https://doi.org/10.2307/800039

Fudge, J. (2014). Feminist reflections on the scope of labour law: Domestic work, social reproduction, and jurisdiction. *Feminist Legal Studies*, *22*(1), 1–23. https://doi.org/10.1007/s10691-014-9256-2

Goods, C., Veen, A., & Barratt, T. (2019). "Is your gig any good?" Analysing job quality in the Australian platform-based food-delivery sector. *Journal of Industrial Relations*, *61*(4), 502–527. https://doi.org/10.1177/0022185618817069

Gornick, J. C., Meyers, M., & Wright, E. O. (Eds.). (2009). *Gender equality: Transforming family divisions of labor*. Verso.

Imana, B., Korolova, A., & Heidemann, J. (2021). Auditing for discrimination in algorithms delivering job ads. In *Proceedings of the 2021 World Wide Web Conference (WWW '21)* (pp. 3760–3771). https://doi.org/10.1145/3442381.3450077

International Labour Organization. (2021). *Working from home: From invisibility to decent work*. Author.

Kalleberg, A. L. (2009). Precarious work, insecure workers: Employment relations in transition. *American Sociological Review*, *74*(1), 1–22. https://doi.org/10.1177/000312240907400101

Karamessini, M., & Rubery, J. (2013). Economic crisis and austerity: Challenges to gender equality. In M. Karamessini & J. Rubery (Eds.), *Women and austerity: The economic crisis and the future for gender equality* (pp. 314–351). Routledge. https://doi.org/10.4324/9780203066294

Leschke, J., & Watt, A. (2014). Challenges in constructing a multi-dimensional European job quality index. *Social Indicators Research, 118*(1), 1–31. https://doi.org/10.1007/s11205-013-0405-9

Murphy, E., & Oesch, D. (2016). The feminization of occupations and change in wages: A panel analysis of Britain, Germany, and Switzerland. *Social Forces*, *94*(3), 1221–1255. https://doi.org/10.1093/sf/sov099

Nilsson, M., Mazumdar, I., & Neunsinger, S. (Eds.). (2022). *Home-based work and home-based workers (1800–2021)*. Brill. https://doi.org/10.1163/9789004499614

Nivakoski, S., & Mascherini, M. (2021). Gender differences in the impact of the COVID-19 pandemic on employment, unpaid work and well-being in the EU. *Intereconomics*, *56*(5), 254–260. https://doi.org/10.1007/s10272-021-0994-5

Organisation for Economic Co-operation and Development. (2017). *Going digital: The future of work for women*. Policy brief on the future of work.

Pateman, C. (1988). *The sexual contract*. Stanford University Press.

Piasna, A. (2023). *Job quality in turbulent times* (Working Paper 2023.05). ETUI.

Piasna, A. (2024). Algorithms of time: How algorithmic management changes the temporalities of work and prospects for working time reduction. *Cambridge Journal of Economics*, *48*(1), 115–132. https://doi.org/10.1093/cje/bead017

Piasna, A., & Drahokoupil, J. (2017). Gender inequalities in the new world of work. *Transfer: European Review of Labour and Research, 23*(3), 313–332. https://doi.org/10.1177/1024258917713839

Piasna, A., & Drahokoupil, J. (2021). Flexibility unbound: Understanding the heterogeneity of preferences among food delivery platform workers. *Socio-Economic Review, 19*(4), 1397–1419. https://doi.org/10.1093/ser/mwab029

Piasna, A., Zwysen, W., & Drahokoupil, J. (2022). *The platform economy in Europe: Results from the second ETUI Internet and Platform Work Survey (IPWS)* (Working Paper 2022.05). ETUI. https://doi.org/10.2139/ssrn.4042629

Prassl, J. (2018). *Humans as a service: The promise and perils of work in the gig economy*. Oxford University Press. https://doi.org/10.1093/oso/9780198797012.001.0001
Rubery, J. (2011). Towards a gendering of the labour market regulation debate. *Cambridge Journal of Economics*, *35*(6), 1103–1126. https://doi.org/10.1093/cje/ber001
Rubery, J. (2015). Change at work: Feminisation, flexibilisation, fragmentation and financialisation. *Employee Relations*, *37*(6), 633–644. https://doi.org/10.1108/ER-04-2015-0067
Rubery, J., & Rafferty, A. (2013). Women and recession revisited. *Work, Employment & Society*, *27*(3), 414–432. https://doi.org/10.1177/0950017012460314
Sevilla, A., & Smith, S. (2020). Baby steps: The gender division of childcare during the COVID-19 pandemic. *Oxford Review of Economic Policy*, *36*(Supplement 1), S169–S186. https://doi.org/10.1093/oxrep/graa027
Sewell, G., & Taskin, L. (2015). Out of sight, out of mind in a new world of work? Autonomy, control, and spatiotemporal scaling in telework. *Organization Studies*, *36*(11), 1507–1529. https://doi.org/10.1177/0170840615593587
Stojmenovska, D., Steinmetz, S., & Volker, B. (2021). The gender gap in workplace authority: Variation across types of authority positions. *Social Forces*, *100*(2), 599–621. https://doi.org/10.1093/sf/soab007
Tomei, M. (2021). Teleworking: A curse or a blessing for gender equality and work-life balance? *Intereconomics*, *56*(5), 260–264. https://doi.org/10.1007/s10272-021-0995-4
Valenduc, G., & Vendramin, P. (2016). *Work in the digital economy: Sorting the old from the new* (Working Paper 2016.03). ETUI. https://doi.org/10.2139/ssrn.2770405
Vandaele, K., & Piasna, A. (2023). Sowing the seeds of unionisation? Exploring remote work and work-based online communities in Europe during the Covid-19 pandemic. In N. Countouris, V. De Stefano, A. Piasna & S. Rainone (Eds.), *The future of remote work* (pp. 103–126). ETUI.
Vosko, L. F. (2000). *Temporary work: The gendered rise of a precarious employment relationship*. University of Toronto Press. https://doi.org/10.3138/9781442680432
Wajcman, J. (2004). *TechnoFeminism*. Polity.
Wood, A. J., Graham, M., Lehdonvirta, V., & Hjorth, I. (2019). Good gig, bad gig: Autonomy and algorithmic control in the global gig economy. *Work, Employment and Society*, *33*(1), 56–75. https://doi.org/10.1177/0950017018785616
Yerkes, M. A., Remery, C., André, S., Salin, M., Hakovirta, M., & van Gerven, M. (2022). Unequal but balanced: Highly educated mothers' perceptions of work–life balance during the COVID-19 lockdown in Finland and the Netherlands. *Journal of European Social Policy*, *32*(4), 376–392. https://doi.org/10.1177/09589287221080411

13

UNMASKING GENDER DISPARITIES IN THE DIGITAL ECONOMY

Beyond access and numbers

Uma Rani, Nora Gobel and Sueda Uludag

Introduction

The rapid expansion of the platform economy, further accelerated by the Covid-19 pandemic, has led governments worldwide to embrace digitalisation as a potential solution to high unemployment rates, particularly among women and youth. Digital platforms are increasingly presented as mechanisms for economic development and, specifically, women's economic empowerment, particularly in developing countries. This narrative, however, often overlooks the complex and frequently contradictory relationship between gender and digital labour platforms. This chapter critically examines this narrative, arguing that platforms, rather than simply creating unprecedented opportunities, often function as mechanisms of institutional transformation. Echoing the work of Vallas and Schor (2020, p. 282), the chapter posits that platforms can act as "permissive potentates", which externalise responsibility while still exercising concentrated power, allowing them to rework existing neoliberal institutions from within. Further, the chapter aligns with Piletić (2023, p. 438), who argues that platforms consolidate their dominance through neoliberal "innovations" in labour markets, leveraging a flexible workforce and pre-existing institutions, such as unregulated sectors of the economy, to achieve their aims; and with Rodríguez-Modroño et al. (2024), who highlight how these business models increase power imbalances and reinforce exploitative employment practices, further entrenching neoliberal trends of deregulation and commodification.

Building on a growing body of evidence, this chapter argues that digital platforms do not inherently offer equal opportunities for all; rather, intersectional factors such as race, caste, religion, class and migrant status continue to shape access to and outcomes within the digital economy, mirroring and often exacerbating

DOI: 10.4324/9781003528210-17

existing inequalities. This chapter analyses the implications of these complex dynamics for gender equality as part of broader dynamics of the digital transition (see also Piasna, 2026, this volume, for an analysis of the gendered dynamics of remote work). The rise of digital labour platforms represents a significant transformation in the world of work, fundamentally impacting employment relationships, job quality and reshaping social reproduction. Specifically, this chapter argues that while digital platforms might offer some new avenues for income generation, they also exacerbate existing inequalities and create new challenges for women. We analyse how algorithmic management, precarious work arrangements and intensified global competition, characteristics of these platforms, intersect with gendered patterns of vulnerability and opportunity.

Drawing on quantitative and qualitative data from ILO surveys (2017–2023) across various sectors, both male- and female-dominated, covering a range of countries from the Global South and North, this chapter moves beyond simplistic narratives of access and participation to reveal the nuanced, gendered implications of digitalisation for women's lives, livelihoods and economic security. In addition, this chapter draws upon a multi-faceted body of literature to analyse the complex interplay between digital labour platforms and gender. It pays particular attention to the often-invisible gendered labour of social reproduction, highlighting how the demands of platform work can clash with women's caregiving responsibilities.

The promise and paradox of platform work for women

Digital platforms are often presented as a transformative force in the labour market, promising increased employment opportunities, flexibility and a pathway to economic empowerment for women, particularly in developing countries where traditional employment opportunities may be limited (OECD, 2018; UN Women, 2020; World Bank, 2021; World Economic Forum, 2021). This optimistic narrative, often promoted by multinational platform companies and international development institutions, aligns with broader discourses of digitalisation as a key driver of economic development and a tool for bridging the digital gender divide. However, a growing body of research challenges this narrative and reveals a more complex and often contradictory reality (Rani et al., 2022; Rodríguez-Modroño et al., 2024; Vallas & Schor, 2020). Contrary to the promise of empowerment, these platforms often replicate and exacerbate existing gender inequalities, highlighting a significant gap between the rhetoric and the reality of digital work.

This raises critical questions about the nature and extent of their empowerment potential, especially when considering the persistent burden of social reproduction and unpaid care work shouldered by women. In the context of care work, this often involves exploiting existing global or colonial care chains to access a readily available and inexpensive workforce – a highly feminised and racialised reserve army of labour (Rodríguez-Modroño et al., 2022). The digital care platforms, rather than offering innovative solutions to the care crisis, often exacerbate the problem by further commodifying and devaluing care work while obscuring the structural causes of the crisis itself (Rodríguez-Modroño et al., 2024).

One of the central critiques of the platform empowerment narrative is that platforms largely mediate existing tasks and occupations rather than creating genuinely new tasks or occupations (Cook & Rani, 2024; ILO, 2021). The nature of work in sectors like transportation (e.g., ride-hailing), delivery, domestic work, caregiving and beauty services remains fundamentally unchanged; rather, platforms' innovation lies fundamentally in altering how this work is performed and managed using digital tools and algorithmic management. This shift in organisation, while potentially offering some benefits in terms of access and reach, often fails to address the underlying structural issues that perpetuate gender inequality in these sectors. For instance, in the case of domestic work, platforms like SweepSouth in South Africa, which may initially offer potentially higher wages than traditional arrangements, still rely on a workforce composed almost exclusively of women, replicating existing gendered divisions of labour (Hunt et al., 2019; Kalla, 2022; Sibiya & du Toit, 2022). Initial evidence also suggests that platform participation rates and occupational segregation often mirror existing patterns in traditional labour markets (see ILO, 2021 for freelance and microtask work), raising doubts about the transformative capacity of platforms for women's employment and challenging the assumption that mere access to platforms translates into meaningful empowerment and structural transformation.

Furthermore, the promised flexibility of platform work, often presented as a boon for women seeking to balance paid work with family responsibilities, frequently proves to be a myth. Instead of providing genuine control over work schedules, this "flexibility" can become a tool to legitimise double shifts or a burden for women and can deepen their vulnerability (Kwan, 2022), forcing them to navigate unpredictable schedules and client demands, while intensifying the pressure on them to juggle paid and unpaid platform work with unpaid caregiving and household responsibilities (Dattani, 2021; Kalla, 2022; Sibiya & du Toit, 2022; Ticona et al., 2018).

While flexibility is often a key motivator for joining platforms (ILO, 2024; Hunt & Samman, 2020), research reveals significant constraints. Hunt and Samman (2020) found that the ad-hoc nature of bookings and cancellations, particularly on on-demand platform operating models, undermined flexibility and created instability for domestic workers in South Africa. Kalla (2022) and Sibiya and du Toit (2022) similarly found that the pressure to maintain high ratings on platforms like SweepSouth forced workers to accept almost all bookings, regardless of personal commitments, and were penalised for declining work, thereby restricting their flexibility and autonomy. This constrained flexibility is further exacerbated by algorithmic management practices, such as penalties for off-platform work and short notice periods for bookings (Ticona et al., 2018), which intensify worker precarity and limit control over their schedules. Ultimately, the pursuit of flexibility on platforms often undermines worker agency and well-being, reinforcing gender inequalities by obscuring the exploitative realities of this type of work.

Women's narratives across various sectors reveal that they often end up working longer hours, at irregular times, and under precarious conditions to meet income targets and maintain platform ratings, leaving them with little time or energy for their families and personal lives. For example, delivery workers in Mexico City, many of whom are women, reported working long hours six days a week to earn enough to support themselves and their families, highlighting the demanding nature of platform work and the limited flexibility it actually offers (Centeno et al., 2022). This constant juggling act between paid and unpaid work can lead to increased stress, burnout and a further entrenchment of traditional gender roles, where women continue to be primarily responsible for domestic and caregiving duties. This is particularly evident from studies in India, Kenya, South Africa and Uganda where women platform workers remained overwhelmingly responsible for household chores and childcare, despite also engaging in paid platform work (Ghosh et al., 2022; Hunt et al., 2019; ILO, 2024a, 2024b).

The dominant narrative promoting platform work as a pathway to women's empowerment often relies on a neoliberal framework that emphasises individual agency, entrepreneurship and market-based solutions (Rani et al., 2022). This perspective often overlooks the deeply ingrained structural gender inequalities, power dynamics and patriarchal norms that continue to constrain women's economic opportunities. Simply providing access to digital technologies and platforms, without addressing these underlying structural barriers, is insufficient for achieving genuine empowerment or bringing about structural transformation, especially in developing economies. As Dattani (2021) highlights in her study of on-demand domestic workers in India, factors like limited access to smartphones, low digital literacy, safety concerns and patriarchal social norms can restrict women's ability to fully utilise platform opportunities. Furthermore, the precarious realities of platform work – low and unpredictable income, long hours, lack of social protection and the constant pressure through algorithmic management practices – often undermine the very autonomy and flexibility that are touted as key benefits for women.

This creates a paradoxical lose-lose situation: women are either excluded from platforms due to existing inequalities or face precarious working conditions upon entry. This highlights the limitations of a purely market-based approach to women's economic empowerment and reinforces the need to address underlying structural inequalities. Therefore, a critical and intersectional approach that moves beyond simplistic notions of empowerment and acknowledges the complex interplay of structural inequalities, social reproduction and platform dynamics is crucial for understanding the actual impact of the platform economy on women's lives and livelihoods.

Data and methods

The analysis in this chapter draws on data from multiple surveys conducted by the ILO between 2017 and 2023, globally and at the country-level (Table 13.1). The surveys include quantitative and qualitative questions, including open-ended questions that have been harmonised across the different sectors in both developed and developing country contexts to allow for a deeper understanding of worker experiences in different situations. Platforms can be categorised into location-based platforms such as domestic work, healthcare, beauty services, taxi and delivery services and online platforms such as microtask and freelance work. Work on location-based platforms is carried out in a specific physical location, and the tasks are typically mediated by platforms but performed offline, often in clients' homes or public spaces. Work on online platforms involves tasks performed and delivered through digital means, allowing workers to connect with clients across borders through platforms.

TABLE 13.1 Types of Digital Labour Platforms, Country and Year Coverage of ILO Global and Country-Level Surveys

Type of Platforms	*Countries Covered and Year of Survey*	*Sample Size*
Online platforms		
Freelance	Global survey: 31 developed and 48 developing countries (2019–2020) Country survey: India (2022–2023), Kenya (2022–2023), Uganda (2023)	993
Microtask	Global survey: 35 developed and 39 developing countries (2017) Country survey: India (2022–2023), Kenya (2022–2023)	2,774
Location-based platforms		
Taxi drivers	Chile, Ghana, India, Indonesia, Kenya, Lebanon, Mexico, Morocco, Ukraine (2019–2020) and Uganda (2023)	2,318
Delivery workers	Argentina, Chile, China, Ghana, India, Indonesia, Kenya, Lebanon, Mexico, Morocco, Ukraine (2019–2020) and Uganda (2023)	3,098
Beauty workers	India (2022–2023), Kenya (2022–2023)	283
Domestic workers	Kenya (2022–2023)	85
Healthcare workers	India (2022–2023), Kenya (2022–2023)	143
Personal services	Kenya (2022–2023)	100

Source: Own elaboration based on ILO global and country-level surveys on digital labour platforms

Country-level surveys of location-based platforms

Country-level surveys were conducted in collaboration with local researchers and research institutes.[1] To ensure cultural and linguistic relevance, questionnaires were adapted to the local context and translated into local languages as needed, following consultation with researchers in the respective country. Before the main data collection, a pilot test of the questionnaires was conducted in each country to identify and address any potential issues.

Interviews were administered using computer-assisted personal interviewing (CAPI) on mobile devices, such as mobile phones and tablets. This technology included built-in validation rules to ensure data quality.[2] Respondents received a fixed, country-specific payment upon completion of the interview to compensate them for their time.[3] On average, the survey took approximately 40 minutes for workers to complete.

Due to the lack of official statistics on the number and characteristics of platform workers, a traditional random sampling frame was not available. Therefore, the primary goal was to obtain a sample that was as representative of the target population as possible. The target population included any individual aged 18 or older who had worked in the relevant sector for at least three months, a criterion established to ensure they could provide informed responses.

Recruitment strategies varied by sector. For instance, to find taxi drivers, enumerators targeted locations such as petrol stations, office complexes, shopping malls, airports, railway stations, platform company support offices and taxi stands. Delivery workers were primarily recruited near restaurants, shopping malls and other common waiting areas. Beauty workers were identified through Facebook advertisements, and some platforms provided lists of workers who had consented to be contacted for research. Healthcare respondents were initially reached through personal contacts and referrals, with subsequent participants recruited using a snowball sampling method.

Global surveys of online platforms

The 2017 global survey of microtask workers and the 2019–2020 freelance survey were conducted with the assistance of SoundRocket, a social science survey research firm. The microtask survey was posted as a paid task on five different platforms. Participation was open to all, with the exception of Amazon Mechanical Turk (AMT), where the survey specifically targeted workers from India and the United States. To ensure a diverse sample, the survey was posted in small batches at various times of the day, and workers could self-select to participate.

For the freelance survey, several recruitment models were evaluated. The final strategy involved recruiting directly on the freelance platform (90%), identifying workers through other digital platforms like AMT (8%), and targeting individuals through online advertisements (2%). All participants who completed the questionnaire received compensation for their time and they took 60 minutes on average to complete the survey.

The data presented in this chapter are disaggregated by gender, country, sector and platform type (online or location-based). Country-level data are used for location-based platforms and for the online platform surveys in Kenya and India, while data from the global surveys on microtask and freelance platforms are presented by region, distinguishing between developed and developing countries.

Reproducing and exacerbating inequalities: the gendered dynamics of platform work

This section on findings from research draws both on the quantitative and qualitative results from the ILO surveys listed in Table 13.1, and a growing number of country and sector-specific case studies of platform work. One of the key messages from these diverse but extensive surveys and a growing body of empirical evidence is that digital labour platforms, despite claims of neutrality, often reproduce and exacerbate existing gender inequalities. This can be seen to occur through four interconnected dynamics: occupational segregation, educational disparities, persistent gendered differentials in earnings and the inherent precarity generated by user-driven pay negotiation. These dynamics, deeply embedded within the platform economy, interact to create significant barriers for women seeking decent work and economic security in the platform economy.

Occupational segregation

A key feature of traditional labour markets, occupational segregation, is replicated and often intensified within the platform economy. Platforms have been found to frequently mirror and reinforce traditional gendered divisions of labour, where women are concentrated in lower-paying sectors like domestic and care work (Dattani, 2021; Hunt et al., 2019). These platforms capitalise on societal expectations about "women's work", offering tasks like cleaning, childcare and eldercare that align with these ingrained stereotypes.

The ILO surveys confirm the presence of strong gender segregation in terms of tasks and occupations. In the taxi sector, women constituted an average of 5% of the survey samples, with relatively higher representation in Chile (18%) and Indonesia (13%), but with 5% or lower in Ghana, India, Kenya, Lebanon, Mexico, Morocco and Ukraine (Figure 13.1). The participation of women on delivery platforms was slightly higher (8% on average), reaching about 25% in Indonesia, followed by 19% in Ukraine, about 13–15% in Argentina, Chile and China, while it was lower in Ghana, India, Kenya, Lebanon, Mexico and Morocco. While these occupations remain gendered, qualitative data have indicated that some taxi

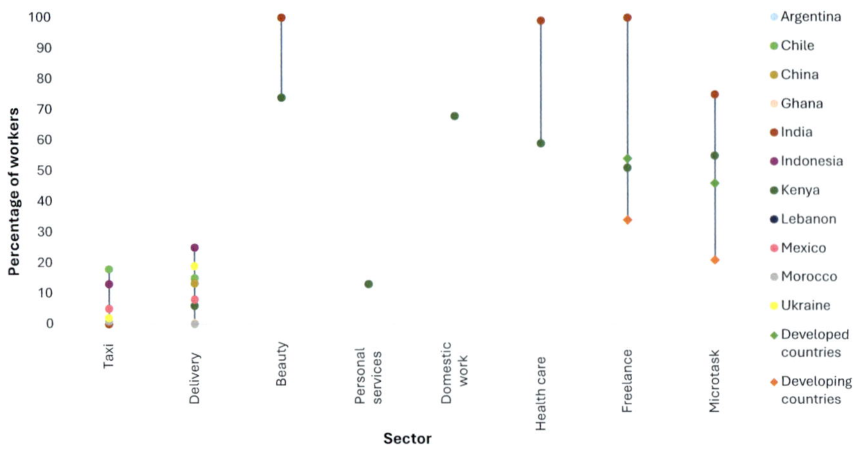

FIGURE 13.1 Percentage of Female Respondents, by Sector and Country.

Source: Own elaboration based on ILO global and country-level surveys on digital labour platforms.

and delivery platforms have attempted to diversify their workforces by actively encouraging and incentivising women to join. Conversely, beauty, healthcare and domestic work are largely female-dominated sectors, although in some country contexts such as India and Kenya, some male workers are entering these sectors, often to perform specific tasks.

Even when women enter male-dominated occupations on platforms, such as taxi and delivery work, they often face unique challenges such as direct discrimination from clients or passengers (Kwan, 2022; Micha et al., 2022). Kwan (2022, p. 559), in her study of female taxi drivers in China, found that passengers often cancelled rides due to the perception that "women are not safe drivers", subsequently giving them negative reviews and low ratings. These biases and discriminatory practices create significant barriers for women attempting to enter male-dominated sectors on platforms. As discussed later in the chapter, algorithmic management practices, including rating systems, can exacerbate gender inequalities.

Women's participation rates on online platforms also remain limited in developing countries (21% on microtask platforms and 34%t on freelance platforms), while participation rates are higher in developed countries, reflecting participation patterns in traditional labour markets (Figure 13.1). Online freelance platforms also replicate occupational segregation, with men largely performing tasks related to technology, data analytics and creative design, while women perform tasks that are largely related to business services, professional services and sales and marketing (ILO, 2021; Rani et al., 2022; Shevchuk & Strebkov, 2021). This mirrors the traditional labour market, as many tasks previously performed in such settings are now outsourced through platforms.

As shown in the qualitative data from the ILO survey, this task segregation is further reinforced by client discrimination, including instances where female workers were deemed unsuitable for certain tasks related to IT or data analytics based on their gender. This discriminatory behaviour limits women's earning potential and restricts access to career advancement, perpetuating economic inequality (Aleksynska et al., 2021; Beerepoot & Lambregts, 2015; Hermann et al., 2023; ILO, 2021).

Educational disparities

A persistent labour market challenge is matching workers with appropriate jobs. Ironically, while platforms are designed to connect workers with clients directly, based on education, their specific occupational skills and experience, many workers on freelance and microtask platforms experience a disconnect between their educational experience and the tasks they perform (Rani et al., 2022). Though many platforms do not require formal educational credentials, success on them hinges on possessing relevant skills and knowledge (Hermann et al., 2023). The ILO surveys show that educational attainment among platform workers varies by platform type. The proportion of workers on location-based platforms with graduate or postgraduate degrees is comparatively lower than those engaged on online labour platforms (Figure 13.2).

Overall, gender differences among the survey respondents' educational attainment are quite mixed depending on the sector and country. For instance, in countries where women participate in male-dominated sectors such as taxi (Chile, Indonesia and Mexico) or delivery (Argentina, Chile, China, Kenya and Ukraine), they often have higher educational attainment than their male counterparts (Figure 13.2).

Women on online platforms also tend to be highly educated. According to the ILO global survey, over 60% of them hold graduate or postgraduate degrees. In

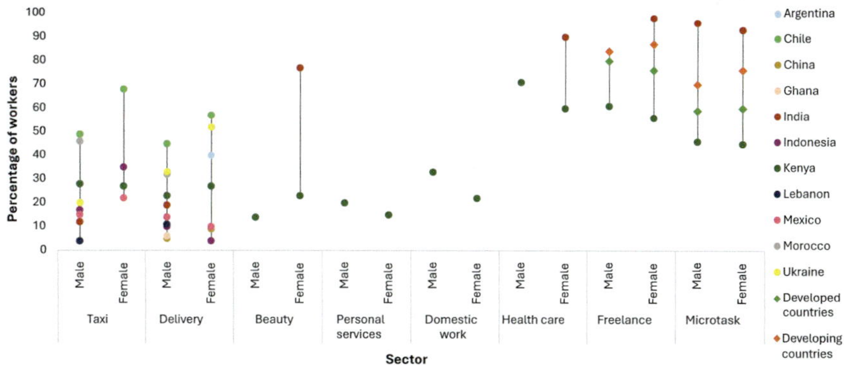

FIGURE 13.2 Percentage of Respondents with University Degree, by Gender, Sector and Country.

Source: Own elaboration based on ILO global and country-level surveys on digital labour platforms.

developing countries, a higher proportion of women than men are highly educated, with approximately 76% and 87% holding undergraduate or postgraduate degrees on microtask and freelance platforms, respectively (Figure 13.2). On average, women in developing countries are also more highly educated than their female counterparts in developed countries engaging in platform work. Men with higher education are predominantly concentrated in science, technology, engineering and medicine (STEM) fields, particularly in developing countries (51% on freelance and 62% on microtask platforms). While this share is lower among women, with 32% and 40% holding STEM degrees on freelance and microtask platforms, respectively, a slightly higher percentage of women on microtask platforms reported having training in medicine and natural sciences. Instead, women more commonly hold degrees in economics or other social sciences (42% on microtask and 55% on freelance platforms).

There seems to be a disconnect between education levels and participation on platforms for all workers, including for women, which raises concerns about potential underemployment among highly qualified workers, particularly women. This suggests that many may be taking these jobs due to a lack of other employment opportunities in the labour market. In addition, it also suggests that access to higher education does not automatically translate into higher-quality or better-paying platform work for women, particularly in developing countries. Instead, it reinforces the argument that barriers to women's participation in the labour market are shaped by deeper gendered norms, platform design and undervaluation of women's work, regardless of their qualifications.

Persistent gender disparities in earnings

Despite the potential for digital labour platforms to create more equitable labour markets, significant gender disparities persist, particularly in earnings and access to opportunities. These disparities often mirror and exacerbate existing inequalities in traditional labour markets, highlighting how platforms can reinforce rather than dismantle discriminatory structures.

One key issue is the undervaluing of women's work, particularly in care and domestic sectors (Grimshaw & Rubery, 2007). Platforms in these sectors often perpetuate traditional gender divisions of labour, where technical jobs (frequently perceived as male roles) command higher wages, while care-related tasks, typically associated with women, remain undervalued (Hunt et al., 2019; Rodríguez-Modroño et al., 2024). By emphasising the supposedly intrinsic rewards of care work, these platforms legitimise unpaid or underpaid labour as a social contribution rather than a recognised profession, further devaluing women's skills and contributions. This practice perpetuates historical patterns of exploitation, as seen in the South African domestic work sector, where platforms continue a legacy of poor conditions and inadequate pay for Black women (Kalla, 2022; Sibiya & du Toit, 2022).

This undervaluation of women's work is not only a matter of societal attitudes; it is reflected in concrete earnings disparities, as shown in Figure 13.3. Domestic workers recorded the lowest average hourly earnings across all online and location-based sectors (including paid and unpaid working hours). Additionally, women in taxi and delivery sectors earn less than men in most countries surveyed, despite performing comparable tasks under similar conditions. This disparity could be partly due to women workers not being available to work during peak hours due to household and caregiving responsibilities, as observed in Argentina, which penalises them and has an impact on their earnings (Micha et al., 2022).

Gender pay gaps also exist on online platforms, with the gaps varying depending upon the nature of the tasks performed and whether the workers reside in developed or developing countries. The average hourly earnings (including both paid and unpaid working hours) of women on freelance platforms were lower than men's in advanced economies while they were higher in developing countries (Figure 13.3). The higher earnings among women in these countries could be due to their higher levels of education compared to men, as shown in Figure 13.2, potentially enabling them to access better-paid tasks. A number of studies in Europe reveal significant gender pay gaps on online labour platforms, influenced by various factors including type of tasks, platform type and geographical location (Aleksynska et al., 2021; Herrmann et al., 2019). While some of this disparity can be attributed to occupational segregation (Beerepoot & Lambregts, 2015; Chan & Wang, 2018), the persistence of gender pay gaps even within the same task categories points to the enduring influence of discrimination and bias.

In addition, the ILO's global surveys on freelance platforms found a stark global North–South disparity in earnings. Women in developing countries earn 50% less than their female counterparts in developed countries for similar tasks

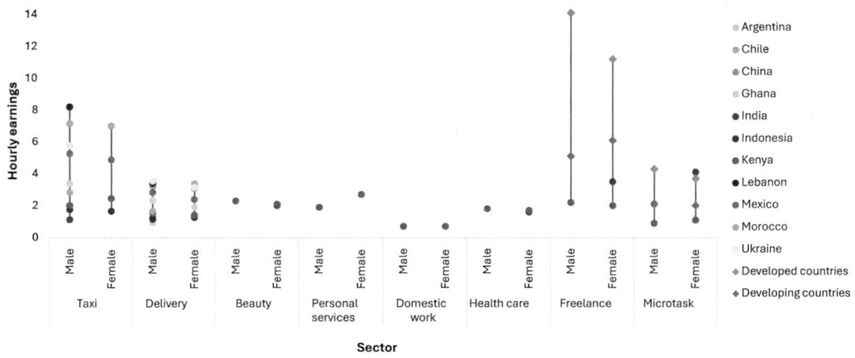

FIGURE 13.3 Average Hourly Earnings of Respondents for Total Work (Paid and Unpaid Time) (in US$), by Gender, Sector and Country.

Source: Own elaboration based on ILO global and country-level surveys on digital labour platforms.

(Figure 13.3). This discrepancy likely stems from factors such as an oversupply of labour, leading workers, particularly women in developing countries, to underbid or accept lower rates to build their profiles and reputations (Rani et al., 2023). This competitive pressure disproportionately impacts women, especially those in the global South, and risks further depressing wages if proper institutional mechanisms are not in place.

Price of precarity

A strong profile and reputation are crucial for securing work and commanding competitive prices on digital labour platforms. However, low barriers to entry and often inadequate vetting processes create an oversupply of workers, intensifying competition. The precarious nature of platform work, often characterised by a lack of traditional employment protections and benefits, is further compounded by user-driven pay negotiation models, especially in sectors likely to be female-dominated. Unlike ride-hailing or food delivery platforms that typically use dynamic pricing or fixed per-task rates set by the platforms, some platforms in female-dominated sectors, such as care and domestic work, often rely on individualised pay negotiation, mirroring practices often seen in traditional informal labour markets such as domestic cleaning (Tandon & Sekharan, 2022). This means that workers and clients are left to negotiate wages, working hours and working conditions independently, often based on client budgets and perceived skill levels for the tasks, which creates a potential for exploitative practices. In addition, women workers with small children who try to increase their hourly fee to include costs of childcare face stiff competition from other workers who have no childcare responsibilities (James, 2022), and might lose out on accessing work or effectively have low net incomes.

On freelance platforms, which are global in nature with an oversupply of labour, this dynamic incentivises underbidding and accepting tasks for low pay. An ILO global survey on freelance platforms reveals that despite facing greater economic pressures, a smaller proportion of workers in developing countries (36%) reported accepting work they would otherwise decline, compared to their counterparts in developed countries (48%), and the proportion was higher among women in both these settings by more than 10 percentage points. About two-thirds of the workers in both developed and developing countries were underbidding for the tasks or projects, and there were no differences between genders (Rani et al., 2025).

This decentralised approach to setting wages intensifies competition among workers and can create a "race to the bottom", where workers are pressured to undercut each other to secure bookings or to receive tasks, ultimately suppressing wages for everyone, especially for women (Hunt et al., 2019; International Finance Corporation & European Union, 2020; Rani et al., 2025; Sibiya & du Toit, 2022). This lack of standardised pricing, exacerbated by platforms like Helpling that allow clients to directly compare worker profiles based on price (van Doorn,

2020), can be particularly detrimental to workers, especially women who may be socialised to avoid assertive negotiation and are thus more likely to accept lower wages.

The constant pressure to accept low-paying offers to maintain a steady income stream traps many women in a cycle of precarity. Further, workers on domestic, care and beauty services platforms also have to commute to reach their clients' homes, which increases their unpaid hours and adds the burden of deducting transportation costs from their earnings (ILO, 2024). This precarious payment structure, combined with the irregular and unpredictable nature of platform work and the associated overhead costs (e.g., transportation, internet access), makes it difficult for women to achieve economic security and build sustainable livelihoods. In addition, the absence of work-related benefits such as maternity leave on platforms often forces women to postpone having a family or children until they find secure, formal employment (James, 2022). The lack of sufficient income and the constant pressure to secure more work can create significant stress and undermine women's ability to plan for the future (James, 2022), including saving or investing in their own professional development, such as further education or training.

Formalising transactions, informalising labour

A central paradox of platform work is the simultaneous formalisation of economic transactions and the informalisation of labour relations. While platforms create a structured system for payments and service exchanges, they often circumvent traditional labour regulations by classifying workers as independent contractors (ILO, 2021; Nhleko, 2023; Pulignano et al., 2023). This classification denies workers access to standard employment protections and social security systems, exposing them to greater vulnerability and precarity across various sectors and geographical contexts.

Nhleko (2023) highlights how platforms like SweepSouth in South Africa intensify informality by denying workers legal protections and benefits, even while promoting a narrative of formalisation. This resonates with pre-existing patterns of informalisation in domestic and care work in the traditional labour market as well as historically, particularly for women and racialised migrant workers. While some workers leverage platforms as networking tools to find offline clients and achieve better working conditions, this strategy ultimately reinforces informality and undermines efforts to achieve decent work standards, particularly for these vulnerable groups.

Similarly, Rodríguez-Modroño et al. (2022) find that on-demand platforms in the domestic and home care sector in Spain, operating within an already precarious and often racialised migrant-dominated care labour market, often do not provide workers with formal labour contracts and these migrant women have limited access to labour rights and social protection. This precarious status, often intersecting with irregular migration statuses, further complicates workers' ability to renew residency permits, highlighting the interconnectedness of labour precarity, migration status and gendered and racialised inequalities. Even in long-term care arrangements facilitated by platforms, workers are often classified as non-specialised domestic workers, denying them the rights and protections such as paid and sick leave, afforded to formal care workers.

The misclassification of workers as independent contractors is a widespread issue with significant consequences. This practice allows platforms to circumvent labour laws, denying workers access to minimum wage, sick leave, paid leave and other benefits (Hunt et al., 2019; Hunt & Samman, 2020; International Finance Corporation & European Union, 2020; ILO, 2021; Kalla, 2022; Sibiya & du Toit, 2022; van Doorn, 2017, 2020). While platforms often highlight the flexibility afforded by this arrangement, this "flexibility" often comes at the cost of job security and social protection, further marginalising women workers. Additionally, Kluzik (2022) argues that digital platforms further commodify and fragment care work, reducing it to a series of discrete, marketable tasks. This fragmentation can undermine the holistic and relational nature of care, potentially impacting both the quality of care provided and the well-being of care workers.

Ticona and Mateescu's (2018) study on the United States demonstrates how care work platforms attempt to formalise certain aspects of the employment relationship, such as providing payment infrastructure and tax tools, while simultaneously undermining formal employment relationships and failing to enforce decent working conditions. This creates a situation where platforms act as "cultural entrepreneurs", promoting a narrative of formalisation while perpetuating and promoting informal and precarious working conditions. Even in more regulated contexts like the EU, Trojansky (2020) notes that long-term home care platforms can undermine formalisation efforts by classifying workers as self-employed, limiting their access to social protection and creating challenges for maintaining work-life balance.

Moreover, platforms often shift operational costs and risks onto workers (ILO, 2024a, 2024b; McDonald et al., 2021; van Doorn, 2017) while limiting their capacity to challenge unfair practices through restrictive terms of service and information asymmetry. These findings collectively challenge the notion that platforms are inherently drivers of formalisation. In addition, the isolated nature of much platform-based care and domestic work, coupled with the lack of collective representation, further intensifies worker precarity and hinders efforts to improve working conditions (Rodríguez-Modroño et al., 2024; van Doorn, 2020).

Algorithmic control and the erosion of worker agency

Algorithmic management, a defining feature of digital labour platforms, exerts significant control over workers, impacting their access to work, income and job security. While often presented as a neutral and efficient management tool, algorithmic systems can perpetuate and even worsen gender inequalities. Rating systems, a core component of algorithmic management, are particularly influential, shaping workers' reputations and determining their access to future opportunities (Hunt et al., 2019; Khethisa et al., 2020; McDonald et al., 2021; Ticona & Mateescu, 2018). Kalla (2022), for instance, highlights how arbitrary dismissals and unfair ratings on the SweepSouth platform contribute to worker precarity.

Similarly, Rodríguez-Modroño et al. (2022) demonstrate how on-demand platforms in domestic and home care work in Spain utilise algorithms to control workers' time and restrict their autonomy. This is not sector-specific; van Doorn (2017) demonstrates how platforms across various service sectors, from on-demand services to task-based platforms like TaskRabbit, draw on historical patterns of control and exploitation of racialised and feminised labour. This includes undervaluing tasks traditionally performed by women, restricting their autonomy, and perpetuating gendered power imbalances within platform work. They also exert control through monitoring, performance metrics and behavioural nudges, creating a system where workers are dispensable and easily replaced. This control is often compounded by the platform's role as an intermediary that prioritises client satisfaction over worker well-being (Ticona & Mateescu, 2018; van Doorn, 2017, 2020), creating a power imbalance that limits workers' ability to fight for their rights.

The impact of algorithmic management can be particularly disadvantageous for women, especially in male-dominated sectors. Algorithms can perpetuate gender bias by penalising women for behaviours linked to caregiving and household responsibilities; as already mentioned, in the ride-hailing sector in both Argentina and China (Kwan, 2022; Micha et al., 2022) the consequence of cancelling rides or declining long-distance trips was lower ratings and reduced earnings. This algorithmic bias, along with the platform's control over workers' working time such as arrival and departure times, restricting communication channels and penalising last-minute cancellations while offering limited recourse for client cancellations (Rodríguez-Modroño et al., 2022), reinforces gender disparities in income and working hours.

James (2022) also shows how women on online labour platforms who do not remain active or do not respond to clients immediately due to caregiving responsibilities can face repercussions, including lower ratings and reduced access to work. The failure of these systems to account for the gendered labour of social reproduction, including care and household responsibilities, further marginalises women and exacerbates precarity, especially for those already facing multiple forms of discrimination (Centeno et al., 2022; Micha et al., 2022). This asymmetrical power dynamic, coupled with information asymmetry regarding client fees and worker pay, reinforces worker vulnerability and platform control.

The lack of transparency and accountability in algorithmic management poses a significant challenge for workers seeking to contest unfair or discriminatory outcomes (ILO, 2021). The opacity of these systems makes it difficult for workers to understand how algorithms are making decisions and to challenge those decisions when they perceive them as biased or unjust. While some workers have found ways to navigate these opaque and often discriminatory systems through collective action and information sharing via platforms like WhatsApp (Tandon & Sekharan, 2022), addressing the fundamental power imbalance inherent in algorithmic management requires systemic change and greater worker agency in the design and deployment of these technologies.

Intersectionality: exposing multiple vulnerabilities

An intersectional lens (Collins, 2019; Crenshaw, 1989) is crucial for understanding the nuanced and varied experiences of women in the platform economy. Gender intersects with other social categories like race, class, migration status, education and digital literacy, creating unique vulnerabilities and shaping how different groups of women interact with digital labour platforms. This intersectional approach is essential for developing effective policies that address the specific challenges faced by diverse groups of women.

Empirical evidence shows that platform-based work, particularly in domestic and care work, can reinforce existing racial and class inequalities (Kalla, 2022; Khethisa et al., 2020; Rodríguez-Modroño et al., 2022; Sibiya & du Toit, 2022; van Doorn, 2017). For example, in South Africa, Black African women are disproportionately represented in precarious and low-paying platform-based domestic work, further entrenching existing disparities. Furthermore, the digital divide, characterised by unequal access to technology and digital literacy skills, creates significant barriers. Studies in India and South Africa reveal that many women are excluded from platform work because they lack smartphones or the ability to use the required apps (Dattani, 2021; Hunt & Machingura, 2016).

Migrant women, often drawn to platform work for its flexibility, are particularly vulnerable to exploitation in the platform economy – as they are more generally in the labour market (see Steinmetz & Guarnerio, 2026, this volume). This precarious position is often compounded by language barriers, limited legal resources, and uncertain immigration status (Khethisa et al., 2020; Rodríguez-Modroño et al., 2022; van Doorn, 2020), demonstrating that platform work, while appealing, is not a panacea for the challenges migrant workers face. Rodríguez-Modroño et al. (2022) illustrate the challenges faced by migrant domestic workers in Spain who encounter difficulties renewing residency permits, often due to a lack of formal labour contracts. Van Doorn (2020) also notes how platforms like Handy exploit the precarious status of migrant workers by charging high fees for starter kits and siding with clients in disputes, further diminishing worker power.

Harassment and violence pose significant threats to women platform workers, especially in sectors like domestic and care work, where work takes place in private homes and often involves isolated interactions with clients. Unlike traditional arrangements based on referrals or placement agencies, which often provide a degree of pre-vetting or background information about clients, platform work often involves interacting with individuals about whom the workers have very limited information, increasing the potential for risk. Workers are often left to assess the safety of each gig independently, taking personal precautions like notifying family members (Hunt et al., 2019).

Several studies document instances of harassment, abuse and even violence against black African women platform workers on SweepSouth, often with limited recourse or support from platforms (Kalla, 2022; International Finance Corporation & European Union, 2020; Sibiya & du Toit, 2022). Khethisa et al. (2020) further document the challenges faced by migrant domestic workers in Cape Town, including threats of violence and abuse, coupled with poor communication and support from platforms. The opaque nature of platform operations, coupled with the lack of platform moderation, forces workers to bear the responsibility for their own safety, adding an unpaid emotional and logistical burden to their work (Pulignano et al., 2023; Ticona & Mateescu, 2018). Kwan's (2022) research in China exposes how platforms fail to provide adequate safety measures, leaving women workers vulnerable to gender-based violence, including sexual harassment and unsafe rides, particularly during late-night hours. This lack of protection exacerbates existing gender inequalities and intensifies precarity for women in the platform economy. These intersecting vulnerabilities underscore the need for comprehensive policies and interventions that address not only gender inequality but also the specific risks faced by women in the platform economy.

Towards a more equitable platform economy

The gig economy raises fundamental questions about the future of work in an increasingly globalised and digitised world. The power of multinational corporations, the ownership and control of data, the influence of venture capital and international financial institutions and the need for effective platform regulation are all critical issues that require ongoing attention. This chapter has demonstrated how digital labour platforms, while offering new income-generating opportunities, can reproduce and exacerbate existing gender inequalities. Women's work remains undervalued, and despite high levels of education, they continue to face barriers to accessing better-paid tasks. The algorithmic management and client-centric rating systems prevalent on these platforms often perpetuate power imbalances, leaving workers, particularly women, with limited recourse against exploitation. These vulnerabilities are further intensified by the lack of adequate social protection and labour rights, impacting women, particularly those who are primary breadwinners for their families, most acutely. Moreover, it is crucial to recognise that these challenges intersect with other forms of discrimination based on race, class, migration status and other social identities, and addressing them requires a multifaceted, gender-sensitive approach.

Classifying the platform workers as "employees" based on their autonomy and control is essential for extending fundamental principles and rights at work and labour protections – minimum wage, paid time off, social security – to platform workers (ILO, 2021). Strengthening collective bargaining rights is important for empowering women to negotiate fair wages, safe conditions and policies that address their specific needs. These needs include access to affordable childcare, challenging the assumption that working from home eliminates the need for external childcare support, as women still need to perform their paid tasks, and the need for protection against gender-based violence and harassment within the digital workplace. Algorithmic transparency and accountability, including auditing algorithms for gender bias, providing clear explanations of how they function and establishing accessible redress mechanisms are essential for mitigating discriminatory outcomes. Portable social security benefits can ensure that all platform workers, including women, have access to social security, healthcare and other benefits, irrespective of their employment status. Bridging the gender digital divide through targeted training and support programmes is equally crucial for enhancing women's opportunities in the digital economy. Finally, social dialogue and coordination are essential at the international level to address the cross-border nature of many platforms and to ensure that all workers, irrespective of their employment status, are provided with labour and social protections.

While technology itself is not inherently problematic, how it is used or deployed and governed determines its impact on social and economic inequalities, as well as its impact on gender equality. As Huws (2019) argues, there is a need for more bottom-up design of technologies to ensure they serve the interests of the workers, rather than those of big tech companies. Further, social dialogue and worker organising have a critical role to play in achieving a more equitable platform economy. Platforms, governments and workers must engage in constructive dialogue to address the challenges of platform work and co-create solutions that promote decent work and gender equality. Supporting the development of worker collectives and unions can empower platform workers to advocate for their rights and negotiate for better working conditions.

Acknowledgements

This work was supported by the Bill and Melinda Gates Foundation GRANT AGREEMENT Investment ID INV-006223 – Understanding and improving women's work on digital labour platforms. This work would not have been possible without the colleagues and consultants who implemented, coordinated and analysed the diverse set of surveys and interviews conducted by the ILO globally as well as specific countries between 2017 and 2023. Any view expressed or conclusions drawn in this chapter represent the views of the authors and do not necessarily represent ILO views or ILO policy. The views expressed herein should be attributed to the authors and not to the ILO, its management, or its constituents.

Notes

1 For more details about the ILO global and cross-sectional surveys, sampling and implementation, see Berg et al. (2018, Appendix 2); ILO (2021, Appendix 4); and (ILO, 2024a, 2024b, Appendix 3).
2 The surveys were implemented on KoBoToolbox, an open-source survey tool: https://www.kobotoolbox.org/
3 The amounts were set in consideration of the country's minimum wage and also based on the peak earnings of taxi drivers or delivery workers.

References

Aleksynska, M., Shevchuk, A., & Strebkov, D. (2021). Online platform work in Russia and Ukraine: Gender differences in earnings and work satisfaction. In T. Karabchuk, K. Kumo, K. Gatskova, & E. Skoglund (Eds.), *Gendering post-Soviet space* (pp. 277–299). Springer. https://doi.org/10.1007/978-981-15-9358-1_13

Beerepoot, N., & Lambregts, B. (2015). Competition in online job marketplaces: Towards a global labour market for outsourcing services? *Global Networks*, *15*(2), 236–255. https://doi.org/10.1111/glob.12051

Berg, J., Furrer, M., Harmon, E., Rani, U., & Silberman, M. S. (2018). *Digital labour platforms and the future of work: towards decent work in the online world*. ILO.

Centeno, L. A., Tejada, A. H., Rodríguez Martínez, A., Rodríguez Leal-Isla, A. L., Jaramillo-Molina, A. M., & Rivera-González, R. C. (2022). Food delivery workers in Mexico City: A gender perspective on the gig economy. *Gender & Development*, *30*(3), 601–617. https://doi.org/10.1080/13552074.2022.2131253

Chan, J., & Wang, J. (2018). Hiring preferences in online labor markets: Evidence of a female hiring bias. *Management Science*, *64*(7), 2973–2994. https://doi.org/10.1287/mnsc.2017.2756

Collins, P. H. (2019). The difference that power makes: Intersectionality and participatory democracy. In O. Hankivsky & J. S. Jordan-Zachery (Eds.), *The Palgrave handbook of intersectionality in public policy. The politics of intersectionality* (pp. 167–192). Palgrave Macmillan. https://doi.org/10.1007/978-3-319-98473-5_7

Cook, S., & Rani, U. (2024). Platform work in developing economies: Can digitalisation drive structural transformation? *The Indian Journal of Labour Economics*, *68*, 395–416. https://doi.org/10.1007/s41027-024-00541-1

Crenshaw, K. (1989). Demarginalizing the intersection of race and sex: A black feminist critique of antidiscrimination doctrine, feminist theory and antiracist politics. *University of Chicago Legal Forum*, *1989*(1), 139–167. https://chicagounbound.uchicago.edu/uclf/vol1989/iss1/8

Dattani, K. (2021). Platform "glitch as surprise". *City*, *25*(3–4), 376–395. https://doi.org/10.1080/13604813.2021.1935786

Ghosh, A., Zaidi, M., & Ramachandran, R. (2022). Locating women workers in the platform economy in India – old wine in a new bottle? *Gender & Development*, *30*(3), 765–784. https://doi.org/10.1080/13552074.2022.2131258

Grimshaw, D., & Rubery, J. (2007). *Undervaluing women's work* (EOC Working Paper Series No. 53). Equal Opportunities Commission. https://www.researchgate.net/publication/267854289_Undervaluing_Women's_Work

Hermann, A. M., Zaal, P. M., Chappin, M. M. H., Schemmann, B., & Lühmann, A. (2023). "We don't need no (higher) education" – How the gig economy challenges the education-income paradigm. *Technological Forecasting and Social Change, 186(a)*, 122–136. https://doi.org/10.1016/j.techfore.2022.122136

Herrmann, A. M., Zaal, P., Chappin, M. M. H., & Schemmann, B. (2019). Does education still matter in online labor markets? In D. Wruk, A. Oberg, & I. Maurer (Eds.), *Perspectives on the sharing economy. Newcastle-upon-Tyne* (pp. 64–71). Cambridge Scholars Publishing.

Hunt, A., & Machingura, F. (2016). *A good gig? The rise of on-demand domestic work* (Working Paper 07). Overseas Development Institute. https://odi.org/en/publications/a-good-gig-the-rise-of-on-demand-domestic-work/

Hunt, A., & Samman, E. (2020). Domestic work and the gig economy in South Africa: Old wine in new bottles? *Anti-Trafficking Review, 15,* 102–121. https://doi.org/10.14197/atr.201220156

Hunt, A., Samman, E., Tapfuma, S., Mwaura, G., Omenya, R., Kim, K., Stevano, S., & Roumer, A. (2019). *Women in the gig economy: Paid work, care and flexibility in Kenya and South Africa.* Overseas Development Institute. https://odi.org/en/publications/women-in-the-gig-economy-paid-work-care-and-flexibility-in-kenya-and-south-africa/

Huws, U. (2019). The hassle of housework: Digitalisation and the commodification of domestic labour. *Feminist Review, 123*(1), 8–23. https://doi.org/10.1177/0141778919879725

International Finance Corporation, & European Union. (2020). *SweepSouth* [Case study]. https://documents1.worldbank.org/curated/en/196351614012371793/pdf/SweepSouth-Highlights-the-Pay-and-Working-Conditions-of-Domestic-Workers.pdf

International Labour Organization. (2021). *World employment and social outlook 2021: The role of digital platforms in transforming the world of work.* https://www.ilo.org/publications/flagship-reports/role-digital-labour-platforms-transforming-world-work

International Labour Organization. (2024a). *Digital labour platforms in Kenya: Exploring women's opportunities and challenges across various sectors.* https://www.ilo.org/media/541156/download

International Labour Organization. (2024b). *Platform work in Uganda: Promoting decent work for all.*

James, A. (2022). Women in the gig economy: Feminising "digital labour". *Work in the Global Economy, 2*(1), 2–26. https://doi.org/10.1332/273241721X16448410652000

Kalla, S. (2022). Hacking platform capitalism: The case of domestic workers on South Africa's SweepSouth platform. *Gender & Development, 30*(3), 655–666. https://doi.org/10.1080/13552074.2022.2136838

Khethisa, B. L., Tsibolane, P., & Van Belle, J. P. (2020). Surviving the gig economy in the global South: How Cape Town domestic workers cope. In R. K. Bandi, R. C. R. S. Klein, S. Madon, & E. Monteiro (Eds.), *The future of digital work: The challenge of inequality* (pp. 67–85). Springer International Publishing. https://doi.org/10.1007/978-3-030-64697-4_7

Kluzik, V. (2022). Governing invisibility in the platform economy: Excavating the logics of platform care. *Internet Policy Review, 11*(1), 1–21. https://doi.org/10.14763/2022.1.1636

Kwan, H. (2022). Gendered precarious employment in China's gig economy: Exploring women gig drivers' intersectional vulnerabilities and resistances. *Gender & Development, 30*(3), 551–574. https://doi.org/10.1080/13552074.2022.2118464

McDonald, P., Williams, P., & Mayes, R. (2021). Means of control in the organization of digitally intermediated care work. *Work, Employment and Society, 35*(5), 872–890. https://doi.org/10.1177/0950017020969107

Micha, A., Poggi, C., & Pereyra, F. (2022). When women enter male-dominated territories in the platform economy: Gender inequalities among drivers and riders in Argentina. *Gender & Development*, *30*(3), 575–600. https://doi.org/10.1080/13552074.2022.2117931

Nhleko, T. (2023). The "platformisation" of domestic work in South Africa: A shift towards marginal formalisation and deepening informalisation of domestic work employment. *The Thinker*, *96*(3), 87–98. https://doi.org/10.36615/the_thinker.v96i3.2678

Organisation for Economic Co-operation and Development. (2018). *Bridging the digital gender divide: Include, upskill and innovate.* https://www.oecd.org/digital/bridging-the-digital-gender-divide.pdf

Piasna, A. (2026). Digitalisation and remote work: Gendered outcomes in job quality and the role of persistent gender inequalities in paid and unpaid work. In J. Rubery, N. Sánchez-Mira, & V. Insarauto (Eds.), *Women in turbulent times. Crises, transitions, and challenges for gender equality* (pp. 257–274). Routledge.

Piletić, A. (2023). Continuity or change? Platforms and the hybridization of neoliberal institutional contexts. *Review of International Political Economy, 31*(2), 1–25. https://doi.org/10.1080/09692290.2023.2220088

Pulignano, V., Mará, C., Franke, M., & Muszynski, K. (2023). Informal employment on domestic care platforms: A study on the individualisation of risk and unpaid labour in mature market contexts. *Transfer*, *29*(3), 323–338. https://doi.org/10.1177/10242589231177353

Rani, U., Castel-Branco, R., Satija, S., & Nayar, M. (2022). Women, work, and the digital economy. *Gender & Development*, *30*(3), 421–435. https://doi.org/10.1080/13552074.2022.2151729

Rani, U., Dhir, R. K., & Gobel, N. (2023). Work on online labour platforms: Does formal education matter? In U. Huws & A. Surie (Eds.), *Platformization and informality: Pathways of change, alteration and transformation* (pp. 47–87). Routledge. https://doi.org/10.1007/978-3-031-11462-5

Rani, U., Dhir, R., & Gobel, N. (2025). Digital labour platforms and their contribution to development outcomes. In M. Moore, C. Scherrer, & M. van der Linden (Eds.), *The Elgar companion to decent work and the Sustainable Development Goals* (pp. 562–575). Edward Elgar. https://doi.org/10.4337/9781035300907.00056

Rodríguez-Modroño, P., Agenjo-Calderón, A., & López-Igual, P. (2022). Platform work in the domestic and home care sector: New mechanisms of invisibility and exploitation of women migrant workers. *Gender & Development*, *30*(3), 619–635. https://doi.org/10.1080/13552074.2022.2121060

Rodríguez-Modroño, P., Agenjo-Calderón, A., & López-Igual, P. (2024). A social reproduction analysis of digital care platform work. *New Political Economy*, *29*(4), 616–627. https://doi.org/10.1080/13563467.2024.2317703

Shevchuk, A., & Strebkov, D. (2021). Digital platforms and the changing freelance workforce in the Russian Federation: A ten-year perspective. *International Labour Review*, *162*(1), 1–22. https://doi.org/10.1111/ilr.12232

Sibiya, W., & du Toit, D. (2022). Sweeping up decent work: Paid domestic work and digital platforms in South Africa. *Gender & Development*, *30*(3), 637–654. https://doi.org/10.1080/13552074.2022.2126199

Steinmetz, S., & Guarnerio, M. (2026). Intersecting inequalities. The role of gender and migration background in women's labour market vulnerability during crises. In J. Rubery, N. Sánchez-Mira, & V. Insarauto (Eds.), *Women in turbulent times. Crises, transitions, and challenges for gender equality* (pp. 29–51). Routledge.

Tandon, A., & Sekharan, A. (2022). Labouring (on) the app: Agency and organisation of work in the platform economy. *Gender & Development*, *30*(3), 687–706. https://doi.org/10.1080/13552074.2022.2130515

Ticona, J., & Mateescu, A. (2018). Trusted strangers: Carework platforms' cultural entrepreneurship in the on-demand economy. *New Media & Society*, *20*(11), 4384–4404. https://doi.org/10.1177/1461444818773727

Ticona, J., Mateescu, A., & Rosenblat, A. (2018). *Beyond disruption: How tech shapes labor across domestic work and ridehailing.* Data & Society. https://datasociety.net/library/beyond-disruption/

Trojansky, A. (2020). Towards the "Uber-isation" of care? Platform work in the sector of long-term home care and its implications for workers' rights. *European Economic and Social Committee.* https://www.eesc.europa.eu/en/our-work/publications-other-work/publications/towards-uber-isation-care#downloads

UN Women. (2020). *The digital revolution: Implications for gender equality and women's rights 25 years after Beijing.* https://www.unwomen.org/en/digital-library/publications/2020/08/discussion-paper-the-digital-revolution-implications-for-gender-equality-and-womens-rights

Vallas, S., & Schor, J. B. (2020). What do platforms do? Understanding the gig economy. *Annual Review of Sociology*, *46*, 273–294. https://doi.org/10.1146/annurev-soc-121919-054857

van Doorn, N. (2017). Platform labour: On the gendered and racialized exploitation of low-income service work in the "on-demand" economy. *Information, Communication & Society*, *20*(6), 898–914. https://doi.org/10.1080/1369118X.2017.1294194

van Doorn, N. (2020). Stepping stone or dead end? The ambiguities of platform-mediated domestic work under conditions of austerity. Comparative Landscapes of Austerity and the Gig Economy. In D. Baines & I. Cunningham (Eds.), *Working in the context of austerity: Challenges and struggles* (pp. 49–70). Bristol University Press. https://doi.org/10.46692/9781529208689.003

World Bank. (2021). *Accelerating gender equality in digital development.* https://thedocs.worldbank.org/en/doc/61714f214ed04bcd6e9623ad0e215897-0400012021/related/Digital-Development-Note-on-Gender-Equality-November2021-final.pdf

World Economic Forum. (2021). *Global gender gap report 2021: Insights report, March 2021.* World Economic Forum. https://www.weforum.org/reports/global-gender-gap-report-2021

14

UNPACKING THE GREEN ECONOMY

Worker justice without gender justice?

Jack Daly, Vera Trappmann, Ioulia Bessa and Jennifer Tomlinson

Introduction

The climate crisis represents the greatest crisis for humankind.[1] The sustainability of current economic models is under scrutiny as industries face increasing political and social pressure to transition to a greener, decarbonised economy. This transition is often conceptualised as involving the expansion of specific industries, such as renewable energies and sustainable transport, alongside the contraction or transformation of high-polluting industries such as heavy manufacturing and fossil-fuel extraction. There is, therefore, a pressing need for a "just transition"; one that, among other goals, ensures that workers subject to job losses can be redeployed into a green economy. Moreover, the transition to a green economy could present the opportunity to address other pressing environmental and social challenges, like plastic pollution, biodiversity loss, the reach of other planetary boundaries as well as the care crisis. However, mainstream debates and policies are focusing narrowly on technological innovation for an energy transition as a response to global warming, in which the environment remains a resource to exploit, whilst pursuing market growth (Djoudi et al., 2016; Irving & Helin, 2018; MacGregor, 2009). This narrow focus on what constitutes a green economy as only an energy transition risks reinforcing existing gender inequalities in both the labour market and the household. What is missing is a gendered analysis that seeks to challenge the economic structures that drive climate change. Such analyses are not widespread in mainstream academic and political debates (Djoudi et al., 2016; MacGregor, 2010) but are more prevalent in feminist ecological economics where the connection between human and non-human exploitation is expressed more explicitly. This is illustrated in arguments that measures of Gross Domestic Product discount both the unpaid work of care and subsistence production and

DOI: 10.4324/9781003528210-18

ecosystem services while counting human and environmental depletion and degradation as value-producing (Barca, 2020; Rodriguez Acha, 2016; Waring, 1999).

In this chapter, we examine the current mainstream debates on and policies for the transition to a green economy regarding gender equality. We review important debates in the gender and climate change literatures. First, we explore how gender is positioned within climate change debates. We then examine the construction and visibility of gender in the current green economy and decarbonisation goals within the United Kingdom and EU, before reviewing how gender plays out within just transition policies and the green economy. In conclusion, we look to refine how the transition to a green economy could be achieved with a more gender-sensitive approach contributing to the debate on the need for gender mainstreaming of the green economy.

Gender and the climate change debate

The climate crisis is interwoven with gendered, racial and class-based power structures (Olofsson et al., 2016). Women are more vulnerable to climate change: impacts from heatwaves on pregnant women are more severe (WHO Europe, 2023), and often extreme weather hazards lead to greater demand for paid and unpaid care work, disproportionately shouldered by women (European Institute for Gender Equality [EIGE], 2023). Gender-sensitive analyses of the climate crisis often focus on women in the Global South, mainly in studies on climate adaptation, addressing the effects of climate change (MacGregor, 2010). Women in the Global South are more vulnerable to weather-related events, displacements, loss of employment and food scarcity and face higher risks to health and life (Mbuli et al., 2021; Sen Roy, 2018; Stronzake & Wolford, 2016). However, vulnerabilities are not intrinsic to women but rather rooted within the gendered divisions of land, labour and other resources (Pearse, 2017). Insisting on generalised women's vulnerabilities to the outcome of climate change denies women's agency to instigate change (Arora-Jonsson, 2011; Sultana, 2022). Indeed, women, low-income groups and Indigenous communities could be at the forefront of discussions on climate change mitigation and adaptation, offering diverse perspectives, innovations and knowledge of local resources and economies (Djoudi & Brockhaus, 2011; Huyer et al., 2020).

Studies on climate change mitigation within sociology of work have rarely addressed gender issues (Djoudi et al., 2016), with some recent exceptions. Middlemiss et al. (2023) emphasize the problem of a universal policy climate change response, without taking present-day diversity of experience into account. Other studies focus on observed behavioural differences between men and women and why women express greater concern over climate change compared to men (e.g., Ali et al., 2022; Yarosh, 2024; Zafar & Ammara, 2024). Likewise, there is a dominant focus on exploring women's greater engagement in pro-environmental behaviours within the domestic division of labour through ethical consumption and resource efficiency (e.g., Briscoe et al., 2019; Dzialo, 2017; Kennedy & Kmec, 2018). In contrast, men often express greater levels of climate scepticism than women (e.g., McCright & Dunlap, 2011, 2013; Pearse, 2017; Tranter & Booth, 2015), and prioritise technological and economic solutions over environmental justice (e.g. Swim et al., 2018). However, without gender-based perspectives on power relations and knowledge construction, such empirical analyses do little to challenge the gender inequalities that underpin the causes and consequences of the climate crisis (Arora-Jonsson, 2011; Djoudi et al., 2016). Furthermore, without a feminist critique of the underpinning gendered power structures of capitalism that drive climate change, there is the risk that essentialist gender norms are reinforced (MacGregor, 2010; Shaheen Moosa & Tuana, 2014).

Thus, studies in employment relations and sociology of work that deal with climate change would benefit from considering perspectives from feminist ecological economics and other contributions from more radical environmental labour studies as well as applying the conceptual tools of gender mainstreaming. This way, more normative framings of a gender-just green transition could be provided. While arguments for greater gender diversity within climate decision-making functions are made (e.g., Grub & Wentworth, 2023; International Labour Organization [ILO], 2015), women's inclusion in climate change decision making should not be based on normative assumptions of gender: that women provide unique insight as they are assumed to be more nurturing and nature-conscious than men. However, empirical evidence does show a positive link between increased women's representation in decision-making roles and sustainable performance (Bear et al., 2010; Ben-Amar et al., 2017; Özparlak & Gürol, 2023; Post et al., 2011).

Gender and the transition to a green economy

Defining the green economy is complex. A narrow understanding comprises sectors like renewable energy, environmental protection and renaturation, alternative fuel production, energy-efficient construction, low-emission transport, electric vehicles (EVs), recycling and waste management, including economic activities, infrastructure and assets that "allow reduced carbon emissions and pollution, enhanced energy and resource efficiency, and prevention of the loss of biodiversity and ecosystem services" (United Nations Environment Programme, 2018). A wider and more encompassing definition of the green economy is "one that results in improved human well-being and social equity, while significantly reducing environmental scarcities" (United Nations Environment Programme, 2011) in which sectors like care and education could also be perceived as "green". How to achieve a net-zero economy is the subject of extensive debate. We claim that a broader notion of the green economy is necessary. Conventional approaches envision market-based, technology-driven solutions to climate change that reflect a masculine-centric green economy in which already male-concentrated sectors like energy and foundations expand or change (Swim et al., 2018). Radical approaches argue that a net-zero economy is not possible under conditions of economic growth. Such an approach proposes a decoupling of economic growth from resource consumption, envisioning degrowth or post-growth economic alternatives (Georgeson, 2017; Söderholm, 2020), providing for critical infrastructures in transport, housing, or health and proposing the provision of basic services (Büchs 2021). Feminists argue that the green economy requires a shift away from energy-intensive industries and a move towards investment in the decarbonisation of physical infrastructure. In parallel, they demand an expansion of social infrastructure to improve investment in low-carbon, female-concentrated sectors, including social care and early education and childcare, which are urgently in need of greater funding (Cohen & MacGregor, 2020; Diski, 2022). We claim that a broader notion of the green economy is necessary to cater not only for an energy transition but the progressive society that an economic transition should aim for – one in which care will play a vital role.

Furthermore, there has been a political assumption that the transition to a green economy comes at the expense of jobs within high-polluting sectors (Räthzel & Uzzell, 2011). While there will undoubtedly be a decline in high-polluting jobs, there is now a general agreement that a green transition should generate net job growth (Cutter et al., 2022) irrespective of whether the transition to a green economy is narrowly or broadly defined.

In the United Kingdom, there is targeted investment into green/low-carbon industries such as renewable energy, waste management, recycling, agriculture, environmental conservation and sustainable transport (Department for Business, Energy & Industrial Strategy, 2021; Green Jobs Taskforce, 2021) that aims to deliver 480,000 skilled green jobs. A similar scheme in the EU aims to deliver one million skilled green jobs in these industries (Vandeplas et al., 2022). As such, the transition to a green economy is expected to result in a predicted 1.2% increase in green employment by 2030, related to the implementation of the European Green Deal (European Centre for the Development of Vocational Training [CEDEFOP], 2021). In the United Kingdom, there has already been a 3.6% increase in green jobs (Simmonds & Lally, 2024). However, much of this job creation and investment is located in male-dominated occupations.

Channelling investment solely into male-dominated sectors risks deepening established gender inequalities in jobs, skills and training for men and women (Pollin & Callaci, 2018). For example, the United Kingdom's foundation industries – representing cement, metal, glass, chemicals, paper and ceramics – have a highly male-concentrated workforce and are struggling to recruit and retain women and young workers (Enterprise Research Centre [ERC], 2021; TFI Network+, 2022). The foundation industries have signalled the need for greater support to identify and remove any barriers to entry for women into the sector to future-proof the workforce and attract the skills required, such as digitalisation and automation, to capitalise on the green transition (Stanfield, 2023). As shown in Figure 14.1, there has been only modest improvement in terms of women's representation in these

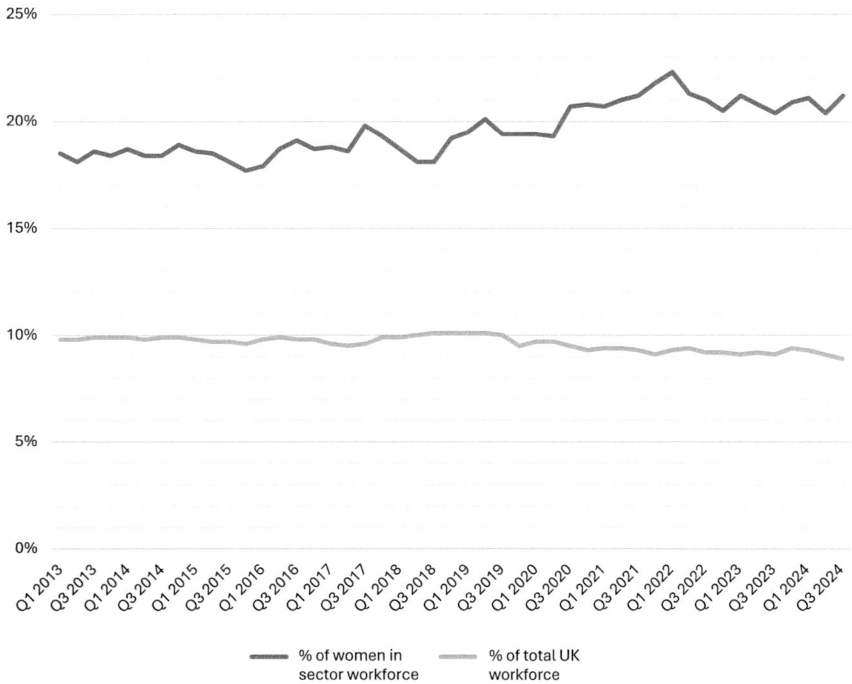

FIGURE 14.1 The Incremental Growth of Women's Representation Coinciding with the Decline of Total Workforce in the Automotive, Fossil Fuels and Foundation Industries in the UK.

Source: Labour Force Survey 2013–2024.

sectors over the last decade. Without a deeper focus on removing barriers to entry and retention of women within male-concentrated sectors, alongside investment in low-carbon mixed or female-concentrated sectors, there is a risk of a green transition lacking the "just" element in terms of gender equity (Samman, 2024). However, within the EU, there are already positive examples, including the disappearance of a gender employment gap in the renewable energy sector in Spain (Rodriguez Acha, 2016).

In the following sections, we further develop our concerns in terms of how a narrow definition of a green economy risks replicating and deepening existing gender inequalities within industrial policy, just transitions and skills.

Public and industrial policy

The United Kingdom has set a goal of reaching net-zero greenhouse gas emissions by 2050 through carbon budgeting, expanding the green energy sector while concurrently reducing reliance on fossil fuel production, promoting electric vehicle use and investing in green technologies such as carbon capture and storage (Burnett et al., 2024; Department for Energy Security and Net Zero, 2023). The EU's Green Deal takes a more comprehensive approach to achieving the target of net-zero emissions by 2050. In addition to expanding the green energy sector, it targets investment in clean transportation, including public transport infrastructure, pursuing a circular economy and addressing key environmental challenges such as pollution and biodiversity loss (European Commission, 2023). Furthermore, the Green Deal provides a more expansive strategy to facilitate a just transition, allocating €55 billion between 2021 and 2027 to support regions and sectors most dependent on fossil fuels and high-polluting industries (European Commission, 2021).

Despite both strategies articulating the need for an inclusive transition, there is little evidence of the mainstreaming of gender in net-zero policies (Carroll, 2022; Rubery et al., 2024). The Gender Equality Index 2023 prepared by the EU's Gender Institute (EIGE, 2023) has presented some information on gender equality related to the need for a socially fair transition of the European Green Deal, in line with the Paris Agreement asking for gender-responsive climate policies (Heinzel, 2024). The EU has also declared its commitment to gender-sensitive climate policies (European Union [EU], 2024) and Germany has recently published an Equality Report just on the socio-ecological transformation (Sachverständigenkommission für den Vierten Gleichstellungsbericht der Bundesregierung, 2025). However, in doing so, it stresses that gender equality is not yet implemented in relevant programmes of the socio-ecological transformation.

As such, all too often, climate change is still framed around potential technical and market-based solutions in which gender inequalities are seen as a parallel challenge rather than interconnected (Allwood, 2020). In the EU, there is recognition that the transition to a green economy has an opportunity to concurrently tackle gender inequalities rather than solely focusing on high-polluting sectors (Casert & Simon, 2023). Yet, the transition is once again presented as an opportunity to challenge gender inequalities rather than a firm commitment to do so (Casert & Simon, 2023).

Critically, climate crisis solutions are still largely framed by advancements in technological innovations, with little consideration as to how this may further reinforce inequalities (Walk, 2024). Critiquing the Green Deal in the EU and the Inflation Reduction Act in the United States, Cohn and Duncanson (2023) argue that the focus on creating green jobs pays little attention to the gender demographics of the groups who will benefit and who will lose jobs. The transition from "dirty" to "clean" energy jobs assumes that existing workers will be reskilled and transitioned over into the green economy, such sectors in which women are underrepresented and face significant barriers to entry (ERC, 2021; Organisation for Economic Co-operation and Development [OECD], 2023). In the United Kingdom, women's representation in the automotive, fossil fuels and foundation industries has increased by just 2.7% since 2013, and women account for only 21.2% of the workforce (Figure 14.1). This coincides with a marginal contraction in these industries aligned with the phasing out of high-polluting sectors (Figure 14.1). In contrast, women represent 77% of employment in health and social work in the United Kingdom (Francis-Devine et al., 2025) and 78% in the EU (Eurostat, 2021) – two sectors omitted from the parameters of the narrow definition of a green economy.

In the United Kingdom, the social care system is under strain through underfunding and privatisation (Goodair et al., 2024; Harding, 2017). As such, investment is required to reconcile the labour shortage of approximately 131,000 vacancies in care in the United Kingdom. Equally, 98% of staff in early years education and care are women, and this sector faces a crisis in recruitment, employment precarity and stagnant low pay that is driving large swathes of staff to consider leaving the sector (Foley & Roberts, 2024; Hardy et al., 2023). Transformative interventions are required not only to reshape this sector but to ensure the predicted increase in vacancies is filled in line with the planned expansion of the sector in the United Kingdom (Hardy et al., 2023; National Audit Office, 2024). Despite being a low-carbon sector that demands investment, social care and early years education are not currently considered "green jobs" and therefore do not benefit from any investment through any just transition funds (Diski, 2022). As such, scarce public funding will most likely benefit men more than women in terms of job creation and skill enhancement.

Furthermore, Cohn and Duncanson (2023) argue that by neglecting the unpaid care work undertaken by women, Green Deals fail to consider how the solutions to the climate crisis risk increasing the burden placed on women. For instance, the advocacy of reduced working hours is often justified by reference to an increase in leisure time and the ability to retrain for new green sectors whilst concurrently reducing carbon emissions (Gunderson, 2018; Kallis et al., 2013; King & van den Bergh, 2017). However, there is a risk that without a change in the gendered division of labour, women will continue to do more unpaid domestic labour related to environmentally conscious changes towards low-carbon domestic practices, e.g., more homemade production, more repairs (Bloodhart & Swim, 2020; Godin & Langlois, 2021; Onaran & Jump, 2022; Pansera et al., 2024).

Finally, how decarbonisation in the Global North may come at the expense of resource exploitation and environmental damage in the Global South demands consideration. As Cohn and Duncanson (2023) argue, the primary focus on technological innovations as a primary solution to the climate crisis requires the ongoing resource extraction of raw materials from countries in the Global South. The decarbonisation of public transport and the expansion of electric vehicles, considered to be at the forefront of the green economy, is dependent on raw materials extracted from the Global South that involve the exploitation of workers, child labour, destruction of land and pollution of natural resources (Boyle, 2023; Bringel & Svampa, 2024; Jarez et al., 2021). Pursuing technological climate crisis solutions risks perpetuating a neo-colonialism in which the Global North attempts to achieve a green transition based on the extraction and commodification of resources in the Global South (Sultana, 2022), reinforcing existing global inequalities (Bringel & Svampa, 2024). The effect again varies according to gender as men dominate and profit from extractivist sectors (Federici, 2004; Stöcker, 2024), while the impact of extractivism, such as water shortage and restricted access to land, increases the level of burden for women (Hailemariam et al., 2021).

Just transition

Just transition is a concept used in the international policy domain to ensure that workers and communities affected by transitions are treated fairly and humanely (Stevis, 2023). Originally, the concept of "just transition" goes back to US labour unions advocating for environmental justice in the 1970s, calling for healthy working conditions in the fossil fuel and chemicals sector (Rector, 2018). More recently, just transition was mentioned in the Paris Agreement (United Nations Framework Convention on Climate Change [UNFCCC, 2015]) and the COP2018 "Solidarity and Just Transition Declaration" (UNFCCC, 2018), documenting the will of governments to enable future employment for workers affected by socio-ecological transformation (Stevis et al., 2020).

However, there is huge variation envisaged in the scope, in the scale (workplace, sectoral, national, global) and in the depth of the proposed green transition, including the extent to which policies intervene in existing structures (Stevis & Felli, 2020). At policy level this translates into a just transition understanding that it is a process that leads to "a future where all jobs are green and decent, greenhouse gas emissions are at net-zero, poverty is eradicated, and communities are thriving and resilient" (Just Transition Centre and B-Team, 2018). This represents a movement towards a more encompassing just transition that comprises "a just transition for all towards an environmentally sustainable economy (…) which needs to be well managed and contribute to the goals of decent work for all, social inclusion, and the eradication of poverty" (ILO, 2016). Comparing "just transition" initiatives across countries, it is evident that most are narrow in scope and depth. They primarily address workers in fossil-fuel sectors, restating the expectations of employment growth due to greener technologies without transforming more comprehensively how production is organised in society with much wider justice implications (Trappmann & Eversberg, 2025).

Actual initiatives are much narrower than the official ILO definition quoted above. A clear gender-sensitive perspective has been introduced in the Spanish case with Just Transition Territorial Agreements, stating "special attention should be paid to the challenges and opportunities for women's employment and well-being in areas where Just Transition Agreements are developed" (Instituto para la transición justa, 2023, p. 66). In practice, this means evaluation criteria for public spending on climate change that prioritise projects that promote women's employment, which contribute to economic revitalisation led by women, or that promote the development of infrastructures reducing the digital divide between women and men or boost women's access to new technologies.

However, spatial and class injustices occur. For example, the reallocation of employment from high-to-low emission firms and sectors (Mohammed, 2021; Niggli & Rutzer, 2021) risks penalising medium-skilled male workers as labour is reallocated to geographical areas with more highly skilled labour (Vandeplas et al., 2022). In the United Kingdom, for example, as demonstrated by Simmonds and Lally (2024), oil and gas jobs are phased out along the east coast of England while most new green jobs emerge in London and the Southeast.

Thus, there is a pressing need to expand the notion of a just transition to go beyond that solely of job protection for those working in high-pollution sectors that are vulnerable to job loss towards one that recognises the effects of transition and also mainstreams gender so that it is visible throughout approaches to transition (Friedrich-Ebert Stiftung, 2020). Gender-just accounts at a policy level range from increasing the proportion of women on the boards of green industries to a fundamental shift away from a growth-based economic system (Walk, 2024) and expanding low-carbon jobs that make up the social infrastructure of production and reproduction (Samman, 2024). Radical understandings of just transition call for abandoning capitalism as the best way of addressing inequalities, including gender inequalities (Lahiri-Dutt, 2023).

Skill requirements for current conceptualisations of a green transition

There is consensus that any green transition requires significant investments in training and skills. Without protective interventions for workers most affected by decarbonisation, labour is likely to shift between geographical areas where a lack of skills provisions restricts access to green jobs for all. Green skills are defined as the knowledge, abilities, values and attitudes needed to live in, develop and support a society that reduces the impact of human activity on the environment (Simmonds & Lally, 2024). Green jobs, as currently defined, typically demand higher-level cognitive and interpersonal skills, requiring higher human capital (Consoli et al., 2016). They can offer highly skilled work with associated benefits through health insurance and strong pension schemes (Broome et al., 2022; Peters, 2013). However, the failure to establish formal skills programmes risks restricting entry into green jobs to those who already hold green skills. For example, Bosch (2023) argues that the failure to provide adequate training on green skills in German car manufacturing restricts workers' ability to capitalise on the transition to a green economy. As the sector undergoes concurrent decarbonisation, existing workers do not hold the required skills, and the sector risks substantial job losses without large levels of investment into training and apprenticeship schemes. Similarly, Snell (2018) argues that failing to retrain and redeploy Australian coal workers into new, green sectors has resulted in employment instability. As coal is phased out, large segments of employment have become vulnerable to job loss, as workers often hold little formal qualification but possess highly specialised, non-transferable skills. In the absence of skills and training regimes for vulnerable workers, Snell (2018) demonstrates how workers move into temporary and part-time positions in alternative fossil fuel industries, facing the same instability rather than transitioning to the green economy.

Moreover, barriers to entry to the green economy are compounded by a lack of focused labour market and sector policies designed to combat the marginalisation of women and young workers (Hofman et al., 2022; Sulich et al., 2020). The cost of [re]training into green sectors, concerns about job security at entry levels, and the perceived pre-existing lack of diversity restrict women's entry into the green and transitioning economies (Godinho, 2022; Stanfield, 2023). Existing inequalities in STEM education hamper women's ability to benefit from the transition to a green economy. Despite women workers being both ready and willing to work in green jobs and sectors, research shows that a lack of clarity about the jobs available in the green economy limits their entry (Simmonds & Lally, 2024; Trappmann et al., 2023). Where women do undertake related apprenticeships, this may not transfer into permanent careers due to a lack of mentoring, limited progression opportunities and highly masculine cultures (Andrew, 2009; Bamberry et al., 2022). Thus, the focus on upskilling and retraining existing workers risks ringfencing jobs within the transitioning sectors to those already within them rather than opening avenues of entry to those looking to enter the green economy. Policy suggestions to counteract this include a gender quota for green sectors (Rodriguez Acha, 2016). More generally, the narrow definition of a green transition fails to integrate the skill needs of other sectors that will be growing in a low-carbon economy, and which are already, often female-dominated sectors like care and education.

Conceptualising a gender inclusive green transition

The climate crisis presents the opportunity to refocus and reframe work and employment in more gender inclusive terms. However, the transition to a green economy to date lacks sufficient gender sensitivity in policy and analysis of investment impacts, which risks reinforcing existing gender inequalities in both the labour market and the domestic division of labour. The imagined solutions to the climate crisis remain rooted within techno-managerial innovation, with the market assumed to solve the challenges faced, balancing economic growth with environmental sustainability. Despite the growing recognition that the climate crisis and the transition to a green economy have intersectional effects, an inclusive transition remains absent. As such, how societies inclusively transition to a green economy demands consideration and greater attention to gender and wider social inequalities and demands a wide range of feminist perspectives on the economy and society.

Perhaps the highest priority for an inclusive transition is the expansion of how we define the green economy to one that includes already low-carbon sectors and jobs. There is a pressing need to recognise and redistribute inequalities in unpaid care and domestic labour, alongside the investment in the social infrastructure, including care, social care and early years education (Cohen & MacGregor, 2020;

Cohn & Duncanson, 2023). Redefining the green economy to include already low-carbon activities such as social care could support investment in female-concentrated sectors (Sofroniou & Anderson, 2020) and improve the quality of social infrastructure for a post-capitalist green economy.

Secondly, there is an urgent need to include feminist voices and perspectives in public policy at the point of inception to ensure gender is visible in debates at every stage of the green transition. We argue that the inclusion of women in the green economy needs to go beyond a focus on increasing women's representation in existing male-dominated sectors and green jobs. Gender mainstreaming (e.g., Mehra & Gupta, 2006; Rubery, 2002) can help visualise the gendered impact of the green transition through policy formulation and economic strategy. We must recognise the potential constraints on gender mainstreaming, including backlash related to the perceived disruption to existing structures, a lack of political will and pre-existing institutional resistance (Fraser, 2013; Vida, 2021; Walby, 2011). However, the incremental increase of women within these spaces could help to embed gender equality in the green transition (Allwood, 2020).

Finally, we have demonstrated a pressing need for a greater interrogation of gender dynamics within climate change. For many feminists, the economy should be organised to serve the purpose of care for both humans and ecosystems. More than valuing caring labour, this perspective takes care as a central ethic; it recognises that care is at the heart of what we all need to survive and thrive, be it for the planet or for humans (Cohn & Duncanson, 2023). A feminist intersectional analysis of the climate crisis helps unveil inequalities in current public policy strategies to meet skill needs and ensure any low-carbon transition can happen in a just and fair way. In doing so, we can expand the conceptualisation of a green economy to one that is gender-inclusive and transformative.

Note

1 The authors would like to thank Jo Cutter and Dennis Eversberg and the editors for helpful comments on earlier drafts.

References

Ali, Q., Parveen, S., Yaacob, H., Rani, A., & Zaini, Z. (2022). Environmental beliefs and the adoption of circular economy among bank managers: Do gender, age, and knowledge act as moderators? *Journal of Cleaner Production*, *361*, 132276. https://doi.org/10.1016/j.jclepro.2022.132276

Allwood, G. (2020). Mainstreaming gender and climate change to achieve a just transition to a climate-neutral Europe. *Journal of Common Market Studies*, *58*(S1), 173–186. https://doi.org/10.1111/jcms.13082

Andrew, A. (2009). Challenging boundaries to "employability": Women apprentices in a non-traditional occupation. *Social Policy and Society*, *8*(3), 347–359. https://doi.org/10.1017/S1474746409004898

Arora-Jonsson, S. (2011). Virtue and vulnerability: Discourses on women, gender, and climate change. *Global Environmental Change*, *21*(2), 744–751. https://doi.org/10.1016/j.gloenvcha.2011.01.005

Bamberry, L., Bridges, D., Wulff, E., & Krivokapic-Skoko, B. (2022). Inequality regimes in male-dominated trades: What role do apprenticeship intermediaries (GTOs) play? *The Economic and Labour Relations Review*, *33*(3), 547–565. https://doi.org/10.1177/10353046221096270

Barca, S. (2020). *Forces of reproduction*. Cambridge University Press.

Bear, S., Rahman, N., & Post, C. (2010). The impact of board diversity and gender composition on corporate social responsibility and firm reputation. *Journal of Business Ethics*, *97*(2), 207–221. https://doi.org/10.1007/s10551-010-0505-2

Ben-Amar, W., Chang, M., & McIlkenny, P. (2017). Board gender diversity and corporate responses to sustainable initiatives: Evidence from the Carbon Disclosure Project. *Journal of Business Ethics*, *142*(2), 369–383. https://doi.org/10.1007/s10551-015-2759-1

Bloodhart, B., & Swim, J. (2020). Sustainability and consumption: What's gender got to do with it? *Journal of Social Issues, 76*(1), 101–113. https://doi.org/10.1111/josi.12370

Bosch, G. (2023). Employment policy for a just transition: The example of Germany. *Transfer: European Review of Labour and Research*, *29*(3), 405–421. https://doi.org/10.1177/10242589231188680

Boyle, L. (2023, February 23). "Here it is better not to be born": Cobalt mining for Big Tech is driving child labor, deaths in the Congo. *The Independent*. https://www.independent.co.uk/climate-change/news/phone-electric-vehicle-congo-cobalt-mine-b2277665.html

Bringel, B., & Svampa, M. (2024). Energy transition and the new shape of green colonialism: The emergence of decarbonisation consensus. In A. Mangelli, F. Maia, & P. Martins (Eds.), *Dependency theories in Latin America: An intellectual reconstruction* (1st ed., pp. 242–258). Routledge.

Briscoe, M., Givens, J., Hazboun, S., & Krannich, R. (2019). At home, in public, and in between: Gender differences in public, private and transportation pro-environmental behaviours in the US intermountain west. *Environmental Sociology*, *5*(4), 374–392. https://doi.org/10.1080/23251042.2019.1628333

Broome, M., Cellini, S., Henehan, K., McCurdy, C., Riom, C., Valero, A., & Ventura, G. (2022). *Net zero jobs: The impact of the transition to net zero on the UK labour market*. The Resolution Foundation.

Büchs, M. (2021). Sustainable welfare: How do universal basic income and universal basic services compare? *Ecological Economics*, *189*, 107152. https://doi.org/10.1016/j.ecolecon.2021.107152

Burnett, N., Hinson, S., & Stewart, I. (2024). *The UK's plans and progress to reach net zero by 2050*. House of Commons Library. https://researchbriefings.files.parliament.uk/documents/CBP-9888/CBP-9888.pdf

Carroll, P. (2022). Gender mainstreaming and the European Union energy transition. *Energies*, *15*(21), 8087. https://doi.org/10.3390/en15218087

Casert, C., & Simon, J. (2023). *Considering gender in regional transformations: A toolkit for just transition regions*. European Commission. https://ec.europa.eu/regional_policy/sources/funding/just-transition-fund/toolkit-considering%20gender%20in%20regional%20transformations.pdf

Cohen, M., & Macgregor, S. (2020). *Towards a feminist green new deal for the UK*. Women's Budget Group. https://wbg.org.uk/wp-content/uploads/2020/05/Feminist-Green-New-Deal.pdf

Cohn, C., & Duncanson, C. (2023). Critical feminist engagements with green new deals. *Feminist Economics*, *29*(3), 15–39. https://doi.org/10.1080/13545701.2023.2184844

Consoli, D., Marin, G., Marzucchi, S., & Vona, F. (2016). Do green jobs differ from non-green jobs in terms of skills and human capital? *Research Policy*, *45*(5), 1046–1060. https://doi.org/10.1016/j.respol.2016.02.007

Cutter, J., Trappmann, V., & Krause, D. (2022). "Just transition": The tension between work, employment, net zero and climate change. In S. Russell & R. Padfield (Eds.), *A research agenda for sustainability and business* (pp. 69–79). Edward Elgar Publishing Ltd.

Department for Business, Energy & Industrial Strategy. (2021). *Net zero strategy: Build back greener* [White Paper]. HM Government. https://assets.publishing.service.gov.uk/media/6194dfa4d3bf7f0555071b1b/net-zero-strategy-beis.pdf

Department for Energy Security and Net Zero. (2023). *Powering up Britain: Net zero growth plan* [White Paper]. HM Government. https://www.gov.uk/government/publications/powering-up-britain/powering-up-britain-net-zero-growth-plan#reducing-emissions-across-the-economy

Diski, R. (2022). *A green and caring economy: Final report.* Women's Budget Group. https://wbg.org.uk/wp-content/uploads/2022/11/A-Green-and-Caring-Economy-Report-FINAL.pdf

Djoudi, H., & Brockhaus, M. (2011). Is adaptation to climate change gender neutral? Lessons from communities dependent on livestock and forests in northern Mali. *The International Forestry Review*, *13*(2), 123–135. https://www.jstor.org/stable/24310663

Djoudi, H., Locatelli, B., Vaast, C., Asher, K., Brockhaus, M., & Basnett Sijipati, B. (2016). Beyond dichotomies: Gender and intersecting inequalities in climate change studies. *Ambio*, *45*(Suppl. 3), S248–S262. https://doi.org/10.1007/s13280-016-0825-2

Dzialo, L. (2017). The feminization of environmental responsibility. *Environmental Sociology*, *3*(4), 427–437. https://doi.org/10.1080/23251042.2017.1327924

Enterprise Research Centre. (2021). *Equality, diversity, and inclusion in UK foundation industries.* Enterprise Research Centre. https://www.enterpriseresearch.ac.uk/wp-content/uploads/2021/06/ERC-Report-EDI-in-UK-Foundation-Industries.pdf

European Centre for the Development of Vocational Training [CEDEFOP]. (2021). *The green employment and skills transformation: Insights from a European Green Deal skills forecast scenario.* European Centre for the Development of Vocational Training. https://www.cedefop.europa.eu/files/4206_en.pdf

European Commission. (2021). *The just transition mechanism: Making sure no one is left behind* [White Paper]. European Commission. https://commission.europa.eu/strategy-and-policy/priorities-2019-2024/european-green-deal/finance-and-green-deal/just-transition-mechanism_en#:~:text=Who%20will%20benefit?-,Introduction,chance%20to%20become%20a%20reality

European Commission. (2023). *A green deal industrial plan for the net-zero age* [White Paper]. European Commission. https://eur-lex.europa.eu/legal-content/EN/TXT/PDF/?uri=CELEX:52023DC0062

European Institute for Gender Equality. (2023). *Gender equality index 2023: Green deal in the European Union.* Publications Office of the European Union. https://eige.europa.eu/gender-equality-index/thematic-focus/green-deal

European Union. (2024). *Statement at COP29 on the importance of an ambitious outcome on gender and climate change.* https://climate.ec.europa.eu/document/download/d3da8b83-0f61-4f2e-9225-df164b306f18_en?filename=Common%20Statement%20at%20COP29%20on%20Gender%20and%20Climate%20Change_final%20version.pdf

Eurostat. (2021). *Majority of health jobs held by women*. Eurostat. https://ec.europa.eu/eurostat/web/products-eurostat-news/-/edn-20210308-1#:~:text=In%209%20EU%20Member%20States,share:%20Luxembourg%20(43%25).&text=In%20Q3%20 2020%2C%20the%20vast,20%25)%20in%20the%20Netherlands

Federici, S. (2004). Women, land-struggles and globalization: An international perspective. *Journal of Asian and African Studies*, *39*(1–2), 47–62.

Foley, N., & Roberts, N. (2024). *Childcare workforce in England* (Research Briefing No. 09948). House of Commons Library. https://researchbriefings.files.parliament.uk/documents/CBP-9948/CBP-9948.pdf

Francis-Devine, B., Zaidi, K., & Murray, A. (2025). *Women and the UK economy* (Research Briefing No. 6838). House of Commons Library. https://researchbriefings.files.parliament.uk/documents/SN06838/SN06838.pdf

Fraser, N. (2013). *Feminism, capitalism and the cunning of history*. https://shs.hal.science/halshs-00725055v1

Friedrich-Ebert-Stiftung, & Social Europe (Eds.). (2020). *Just transition: A social route to sustainability* (Social Europe Dossier). Social Europe.

Georgeson, L., Maslin, M., & Poessinouw, M. (2017). The global green economy: A review of concepts, definitions, measurement methodologies and their interactions. *Geography and Environment*, *4*(1), e00036. https://doi.org/10.1002/geo2.36

Godin, L., & Langlois, J. (2021). Care, gender and change in the study of sustainable consumption: A critical review of the literature. *Frontiers in Sustainability*, *2*, 725753. https://doi.org/10.3389/frsus.2021.725753

Godinho, C. (2022). What do we know about the employment impacts of climate policies? A review of the ex post literature. *WIREs Climate Change*, *13*(6), e794. https://doi.org/10.1002/wcc.794

Goodair, B., McManus, A., Esposti, M. D., & Back-Mortensen, A. (2024). How outsourcing has contributed to England's social care crisis. *British Medical Journal*, *387*, e080380. https://doi.org/10.1136/bmj-2024-080380

Green Jobs Taskforce. (2021). *Green Jobs Taskforce: Report to government, industry and the skills sector* [White Paper]. Green Jobs Taskforce. https://assets.publishing.service.gov.uk/media/650466aadec5be000dc35f85/green-jobs-taskforce-report-2021.pdf

Grub, H., & Wentworth, J. (2023). *What is a just transition for environmental targets?* Parliamentary Office of Science and Technology. https://researchbriefings.files.parliament.uk/documents/POST-PN-0706/POST-PN-0706.pdf#

Gunderson, R. (2018). Work time reductions and economic democracy as climate change mitigation strategies: Or why the climate needs a renewed labor movement. *Journal of Environmental Studies and Sciences*, *9*, 35–44. https://doi.org/10.1007/s13412-018-0507-4

Hailemariam, A., Kalsi, J., & Mavisakalyn, A. (2021). Climate change and gender equality. In R. Baikady, S. M. Sajid, J. Przeperski, V. Nadesan, M. R. Islam, & J. Gao (Eds.), *The Palgrave handbook of global social problems* (pp. 1–15). Springer International Publishing. https://doi.org/10.1007/978-3-319-90377-4_84-1

Harding, R. (2017). A relational (re)view of the UK's social care crisis. *Palgrave Communications*, *3*, 17096. https://doi.org/10.1057/palcomms.2017.96

Hardy, K., Stephens, L., Tomlinson, J., Whittaker, X., Norman, H., & Robyn, M. (2023). *Retention and return: Delivering the expansion of early years entitlement in England*. Early Education and Childcare Coalition. https://static1.squarespace.com/static/646ca30371a2ef6a657e9309/t/65482050ded6710668b8b62a/1699225681784/Retention+and+Return.pdf

Heinzel, C. (2024, February 15). Feministische Ansätze in der Klimarahmenkonvention und Biodiversitätskonvention. *Recht Nachhaltig Denken, Junges Forum Umweltrecht.*

Hofman, J., Bruckmayer, M., Feyerabend, K., Larmour, D., Reed, M., & Lymperis, L. (2022). *Green jobs and skills development for disadvantaged groups.* RAND Europe. https://www.rand.org/pubs/research_reports/RRA1603-1.html

Huyer, S., Acosta, M., Gumucio, T., & Ilham, I. J. (2020). Can we turn the tide? Confronting gender inequality in climate policy. *Gender & Development, 28*(3), 571–591. https://doi.org/10.1080/13552074.2020.1836817

Instituto para la Transición Justa. (2023). *Spain: 4 years towards a just energy transition.* https://www.transicionjusta.gob.es/Documents/Publicaciones%20ES%20y%20EN/Spain_4%20years%20towards%20a%20just%20energy%20transition.pdf

International Labour Organization. (2015). *Gender equality and green jobs* [Policy Brief]. Author. https://www.ilo.org/publications/gender-equality-and-green-jobs

International Labour Organization. (2016). *Guidelines for a just transition towards environmentally sustainable economies and societies for all.* Author. https://www.ilo.org/sites/default/files/wcmsp5/groups/public/%40ed_emp/%40emp_ent/documents/publication/wcms_432859.pdf

Irving, S., & Helin, J. (2018). A world for sale? An ecofeminist reading of sustainable development discourse. *Gender, Work & Organization, 25*(3), 264–278. https://doi.org/10.1111/gwao.12196

Jarez, B., Garcés, I., & Torres, R. (2021). Lithium extractivism and water injustices in the Salar de Atacama, Chile: The colonial shadow of green electromobility. *Political Geography, 87*, 102382. https://doi.org/10.1016/j.polgeo.2021.102382

Just Transition Centre, & B Team. (2018). *Just transition: A business guide from the Just Transition Centre and the B Team.* https://the-bteam.files.svdcdn.com/production/assets/reports/Just-Transition-A-Business-Guide.pdf

Kallis, G., Kalush, M., O'Flynn, H., Rossiter, J., & Ashford, N. (2013). "Friday off": Reduced working hours in Europe. *Sustainability, 5*(4), 1545–1567. https://doi.org/10.3390/su5041545

Kennedy, E., & Kmec, J. (2018). Reinterpreting the gender gap in household pro-environmental behaviour. *Environmental Sociology, 4*(3), 299–310. https://doi.org/10.1080/23251042.2018.1436891

King, L., & van den Bergh, J. (2017). Worktime reduction as a solution to climate change: Five scenarios compared for the UK. *Ecological Economics, 132*, 124–134. https://doi.org/10.1016/j.ecolecon.2016.10.011

Lahiri-Dutt, K. (2023). Framing a gender transformative post-coal future for just transition: A feminist manifesto. *Energy Research & Social Science, 100*, 103097. https://doi.org/10.1016/j.erss.2023.103097

MacGregor, S. (2009). A stranger silence still: The need for feminist social research on climate change. *The Sociological Review, 57*(2), 124–140. https://doi.org/10.1111/j.1467-954X.2010.01889.x

MacGregor, S. (2010). "Gender and climate change": From impacts to discourses. *Journal of the Indian Ocean Region, 6*(2), 223–238. https://doi.org/10.1080/19480881.2010.536669

Mbuli, C., Fonjong, L., & Fletcher, A. (2021). Climate change and small farmers' vulnerability to food insecurity in Cameroon. *Sustainability, 13*(3), 1523. https://doi.org/10.3390/su13031523

McCright, A., & Dunlap, R. (2011). Cool dudes: The denial of climate change among conservative white males in the United States. *Global Environmental Change, 21*(4), 1163–1172. https://doi.org/10.1016/j.gloenvcha.2011.06.003

McCright, A., & Dunlap, R. (2013). Bringing ideology in: The conservative white male effect on worry about environmental problems in the USA. *Journal of Risk Research*, *16*(2), 211–226. https://doi.org/10.1080/13669877.2012.726242

Mehra, R., & Gupta, G. (2006). *Gender mainstreaming: Making it happen*. International Centre for Research on Women. https://www.icrw.org/wp-content/uploads/2016/10/Gender-Mainstreaming-Making-It-Happen.pdf

Middlemiss, L., Snell, E., Chzhen, A., Owen, A., Kennedy, K., Theminimulle, S., & Carregha, T. (2023). Conceptualising socially inclusive environmental policy: A just transition to net zero. *Social Policy and Society*, *22*(4), 763–783. https://doi.org/10.1017/S1474746423000180

Mohammed, A. (2021). *Environmental effects of environmental policies: Evidence from firm-level data* (IMF Working Papers 2021/140). International Monetary Fund. https://www.imf.org/en/Publications/WP/Issues/2021/05/14/Employment-Effects-of-Environmental-Policies-Evidence-From-Firm-Level-Data-50236

National Audit Office. (2024). *Future rollout of new early years entitlements faces challenges* [Press release]. National Audit Office. https://www.nao.org.uk/press-releases/future-rollout-of-new-early-years-entitlements-faces-challenges/

Niggli, M., & Rutzer, C. (2021). *Environmental policy and heterogeneous labor market effects: Evidence from Europe* (WWZ Working Paper 2020/09). University of Basel. https://www.econstor.eu/bitstream/10419/240418/1/2020-09.pdf

Olofsson, A., Öhman, S., & Nygren, K. (2016). An intersectional risk approach for environmental sociology. *Environmental Sociology*, *2*(3), 346–354. https://doi.org/10.1080/23251042.2016.1246086

Onaran, Ö., & Jump, R. (2022). *A shorter working week as part of a green caring economy* [Policy brief]. Women's Budget Group. https://wbg.org.uk/wp-content/uploads/2022/02/Shorter-Working-Week-Report.pdf

Organisation for Economic Co-operation and Development. (2023). *Job creation and local economic development 2023: Bridging the great green divide* [White Paper]. OECD Publishing. https://www.oecd.org/content/dam/oecd/en/publications/reports/2023/03/job-creation-and-local-economic-development-2023_ab3b49a8/21db61c1-en.pdf

Özparlak, G., & Gürol, B. (2023). The role of diversity on the environmental performance and transparency. *Environment, Development and Sustainability*, *27*, 483–507. https://doi.org/10.1007/s10668-023-04193-x

Pansera, M., Barca, S., Martinez Alvarez, B., Leonardi, E., D'Alisa, G., Meira, T., & Guillibert, P. (2024). Toward a just circular economy: Conceptualizing environmental labor and gender justice in circularity studies. *Sustainability: Science, Practice and Policy*, *20*(1), 2338592. https://doi.org/10.1080/15487733.2024.2338592

Pearse, R. (2017). Gender and climate change. *WIREs Climate Change*, *8*(2), e451. https://doi.org/10.1002/wcc.451

Peters, D. (2013). Understanding green occupations from a task-based approach. *Applied Economic Perspectives and Policy*, *38*(2), 238–264. https://doi.org/10.1093/aepp/ppt026

Pollin, R., & Callaci, B. (2018). The economics of just transition: A framework for supporting fossil fuel-dependent workers and communities in the United States. *Labor Studies Journal*, *44*(2), 93–138. https://doi.org/10.1177/0160449X18787051

Post, C., Rahman, N., & Rubow, J. (2011). Green governance: Board of directors' composition and environmental corporate social responsibility. *Business and Society*, *50*(1), 189–223. https://doi.org/10.1177/0007650310394642

Räthzel, N., & Uzzell, D. (2011). Trade unions and climate change: The jobs versus environment dilemma. *Global Environmental Change*, *21*(4), 1215–1233. https://doi.org/10.1016/j.gloenvcha.2011.07.010

Rector, J. 2018. The spirit of Black Lake: Full employment, civil rights, and the forgotten early history of environmental justice. *Modern American History*, *1*(1), 45–66. https://doi.org/10.1017/mah.2017.18

Rodriguez Acha, M. (2016). *Gender equality & just transition* (WEDO Discussion Paper). https://wedo.org/wp-content/uploads/2016/08/gjtransition.pdf

Rubery, J. (2002). Gender mainstreaming and gender equality in the EU: The impact of the EU employment strategy. *Industrial Relations Journal*, *33*(5), 500–522. https://doi.org/10.1111/1468-2338.00250

Rubery, J., Insarauto, V., & Sánchez-Mira, N. (2024). *Gender equality in the EU: Why we need a renewed commitment to gender mainstreaming* (ETUI Policy Brief: 2024.08). European Trade Union Institute. https://doi.org/10.2139/ssrn.5026011

Sachverständigenkommission für den Vierten Gleichstellungsbericht der Bundesregierung. (2025). *Gleichstellung in der sozial-ökologischen Transformation. Gutachten für den Vierten* Gleichstellungs-bericht *der Bundesregierung.* Bundesstiftung Gleichstellung. https://www.bmfsfj.de/resource/blob/257402/3138aa35a1d31fc369771b2a376200f0/vierter-gleichstellungsbericht-data.pdf

Samman, E. (2024). *Women and just transition: Steps trade unions can take to promote gender justice*. The Norwegian Confederation of Trade Unions. https://www.lo.no/globalassets/internasjonalt/women-and-just-transition-2024-04-03.pdf

Sen Roy, S. (2018). *Linking gender to climate change impacts in the global south.* Springer Climate.

Shaheen Moosa, C., & Tuana, N. (2014). Mapping a research agenda concerning gender and climate change: A review of the literature. *Hypatia*, *29*(3), 677–694. https://doi.org/10.1111/hypa.12085

Simmonds, P., & Lally, C. (2024). *Green skills in education and employment* [UK Parliament Post No. 711]. House of Commons Library. https://researchbriefings.files.parliament.uk/documents/POST-PN-0711/POST-PN-0711.pdf

Snell, D. (2018). "Just transition"? Conceptual challenges meet stark reality in a 'transitioning' coal region in Australia. *Globalizations*, *15*(4), 550–564. https://doi.org/10.1080/14747731.2018.1454679

Söderholm, P. (2020). The green economy transition: The challenges for technological change for sustainability. *Sustainable Earth*, *3*, 6. https://doi.org/10.1186/s42055-020-00029-y

Sofroniou, N., & Anderson, P. (2020). The green factor: Unpacking green job growth. *International Labour Review*, *160*(1), 21–41. https://doi.org/10.1111/ilr.12176

Stanfield, J. (2023). *State of equality, diversity, and inclusion in the UK foundation industries 2022.* Transfire. https://transfire-hub.org/wp-content/uploads/2023/02/State-of-Equity-Diversity-and-Inclusion-in-the-UK-Foundation-Industries-2022.pdf

Stevis, D. (2023). *Just transitions: Promise and contestation.* Cambridge University Press.

Stevis, D., Edouard, M., & Dunja, K. (2020). Introduction: The genealogy and contemporary politics of just transitions. In E. Morena, D. Krause, & D. Stevis (Eds.), *Just transitions: Social justice in the shift to a low-carbon world* (pp. 1–31). Pluto Press.

Stevis, D., & Felli, R. (2020). Planetary just transition? How inclusive and how just? *Earth System Governance*, *6*, 100065. https://doi.org/10.1016/j.esg.2020.100065

Stöcker, C. (2024). *Männer, die die Welt verbrennen. Der entscheidende Kampf um die Zukunft der Menschheit* (2. Auflage). Ullstein.

Stronzake, J., & Wolford, W. (2016, Spring). Brazil's landless workers rise up. *Dissent Magazine*. https://dissentmagazine.org/article/brazils-landless-workers-rise-mst-land-occupation/

Sulich, A., Rutkoska, M., & Popławski, Ł. (2020). Green jobs, definitional issues, and the employment of young people: An analysis of three European Union countries. *Journal of Environmental Management, 262*, 119314. https://doi.org/10.1016/j.jenvman.2020.110314

Sultana, F. (2022). Critical climate justice. *The Geographical Journal*, *188*(1), 118–124. https://doi.org/10.1111/geoj.12417

Swim, J., Vescio, T., Dahl, K., & Zawadzki, S. (2018). Gendered discourse about climate change policies. *Global Environmental Change*, *48*, 216–225. https://doi.org/10.1016/j.gloenvcha.2017.12.005

TFI Network+. (2022). *Equality, diversity, and inclusion in the foundation industries: Workshop report March 2022*. TFI Network+. https://tfinetworkplus.org/wp-content/uploads/2022/06/EDI-workshop-final-report-1.pdf

Tranter, B., & Booth, K. (2015). Scepticism in a changing climate: A cross-national study. *Global Environmental Change, 33*, 154–164. https://doi.org/10.1111/irj.12467

Trappmann, V., & Eversberg, D. (2025). *Union and worker initiatives for fair climate policies*. Bristol University Press. (In press)

Trappmann, V., Cutter, J., Schulz, F., Daly, J., & Balderson, U. (2023). *Climate change, green economy, and work: The perception of workers in Germany and the UK*. University of Leeds.

United Nations Environment Programme. (2011). *Towards a green economy: Pathways to sustainable development and poverty eradication*. United Nations.

United Nations Environment Programme. (2018). *Green economy*. United Nations Environment Programme. https://www.unep.org/regions/asia-and-pacific/regional-initiatives/supporting-resource-efficiency/green-economy

United Nations Framework Convention on Climate Change. (2015). *Paris Agreement*. United Nations. https://unfccc.int/sites/default/files/english_paris_agreement.pdf

United Nations Framework Convention on Climate Change. (2018). *Solidarity and just transition Silesia declaration*. United Nations.

Vandeplas, A., Vanyolos, I., Vigani, M., & Vogel, L. (2022). *The possible implications of the green transition for the EU labour market* (European Commission Discussion Paper No. 176). European Commission.

Vida, B. (2021). Policy framing and resistance: Gender mainstreaming in Horizon 2020. *European Journal of Women's Studies*, *28*(1), 26–41. https://doi.org/10.1177/1350506820935495

Walby, S. (2011). *The future of feminism*. Polity Press.

Walk, P. (2024). From parity to degrowth: Unpacking narratives of a gender just transition. *Energy Research & Social Science*, *112*, 103513. https://doi.org/10.1016/j.erss.2024.103513

Waring, M. (1999). *Counting for nothing: What men value and what women are worth*. University of Toronto Press.

WHO Europe. (2023). *Declaration of the Seventh Ministerial Conference on Environment and Health*. World Health Organization Regional Office for Europe. https://www.who.int/europe/publications/i/item/EURO-Budapest2023-6

Yarosh, J. (2024). Does racial and gender bias shape perception? Examining how others' pro-environmental behaviours are viewed. *Environmental Sociology*, *10*(4), 1–11. https://doi.org/10.1080/23251042.2024.2361199

Zafar, S., & Ammara, S. (2024). Variation in climate change views across Europe: An empirical analysis. *Journal of Cleaner Production*, *442*, 141157. https://doi.org/10.1016/j.jclepro.2024.141157

Conclusions

15

THE FUTURE OF GENDER EQUALITY IN TURBULENT TIMES

Why we need a gender lens on polycrisis

Núria Sánchez-Mira, Jill Rubery and Valeria Insarauto

When we began this book project in mid-2022, the world was still grappling with the aftermath of the Covid-19 pandemic and the recent outbreak of the war in Ukraine. In that context, it seemed both relevant and necessary to offer a long-term examination of how a succession of crises – starting with the 2008 financial and austerity crisis and extending to more recent disruptions – had intersected with trends towards gender equality in both waged and unwaged work, following the approach of earlier related volumes (Rubery, 1988; Karamessini & Rubery, 2014). However, as the introductory chapter already explains (Rubery et al., 2026), we soon recognised the need to expand this agenda. The cost-of-living crisis was unfolding rapidly on the back of the Covid-19 pandemic and the war in Ukraine, while debates on a global state of "permacrisis" (Brown et al., 2023) and "polycrisis" (Lawrence et al., 2024, Parnell et al., 2024) were gaining traction in political and academic circles. Moreover, the turbulence triggered by shocks – whether in the financial system, health-related or geopolitical – was clearly occurring alongside and in interaction with other concomitant transformations, such as the digital and green transitions, that were adding pressures on the employment system. These concerns led us to broaden the initial scope of the volume and bring these other processes of change and transformation into the picture.

The journey of bringing this project to completion has not only broadened the scope of the volume but, more fundamentally, prompted deeper reflection on how we conceptualise the different processes under study and their interconnections from a gender perspective. In this concluding chapter, we build on the analytical and empirical insights of the chapters in the volume to develop a broader discussion that engages with the mainstream debate on polycrisis in a timely manner. Our contribution is twofold.

DOI: 10.4324/9781003528210-20

First, we argue that a gender perspective needs to be conceptually woven into this debate, where it has so far been virtually absent. Accordingly, any analysis of polycrisis should incorporate the tensions at the boundaries of production and social reproduction as a core component to capture the dynamics of current turbulence. Several chapters point to the centrality of this issue (Baxter et al., 2026; Karamessini, 2026; Larsen et al., 2026; Lopezlira & Hunter, 2026; Marx et al., 2026; Plomien & Schwartz, 2026) and illustrate how it intersects with the digital and green transformations (Daly et al., 2026; Piasna, 2026; Rani et al., 2026), enriching the discussion with diverse perspectives and focuses.

Second, the contributions in this volume empirically showcase the importance of considering how gender intersects with other axes of social stratification. Authors were encouraged to adopt an intersectionally aware perspective to trace the impacts of the processes studied across gender groups. A number of chapters (Bashevska & Dotti Sani, 2026; Figueiredo & López-Andreu, 2026; Steinmetz & Guarnerio, 2026; Torres & Warren, 2026) show that gendered outcomes are further stratified along different social divides, such as education, social class and migration status. These findings reinforce the argument that, to capture the full picture of polycrisis, it is essential to analyse not only gender differences but also who within each gender benefits or loses under turbulence. Relatedly, this concluding chapter also addresses differences in experiences of crises within genders in light of spatial variations. Although most contributions focus on the Global North, we draw on their insights to discuss how the processes under study produce unequal distributions of risks between the Global North and the Global South and their interconnections – as illustrated, for example, in Rani et al.'s (2026) chapter on platform work in the Global South.

What follows elaborates on these two contributions. We begin by outlining the theoretical reasons for introducing the gender perspective into the polycrisis debate and argue why the crisis of social reproduction should be considered an essential component of turbulence. We then discuss how the acceleration and layering of crises are linked to the systematic exposure of disadvantaged groups, while acknowledging that the political discussion of global polycrisis remains heavily influenced by views stemming from the Global North. Next, we review the empirical contributions of the different chapters in the volume against these theoretical framings, focusing on how they inform the polycrisis debate and underscore the centrality of the social reproduction crisis. These chapters also reveal how gendered outcomes intersect with other forms of social and spatial inequality, feeding into intersectional debates and opening pathways toward more inclusive and global understandings of turbulence. At the same time, the insights from these contributions are woven into the broader evidence from the literature in the field, setting the stage for the concluding discussion on what these uncertain times might herald for gender inequality in the future.

Gendering the polycrisis

The terms "permacrisis" and "polycrisis", now widely used in academic and political debates, convey that it is no longer possible to speak of periods of crisis followed by phases of stability. Describing the current period as turbulent denotes the experience of multiple, simultaneous crises that may be interrelated – a reality better captured by the term "polycrisis" than "permacrisis", since the latter overlooks the interlocked nature of these processes (Parnell et al., 2024). The "polycrisis" perspective emphasizes that crises unfold in a cumulative manner, interacting, exacerbating, accelerating and reshaping one another, and therefore cannot be analysed in isolation (Lawrence et al., 2022; Parnell et al., 2024). Crises may combine to worsen conditions, as seen when the Covid-19 pandemic, the war in Ukraine and Brexit together drove the United Kingdom's cost-of-living crisis. Responses to one crisis may also generate adverse effects elsewhere – for example, efforts to alleviate energy poverty by returning to fuel fossils (Brown et al., 2023). Conversely, synergies are possible, as illustrated by measures addressing the care crisis that simultaneously support a low-carbon economy (Jones et al., 2024).

Scholars engaged in this debate have suggested that the stability attributed to previous periods may have been overstated. Yet, there is broad agreement that what makes the present epoch distinctive is the speed and scope of the multiple challenges we face (Henig & Knight, 2023). In a world that is more interconnected than in previous intersecting crises (Lawrence et al., 2024), what appears unprecedented is the accelerating pace, the density of the events and the thickening of the layering of crises underway (Brown et al., 2023; Henig & Knight, 2023). Together, these dynamics warrant the use of the term "polycrisis" for the current period. From a long-term perspective, today's turbulence can also be seen as an entanglement of crises spiralling from the 2008 financial crash and, within a longer-term outlook, resulting from the post–Second World War acceleration in socioeconomic and earth system trends, exacerbated by neoliberal globalisation (Henig & Knight, 2023). The temporal frame is even more extended for other current issues, namely the environmental crisis. This prolonged state of turbulence questions the usefulness of the very definition of crises as unexpected ruptures of the normal progression of things and invites us to think of current challenges as long-term, chronic or systemic features of the economic and social system (Henig & Knight, 2023; Mrozowicki et al., 2025).

Current turbulence can also be understood as an inherent feature of capitalism, intensified in its neoliberal form, which was partially contained by the relative stability of the political world order under American hegemony during the post-Cold War period. Although that dominance is increasingly contested, it is still being reinforced in some areas – for instance, through reliance on US-owned technology firms. Yet China's growing technological capacity is poised to challenge the United States' power even in this domain. Overall, multiple and diverse sources of "chronic" crises are generating turbulence across economic, social and political systems, as a realignment of the global political and economic order takes place.

The lively theoretical discussions around polycrisis have, however, been strikingly gender-blind. Focused on social rupture and unexpected events, scholarly and political attention has centred on finance, energy, war, migration and political crises. Even apparent efforts to map all sources of crises and interactions across economic, social and political domains (Tooze, 2021; Williams & Erickson, 2024) omit the crucial site for analysing the gendered impacts of polycrisis: the intersection between the spheres of production and social reproduction. In this way, the debate on polycrisis has been disconnected from a rich body of feminist scholarship that has, for over a decade, highlighted the existence of a "crisis of care" (Dowling, 2021; Hess, 2013). Earlier research already showed how households and especially women had become increasingly pressed for time, due to longer work hours and stagnant gendered labour divisions (Schor, 1991). Concepts such as the "time bind" (Hochschild, 1997) or "time squeeze" (Clarkberg & Moen, 2001) capture the consequences of insufficient changes in care arrangements to support women's growing labour market participation. This mismatch strains social capacities to raise children, care for dependants and sustain households and broader communities. The fragility of care systems was further compounded by austerity and privatisation (Dowling, 2021) and intensified by the Covid-19 pandemic (Armstrong et al., 2024).

Following Nancy Fraser (2016), we argue that these tensions reflect not only a crisis of care but a broader crisis of social reproduction as a central and underlying cause of turbulence under advanced capitalism. The fundamental, yet invisible, reliance of the production system on social reproduction means that developments in production that undermine the sustainability of social reproduction could render the capitalist system itself unviable. Hence, a social-reproductive "crisis tendency" lies in every form of capitalist society, a contradiction that emerges not within the separate spheres of production and social reproduction but at the border of their interconnections (Fraser, 2016). In contemporary financialised neoliberal capitalism, this contradiction and the associated need for more working hours to sustain households stem from interrelated pressures across both spheres (Plomien & Schwartz, 2024). In production, wage freezes or reductions are coupled with short- and long-term threats to job security and incomes from the persistent rise of precarious jobs and the gig economy. In social reproduction, rising consumption standards and the accompanying increase in household debt converge with diminished support from public services and mounting time pressures as household members engage more in waged work.

These pressures have led to a dualisation of the organisation of social reproduction: on the one side, greater commodification of domestic work for households who can afford it; on the other, an internalisation of social reproduction within households for those who cannot, with the corresponding burden of unpaid labour mainly falling on women (Fraser, 2016; Huws, 2019). This privatisation of responsibility pushes women, particularly when fathers are absent, to shoulder not only care work but also the financial costs of raising children (England & Folbre, 1999). This underscores the need for collective solutions – such as intergenerational investment in children through the tax system – that would in turn yield high societal returns by supporting the next generation that sustains future pensions for all (England & Folbre, 1999).

Crises in social reproduction were particularly experienced in Eastern European countries (Mrozowicki et al., 2025). One such case is analysed by Plomien and Schwartz (2026) in this volume, who expose the systemic problems following the transition from a socialist to a market economy – a process that neither recognised the dismantling of the pre-existing social reproduction system nor sought to rebuild it to ensure its viability. From a global perspective, the "care gap" that emerged from women's increased recruitment into waged work in richer countries is often filled through the import of migrant workers, transferring traditional female responsibilities to other more vulnerable women, in never-ending "global care chains" (Bettio et al., 2006; Hochschild, 2000). This body of literature underscores both Global North–South interconnections and intersectional inequalities – dimensions largely absent from the polycrisis debate.

This perspective on social reproduction as an underlying, invisible crisis is consistent with recent scholarship that regards the care and public services crisis as chronic and unresolved tensions, as opposed to the mainstream definition of crises as sudden and shorter-term, exogenous shocks (Mrozowicki et al., 2025). This conceptualization is also compatible with Roitman's thesis in "Anti-crisis" (2014), where she argues that the label "crisis" does not merely describe events, but actively shapes how we understand and respond to social challenges. By framing certain developments as urgent and exceptional, and thus demanding action, it curtails other interpretations. For instance, by presenting the financial crisis as a rupture, the crisis discourse contributed to obscuring the structural conditions, as in the financialisation of neoliberal capitalism, that generated it in the first place. While Roitman's (2014) work is not directly concerned with the gendered dimensions of crises, her critique is useful for understanding why the production-social reproduction contradiction remains neglected within the polycrisis discourse. These chronic tensions rarely feature in political agendas and thus remain invisible, despite their importance for understanding the multiple and interacting pressures within economic and social systems and their gendered consequences.

On this basis, a key message from the conclusions of this volume is the need to integrate the tensions in social reproduction into the polycrisis debate as the "social" strand of a more general crisis, including other intersecting economic, ecological and political dimensions. Following Fraser (2016), its centrality means that the other strands cannot be fully understood without considering social reproduction and its gender component. Furthermore, this neglect has led to limited engagement with Polanyi's (1944) influential double movement theory, which argues that an overextension of market relations – and the associated crises in production and social reproduction – may eventually trigger a pushback from wider societal forces. As Ferragina (2019) argues, such social pushback (in Ferragina's case, the demand for more childcare support but financed by cuts to welfare benefits) may only partially alleviate the problem for some groups. Nevertheless, this example underscores the consequences of disregarding social reproduction in analysing forces for change.

Against this background, the collection of chapters in this volume covers different types of processes operating within the context of polycrisis – some more short-term and acute in nature, others more chronic and systemic – all of which can be understood as crises within this framework. Moreover, we follow Mrozowicki et al. (2025) in emphasizing the interconnections between both types of processes: chronic crises reflecting structural problems may be aggravated by acute shocks, as seen in Eastern Europe where the public services crisis was compounded by the Covid-19 pandemic and the sudden arrival of refugees from the war in Ukraine.

Our perspective also entails a critical view of polycrisis, rejecting any pretension of its universality. Global risks are unevenly produced and distributed, and regions experience and respond to them differently, with North–South interconnections playing a crucial role in shaping their dynamics. Discussion of these issues in relation to the processes analysed in this concluding chapter may contribute to a critique of Western-centred definitions of crises as ruptures primarily affecting countries in the Global North. Such a critical view can also make more visible the structural, intersectional inequalities on which crises are grounded. Examining within-gender differences reveals not only how the acceleration and layering of crisis may be reinforcing, reshaping or reducing gender inequalities, but also how other social divides – and their interactions with gender – may be more salient or be gaining importance.

This overarching framework informs our interpretation of the processes examined in the book and their interconnections, as well as our reading of the empirical insights from the different chapters when assessing prospects for gender equality. The discussion that follows develops these points further around the three main themes that mirror the volume's structure: the labour market effects of sudden crises and their situation within broader long-term trends; the different facets of the social reproduction crisis; and the integration of a gender perspective into the digital and green transitions.

Gendered effects of crises on waged work: short-term setbacks, long-term progress – but for whom?

This section reviews the analytical and empirical contributions of the four chapters in the first part of this volume. These chapters primarily address the acute impacts on production systems stemming from those crises – from the financial and the sovereign debt crisis to the Covid-19 pandemic – that have been politically recognised and framed as shocks. While all three crises can be understood as outcomes of systemic tensions in economic and ecological systems, the focus here is on their short-term effects and how these shocks may have disrupted, reversed or accelerated trends in women's position in the labour market. Three chapters examine gendered labour market outcomes (Bashevska & Dotti Sani, 2026; Steinmetz & Guarnerio, 2026; Torres & Warren, 2026), while one explores the evolution of the gender pay gap in the context of changing jobs structures and wage-setting institutions (Figueiredo & López-Andreu, 2026).

A common pattern across all contributions is that shocks tended to intensify pre-existing inequalities, with gender intersecting with other dimensions of social stratification to reinforce the vulnerability of given social groups. For instance, although Bashevska and Dotti Sani (2026, this volume) did not find evidence that the short-term effects of the Covid-19 pandemic led to a generalised she-cession in Europe, the pattern was not uniform across countries, with women in Eastern European countries suffering most from employment losses. Beyond gender, other factors proved more determinant of employment outcomes, with being highly educated or employed in the public sector acting as buffers against labour market shocks.

Some parallels can be drawn with Torres and Warren's (2026) chapter, which also finds stronger impacts of crises on the most vulnerable. In examining trends in women and men's employment outcomes in the United Kingdom from the financial crisis and austerity through the cost-of-living crisis, the authors identify persistent gender gaps in working hours and wages across the different crises. However, their systematic exploration of patterns by social class within genders adds nuance to the picture. In fact, gaps widened between social classes as relative earnings worsened for the working class – particularly during the pandemic and cost-of-living crisis – for both men and women. At the same time, women remained the lowest-paid overall and were disproportionately affected by the sizable expansion of zero-hour contracts that took place in the United Kingdom particularly post-pandemic.

A similar picture also emerges from Steinmetz and Guarnerio's chapter (2026, this volume), which adopts a long-term perspective on the impact of the Great Recession and Covid-19 pandemic on employment, job quality and occupational segregation across 20 European countries, focusing on the intersection between gender and migration status. The authors show that both native men and women were least affected by crises, while it was non-EU migrants and in particular women within this group who suffered the most job losses and reductions in working hours, confirming their role as a "buffer" group absorbing economic shocks. In contrast, EU migrant women experienced some gradual improvements in job quality, signalling partial integration into more resilient labour market segments. Overall, segregation patterns remained largely stable over the period, with non-EU migrant women persistently concentrated in low-skill jobs. This enduring segregation reflects structurally entrenched patterns rather than temporary crisis effects.

A somewhat more positive picture emerges from Figueiredo and López-Andreu's examination of trends in gender pay inequity and wage-setting institutions in Southern Europe (2026). The chapter shows that during the austerity period both Portugal and Spain experienced stagnant or widening gender pay gaps. However, following new centre-left electoral victories in both countries, significant reductions in gender pay gaps were achieved in the post-austerity period, which saw partial reversals of austerity reforms, increases in minimum wages and a revival of public sector employment and pay. However, these declines were not solely driven by efforts to improve gender equality; they also reflected, first, occupational restructuring – such as the contraction of male-dominated jobs in construction and low-tech industry during the financial crisis; and, second, women's rising educational attainment, which favoured entry into expanding professional and knowledge-intensive occupations. Furthermore, in Spain, real wages declined for men throughout both the austerity and post-austerity period, particularly in high-paid jobs, while in Portugal real earnings increased across most deciles for both men and women, with women in low-paid jobs benefiting the most.

Overall, the chapters reviewed in this section underscore the importance of examining who within each gender – and across other social divides – benefits or loses during crises. This perspective makes it more difficult to provide a straightforward answer to the question of the direction of change in gender equality as a consequence of these different waves of crises. Overall, there has been no reversal of progress in women's labour market integration. While the different shocks may have represented temporary setbacks for some groups, women's increasing presence in waged work has proved resilient over the long run. In countries severely affected by recession, strong added-worker effects even led to noticeable increases in female breadwinner households (Marx et al., 2026, this volume; Vitali & Arpino, 2016). Evidence of skill upgrading and women's entry into high level jobs (Figueiredo & López-Andreu, 2026; Steinmetz & Guarnerio, 2026, this volume) also signals progress for women, reflecting longer-term trends towards increased female investment in education and indeed the reversal of the educational gap (Klesment & Van Bavel, 2017). Yet these findings also add to existing evidence that it is mainly highly educated women who are benefiting most from progress in gender equality (Stier & Herzberg-Druker, 2017; Vokić et al., 2019). Not only did the spread of teleworking during the Covid-19 pandemic act to safeguard highly educated workers from job loss (Eurofound, 2022a), but they also benefited from the employment creation concentrated in well-paid, knowledge-intensive sectors in its aftermath (Eurofound, 2022b). The counterpoint of these trends is the widening gaps within genders along class and migration lines, among others. A common pattern across the different crises is in fact the persistent and even deepening vulnerability of lower-skilled and migrant women, who remain disproportionately exposed to precarious work and crisis-sensitive jobs (Bashevska & Dotti Sani, 2026; Steinmetz & Guarnerio, 2026; Torres & Warren, 2026, this volume). Nevertheless, a positive policy environment can mitigate these vulnerabilities, as illustrated by the rise in real wages for lower-skilled women in Portugal (Figueiredo & López-Andreu, 2026, this volume). In this case, minimum wages had an important and stronger impact on wages for women in Portugal than in Spain because they were set closer to the base rates in collective bargaining agreements. This demonstrates that institutions matter, and that intersectional vulnerabilities are not only shaped by structural inequalities but also by the adequacy or failure of policy responses. Ultimately, crisis effects are deeply dependent on country context, including their policy regimes, as Bashevska and Dotti Sani show.

Social reproduction in crisis and the need for a care transition

This section focuses on the chapters presented in the second part of the volume, which address the gendered division of waged and unwaged work at the household level (Marx et al., 2026; Baxter et al., 2026); the impact of transitions towards neoliberal market economies on social reproduction (Plomien & Schwartz, 2026); developments in social care policies (Lopezlira & Hunter, 2026; Karamessini, 2026); and support for women and carers within social protection systems (Larsen et al., 2026). As such, these contributions illuminate different facets of the underlying crisis of social reproduction as a chronic, systemic contradiction intensified under contemporary neoliberal financial capitalism. All suggest that to address this crisis there needs to be a structural transformation of the social reproduction system, including a transition to a new care system. Despite recent waves of economic downturn and associated political responses that have deepened these problems, the crisis in social reproduction has not yet been politically acknowledged as such.

Feminist scholarship on "social depletion" (Elson, 2012; Rai, 2024; Rai et al., 2013) offers a useful lens to conceptualise this crisis, as it puts the focus not only on how essential social reproduction is to the functioning of economies and societies, but also on how its costs are systematically ignored, which leads to depletion at multiple levels. Depletion can occur whenever outflows (labour, time, emotional energy) exceed the inflows (support, rest, compensation), causing harm at the level of individuals (physical and mental exhaustion), households (strained resources and time) and communities (collective support networks) (Rai et al., 2013). Under this framework, different themes covered in the chapters reviewed in this section can be seen as expressions of the tensions across the boundaries of production and reproduction potentially leading to depletion. These themes include the persistent expansion of the dual full-time earner in Europe (Marx et al., 2026), the slow progress in the gendered division of domestic labour (Baxter et al., 2026), the fragility of the social reproduction system with the transition to a new production regime in Eastern European countries (Plomien & Schwartz) and the struggles of care workers to secure their livelihoods in a context of rising costs of living (Lopezlira & Hunter, 2026).

As highlighted in the previous section, despite the notable turbulence of recent decades, one remarkably stable trend has been women's growing integration into waged work, even if with temporary setbacks during specific crises and national contexts. This long-term trend parallels the gradual expansion of the dual full-time earner model, which Marx and coauthors (2026) argue reflects not merely a rise in gender equality, but also a shift in households' provisioning strategies. Adopting a dual source of labour income is gradually becoming a generalised arrangement, amid growing employment insecurity and shifts in consumption standards, coupled with rising costs of living. The authors show that relying on a single (male) earner has become a less financially viable arrangement over the last two decades, as these types of households faced greater economic hardship, especially during the Great Recession, but also recovered less in its aftermath. Moreover, the vulnerability gap between male breadwinner and female breadwinner couples appears to be slowly narrowing as men's labour market position weakens. Successive crises may have temporarily stalled or reversed the upward trend towards dual full-time earners, yet in the longer run they appear to accelerate it, as this arrangement is most resilient against economic turbulence and precarious labour markets.

Overall, these household responses are a core constituent of the processes of social adjustment to polycrisis, although such efforts to stabilise income resources are unlikely in themselves to be sufficient to overcome the chronic crisis in social reproduction. A closely related issue is the slow pace of change in the gender division of unwaged work. As illustrated by Baxter et al.'s (2026) chapter on Australia, time use studies tend to find a gradual but modest convergence between genders over time, alongside short-term widening of gender gaps during the pandemic. Indeed, the authors show that although Covid-19 lockdowns temporarily exacerbated inequalities in unpaid labour, they did not reverse the long-term trend towards reduced gender inequalities in paid and unpaid work. However, and consistent with the broader literature (Sullivan et al., 2018), the gap was found to be closing mainly through women's decreased time spent in housework. While such reduction has been associated with women's higher involvement in paid work, men's increased involvement in care work, even if limited, could be considered more reflective of behavioural or normative change towards some degendering of core routine household tasks (Milkie et al., 2025).

The reorganisation of household waged and unwaged labour is critically situated at the interface of production and social reproduction and hence exposes the tensions across them that are managed mainly by women. From this perspective, the significant and sustained increase in female waged labour without a fundamental reorganisation of the reproduction side has accentuated the "time squeeze" (Clarkberg & Moen, 2001), which constitutes a manifestation of depletion at individual and household levels. This systematic exhaustion of social capabilities to ensure social reproduction is a long-term trend predating the financial crisis. However, already strained household resources and shrinking time for unpaid labour were compounded by austerity and later by the Covid-19 pandemic, reflecting the interaction between chronic processes and ruptures. Austerity policies in Europe in response to the financial crisis led to cuts to public services in health, education and social care and to a stalling of plans to build the necessary care infrastructure to support women's growing participation in paid work. Meanwhile, in the hardest-hit countries, women faced mounting pressures: to take on additional paid work to compensate for male unemployment or reduced wages; to manage social reproduction with fewer public resources; and to accept more precarious and less rewarded work (Elson, 2012; Karamessini & Rubery, 2014). The Covid-19 pandemic further strained health and social systems already weakened by austerity and privatisation (Armstrong et al., 2024; Dowling, 2021). In this context, women's responses proved critical to societal functioning in each of the spheres most affected by the pandemic; not only operating the frontline, especially in health and care, but also holding together social reproduction by providing the bulk of care and homeschooling while increasingly engaging in remote working.

Another example of the failure of neoliberal capitalism to develop sustainable social reproduction and care systems is evidenced in the experiences of transition from state socialism to market economies of Eastern European countries. As shown in the chapter by Plomien and Schwartz (2026), the overwhelming focus of the transition was on creating markets and developing democratic institutions, with little attention to ensuring that workers and their families could survive in the new economic order. Deprived of state socialist support systems, households' only source of income became low-paid and often insecure wage employment. Much of the burden of how to secure a livelihood fell to women, who had to take up full-time work while also doing more domestic and care labour. The struggle to provide also led to large-scale migration by both men and women, creating new vulnerabilities in destination countries due to gender segregation and low pay, while the splitting of families depleted care resources in origin countries. These dynamics, as discussed in the chapter through the examples of Poland and Ukraine, offer broader lessons about the risks of major system transitions – such as those anticipated under new forms of technology – when insufficient attention is given to ensuring the sustainability of social reproduction.

The chapter by Lopezlira and Hunter (2026) provides an example of efforts to mitigate depletion impacts on women undertaking care work. The United States is perhaps the most market-driven advanced economy, with access to basic benefits and medical care tied to employment position and not universal. Furthermore, the generalisation of the dual earner model as a minimum necessary household commitment to wage employment predates the developments we have just described for Europe (Schor, 1991). This imperative has not been matched by the development of adequate support systems enabling women to remain in work when faced with competing demands on their time, particularly for childcare or elder care (Forden et al., 2023). As recounted by the authors, to solve the crisis in elderly care, California introduced the In-Home Supportive Services (IHSS) programme – a social care employment system, which in practice mainly serves those caring for immediate family members (72.1% of all recipients). This is effectively constituting proper wage employment for what in other societies would be unpaid family care work, though in some contexts subsidised through the benefit system (Offenhenden et al., 2025). In California, these jobs are rewarded through a wage structure set through collective bargaining, albeit highly fragmented due to local negotiation and funding disparities across counties. This case illustrates that the need for social support persists even in fully marketised systems, and states may find they have little option but to extend wage labour into traditionally unpaid labour territory as opting out of waged work is no longer financially possible for women.

The Californian case, along with other contributions in the volume, shows that the challenges of social reproduction are not only gendered but also shaped by class, migration and family structure. Hence, as Marx et al. (2026) argue, while dual full-time earning may to some extent reflect the professional aspirations of highly educated women, it is often driven by economic necessity for the lower skilled (see also Sánchez-Mira, 2020). In turn, relying on a second income is not possible for lone parent families, who are generally headed by women and over-represented among low-income households. They were one of the groups who suffered most from the cost-of-living crisis, given that they tend to allocate a larger share of their budget to essentials such as housing, food and energy. These goods experienced the steepest increases between 2021 and 2023, leaving these households particularly exposed to inflation (ILO, 2022; Sologon et al., 2024). Moreover, in the examples of Poland and Ukraine discussed by Plomien and Schwartz (2026), the shift from public to private provisioning and the dismantling of redistributive systems deepened class inequalities, intensifying vulnerability for low-income families. Migration may help mitigate some of that immediate hardship, but perpetuates transnational inequalities and care deficits. In fact, as shown by Lopezlira and Hunter (2026), social care occupations remain highly gendered, racialised and systematically undervalued. With wages persistently situated under a living wage standard and real incomes further eroded during high inflation, workers struggle to meet basic needs.

Overall, the commodification of social reproduction and the deepening of inequalities between households across multiple lines is closely related to the dualisation of social reproduction arrangements: between an externalisation of domestic work for those who can afford it and the internalisation through increased household (female) labour for those who cannot (Fraser, 2016; Huws, 2019). Commodification thus represents an individual solution or "mitigation" strategy (Rai et al., 2013) to alleviate the consequences of depletion and is often the most readily available strategy for households. However, inequality is built into these mitigation strategies, as they displace depletion further down the chain. For instance, women in care jobs often struggle themselves with the combined burden of paid and unpaid work. Relatedly, female migrants who move to fill "care gaps" in the Global North frequently become transnational primary breadwinners while having to navigate conservative gender expectations in their home countries

– expectations that conflict with a role mainly driven by economic need (Bastia, 2011). These dynamics reveal structural imbalances and interconnections across North-South divides, social classes, and racialized groups (Rai et al., 2013).

In contrast, collective responses to counter depletion involve “replenishment”, mainly through state or institutional support, and “transformation”, which entails structural change in gender roles and recognition of social reproduction (Rai et al., 2013). Karamessini’s chapter provides insights on these collective strategies, advocating for a “care transition” to address the insufficient development of institutional support amid women’s growing involvement in wage employment. This transition requires both a defamilialisation – shifting care provision from families to the state and/or the market—and a degenderisation of care – promoting a more equal sharing between men and women. This transition requires thus renewed state intervention, as reliance on private providers risks deepening inequalities in access and causing a trickling of the costs of social reproduction down the line. Degenderisation of care also needs renewed impulse, given the slow rhythm of gender convergence in the division of labour within households (see also Baxter et al., 2026, this volume, above).

Under this framework, Karamessini takes stock of the state of the care transition in the EU, showing that it is uneven and incomplete, particularly in elderly care and in closing gender gaps in unpaid work. Even though there has been a significant expansion of formal childcare since the 1990s, driven by the EU’s Barcelona targets, coverage for children under three years of age remains low in many countries. Moreover, reforms on elderly care have focused on cash-for-care allowances instead of universal service provision, hence favouring supported familialism and informal care arrangements that continue to rely on a migrant and racialised workforce. Austerity policies, involving cuts in childcare and elderly care services, also contributed to a temporary refamilialisation of care. After a long period of stalled development, the EU has recently taken up the baton and sought to accelerate the slow trend towards defamilialised care systems through the European Care Strategy (European Commission, 2022). This declared new turn in EU policy sets revised upward childcare targets, introduces elder care targets for the first time and calls for better working conditions in the care sector in the aftermath of the Covid-19 pandemic. There have also been moves to promote some degendering of care responsibilities through dedicated leave for fathers under the work–life balance directive (European Union, 2019). However, the prospects for realising this strategy appear increasingly uncertain in the current context of return to fiscal stringency and prioritisation of defence expenditure over social priorities.

Complementing Karamessini’s (2026) perspective, Larsen and colleagues (2026) argue in their chapter that a care transition must be accompanied by a more fundamental review of welfare state systems to uncover the different ways in which women’s presumed caring responsibilities remain deeply embedded in benefits and support systems. Without such wider transformation, even better subsidised care provision may fail to create real equal opportunities for men and women to be both carers and workers (Fraser, 1994). The authors show that the assumption of women's primary care responsibility is still built into the social protection system across a variety of EU member states – including the Nordic economies such as Denmark, although to a lesser extent than in the other countries under scrutiny, namely the United Kingdom, Germany and the Netherlands. Gaps in access to social protection for women and levels of benefits remain significant when faced with loss of employment during crises or in other contexts. Moreover, loss of employment may also lead to loss of access to childcare support or paid parental leave. Therefore, women are still being treated in some respects as contingent labour market participants, a condition reinforced by the assumption that they should willingly become full-time carers while searching for a new job. In this way, Larsen and colleagues (2026) reinforce Karamessini's (2026) argument that the care transition must involve not only the defamilialisation of care but also full degendering of care roles, so that women who face problems of job security are not pushed back into essentialised roles as caregivers first and members of the workforce second.

Gendering the digital and green transitions: towards new ways of working and living

Two additional major transformations currently underway are addressed in the third part of this volume. Driven by distinct forces of change, both processes are expected to reshape production systems, labour market structures and institutions and their gendered nature. The first concerns the growing diffusion of digital- and AI-enabled new forms of work, addressed by Piasna (2026) and Rani and colleagues (2026); the second relates to the transition to net-zero emissions as a response to the ecological crisis, examined by Daly et al. (2026). We discuss next their gender implications in this order.

The first challenge – the digitalisation of work – is a market-driven process of change led by large technology organisations, a new oligarchy, with minimal input from nation states, let alone citizens or workforces (Bria & Bautista, 2025). Prior to the pandemic, debates on digitalisation emphasised its potential to further fragment employment under the guise of flexibility, thereby reinforcing gender divides and worsening working conditions for women. Developments such as the platformisation of work are challenging the standard employment relationship and exerting pressure on the institutions built around it, including collective bargaining and social protection systems (De Stefano et al., 2021; Forsyth & McCrystal, 2025). Such fragmentation is likely to undermine gender equality, as the standard employment relationship remains—at least in the Global North—the key instrument for delivering women's rights, such as maternity leave and equal pay, and for providing economic security in employment.

The Covid-19 pandemic brought to the foreground another issue linked to digitalisation by accelerating the spread of digitally-enabled remote work. This diffusion disproportionately affected skilled white collar jobs and women (Eurofound, 2022a), changing the gender profile of the remote worker from male-dominated to more prevalent among women. This transformation sparked intense debate on what greater flexibility in time and location of work might mean for gender equality in highly skilled, protected occupations. This debate, however, paid little attention to other forms of distance work, particularly the rise of online platform work that enables capital in the Global North to reach educated middle class women in the Global South. Two chapters in this volume examine these developments and their broader implications for gender equality. Piasna (2026) analyses the gendered effects of remote and online platform work during and beyond the Covid-19 pandemic across Europe, while Rani and colleagues (2026) look at platform work globally to challenge the dominant narrative that gig work empowers educated women in the Global South.

Piasna's (2026) chapter draws on two European surveys covering both remote platform work and remote working within employment relationships to show that, contrary to promises of levelling the playing field for men and women through improved work-family reconciliation, remote working tends to reproduce and even reinforce gender inequalities. The overarching explanation is that remote working has expanded in a context where strong gender norms and inequalities persist, in both the workplace and the household, meaning that this shift largely mirrors existing gender structures. More specifically, the apparent autonomy to shift working time and location often blurs boundaries between work and home, reinforcing the gendered division of labour. Piasna (2026) finds that mothers with young children experience the greatest increase in unpaid domestic and care work when teleworking regularly, while fathers' behaviour remains largely unchanged. These findings support existing research showing that home-based work increases pressures on women to do more housework and childcare, particularly as they are less likely to work in enclosed workspaces where clearer boundaries can be established (Chung, 2022; Kurowska, 2020). Moreover, Piasna (2026) shows that regular teleworking mothers have the worst promotion chances of all groups, while hybrid workers who telework occasionally enjoy the best pay and promotion opportunities.

Overall, research on telework and working time flexibility has shown that flexible working can have harmful effects when combined with the persistent ideal of a work-centred employee, leading to increased working time (Lott & Chung, 2016), work-to-family encroachment (Yucel et al., 2025) and digital presenteeism replacing physical presenteeism (Howcroft et al., 2024). Following Chung (2022), a renewed ideal worker linked to busyness as a sign of status has contributed to the "flexibility paradox" or the self-exploitation of those working flexibly. This tendency is exacerbated by the flexibility stigma (Williams et al., 2013) and perceptions of employment insecurity, which push workers to work harder and longer to signal productivity and commitment to the company.

All this suggests that remote work is no more a solution to gender inequalities than part-time work has proved to be. Both tend to reinforce rather than transform the gendered division of labour. In professional and high-level jobs, part-time work has confined women to limited career trajectories and stagnant earnings. Meanwhile, in-person part-time service workers often face employer-oriented flexibility, designed to cut costs through flexible scheduling to meet demand variations. Both these traits are emerging in remote and flexible working: while these arrangements allow mothers to remain employed without reducing hours (Chung & Van der Horst, 2017), they do so at the price of widening gaps in pay and opportunities. At the same time, the rise of gig work is deepening the fragmentation of employment already seen in part-time work in service jobs.

Relatedly, there are significant differences in job quality between teleworkers in a traditional employment relationship and those engaged in remote platform work, which is often precarious and poorly paid. Indeed, as Rani and colleagues (2026) show, women are disproportionately represented on platforms with the poorest working conditions, such as clickwork, and less so in professional freelance work. These patterns signal future risks if digitally-mediated tasks are increasingly automated through AI or outsourced to online platforms, stripping home-based workers of employment protections. Gendered occupational segregation may deepen if it is routine tasks that are primarily outsourced, while hybrid or office-based employees retain more skilled areas. Recent research on the potential impact of generative AI reinforces these concerns, showing that women's jobs are twice as likely to be affected by automation, particularly due to the high exposure of clerical work (Gmyrek et al., 2025).

If research on the Global North underscores the need to examine how the gendered effects of digitalisation intersect with inequalities across occupational and skill divides, the chapter by Rani and coauthors (2026) highlights the interconnections of these patterns with Global North–South dynamics. Drawing on extensive ILO surveys and qualitative research, the authors show how online platform work enables capital in the Global North to access educated middle-class women in the Global South. Contrary to narratives of empowerment, digital labour platforms tend to reproduce gender inequalities in occupational segregation and earnings: women are overrepresented in lower-paying, care-related sectors and face algorithmic bias when entering male-dominated fields such as ride-hailing. So-called flexibility comes at a high cost – unpredictable schedules, intensified time pressures, non-guaranteed income and penalties for limited availability due to care responsibilities. Beyond expanding empirical evidence on platform labour globally, the chapter exposes the gendered nature of deskilled work offered through these systems. Women working on online platforms in the Global South are not only more educated than their counterparts in the Global North, but the education gap relative to men is also larger in these regions. This pattern underscores the risk of underutilising women's skills and potential, particularly through freelance and microtask platforms that tap into a highly educated (female) workforce worldwide. The result is a double form of exploitation: employers in the Global North pay lower rates for equivalent work to Global South workers than they offer to labour sourced locally, while simultaneously contributing to the underutilisation of women's skills and talents in their home societies. Far from empowering women, digital labour platforms foster new globalised forms of gendered exploitation and inequality.

We now turn to the second challenge: the environmental crisis, which exposes an even deeper contradiction between the economic system's infrastructural foundations and the sustainability of human and non-human life. As with the care crisis, addressing this challenge demands a transition to new ways of working and living – a shift unlikely to occur without active state intervention at both national and international levels, since markets will not pursue net-zero goals without clear incentives and limits on economic activity. Moreover, the way the transition reorganises economic processes will shape its gender effects. It is therefore crucial to make these potential impacts visible and ensure that women's voices are included in decision-making to steer transformation towards gender equality. The chapter by Daly and coauthors contributes to this debate by showing that gender mainstreaming in policy change discussions remains far from realised.

The limited discussion and awareness of both the risks and opportunities for gender equality in the shift to a net-zero economy partly reflect a dominant belief that the target can be achieved through technological fixes. As Daly et al. note, mainstream debates largely emphasise reskilling workers – primarily men in high-emission sectors – alongside transition to alternative fuel sources. This represents a narrow view of the scale of transformation required to achieve and sustain a green economy. A deeper analysis suggests that this transition could – and should – be as radical as those envisioned in the seemingly more exciting debates around the march of the robots or the replacement of humans by AI chatboxes.

The radical dimensions of a green economy agenda include whether societies should adopt a no-growth or degrowth agenda, the extent to which circular economy models must be developed, and which low-carbon activities merit what may be scarce investment (Daly et al., 2026, this volume). Each of these radical scenarios carries significant implications for the gender division of labour. For instance, both degrowth and circular economy strategies imply an expansion of unpaid labour to extend product life and offset restrictions on market-based additions to raw or basic materials. The risk is that this additional burden will fall disproportionately on women, given prevailing assumptions that they are the primary homemakers. Furthermore, the environmental and care crises may interact in different ways. As Jones-Renaud et al. (2024) note, climate change may intensify care demands through extreme weather events and resource scarcity, while also weakening care systems by damaging care infrastructure and dismantling care networks through forced displacement. Yet positive synergies are also possible: a shift towards less carbon-intensive sectors could offer a response both to the green and the care crises. Care jobs are not only female-dominated but also inherently low-carbon and essential for resilience in the face of climate change, as they strengthen communities' capacity to adapt and recover from climate shocks. A gender-just transition to a net zero economy therefore requires redistributing care responsibilities and recognising care work as a cornerstone of green economies (Jones-Renaud et al., 2024).

These scenarios all raise questions for which answers remain uncertain. However, what Daly et al. argue, and should be acted upon, is that the remaking of the economy to meet net-zero targets will entail changes with profound implications for gender equality, creating opportunities for progress but also risks of regression into traditional gender roles and stereotypes. It is therefore essential to place gender concerns at the centre of the debate and ensure women's voices are included in decision-making processes.

Achieving net-zero must be driven by state action, both at the national level and through coordinated multinational initiatives. A global perspective on the ecological crisis is as critical as that on the other transitions discussed – if not more so – given Global North–South dynamics in this domain, including the export of environmental externalities to the Global South through carbon credit trading and environmental dumping. Interconnections between the environmental crisis and the digital transformation are also increasingly evident in the significant carbon and extractive footprints of digital infrastructures (Brodie, 2023). Political solutions must therefore ensure global equity. Moreover, effective policies will require profound changes to ways of living, demanding collective, collaborative, and coordinated action. Yet the more solutions are framed as technological fixes, the greater the risk that democratic debate on the accompanying societal transformations will be sidelined. Decision-making power may increasingly shift to technology companies – even when public funding remains the primary source of investment. Current geopolitical tensions further undermine optimism about reaching the consensus required for the far-reaching transformations demanded by the green transition, as reflected in the disappointing outcome of the COP30 climate summit in Belém, which concluded as we were finalising these lines. These considerations set the stage for the concluding discussion in the final two sections of the chapter, where we first distil the book's key messages and then discuss future prospects for advancing gender equality in light of recent developments.

Taking stock: challenges in assessing progress towards gender equality in an era of turbulence

When reviewing progress on gender equality over the period of successive crises until the end of the Covid-19 pandemic, it could be tempting to focus on gender gaps and from that conclude that there has been steady progress, albeit slow in some areas. After all, the empirical evidence presented in this volume shows that women's integration into employment has continued to be normalised, with little indication of a reversal in employment rates. The trend towards dual earner households and away from the male breadwinner model is equally persistent. Crises have caused, at most, temporary disruptions for some women, and may even have reinforced women's labour market participation in the long run. Gains have also been made in narrowing gender pay gaps, and there is some convergence in time spent on domestic work – though largely because women have reduced their contribution rather than men increasing theirs. Taken together, these developments might suggest a "satisfactory, could do better" assessment, given that women's access to employment and to higher education appear resilient in the face of repeated shocks.

Yet, when we look beneath these aggregate trends – examining what is happening to different socio-economic groups of women, the interactions between the Global North and the Global South, and the forces reshaping how we work and live – such conclusions quickly appear complacent and blinkered. There are at least four main reasons to adopt a different perspective: three drawn from each of the book's main sections and a fourth rooted in the rapidly changing political climate and other sources of turbulence.

In the first place, much of the apparent progress primarily benefits middle class women in the Global North, with these gains for more privileged women (and their male partners) often relying on female migrant workers who provide essential support to sustain social reproduction. In this sense, the resilience of overall employment rates – especially among higher-educated women – and reductions in gender gaps cannot be taken as unequivocal signs of advancement in gender equality, as they obscure the entrenched segregation and persistent precariousness faced by working class and migrant women (Steinmetz & Guarnerio, 2026, this volume). These groups continue to bear disproportionate risks and burdens, including short working hours, employment insecurity and low wages (Bashevska & Dotti Sani, 2026; Figueiredo & López-Andreu, 2026; Torres & Warren, 2026, this volume). Moreover, narrowing gender gaps – such as in pay – appear partly driven by a weakening of men's position in the labour market, linked to the erosion of labour market institutions such as collective bargaining during crisis periods, hence hardly a win for women (Figueiredo & López-Andreu, 2026, this volume). Relatedly, the reinforcement of a long-term trend towards dual-full-time earning in Europe may signal that this arrangement is increasingly perceived as more financially secure amid growing employment insecurity, rising consumption standards and escalating costs of living (Marx et al., 2026, this volume). This development underscores broader tensions around the boundaries of production and social reproduction.

Second, the emphasis on women's progress in the wage labour market contributes to the invisibility of crises in social reproduction and masks the failures to provide adequate social support to replace women's unpaid domestic labour. This was evident both during the transition to market economies after the collapse of socialism in Eastern Europe and in highly market-driven systems such as the United States, where reliance on the market has proved insufficient for sustaining social reproduction. Even in less market-oriented economies, such as some European countries, care policy strategies have been constrained by the EU's broader neoliberal agenda, which prioritises increasing women's employment without considering the quality of those jobs. Some scholars have argued that the gender equality label has been used to make the promotion of flexible employment across Europe appear more palatable (Stratigaki, 2004), as illustrated by the spread of part-time work in contexts with little appetite for it, such as in Spain (Insarauto, 2021). Moreover, this neoliberal framing fails to challenge the trends towards the extensification and intensification of working time that have accompanied digitalisation and an "always-on" culture driven by performance-based management practices, particularly for higher skilled workers (Burchell et al., 2024; Chung, 2022). In this sense, adopting a "replenishing" strategy – providing more state-supported care – without addressing other fundamental aspects of "transformation" may prove insufficient over the long run, especially if such interventions turn out to be more fragile in times of economic crisis or shifts in value systems (Rai et al., 2013). This tendency was evident during austerity, when women were expected to pick up the slack from cuts in expenditure and cancelling of investments in care infrastructure. Looking ahead, the recent social turn in EU policy may be coming to an end due to new defence-related expenditure pressures, the reinstatement of severe fiscal rules after a brief respite during the Covid-19 pandemic and the immediate recovery period, and a political climate increasingly hostile to gender equality goals.

A third factor limiting optimism is the range of emerging threats to women's progress in the labour market, whether these stem from the neoliberal fixation with flexibility, the technology-enabled expansion of gig work, the heightened risks of job displacement from AI diffusion or indeed the transition to net zero. A crucial concern is that these changes jeopardise the survival of standard employment relationships for both men and women. Yet this risk is rarely linked to the central role of formal employment in sustaining social reproduction – at least in the Global North – not only at the household level but also within national economies. This omission once again renders social reproduction invisible. This importance was briefly acknowledged during the Covid-19 pandemic, when governments across the political spectrum recognised the need to compensate for losses in regular employment income to prevent societal collapse (Rubery & Tavora, 2021). However, that insight has largely vanished from mainstream debates on the future of work, which show little recognition of the need for policies that safeguard guaranteed employment contracts and associated income.

On this point, the digital transition can be seen as compounding the crisis of social reproduction in several ways. First, it reinforces households' difficulties in securing provision through the fragmentation of work and the associated reconfiguration of what is considered paid and unpaid labour. By refusing to take responsibility as employers, platforms shift costs and risks onto workers, including unpaid time spent waiting for gigs, bidding for jobs or maintaining ratings (Mangan et al.,

2023; Pulignano & Domecka, 2025). This promotes a "fragmented" working time regime (Piasna, 2024), where all non-productive labour is squeezed out of paid working time, resulting in scarce and unpredictable earnings that make it difficult to assemble a livelihood from multiple gigs. Such precarity forces platform workers to remain permanently available for work to secure a minimum income, resulting in the paradoxical simultaneous fragmentation and extensification of working time (Piasna, 2024). In this way, the platformisation of work contributes to individual and household depletion of economic and temporal resources. Second, the rise of digital platforms in cleaning and care services accelerates the externalisation and commodification of domestic work as a response to households' time squeezes (Huws, 2019). This process exploits a highly feminised and racialised workforce within colonial care chains (Rodríguez-Modroño et al., 2022) and reinforces the problem by further commodifying, fragmenting and devaluing care work while obscuring its structural causes (Rodríguez-Modroño et al., 2024).

In this sense, within a polycrisis framework that incorporates a gender perspective, digitalisation emerges as a crisis marked by systemic tensions between the development of productive forces, social relations of production and the social reproductive capacities underpinning the accumulation regime. While pressures on the standard employment relationship are long-standing and driven by other fissuring processes – such as outsourcing, temporary agency work or part-time employment – an open question is whether the additional strains introduced by digitalisation may eventually lead to a tipping point (Burchell et al., 2024) – away from the standard employment relationship as the organising principle for work and working time and from its role in providing stability for social reproduction in post-war European societies.

The direction these changes will take depends not primarily on technological advances, but on the political environment in which digitalisation and AI are deployed – whether driven by the interests of dominant tech oligopolies, by a re-assertive regulatory state, or geopolitical power struggles between the United States and China. Similarly, the path to net-zero remains uncertain amid fragmenting political consensus and persistent contentions over who bears the costs and who benefits from the transition.

This uncertainty underscores the fourth main reason why complacency about progress on gender equality is misplaced: current political turmoil undermines the stability and consensus needed to tackle these multiple, interconnected challenges. Agreement on future objectives at global, regional and national level is at risk of collapse, exposing the fragility of earlier commitments to key goals – from gender equality to net-zero. Amid this political polycrisis, any semblance of ethical capitalism is fading as companies that once pledged non-discrimination and low carbon practices abandon sustainability and Equality, Diversity and Inclusion policies to pre-empt political backlash – rolling back initiatives in their US operations under pressure from the Trump administration, while maintaining these principles in Europe where regulatory frameworks, such as gender quotas and pay-gap disclosure laws, still apply (Rogers, 2025). Furthermore, contention persists about how to compensate for the costs of the climate crisis – from Global North countries, which bear primary responsibility, to the Global South, which suffers most from its impacts. Even more troublingly, the world is regressing to disputes over the validity of climate science, with misinformation fuelling these debates (Barcellos de Moraes, 2025). Some actors exploit such arguments as a pretext to pursue short-term vested interests and avoid the systemic disruption required to phase out fossil fuels and prioritise long-term sustainability. Ultimately, the catastrophic consequences of continued climate inaction may be the only force capable of compelling united action.

Looking forward: the future of gender equality in turbulent times

In the previous section, we identified three core analytical insights emerging from the transversal discussion of the chapters in this volume: first, the need to consider the interaction of gender divides with other social cleavages when analysing the effects of crises; second, the centrality of the tensions between production and social reproduction for understanding current turbulence; and third, the challenges posed by ongoing and future labour market transformations to the standard employment relationship as a pillar for the organisation of social reproduction in contemporary Western societies. Together, these three points substantiate our argument that integrating a gender perspective into the polycrisis debate is essential if we are to fully grasp its scope and design inclusive policy responses to the multiple challenges involved. The chapters in this volume, alongside our review of the broader literature, offer numerous examples of "boundary struggles" (Fraser, 2016) at the interface of production and social reproduction as key sites of conflict in capitalist societies – struggles that we contend are crucial components of polycrisis. These conflicts are deeply shaped by gender, in intersection with other forms of stratification, including class, race, ethnicity, as well as migration patterns and North–South interconnections. While assessing prospects for gender equality becomes extremely difficult in the context of profound uncertainty we have portrayed, what seems certain is that any assessment should take these insights into account. From this perspective, three key points can be made looking forward.

First, recognising the chronic or long-term crisis in social reproduction within polycrisis debates is essential to mobilise action not only in favour of gender equality but also for retaining and expanding institutions that support social reproduction – such as formal employment and public services in childcare and eldercare. There is an urgent need to defend and strengthen such institutions, particularly the standard employment relationship which has historically underpinned equality rights and provided a measure of economic security in the Global North. At the same time, new mechanisms are required to deliver universal gender equality rights, including access to social protection such as pensions, paid maternity leave, and childcare. While these concerns have long been central in the Global South, the Global North now faces the challenge of finding innovative ways to ensure more universal protections. A possible positive outcome of current turbulence could be the demise of the neoliberal myth that markets alone can meet the needs of a thriving society. The need for a Polanyian response to decades of neoliberalism was beginning to be recognised during the Covid-19 pandemic, in calls for a renewal of society through valuing essential services such as care. Yet that moment was quickly overshadowed by new forms of turbulence and renewed emphasis on rearmament and other "masculine" priorities. Ultimately, addressing the crisis of social reproduction requires not only renewed state engagement in care provision but also a fundamental restructuring of gender social relations, across the private and public spheres and North–South divides, in a way that recognises the value of reproductive labour, that integrates care work into economic policy and that more fundamentally challenges the dominance of financial concerns over human needs (Elson, 2012; Rai et al., 2013).

Second, polycrisis is likely to persist as a defining feature – even with interludes of apparent stability – until a significant realignment of the world order occurs, a question beyond the scope of this volume. What matters is that we are entering an era of profound change, and now more than ever, we need a renewed commitment to gender mainstreaming. That means embedding a gender lens across all core aspects of institution-building and policy-making. Yet, despite commitments – such as those by the EU, the first institution to pledge this shift to their policy framework – implementation remains limited. Thirty years after gender mainstreaming was endorsed at the Beijing conference, a renewed effort is urgently needed. Moreover, this approach must integrate intersectional perspectives and acknowledge Global North–South dynamics, as recognised in the EU Gender Equality Strategy 2020–2025 (European Commission, 2020). Embedding gender considerations in policy also connects to the broader imperative of rethinking how we work and live to achieve sustainability and net-zero goals. These transformations could enable societies to reorganise in ways that support flourishing human and non-human life. However, such opportunities will be missed – and inequalities perpetuated or deepened – unless gender equality is placed at the centre of political agendas.

The scope for realising gender mainstreaming depends largely on the political climate, which brings us to our third and final point. When writing these lines at the close of 2025, amid widespread attacks on gender equality targets and policies from the United States and the growing influence of right-wing populist parties in Europe and beyond, the EU's role in upholding gender equality as a core value becomes increasingly critical. The current backlash against gender equality is no more a sustained and dominant view than the earlier apparent liberal consensus in favour of greater gender equality. Divergent political views coexist within all societies, and the outcome of these dynamics remains uncertain. Nevertheless, there are well-founded concerns that misogyny is evolving into a deliberate political strategy, amplified during the pandemic through social media and now weaponised to influence policy and mobilise support for anti-gender agendas (Wiens et al., 2025). Much in the end will depend on whether women themselves are willing to adjust their aspirations and behaviours against pressures towards regression. Some political projects may seek a return to traditional gender relations. However, the key question is whether the views of powerful men can put the genie of women's aspirations towards gender equality back in the bottle.

References

Armstrong, P., Armstrong, H., & Choiniere, J. A. (2024). *The labour crisis in long-term care: The right to care*. Edward Elgar Publishing.

Barcellos de Moraes, F. (2025, June 21). *Climate disinformation at the center of geopolitics: COP30 Presidency leads global coordination on the issue*. COP30 Brasil. https://cop30.br/en/news-about-cop30/climate-disinformation-at-the-center-of-geopolitics-cop30-presidency-leads-global-coordination-on-the-issue

Bashevska, M., & Dotti Sani, G. (2026). The gendered impact of the Covid-19 pandemic on labor market outcomes: A comparative European perspective. In J. Rubery, N. Sánchez-Mira, & V. Insarauto (Eds.), *Women in turbulent times. Crises, transitions, and challenges for gender equality* (pp. 52–72). Routledge.

Bastia, T. (2011). Migration as protest? Negotiating gender, class, and ethnicity in urban Bolivia. *Environment and Planning A*, *43*(7), 1514–1529. https://doi.org/10.1068/a43365

Baxter, J., Campbell, A., Lee, R., & Lloyd, M. (2026). Covid-19 and gender gaps in paid and unpaid work. In J. Rubery, N. Sánchez-Mira, & V. Insarauto (Eds.), *Women in turbulent times. Crises, transitions, and challenges for gender equality* (pp. 141–161). Routledge.

Bettio, F., Simonazzi, A., & Villa, P. (2006). Change in care regimes and female migration: The "care drain" in the Mediterranean. *Journal of European Social Policy*, *16*(3), 271–285. https://doi.org/10.1177/0958928706065598

Bria, F., & Bautista, J. (2025). *The authoritarian stack*. https://www.authoritarian-stack.info/

Brodie, P. (2023). Data infrastructure studies on an unequal planet. *Big Data & Society*, *10*(1). https://doi.org/10.1177/20539517231182402

Brown, G., El-Erian, M., Spence, M., & Lidow, R. (2023). *Permacrisis: A plan to fix a fractured world*. Simon and Schuster.

Burchell, B., Deakin, S., Rubery, J., & Spencer, D. A. (2024). The future of work and working time: Introduction to special issue. *Cambridge Journal of Economics*, *48*(1), 1–24. https://doi.org/10.1093/cje/bead057

Chung, H. (2022). *The flexibility paradox: Why flexible working leads to (self-) exploitation* (1st ed.). Bristol University Press. https://doi.org/10.2307/j.ctv2c3k1n8

Chung, H., & van der Horst, M. (2017). Women's employment patterns after childbirth and the perceived access to and use of flexitime and teleworking. *Human Relations*, *71*(1), 47–72. https://doi.org/10.1177/0018726717713828

Clarkberg, M., & Moen, P. (2001). Understanding the time-squeeze: Married couples' preferred and actual work-hour strategies. *American Behavioral Scientist*, *44*(7), 1115–1136. https://doi.org/10.1177/0002764201044007005

Daly, J., Trappmann, V., Bessa, I., & Tomlinson, J. (2026). Unpacking the green economy: Worker justice without gender justice? In J. Rubery, N. Sánchez-Mira, & V. Insarauto

(Eds.), *Women in turbulent times. Crises, transitions, and challenges for gender equality* (pp. 297–315). Routledge.

De Stefano, V., Durri, I., Stylogiannis, C., & Wouters, M. (2021). *Platform work and the employment relationship* (ILO Working Paper No. 27). International Labour Organization. https://www.ilo.org/wcmsp5/groups/public/---ed_protect/---protrav/---travail/documents/publication/wcms_777866.pdf

Dowling, E. (2021). *The care crisis: What caused it and how can we end it?* Verso.

Elson, D. (2012). Social reproduction in the global crisis: Rapid recovery or long-lasting depletion? En P. Utting, S. Razavi, & R. V. Buchholz (Eds.), *The global crisis and transformative social change* (pp. 63–80). Palgrave Macmillan, London. https://doi.org/10.1057/9781137002501_4

England, P., & Folbre, N. (1999). Who should pay for the kids? *The ANNALS of the American Academy of Political and Social Science*, *563*(1), 194–207. https://doi.org/10.1177/000271629956300112

Eurofound. (2022a). *COVID-19 pandemic and the gender divide at work and home.* Publications Office of the European Union.

Eurofound. (2022b). *Recovery from COVID-19: The changing structure of employment in the EU.* Publications Office of the European Union.

European Commission. (2020). *A union of equality: Gender equality strategy 2020–2025* (COM(2020) 152 final). European Commission. https://ec.europa.eu/info/policies/justice-and-fundamental-rights/gender-equality/gender-equality-strategy_en

European Commission. (2022). *Communication from the Commission to the European Parliament, the Council, the European Economic and Social Committee and the Committee of the Regions on the European care strategy* (COM(2022) 440 final). Publications Office of the European Union. https://eur-lex.europa.eu/legal-content/EN/TXT/PDF/?uri=CELEX:52022DC0440

European Union. (2019). *Directive (EU) 2019/1158 of the European Parliament and of the Council of 20 June 2019 on work-life balance for parents and carers and repealing Council Directive 2010/18/EU.* Official Journal of the European Union. https://eur-lex.europa.eu/eli/dir/2019/1158/oj/eng

Ferragina, E. (2019). The political economy of family policy expansion: Fostering neoliberal capitalism or promoting gender equality supporting social reproduction? *Review of International Political Economy*, *26*(6), 1238–1265. https://doi.org/10.1080/09692290.2019.1627568

Figueiredo, H., & López-Andreu, M. (2026). Gender pay inequality and wage setting institutions through crises and recoveries: A Southern European success story? In J. Rubery, N. Sánchez-Mira, & V. Insarauto (Eds.), *Women in turbulent times. Crises, transitions, and challenges for gender equality* (pp. 94–116). Routledge.

Forden, J., Radpour, S., Conway, E., & Ghilarducci, T. (2023). *Reducing the unequal burden of unpaid eldercare work.* Schwartz Center for Economic Policy Analysis, The New School. https://www.economicpolicyresearch.org/resource-library/research/reducing-the-unequal-burden-of-unpaid-eldercare-work

Forsyth, A., & McCrystal, S. (2025). *Collective bargaining and collective action in the platform economy: A 2024 update of developments in legislation, case law and collective agreements* (ILO Working Paper No. 143). International Labour Organization. https://doi.org/10.54394/EMDS2473

Fraser, N. (1994). After the family wage: Gender equity and the welfare state. *Political Theory*, *22*(4), 591–618. https://doi.org/10.1177/0090591794022004003

Fraser, N. (2016, July-August). Contradictions of capital and care. *New Left Review*, *100*, 99–117. https://newleftreview.org/issues/ii100/articles/nancy-fraser-contradictions-of-capital-and-care

Gmyrek, P., Berg, J., & Bescond, D. (2025). Generative AI and jobs: An analysis of potential effects on global employment. *Gospodarka Narodowa: The Polish Journal of Economics*, *323*(3), 6–30. https://doi.org/10.33119/GN/203716

Henig, D., & Knight, D. M. (2023). Polycrisis: Prompts for an emerging worldview. *Anthropology Today*, *39*(2), 3–6. https://doi.org/10.1111/1467-8322.12884

Hess, C. (2013, April). *Women and the care crisis* (Briefing Paper No. 401). Institute for Women's Policy Research. https://iwpr.org/wp-content/uploads/2020/06/C401.pdf

Hochschild, A. R. (1997). *The time bind: When work becomes home and home becomes work*. Metropolitan Books.

Hochschild, A. R. (2000). Global care chains and emotional surplus value. In A. Giddens & W. Hutton (Eds.), *On the edge: Living with global capitalism* (pp. 130–146). Jonathan Cape.

Howcroft, D., Banister, E., Jarvis-King, L., Rubery, J., & Távora, I. (2024). Digitalisation and the remaking of the ideal worker. *Work, Employment and Society*, *39*(3), 703–726. https://doi.org/10.1177/09500170241301015

Huws, U. (2019). The hassle of housework: Digitalisation and the commodification of domestic labour. *Feminist Review*, *123*(1), 8–23. https://doi.org/10.1177/0141778919879742

Insarauto, V. (2021). Women's vulnerability to the economic crisis through the lens of part-time work in Spain. *Work, Employment and Society*, *35*(4), 621–639. https://doi.org/10.1177/09500170211001271

International Labour Office. (2022). *Global wage report 2022–23: The impact of inflation and COVID-19 on wages and purchasing power*. International Labour Office.

Jones-Renaud, L., Panda, A., Robino, C., & Aguilar, M. G. (2024). *Climate change and care work: Integrated solutions for intersecting crises* (Policy brief). The Asia Foundation, International Development Research Centre (IDRC), & Fundación Avina. https://www.wocan.org/wp-content/uploads/2025/01/WEP_Climate-Change-and-Care-Policy-Brief_EN.pdf

Karamessini, M. (2026). The "care transition" in turbulent times. In J. Rubery, N. Sánchez-Mira, & V. Insarauto (Eds.), *Women in turbulent times. Crises, transitions, and challenges for gender equality* (pp. 207–228). Routledge.

Karamessini, M., & Rubery, J. (2014). *Women and austerity: The economic crisis and the future for gender equality*. Routledge. https://doi.org/10.4324/9780203066294

Klesment, M., & Van Bavel, J. (2017). The reversal of the gender gap in education, motherhood, and women as main earners in Europe. *European Sociological Review*, *33*(3), 465–481. https://doi.org/10.1093/esr/jcw063

Kurowska, A. (2020). Gendered effects of home-based work on parents' capability to balance work with non-work: Two countries with different models of division of labour compared. *Social Indicators Research*, *151*(2), 405–425. https://doi.org/10.1007/s11205-018-2034-9

Larsen, T. P., Leschke, J., & Bekker, S. (2026). Unemployment and care risks in times of crisis: Gender (in)equalities at the intersection of unemployment benefits, childcare and leave policies. In J. Rubery, N. Sánchez-Mira, & V. Insarauto (Eds.), *Women in turbulent times. Crises, transitions, and challenges for gender equality* (pp. 229–254). Routledge.

Lawrence, M., Homer-Dixon, T., Janzwood, S., Rockström, J., Renn, O., & Donges, J. F. (2024). Global polycrisis: The causal mechanisms of crisis entanglement. *Global Sustainability*, *7*, Article e6. https://doi.org/10.1017/sus.2024.1

Lawrence, M., Janzwood, S., & Homer-Dixon, T. (2022). *What is a global polycrisis?* (Version 2.0) (Discussion Paper 2022–4). Cascade Institute. https://cascadeinstitute.org/technical-paper/what-is-a-globalpolycrisis/

Lopezlira, E., & Hunter, S. (2026). Enhancing dignity and equity: Homecare workforce challenges amidst the cost of living crisis, with a focus on California. In J. Rubery, N. Sánchez-Mira, & V. Insarauto (Eds.), *Women in turbulent times. Crises, transitions, and challenges for gender equality* (pp. 184–206). Routledge.

Lott, Y., & Chung, H. (2016). Gender discrepancies in the outcomes of schedule control on overtime hours and income in Germany. *European Sociological Review*, *32*(6), 752–765. https://doi.org/10.1093/esr/jcw032

Mangan, D., Muszyński, K., & Pulignano, V. (2023). The platform discount: Addressing unpaid work as a structural feature of labour platforms. *European Labour Law Journal*, *14*(4), 541–569. https://doi.org/10.1177/20319525231210550

Marx, L., Bian, F., & Sánchez-Mira, N. (2026). Crises as drivers of change in couples' paid work arrangements in Europe. In J. Rubery, N. Sánchez-Mira, & V. Insarauto (Eds.), *Women in turbulent times. Crises, transitions, and challenges for gender equality* (pp. 119–140). Routledge.

Milkie, M. A., Sayer, L. C., Nomaguchi, K., & Yan, H. X. (2025). Who's doing the housework and childcare in America now? Differential convergence in twenty-first-century gender gaps in home tasks. *Socius: Sociological Research for a Dynamic World*, *11*. https://doi.org/10.1177/23780231251314667

Mrozowicki, A., Gardawski, J., Burski, J., & Rapacki, R. (2025). Patchwork capitalism and managing the interlinked crises in essential public services in Poland. *International Labour Review*, *164*(1). https://doi.org/10.16995/ilr.18832

Offenhenden, M., Soronellas-Masdeu, M., & Comas-d'Argemir, D. (2025). Ageing at home: Long-term care and the challenges of deinstitutionalisation in Spain. *Dialectical Anthropology*. https://doi.org/10.1007/s10624-025-09786-8

Parnell, T., Van Hout, T., & Del Fante, D. (2024). Critical discursive responses to polycrisis. In T. Parnell, T. Van Hout, & D. Del Fante (Eds.), *Critical approaches to polycrisis* (pp. 1–14). Palgrave Macmillan. https://doi.org/10.1007/978-3-031-76966-5_1

Piasna, A. (2024). Algorithms of time: How algorithmic management changes the temporalities of work and prospects for working time reduction. *Cambridge Journal of Economics*, *48*(1), 115–132. https://doi.org/10.1093/cje/bead017

Piasna, A. (2026). Digitalisation and remote work: Gendered outcomes in job quality and the role of persistent gender inequalities in paid and unpaid work. In J. Rubery, N. Sánchez-Mira, & V. Insarauto (Eds.), *Women in turbulent times. Crises, transitions, and challenges for gender equality* (pp. 257–274). Routledge.

Plomien, A., & Schwartz, G. (2024). Market-reach into social reproduction and transnational labour mobility in Europe. *New Political Economy*, *29*(2), 288-304. https://doi.org/10.1080/13563467.2023.2244448

Plomien, A., & Schwartz, G. (2026). The crisis of social reproduction provisioning: Gender, class and migration in Poland and Ukraine. In J. Rubery, N. Sánchez-Mira, & V. Insarauto (Eds.), *Women in turbulent times. Crises, transitions, and challenges for gender equality* (pp. 162–183). Routledge.

Polanyi, K. (1944). *The great transformation: The political and economic origins of our time*. Beacon Press.
Pulignano, V., & Domecka, M. (2025). *The politics of unpaid labour: How the study of unpaid labour can help address inequality in precarious work*. Oxford University Press.
Rai, S. M. (2024). *Depletion: The human costs of caring*. Oxford University Press.
Rai, S. M., Hoskyns, C., & Thomas, D. (2013). Depletion. The cost of social reproduction. *International Feminist Journal of Politics*, *16*(1), 86–105. https://doi.org/10.1080/14616742.2013.789641
Rani, U., Gobel, N., & Uludag, S. (2026). Unmasking gender disparities in the digital economy: Beyond access and numbers. In J. Rubery, N. Sánchez-Mira, & V. Insarauto (Eds.), *Women in turbulent times. Crises, transitions, and challenges for gender equality* (pp. 275–296). Routledge.
Rogers, T. N. (2025, November 6). *Trump's diversity retreat leaves European companies walking a tightrope*. Financial Times. https://www.ft.com/content/6fd88ef7-e378-400c-9a92-47090c375535
Rodríguez-Modroño, P., Agenjo-Calderón, A., & López-Igual, P. (2022). Platform work in the domestic and home care sector: New mechanisms of invisibility and exploitation of women migrant workers. *Gender & Development*, *30*(3), 619–635. https://doi.org/10.1080/13552074.2022.2121060
Rodríguez-Modroño, P., Agenjo-Calderón, A., & López-Igual, P. (2024). A social reproduction analysis of digital care platform work. *New Political Economy*, *29*(4), 616–627. https://doi.org/10.1080/13563467.2024.2317703
Roitman, J. (2014). *Anti-crisis*. Duke University Press.
Rubery, J. (Ed.). (1988). *Women and recession*. Routledge. https://doi.org/10.4324/9780203832684
Rubery, J., & Tavora, I. (2021). The COVID-19 crisis and gender equality: Risks and opportunities. In B. Vanhercke, S. Spasova, & B. Fronteddu (Eds.), *Social policy in the European Union: State of play 2020* (pp. 71–96). European Trade Union Institute (ETUI) and European Social Observatory (OSE). https://www.etui.org/sites/default/files/2020-12/Social%20policy%20in%20the%20European%20Union%20state%20of%20play%202020-web.pdf
Rubery, J., Insarauto, V. & Sánchez-Mira, N. (2026). Gender equality in turbulent times: From the financial crash to polycrisis. In J. Rubery, N. Sánchez-Mira, & V. Insarauto (Eds.), *Women in turbulent times. Crises, transitions, and challenges for gender equality* (pp. 3–26). Routledge.
Sánchez-Mira, N. (2020). Work–family arrangements and the crisis in Spain: Balkanized gender contracts? *Gender, Work & Organization*, *27*(6), 944–970. https://doi.org/10.1111/gwao.12417
Schor, J. (1991). *The overworked American: The unexpected decline of leisure*. Basic Books.
Sologon, D. M., Doorley, K., & O'Donoghue, C. (2024). *Gender disparities in inflation during the cost-of-living crisis in Europe: A novel decomposition* (IZA DP No. 16860). IZA - Institute of Labor Economics. http://www.jstor.org/stable/resrep68458
Steinmetz, S., & Guarnerio, M. (2026). Intersecting inequalities. The role of gender and migration background in women's labour market vulnerability during crises. In J. Rubery, N. Sánchez-Mira, & V. Insarauto (Eds.), *Women in turbulent times. Crises, transitions, and challenges for gender equality* (pp. 29–51). Routledge.

Stier, H., & Herzberg-Druker, E. (2017). Running ahead or running in place? Educational expansion and gender inequality in the labor market. *Social Indicators Research*, *130*(3), 1187–1206. https://www.jstor.org/stable/48715396

Stratigaki, M. (2004). The cooptation of gender concepts in EU policies: The case of "reconciliation of work and family". *Social Politics: International Studies in Gender, State & Society*, *11*(1), 30–56. https://doi.org/10.1093/sp/jxh025

Sullivan, O., Gershuny, J., & Robinson, J. P. (2018). Stalled or uneven gender revolution? A long-term processual framework for understanding why change is slow. *Journal of Family Theory & Review*, *10*(1), 263–279. https://doi.org/10.1111/jftr.12248

Tooze, A. (2021). *Shutdown: How COVID shook the world economy*. Allen Lane.

Torres, L., & Warren, T. (2026). Working lives and livelihoods in turbulent times: Intersecting inequalities of gender and class in the UK. In J. Rubery, N. Sánchez-Mira, & V. Insarauto (Eds.), *Women in turbulent times. Crises, transitions, and challenges for gender equality* (pp. 73–93). Routledge.

Vitali, A., & Arpino, B. (2016). Who brings home the bacon? The influence of context on partners' contributions to the household income. *Demographic Research*, *35*, 1213–1244. https://doi.org/10.4054/DemRes.2016.35.41

Vokić, N. P., Obadić, A., & Ćorić, D. S. (2019). *Gender equality in the workplace: Macro and micro perspectives on the status of highly educated women*. Springer.

Wiens, B. I., Ruest, N., & MacDonald, S. (2025, June 18). Misogyny has become a political strategy — here's how the pandemic helped make it happen. *The Conversation*. https://theconversation.com/misogyny-has-become-a-political-strategy-heres-how-the-pandemic-helped-make-it-happen-256043

Williams, S., & Erickson, M. (2024). *Crises at work: Economy, climate and pandemic*. Policy Press.

Williams, J. C., Blair-Loy, M., & Berdahl, J. L. (2013). Cultural schemas, social class, and the flexibility stigma. *Journal of Social Issues*, *69*(2), 209–234. https://doi.org/10.1111/josi.12012

Yucel, D., Badawy, P., & Schieman, S. (2025). Working from home and role blurring: The effects of job pressure, organizational support, and caregiving responsibilities. *Community, Work & Family*, 1–26. https://doi.org/10.1080/13668803.2025.2551141

INDEX

Note: Page numbers in **bold** and in *italics* indicate reference tables and reference figures respectively.